TYPHON

PUBLISHER'S NOTE

To start, I'd like to heap thanks upon my contributors for their patience. As they know, it took a little longer to finish TYPHON than I'd originally planned.

This book was initially conceived as the third volume in the Legal Action Comics series. Published in 2001 and 2003, these were benefit anthologies intended to raise public awareness about a certain nuisance lawsuit, (for more information on Rall v. Hellman, see Legal Action Comics Volumes 1 & 2).

The call for submissions letter for Legal Action Comics Volume Three went out at the end of 2004. About a year into the project, I realized that, while I wanted to do another comics anthology, I didn't want to do another book connected with the lawsuit. I was bored with Rall v. Hellman, and it was a pretty safe bet that readers were bored with it as well. I'd also been thinking about adding color to the book, and tweaking the format a bit; it soon became clear that what I had in mind was an altogether different book. Thus, Legal Action Comics Volume Three became TYPHON.

The switch to full color meant that nearly every strip I'd collected up to that point would need to be colored, which would take time. Then came the hand grenade of cuteness that exploded in my life: in the Summer of 2005, my wife Linda announced that she was with child, and in May of 2006, Alice was born.

I've since learned that having a kid is a wonderful thing; I've also learned that it's not easy to put a book together during that sleepless first year with Baby, (those of you with kids are knowingly nodding your heads right about now). After that staggering first year, (which included a move across the East River), our lives settled down a bit, and work on TYPHON resumed.

So who, (or what) is TYPHON? Briefly put, Typhon is creature out of Greek mythology; a frightful, multi-headed monster who does battle with Zeus. Like a lot of kids, I was crazy for Greek Myths, (thanks to the d'Aulaire's classic book), but for some reason, I didn't become aware of Typhon until the mid 1990's, while paging through a collection of Gustav Klimt's paintings. In the section of Klimt's Beethoven Frieze titled "The Hostile Powers," sandwiched between an assortment of grotesque nudes, Klimt paints a

hulking, ape-like beast he calls "Typhon." Being a lifelong sucker for monsters, I was immediately hooked.

Patrick Moriarty does a wonderful job of retelling the Typhon myth, (see "The Bullyrag" on Page 64), and R. Sikoryak's stunning cover illustration gives us a snapshot of Zeus' climactic battle with the terrifying Typhon, viewed through the lens of comics history.

So, after its monstrous four year gestation, we have TYPHON the comics anthology. I hope my contributors will find it worth the wait, and I hope readers will enjoy it well enough to justify further volumes.

I'd like to thank my wife Linda for her gracious understanding. It's a little scary rolling the dice on a comics anthology in the midst of an economic downturn, but her mantra "it's only money" has a distinctly soothing effect, (repeat when necessary).

I also want to thank my friend Paul Hernandez, who always manages to wrap his highly flexible brain around technical challenges that would otherwise leave me curled up on the floor in the fetal position, weeping.

I'm grateful to Gregory Benton for doing a stellar job coloring Tim Lane's strip "Manic Depressive From Another Planet," (Page 157). Gregory's own strips, "Survival of the Fittest: Tastes Like Chicken," (Page 30) and "Deep As The Ocean Goes," (Page 169) are guaranteed to delight.

Special thanks go out to Guy Gonzales, who apparently takes no offense at having been turned into a cartoon character, (see Page 4). I hope readers will get a kick out of seeing some of Guy's splendid drawings, which I'm pleased to present on Page 190.

Finally, for indispensable publishing advice, a tip of the multi-headed Typhonic hat goes to Kristine Anstine, John Kuramoto, Brett Warnock, Chris Staros, Alvin Buenaventura, Chris Oliveros, and Adam Grano. These are the people who bring you good comics; when you see them, buy them a drink.

Danny Hellman
Brooklyn, 2008

"It's broccoli, dear."
"I say it's spinach, and I say it sucks dick."

Dirty Danny gag cartoon by Mark Campos

TYPHON **1**

TYPHON

CONTENTS

TYPHON
CONTENTS

Back Cover illustration by Tim Lane

Dirty Danny Press logo by Sam Henderson
•
TYPHON is edited & designed by Danny Hellman
with production assistance by Paul Hernandez

TYPHON Volume One
Copyright © 2008 Dirty Danny Press

TYPHON
c/o Danny Hellman
P.O. Box 901 Old Chelsea Station
New York, NY 10113-0901

Submissions accepted in photocopy and digital formats only.
No submissions will be returned.

Visit us on the web at: www.dannyhellman.com/typhon

Printed in China

THE TERROR IN PEEP BOOTH FIVE

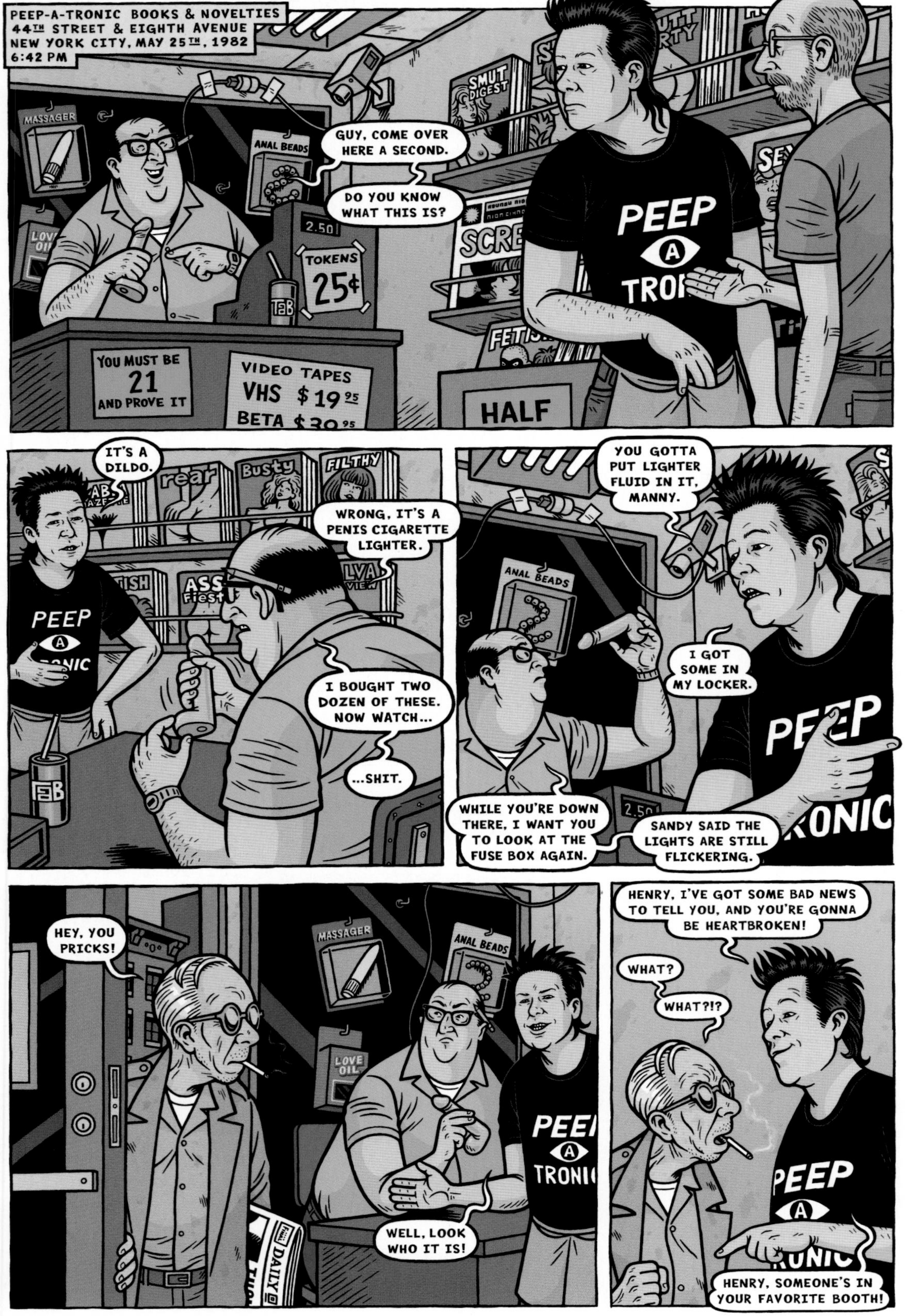
PEEP-A-TRONIC BOOKS & NOVELTIES
44TH STREET & EIGHTH AVENUE
NEW YORK CITY, MAY 25TH, 1982
6:42 PM
GUY, COME OVER HERE A SECOND.
DO YOU KNOW WHAT THIS IS?
MASSAGER
ANAL BEADS
SMUT DIGEST
TOKENS 25¢
YOU MUST BE 21 AND PROVE IT
VIDEO TAPES VHS $19.95 BETA $39.95
HALF
PEEP A TRONIC
IT'S A DILDO.
WRONG, IT'S A PENIS CIGARETTE LIGHTER.
I BOUGHT TWO DOZEN OF THESE. NOW WATCH...
...SHIT.
YOU GOTTA PUT LIGHTER FLUID IN IT, MANNY.
I GOT SOME IN MY LOCKER.
WHILE YOU'RE DOWN THERE, I WANT YOU TO LOOK AT THE FUSE BOX AGAIN.
SANDY SAID THE LIGHTS ARE STILL FLICKERING.
HEY, YOU PRICKS!
WELL, LOOK WHO IT IS!
HENRY, I'VE GOT SOME BAD NEWS TO TELL YOU, AND YOU'RE GONNA BE HEARTBROKEN!
WHAT?
WHAT?!?
HENRY, SOMEONE'S IN YOUR FAVORITE BOOTH!

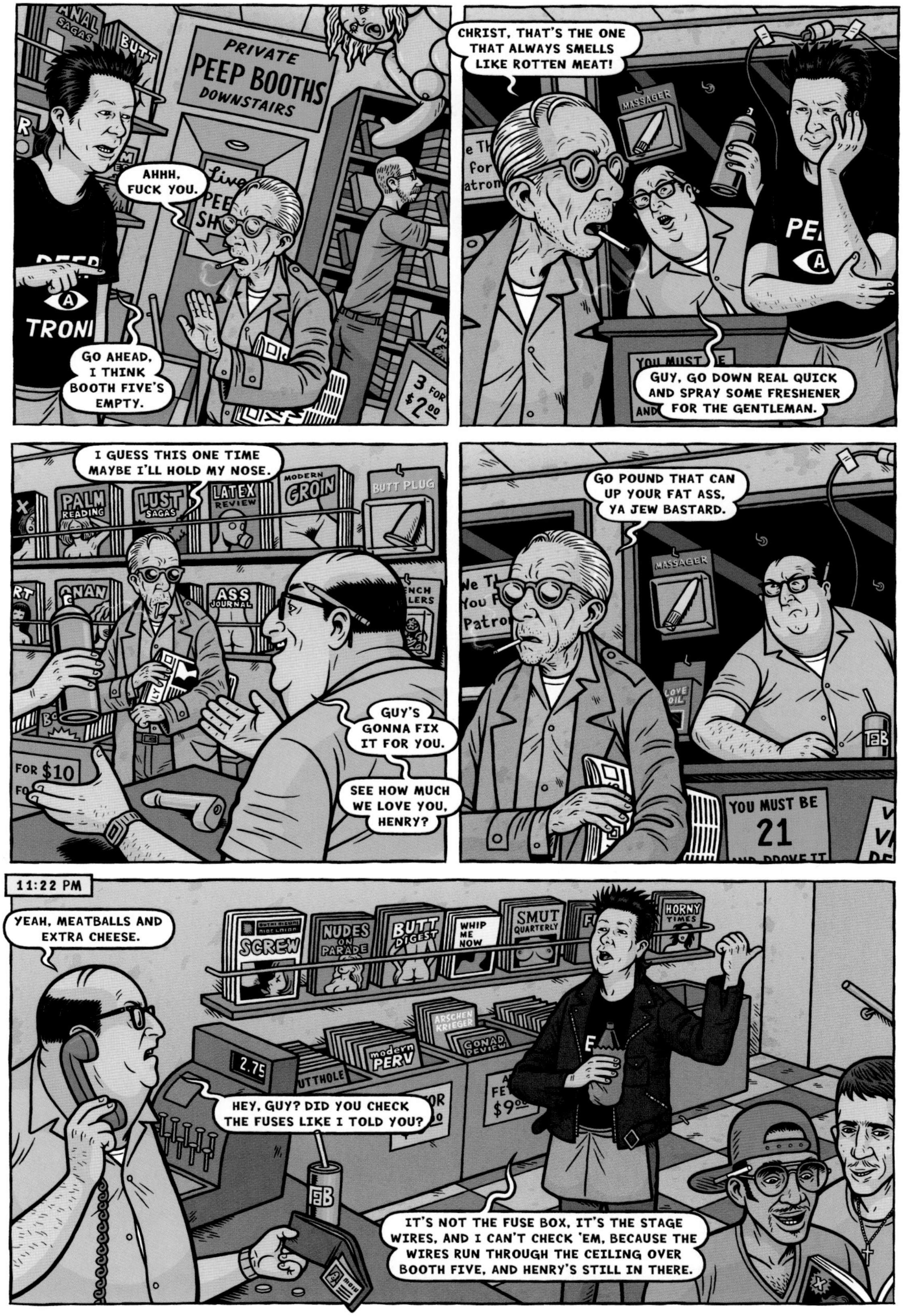
PRIVATE PEEP BOOTHS DOWNSTAIRS
GO AHEAD, I THINK BOOTH FIVE'S EMPTY.
AHHH, FUCK YOU.
3 FOR $2.00
CHRIST, THAT'S THE ONE THAT ALWAYS SMELLS LIKE ROTTEN MEAT!
MASSAGER
GUY, GO DOWN REAL QUICK AND SPRAY SOME FRESHENER FOR THE GENTLEMAN.
I GUESS THIS ONE TIME MAYBE I'LL HOLD MY NOSE.
PALM READING
LUST SAGAS
LATEX REVIEW
MODERN GROIN
BUTT PLUG
ASS JOURNAL
FOR $10
GUY'S GONNA FIX IT FOR YOU.
SEE HOW MUCH WE LOVE YOU, HENRY?
GO POUND THAT CAN UP YOUR FAT ASS, YA JEW BASTARD.
MASSAGER
YOU MUST BE 21
11:22 PM
YEAH, MEATBALLS AND EXTRA CHEESE.
SCREW
NUDES ON PARADE
BUTT DIGEST
WHIP ME NOW
SMUT QUARTERLY
HORNY TIMES
ARSCHEN KRIEGER
MODERN PERV
2.75
HEY, GUY? DID YOU CHECK THE FUSES LIKE I TOLD YOU?
IT'S NOT THE FUSE BOX, IT'S THE STAGE WIRES, AND I CAN'T CHECK 'EM, BECAUSE THE WIRES RUN THROUGH THE CEILING OVER BOOTH FIVE, AND HENRY'S STILL IN THERE.

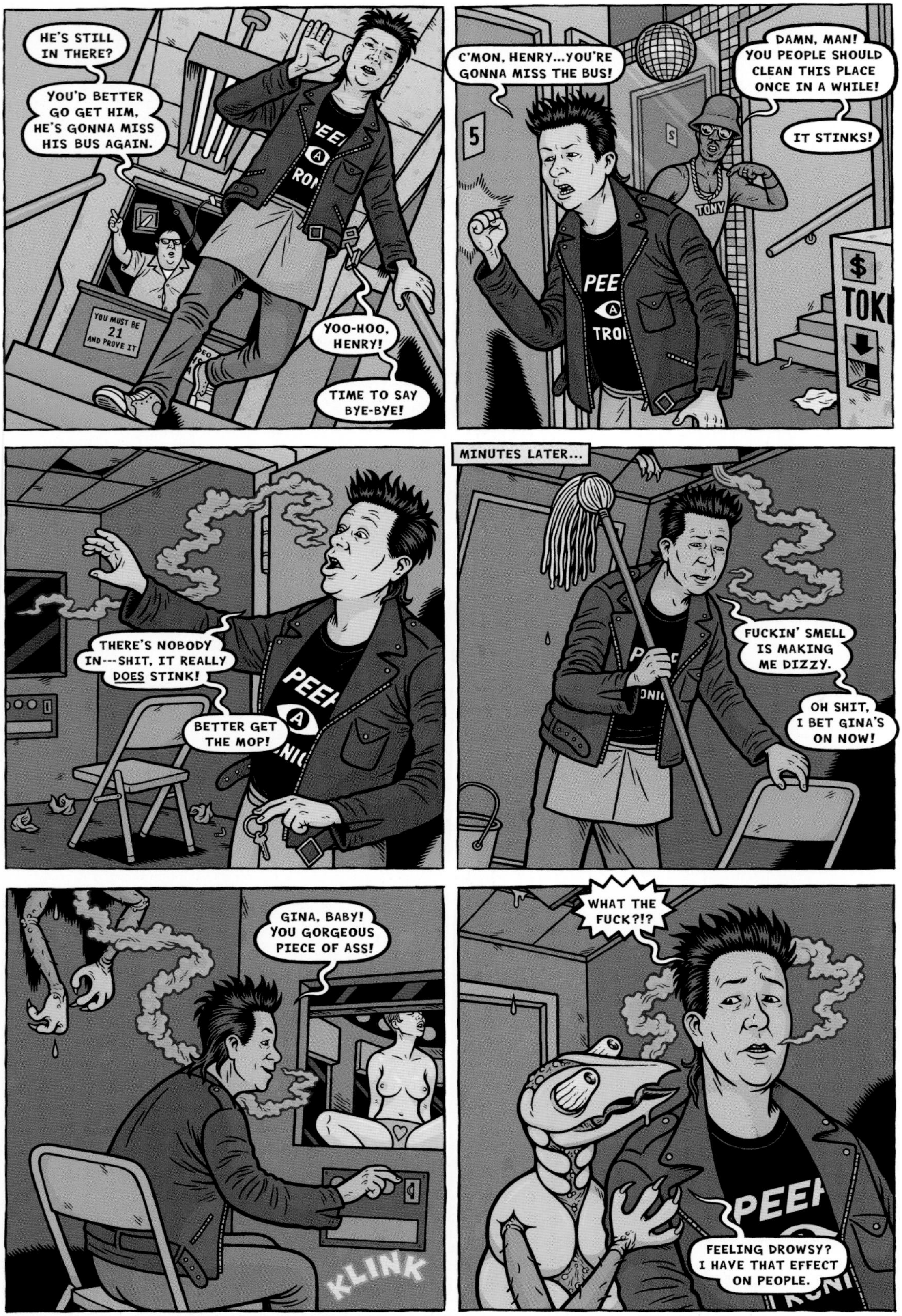
HE'S STILL IN THERE?
YOU'D BETTER GO GET HIM, HE'S GONNA MISS HIS BUS AGAIN.
YOU MUST BE 21 AND PROVE IT
YOO-HOO, HENRY!
TIME TO SAY BYE-BYE!
C'MON, HENRY...YOU'RE GONNA MISS THE BUS!
DAMN, MAN! YOU PEOPLE SHOULD CLEAN THIS PLACE ONCE IN A WHILE!
IT STINKS!
THERE'S NOBODY IN---SHIT, IT REALLY DOES STINK!
BETTER GET THE MOP!
MINUTES LATER...
FUCKIN' SMELL IS MAKING ME DIZZY.
OH SHIT, I BET GINA'S ON NOW!
GINA, BABY! YOU GORGEOUS PIECE OF ASS!
KLINK
WHAT THE FUCK?!?
FEELING DROWSY? I HAVE THAT EFFECT ON PEOPLE.

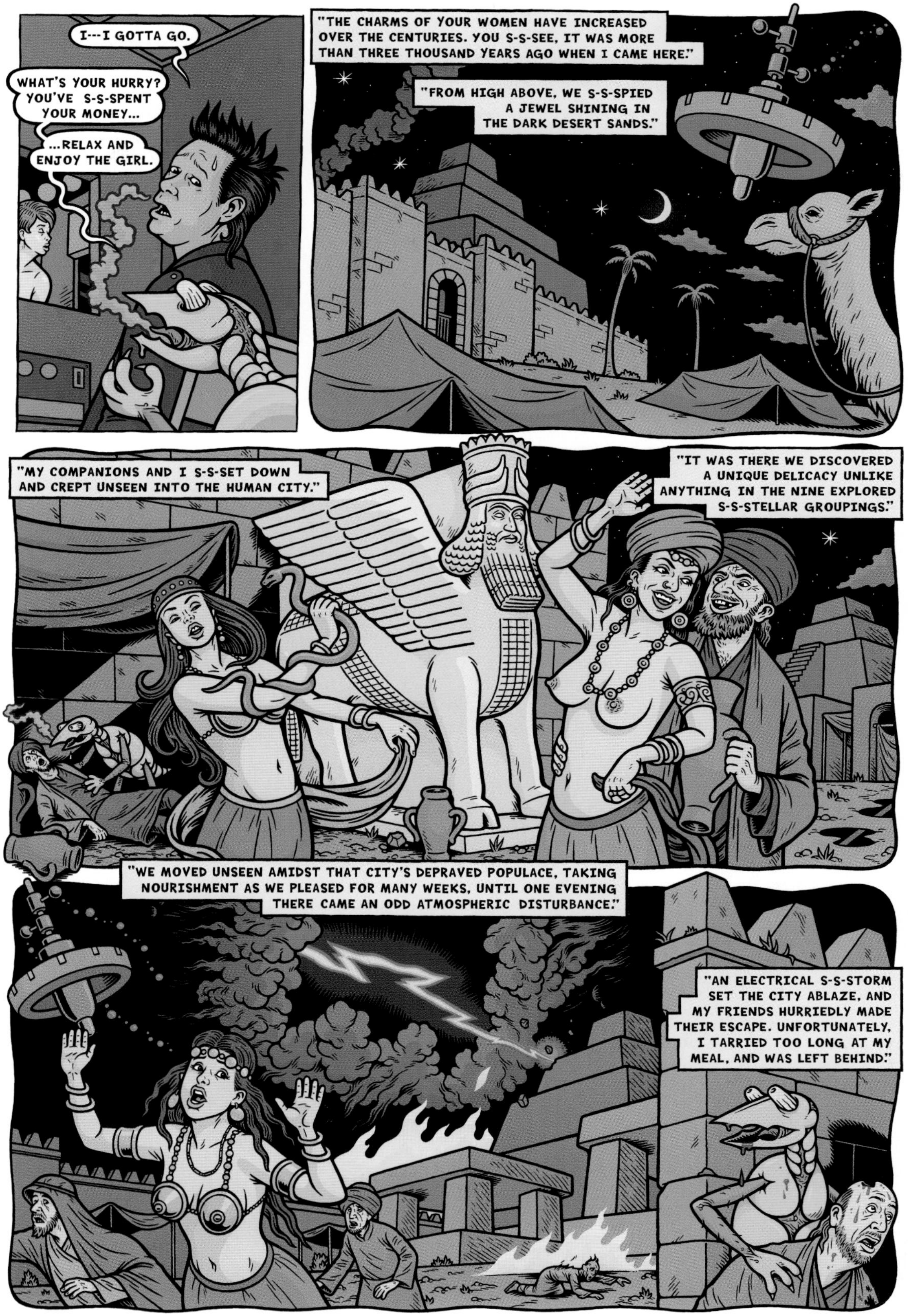
I---I GOTTA GO.
WHAT'S YOUR HURRY? YOU'VE S-S-SPENT YOUR MONEY...
...RELAX AND ENJOY THE GIRL.
"THE CHARMS OF YOUR WOMEN HAVE INCREASED OVER THE CENTURIES. YOU S-S-SEE, IT WAS MORE THAN THREE THOUSAND YEARS AGO WHEN I CAME HERE."
"FROM HIGH ABOVE, WE S-S-SPIED A JEWEL SHINING IN THE DARK DESERT SANDS."
"MY COMPANIONS AND I S-S-SET DOWN AND CREPT UNSEEN INTO THE HUMAN CITY."
"IT WAS THERE WE DISCOVERED A UNIQUE DELICACY UNLIKE ANYTHING IN THE NINE EXPLORED S-S-STELLAR GROUPINGS."
"WE MOVED UNSEEN AMIDST THAT CITY'S DEPRAVED POPULACE, TAKING NOURISHMENT AS WE PLEASED FOR MANY WEEKS, UNTIL ONE EVENING THERE CAME AN ODD ATMOSPHERIC DISTURBANCE."
"AN ELECTRICAL S-S-STORM SET THE CITY ABLAZE, AND MY FRIENDS HURRIEDLY MADE THEIR ESCAPE. UNFORTUNATELY, I TARRIED TOO LONG AT MY MEAL, AND WAS LEFT BEHIND."

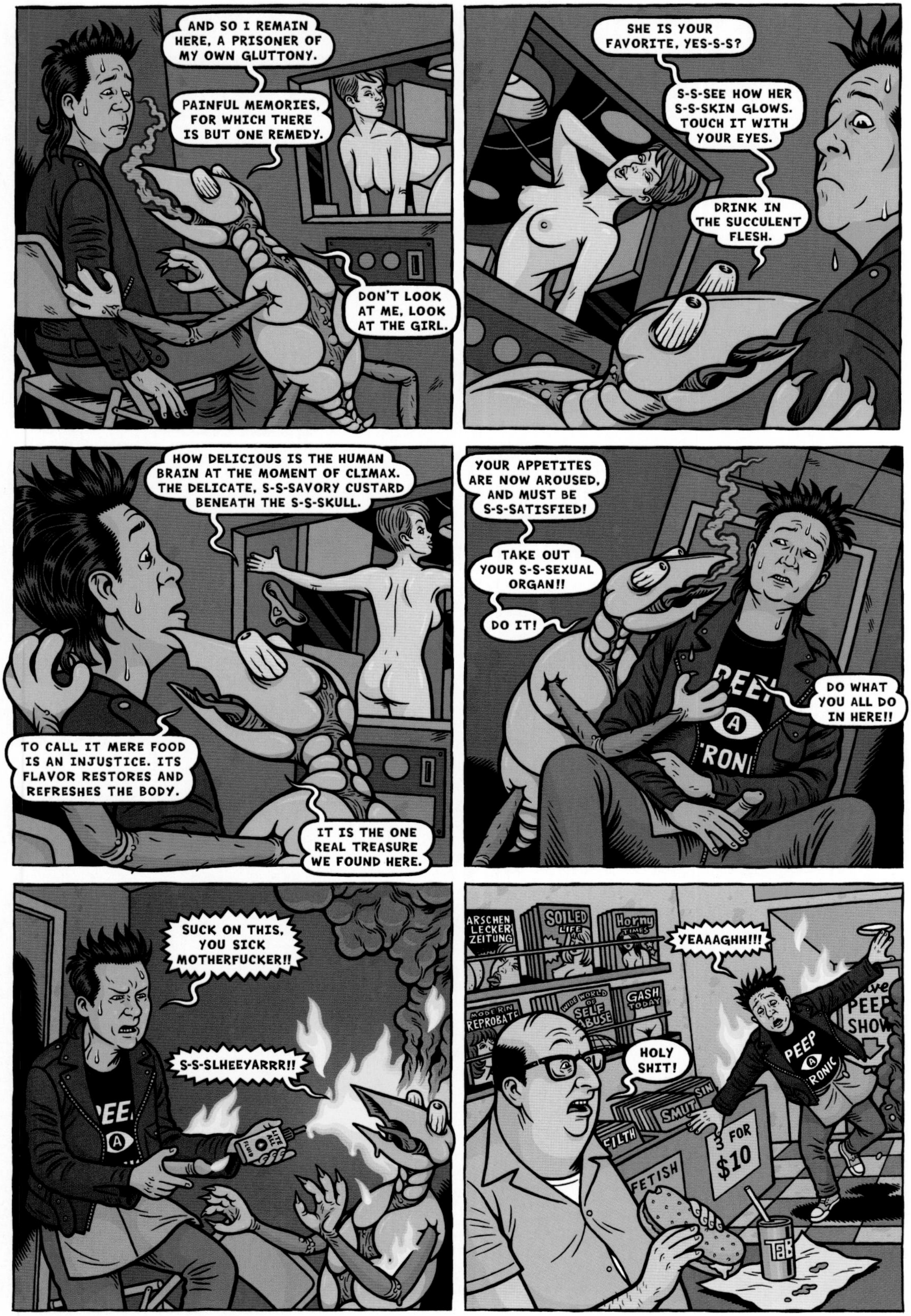
AND SO I REMAIN HERE, A PRISONER OF MY OWN GLUTTONY.
PAINFUL MEMORIES, FOR WHICH THERE IS BUT ONE REMEDY.
DON'T LOOK AT ME, LOOK AT THE GIRL.
SHE IS YOUR FAVORITE, YES-S-S?
S-S-SEE HOW HER S-S-SKIN GLOWS. TOUCH IT WITH YOUR EYES.
DRINK IN THE SUCCULENT FLESH.
HOW DELICIOUS IS THE HUMAN BRAIN AT THE MOMENT OF CLIMAX. THE DELICATE, S-S-SAVORY CUSTARD BENEATH THE S-S-SKULL.
TO CALL IT MERE FOOD IS AN INJUSTICE. ITS FLAVOR RESTORES AND REFRESHES THE BODY.
IT IS THE ONE REAL TREASURE WE FOUND HERE.
YOUR APPETITES ARE NOW AROUSED, AND MUST BE S-S-SATISFIED!
TAKE OUT YOUR S-S-SEXUAL ORGAN!!
DO IT!
DO WHAT YOU ALL DO IN HERE!!
SUCK ON THIS, YOU SICK MOTHERFUCKER!!
S-S-SLHEEYARRR!!
ARSCHEN LECKER ZEITUNG
SOILED LIFE
Horny
YEAAAGHH!!!
MODERN REPROBATE
WIDE WORLD OF SELF ABUSE
GASH TODAY
PEEP SHOW
HOLY SHIT!
PEEP A TRONIC
SMUT
FILTH
FETISH
3 FOR $10
TAB

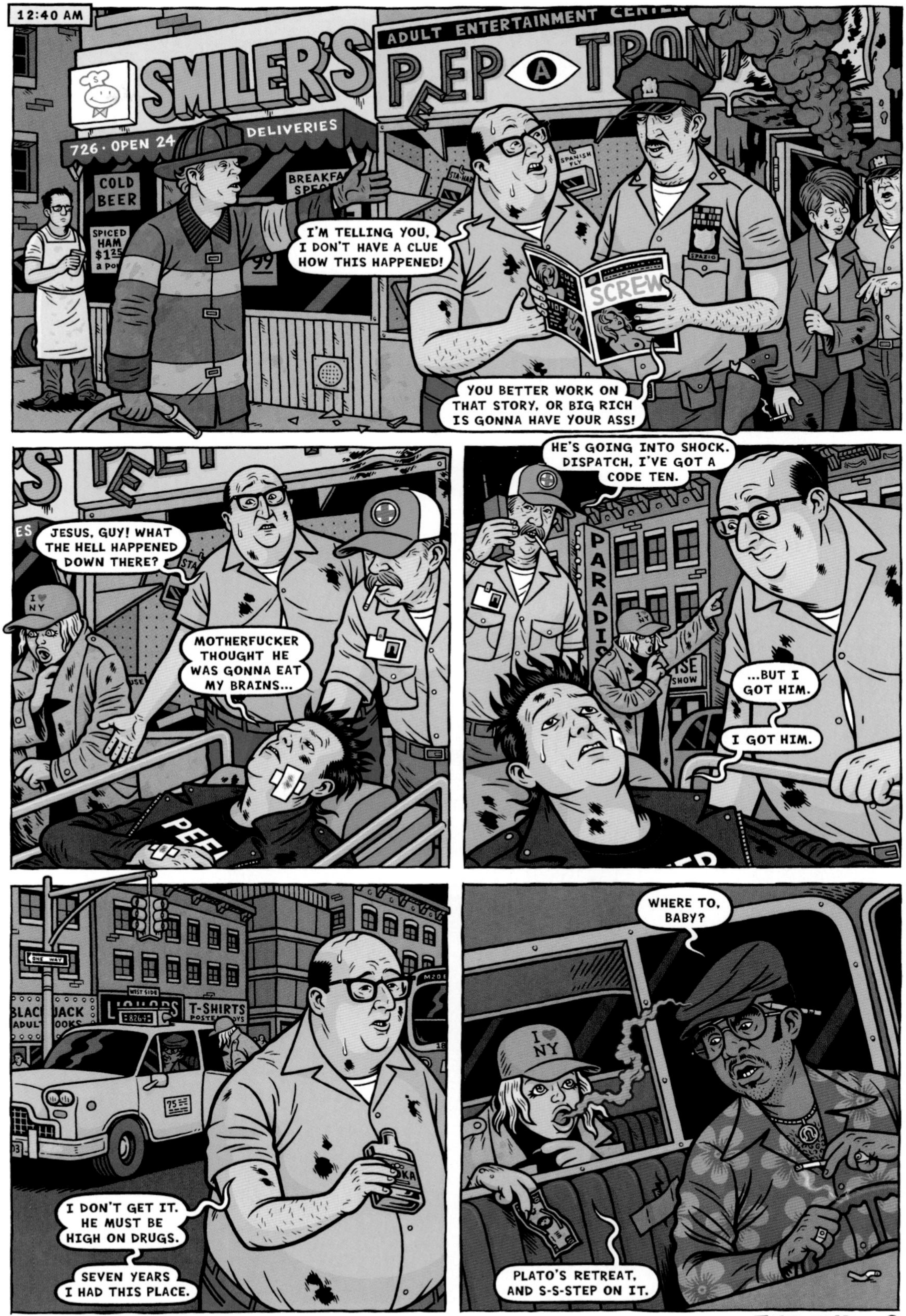
12:40 AM
SMILER'S
726 · OPEN 24
DELIVERIES
COLD BEER
ADULT ENTERTAINMENT CENTER
I'M TELLING YOU, I DON'T HAVE A CLUE HOW THIS HAPPENED!
SCREW
YOU BETTER WORK ON THAT STORY, OR BIG RICH IS GONNA HAVE YOUR ASS!
JESUS, GUY! WHAT THE HELL HAPPENED DOWN THERE?
MOTHERFUCKER THOUGHT HE WAS GONNA EAT MY BRAINS...
HE'S GOING INTO SHOCK. DISPATCH, I'VE GOT A CODE TEN.
...BUT I GOT HIM.
I GOT HIM.
I DON'T GET IT. HE MUST BE HIGH ON DRUGS.
SEVEN YEARS I HAD THIS PLACE.
WHERE TO, BABY?
PLATO'S RETREAT, AND S-S-STEP ON IT.

THE END...?

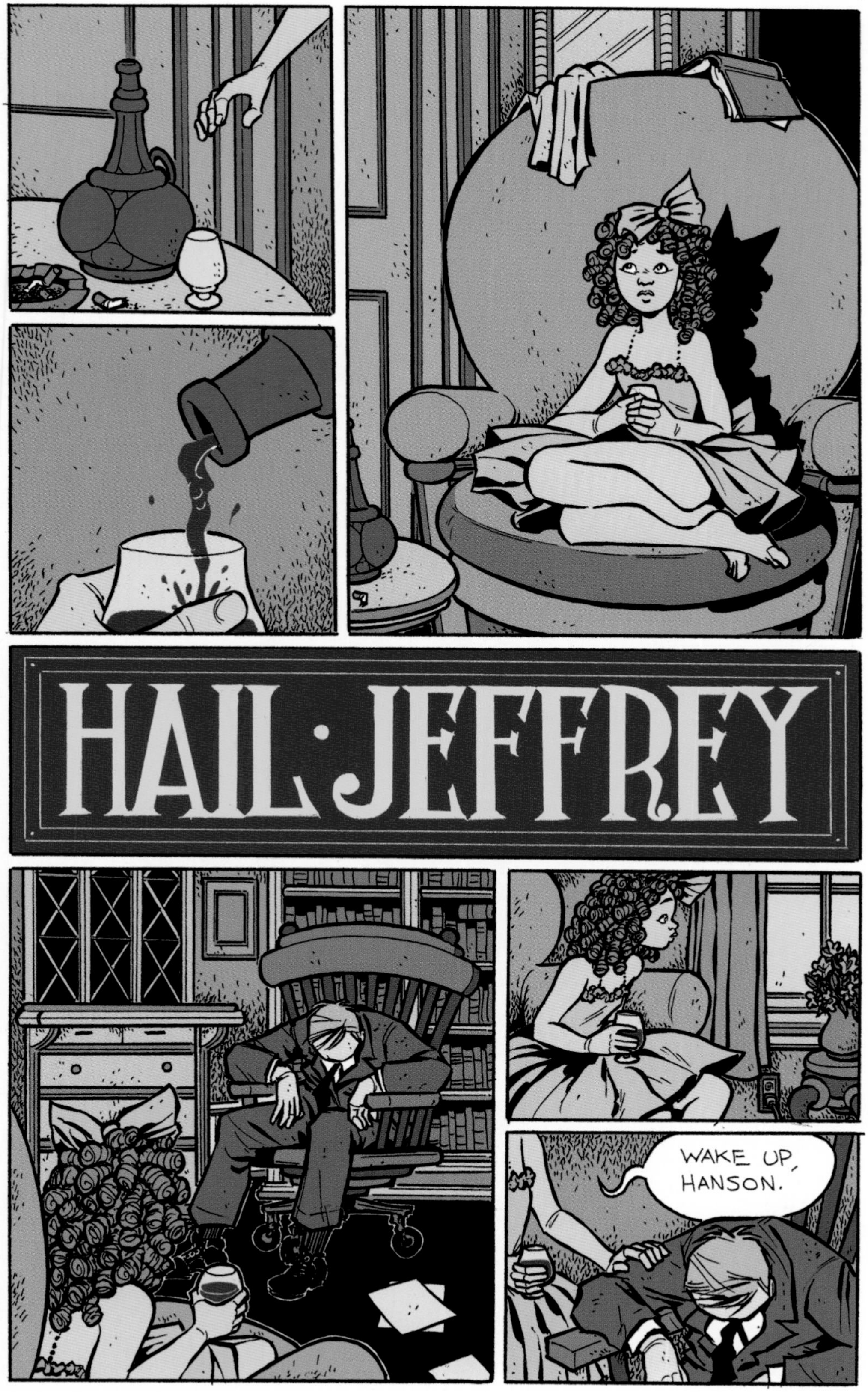
HAIL·JEFFREY
WAKE UP, HANSON.

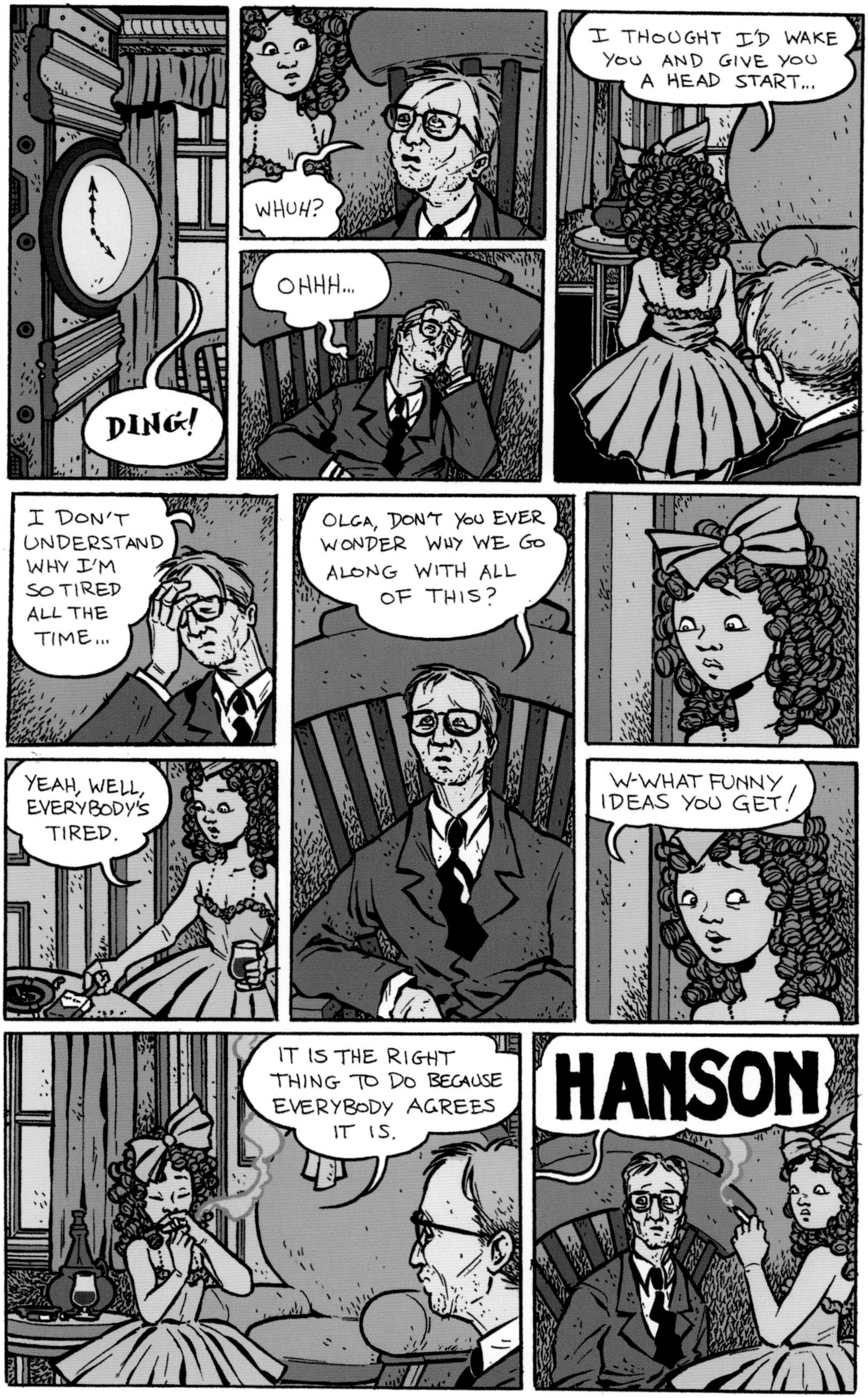
DING!
WHUH?
OHHH...
I THOUGHT I'D WAKE YOU AND GIVE YOU A HEAD START...
I DON'T UNDERSTAND WHY I'M SO TIRED ALL THE TIME...
OLGA, DON'T YOU EVER WONDER WHY WE GO ALONG WITH ALL OF THIS?
YEAH, WELL, EVERYBODY'S TIRED.
W-WHAT FUNNY IDEAS YOU GET!
IT IS THE RIGHT THING TO DO BECAUSE EVERYBODY AGREES IT IS.
HANSON

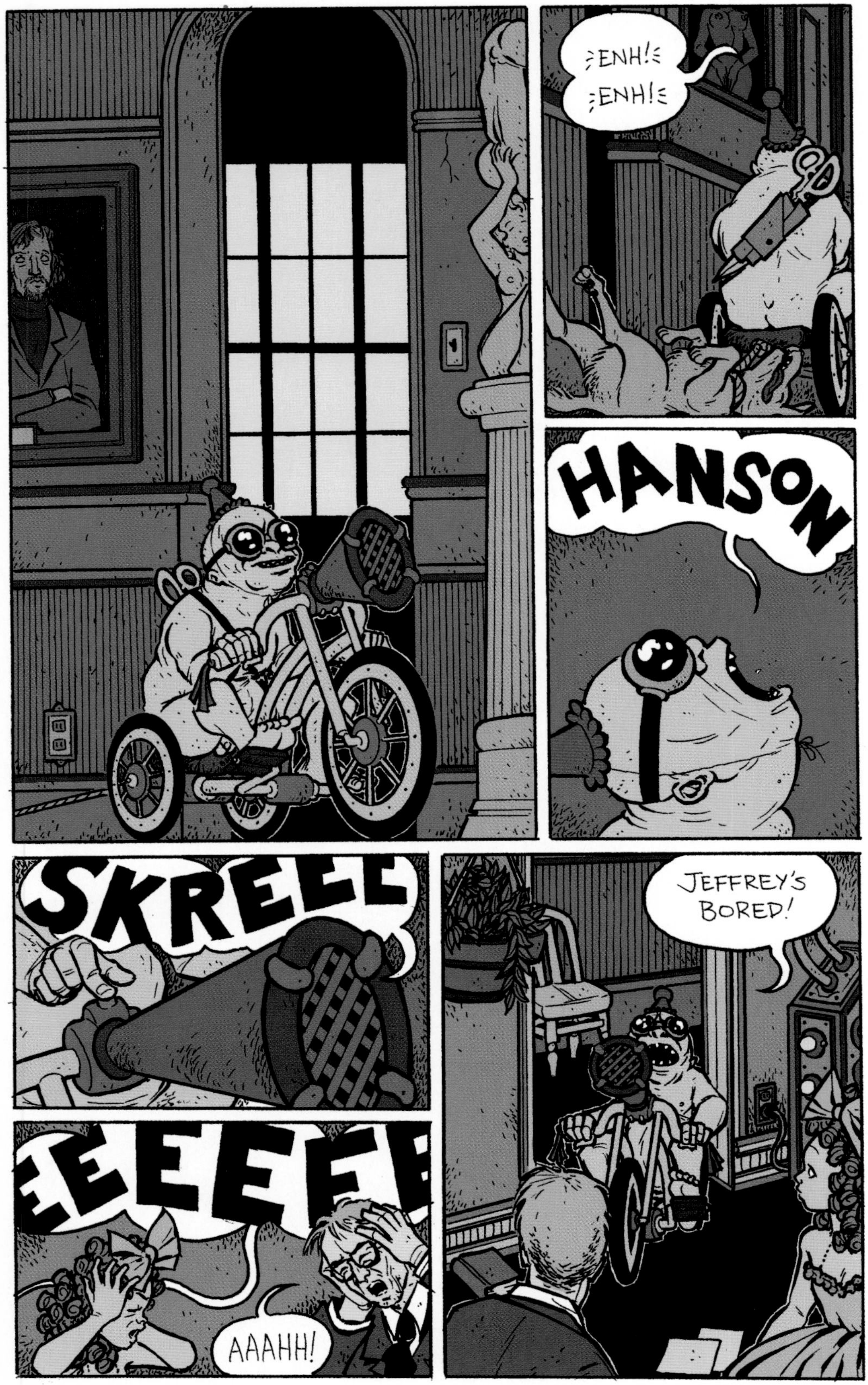
ENH!
ENH!
HANSON
SKREEE
EEEEEE
AAAHH!
JEFFREY'S BORED!

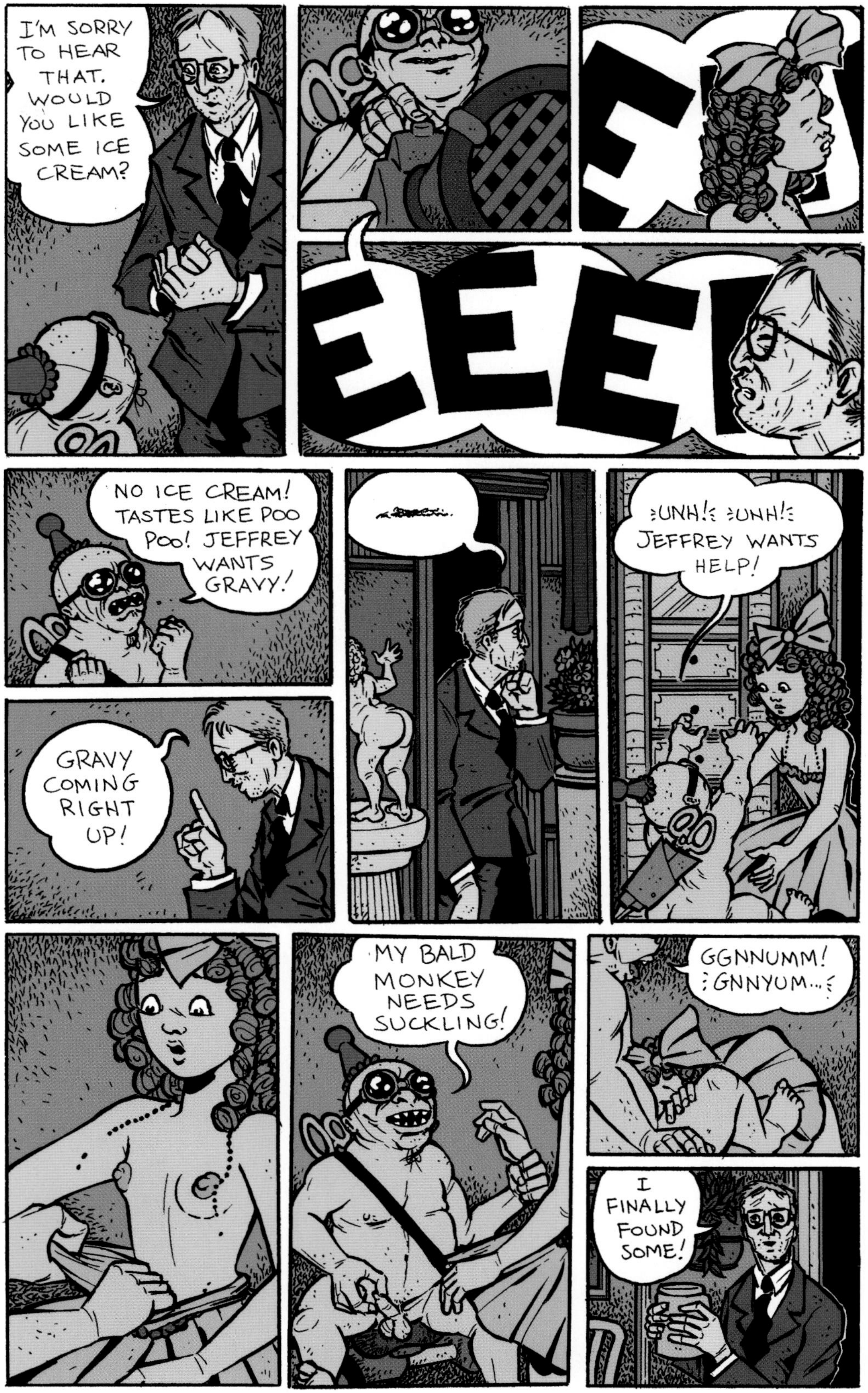
I'M SORRY TO HEAR THAT. WOULD YOU LIKE SOME ICE CREAM?
EEE
NO ICE CREAM! TASTES LIKE POO POO! JEFFREY WANTS GRAVY!
GRAVY COMING RIGHT UP!
UNH! UNH! JEFFREY WANTS HELP!
MY BALD MONKEY NEEDS SUCKLING!
GGNNUMM! GNNYUM...
I FINALLY FOUND SOME!

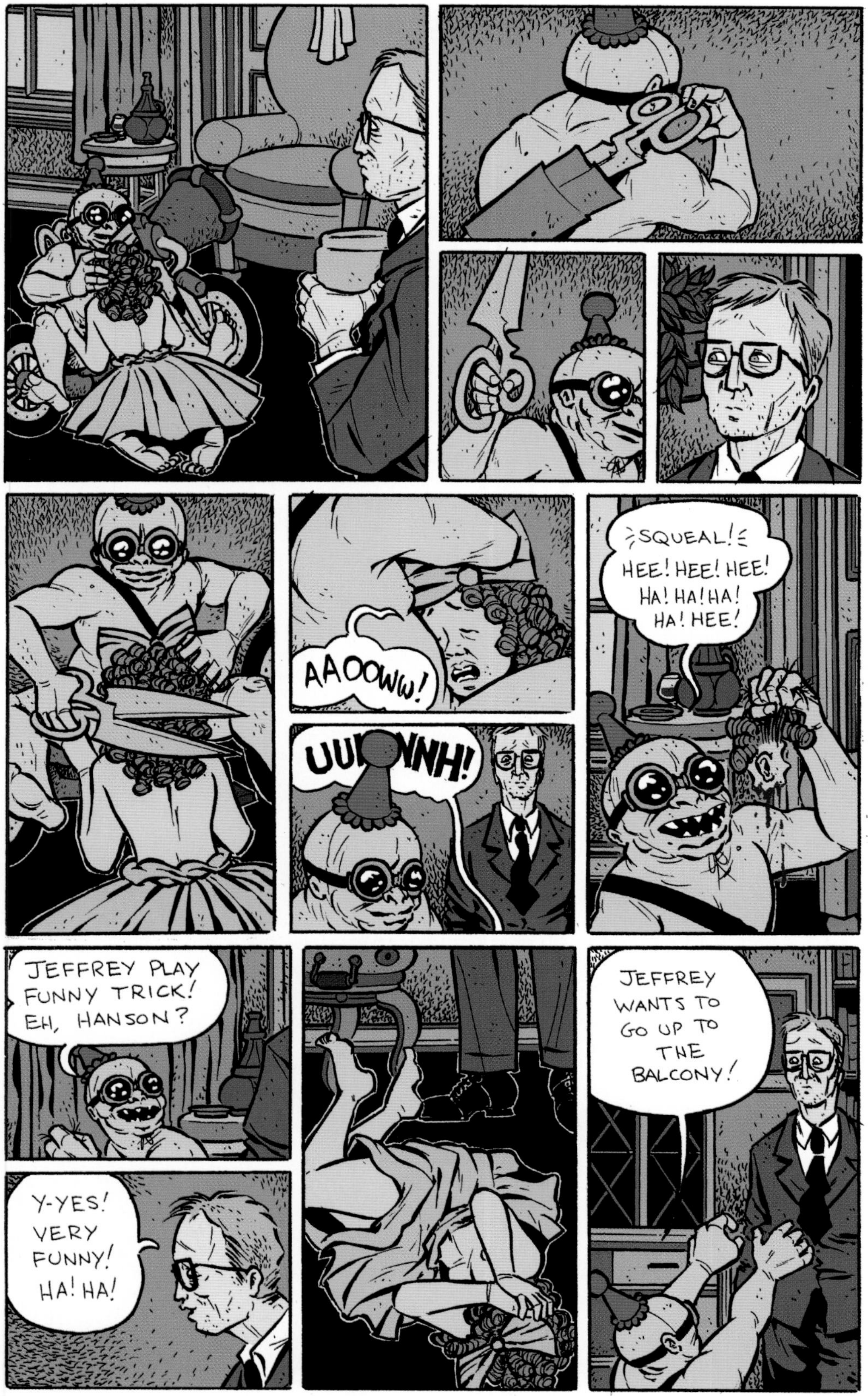
AAOOWW!
UUNNH!
SQUEAL!
HEE! HEE! HEE! HA! HA! HA! HA! HEE!
JEFFREY PLAY FUNNY TRICK! EH, HANSON?
Y-YES! VERY FUNNY! HA! HA!
JEFFREY WANTS TO GO UP TO THE BALCONY!

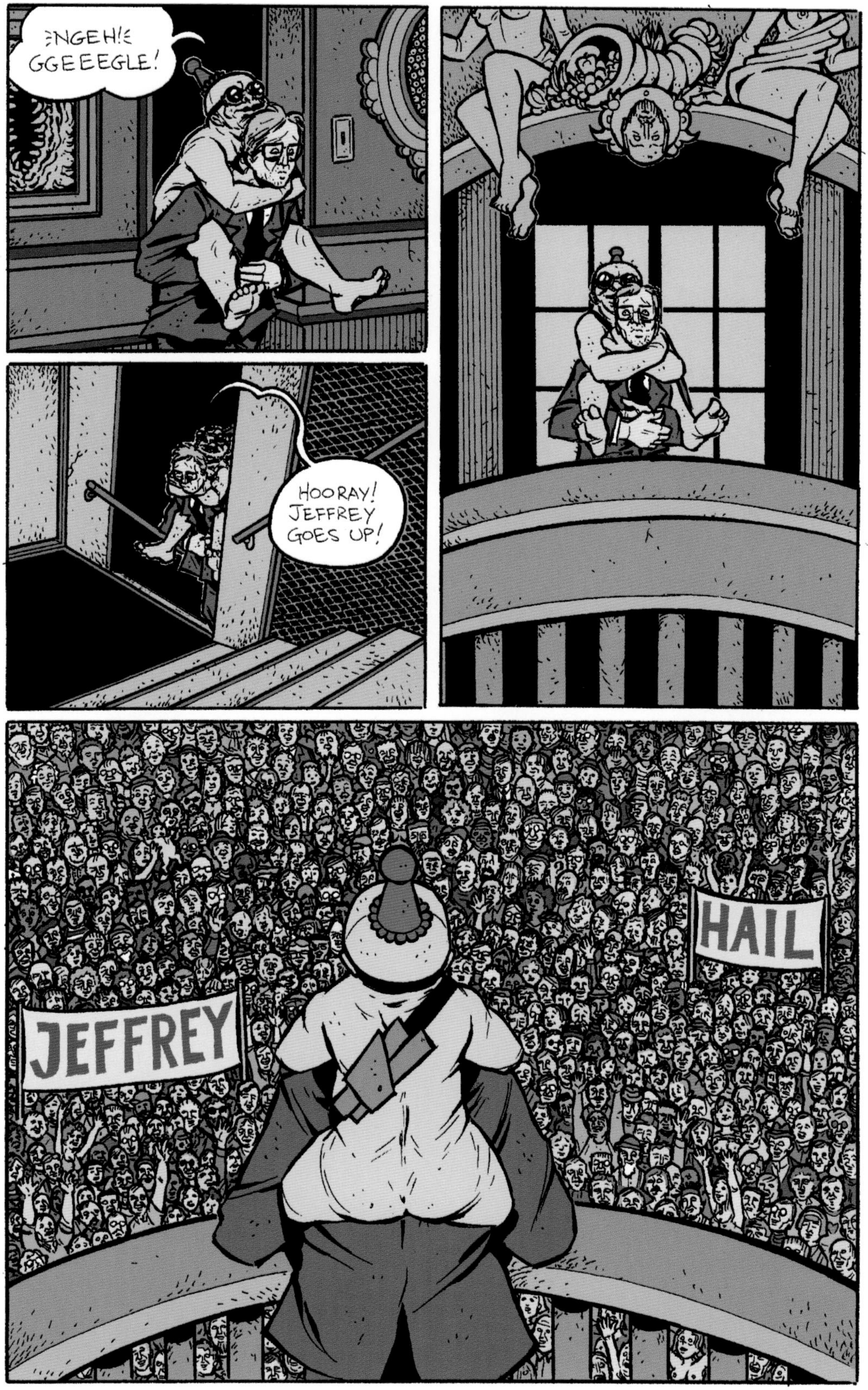
NGEH!
GGEEEGLE!
HOORAY! JEFFREY GOES UP!
HAIL
JEFFREY

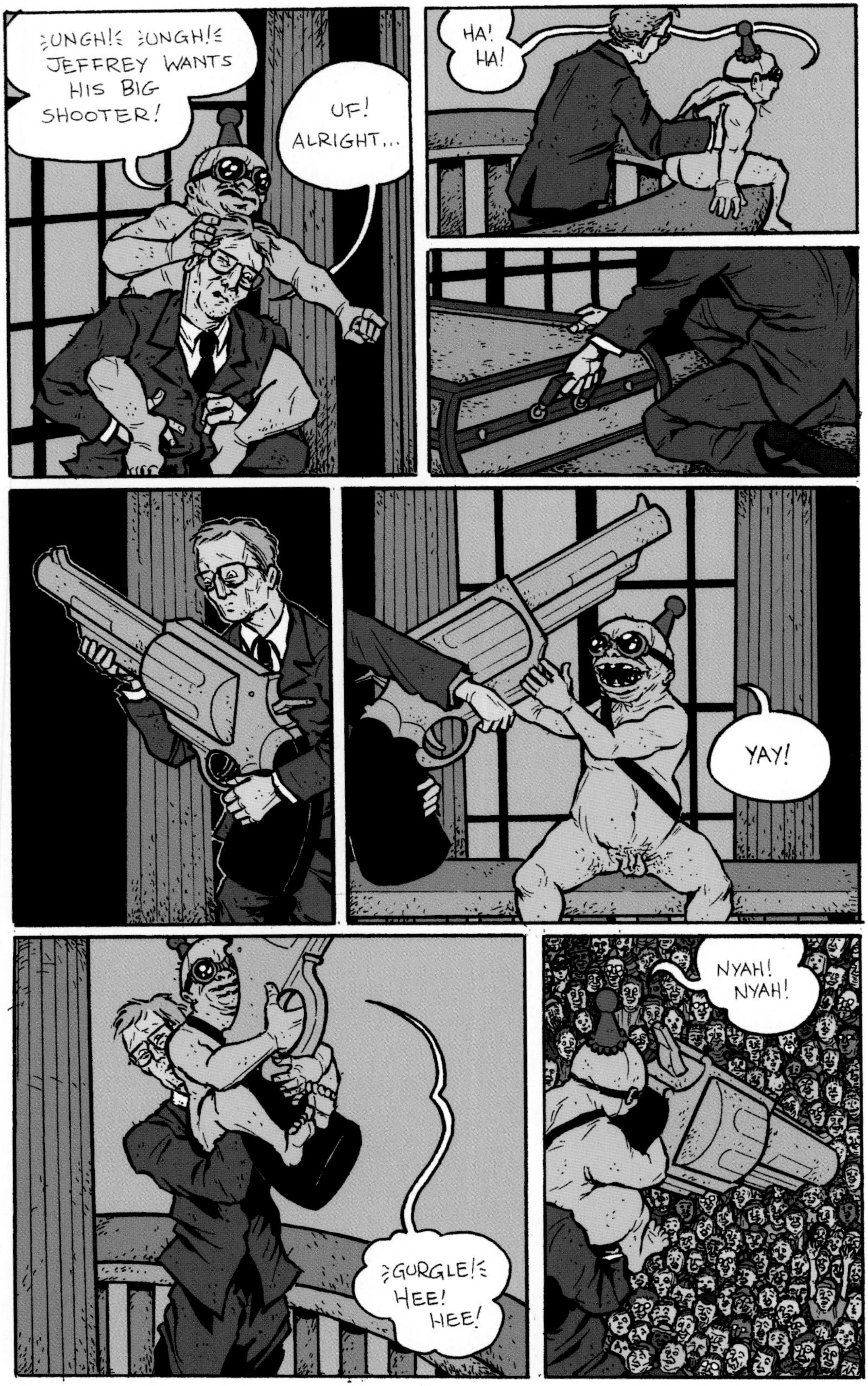

UNGH! UNGH! JEFFREY WANTS HIS BIG SHOOTER!
UF! ALRIGHT...
HA! HA!
YAY!
GURGLE! HEE! HEE!
NYAH! NYAH!

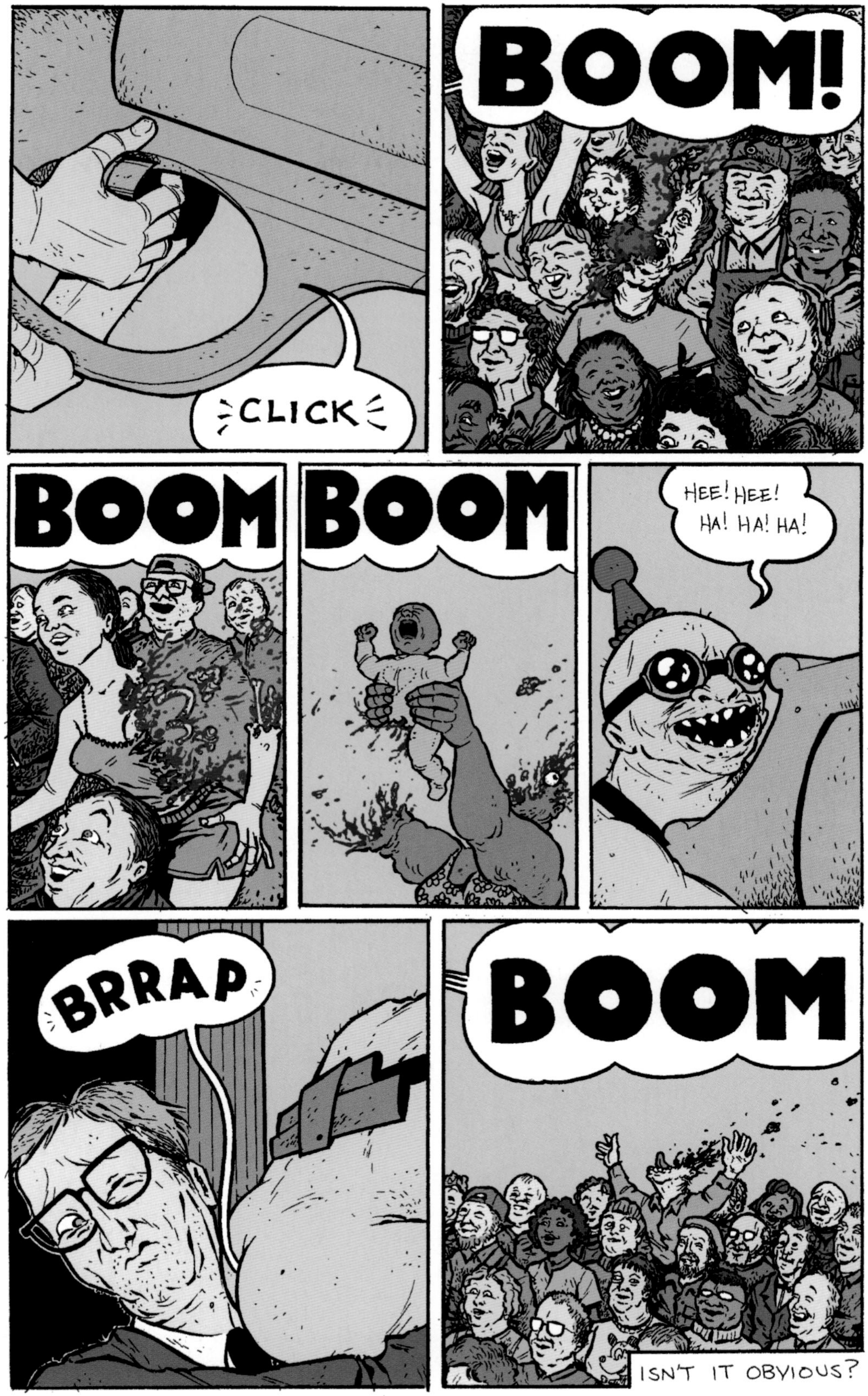
CLICK
BOOM!
BOOM
BOOM
HEE! HEE! HA! HA! HA!
BRRAP
BOOM
ISN'T IT OBVIOUS?

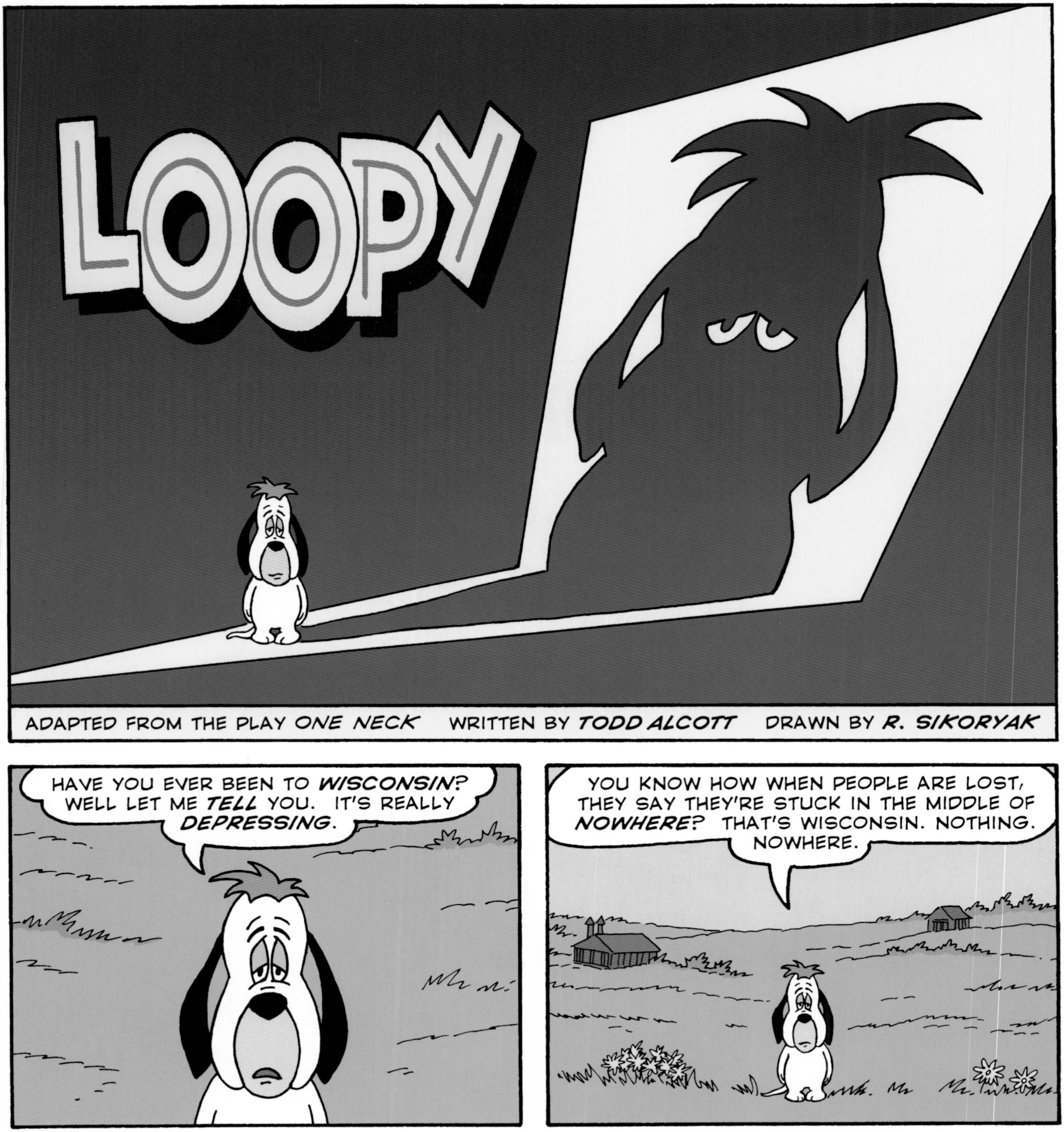
LOOPY
ADAPTED FROM THE PLAY ONE NECK WRITTEN BY TODD ALCOTT DRAWN BY R. SIKORYAK
HAVE YOU EVER BEEN TO WISCONSIN? WELL LET ME TELL YOU. IT'S REALLY DEPRESSING.
YOU KNOW HOW WHEN PEOPLE ARE LOST, THEY SAY THEY'RE STUCK IN THE MIDDLE OF NOWHERE? THAT'S WISCONSIN. NOTHING. NOWHERE.

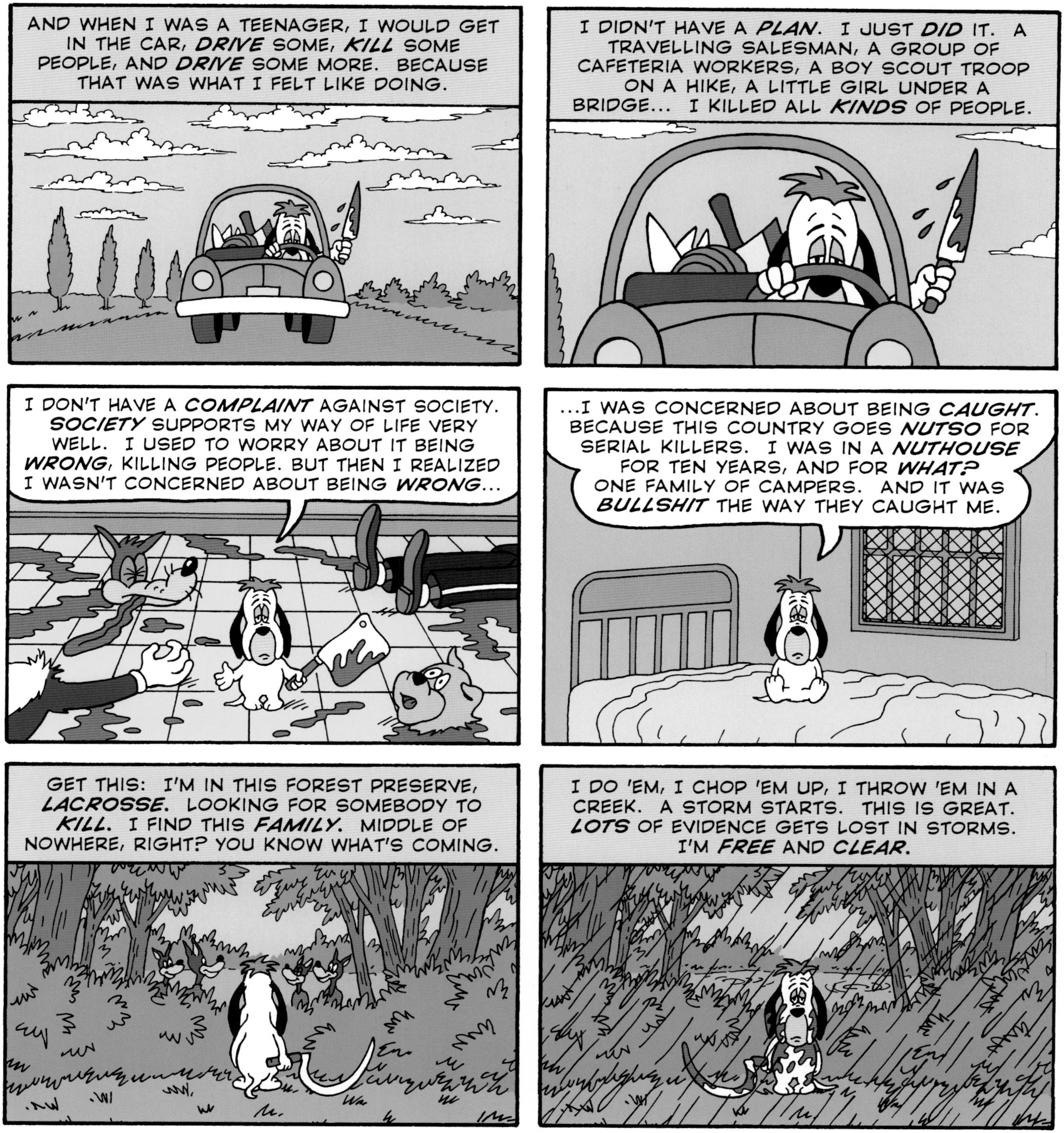
AND WHEN I WAS A TEENAGER, I WOULD GET IN THE CAR, DRIVE SOME, KILL SOME PEOPLE, AND DRIVE SOME MORE. BECAUSE THAT WAS WHAT I FELT LIKE DOING.
I DIDN'T HAVE A PLAN. I JUST DID IT. A TRAVELLING SALESMAN, A GROUP OF CAFETERIA WORKERS, A BOY SCOUT TROOP ON A HIKE, A LITTLE GIRL UNDER A BRIDGE... I KILLED ALL KINDS OF PEOPLE.
I DON'T HAVE A COMPLAINT AGAINST SOCIETY. SOCIETY SUPPORTS MY WAY OF LIFE VERY WELL. I USED TO WORRY ABOUT IT BEING WRONG, KILLING PEOPLE. BUT THEN I REALIZED I WASN'T CONCERNED ABOUT BEING WRONG...
...I WAS CONCERNED ABOUT BEING CAUGHT. BECAUSE THIS COUNTRY GOES NUTSO FOR SERIAL KILLERS. I WAS IN A NUTHOUSE FOR TEN YEARS, AND FOR WHAT? ONE FAMILY OF CAMPERS. AND IT WAS BULLSHIT THE WAY THEY CAUGHT ME.
GET THIS: I'M IN THIS FOREST PRESERVE, LACROSSE. LOOKING FOR SOMEBODY TO KILL. I FIND THIS FAMILY. MIDDLE OF NOWHERE, RIGHT? YOU KNOW WHAT'S COMING.
I DO 'EM, I CHOP 'EM UP, I THROW 'EM IN A CREEK. A STORM STARTS. THIS IS GREAT. LOTS OF EVIDENCE GETS LOST IN STORMS. I'M FREE AND CLEAR.

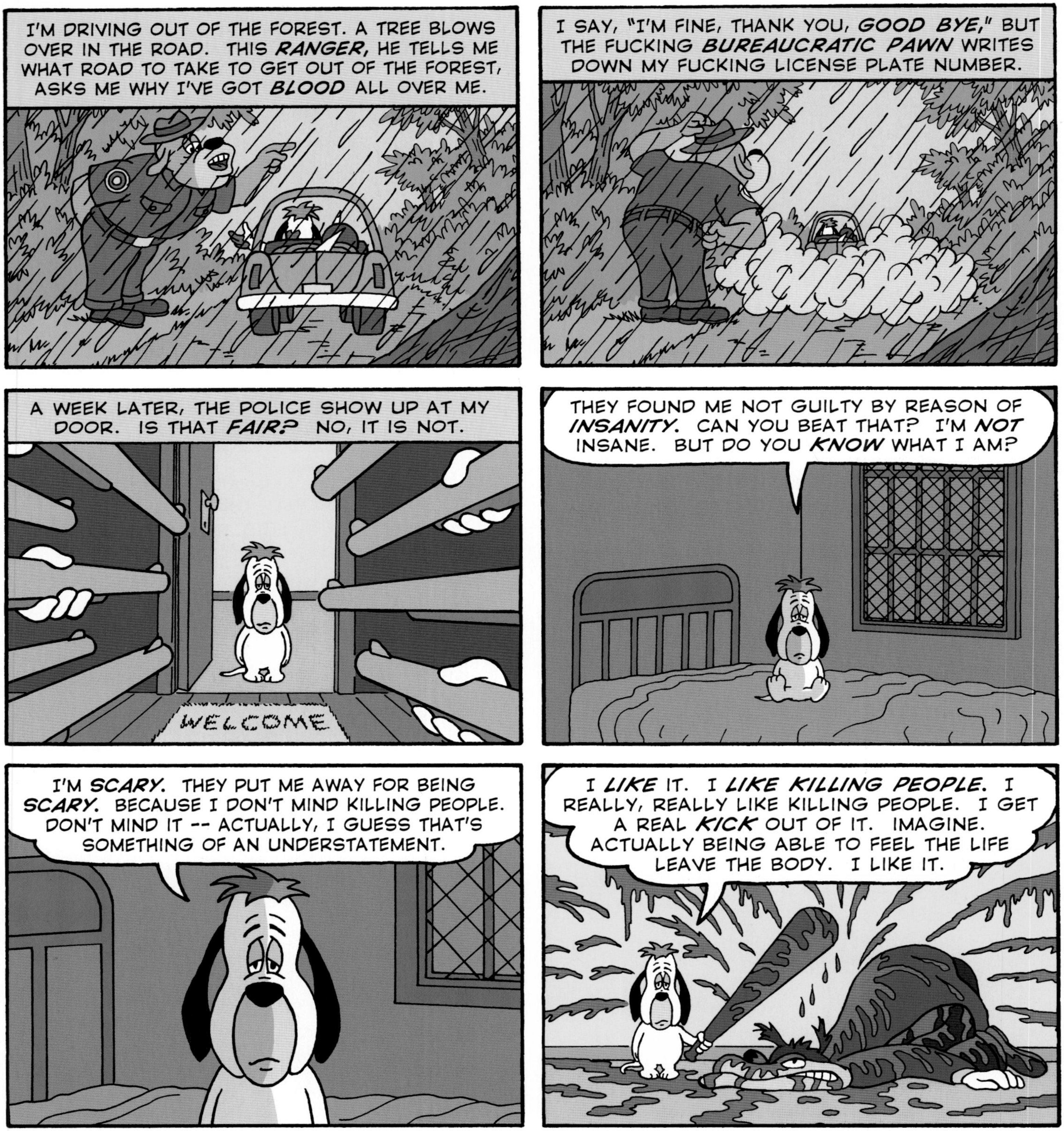
I'M DRIVING OUT OF THE FOREST. A TREE BLOWS OVER IN THE ROAD. THIS RANGER, HE TELLS ME WHAT ROAD TO TAKE TO GET OUT OF THE FOREST, ASKS ME WHY I'VE GOT BLOOD ALL OVER ME.
I SAY, "I'M FINE, THANK YOU, GOOD BYE," BUT THE FUCKING BUREAUCRATIC PAWN WRITES DOWN MY FUCKING LICENSE PLATE NUMBER.
A WEEK LATER, THE POLICE SHOW UP AT MY DOOR. IS THAT FAIR? NO, IT IS NOT.
WELCOME
THEY FOUND ME NOT GUILTY BY REASON OF INSANITY. CAN YOU BEAT THAT? I'M NOT INSANE. BUT DO YOU KNOW WHAT I AM?
I'M SCARY. THEY PUT ME AWAY FOR BEING SCARY. BECAUSE I DON'T MIND KILLING PEOPLE. DON'T MIND IT -- ACTUALLY, I GUESS THAT'S SOMETHING OF AN UNDERSTATEMENT.
I LIKE IT. I LIKE KILLING PEOPLE. I REALLY, REALLY LIKE KILLING PEOPLE. I GET A REAL KICK OUT OF IT. IMAGINE. ACTUALLY BEING ABLE TO FEEL THE LIFE LEAVE THE BODY. I LIKE IT.

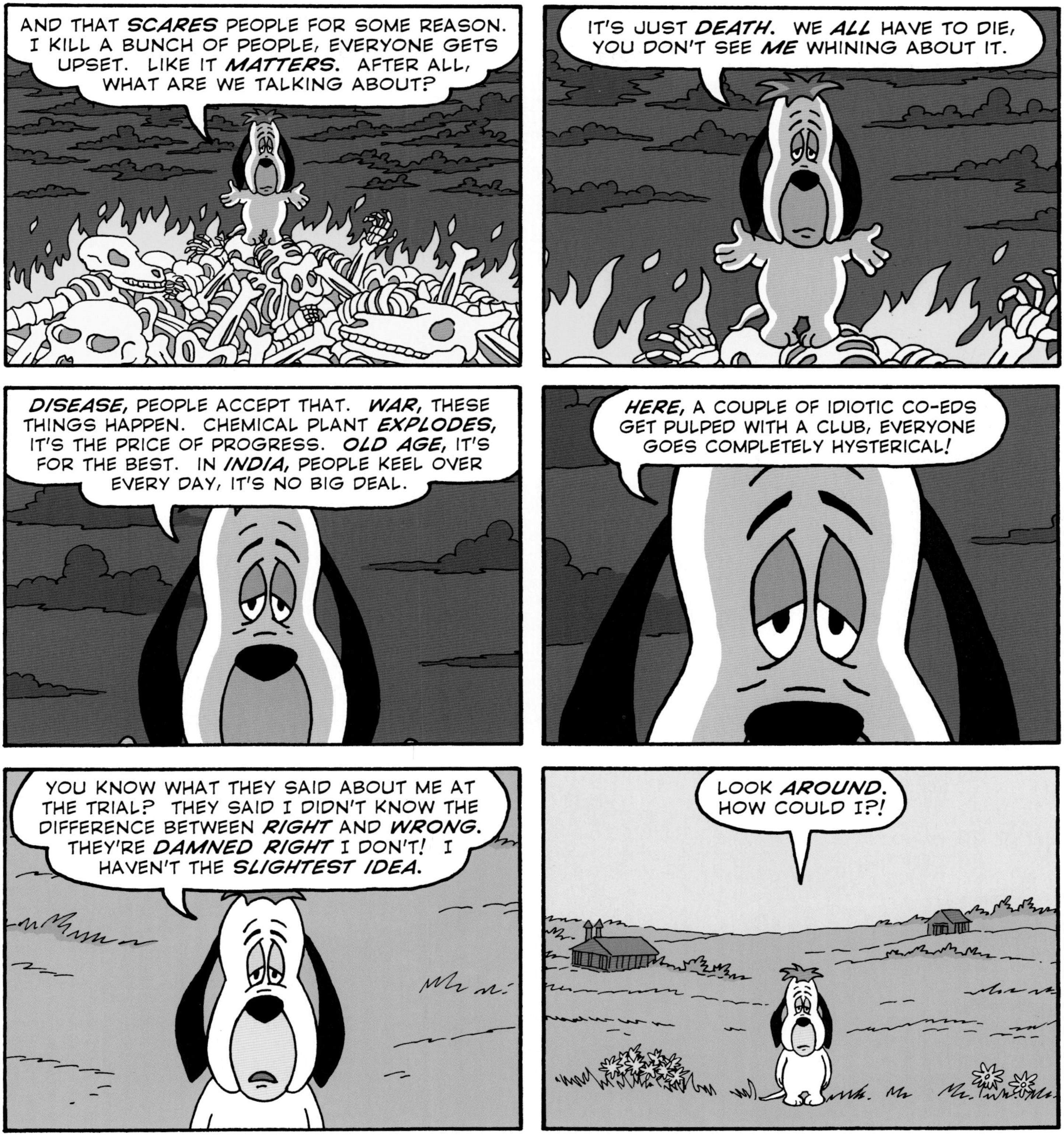
AND THAT SCARES PEOPLE FOR SOME REASON. I KILL A BUNCH OF PEOPLE, EVERYONE GETS UPSET. LIKE IT MATTERS. AFTER ALL, WHAT ARE WE TALKING ABOUT?
IT'S JUST DEATH. WE ALL HAVE TO DIE, YOU DON'T SEE ME WHINING ABOUT IT.
DISEASE, PEOPLE ACCEPT THAT. WAR, THESE THINGS HAPPEN. CHEMICAL PLANT EXPLODES, IT'S THE PRICE OF PROGRESS. OLD AGE, IT'S FOR THE BEST. IN INDIA, PEOPLE KEEL OVER EVERY DAY, IT'S NO BIG DEAL.
HERE, A COUPLE OF IDIOTIC CO-EDS GET PULPED WITH A CLUB, EVERYONE GOES COMPLETELY HYSTERICAL!
YOU KNOW WHAT THEY SAID ABOUT ME AT THE TRIAL? THEY SAID I DIDN'T KNOW THE DIFFERENCE BETWEEN RIGHT AND WRONG. THEY'RE DAMNED RIGHT I DON'T! I HAVEN'T THE SLIGHTEST IDEA.
LOOK AROUND. HOW COULD I?!

SATAN'S SLAVES

EVER SINCE I WAS A CHILD I'VE HAD THIS DEEP, DARK FEAR OF THE DEVIL ~ OR "SATAN" TO BE EXACT ~ IF SUCH A THING EXISTS... BEING A MOVIE-ADDICT SURELY DIDN'T HELP ~ MY BROTHER LOUIE & I WATCHED MANY A HORROR-MOVIE TOGETHER, BUT IF A MOVIE DEALT WITH DEMONIC POSSESSION OR THE PRESENCE OF SATAN, IT SCARED THE WITS OUT OF ME... MY BROTHER SEEMED TO NEVER GET SCARED.

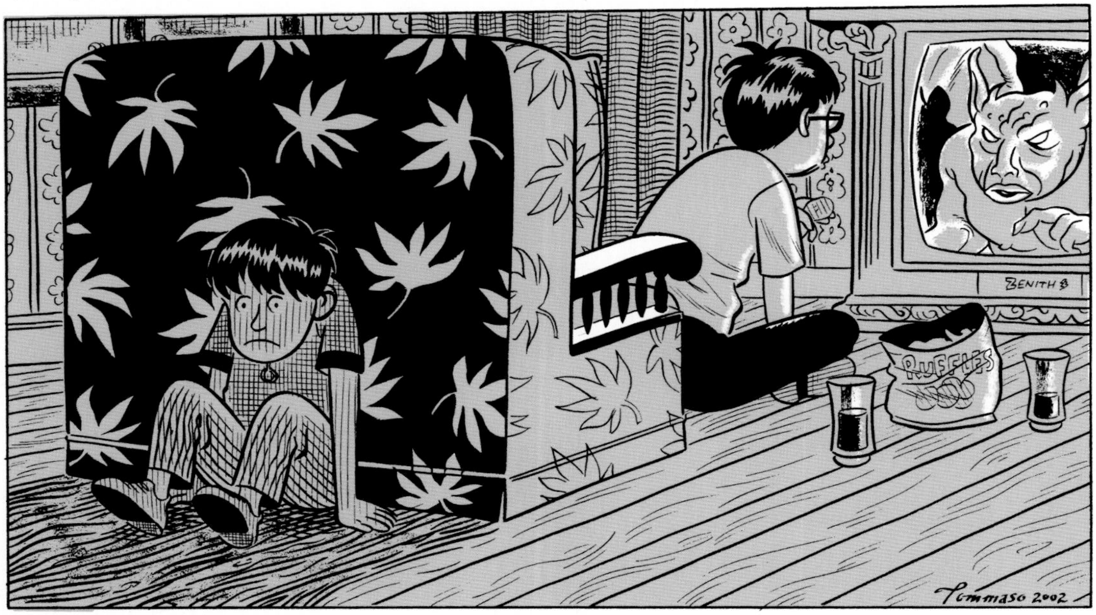
ZENITH
RUFFLES
Tommaso 2002

I GUESS I'VE ALWAYS LIVED IN A "FANTASY-WORLD", WHAT WITH ALL THE HOURS I'D SPENT IN FRONT OF THE T.V. WATCHING MOVIES AS A KID... AT TIMES I GOT TOO EMOTIONALLY CAUGHT-UP IN THE SITUATIONS — AS A RESULT, I BECAME QUITE AN IMPRESSIONABLE CHILD.

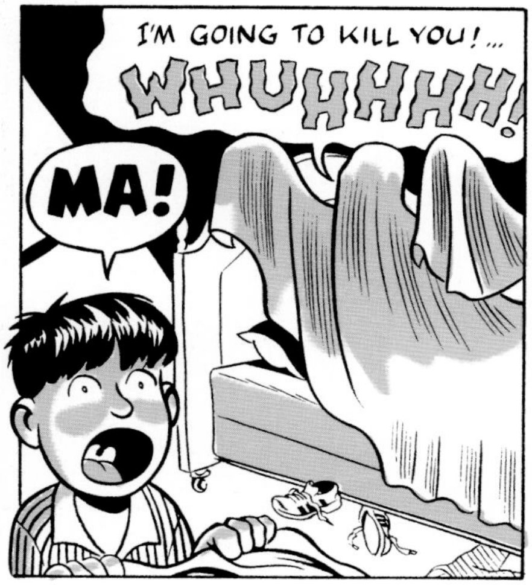
I'M GOING TO KILL YOU!...
WHUHHHH!
MA!

ONCE, WHEN I WAS FIVE YRS. OLD I WAS AWAKENED IN THE MIDDLE OF THE NIGHT, BY WHAT SOUNDED LIKE A DEMON ROAMING THROUGH OUR HOUSE ~ I IMAGINED IT A DEMON BECAUSE EARLIER I'D SEEN "GARGOYLES" ~ A MOVIE ON T.V. ~ & OF COURSE, IT'D FREAKED-ME-OUT. I COULDN'T GET A WINK OF SLEEP THAT ENTIRE NIGHT...

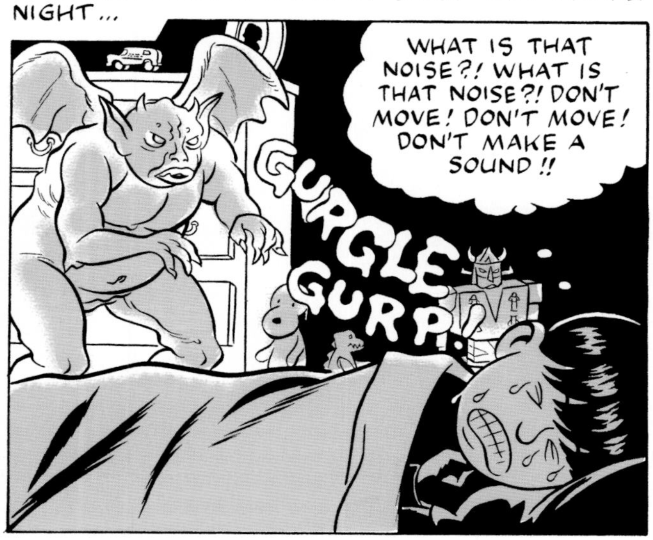
WHAT IS THAT NOISE?! WHAT IS THAT NOISE?! DON'T MOVE! DON'T MOVE! DON'T MAKE A SOUND!!
GURGLE
GURP!

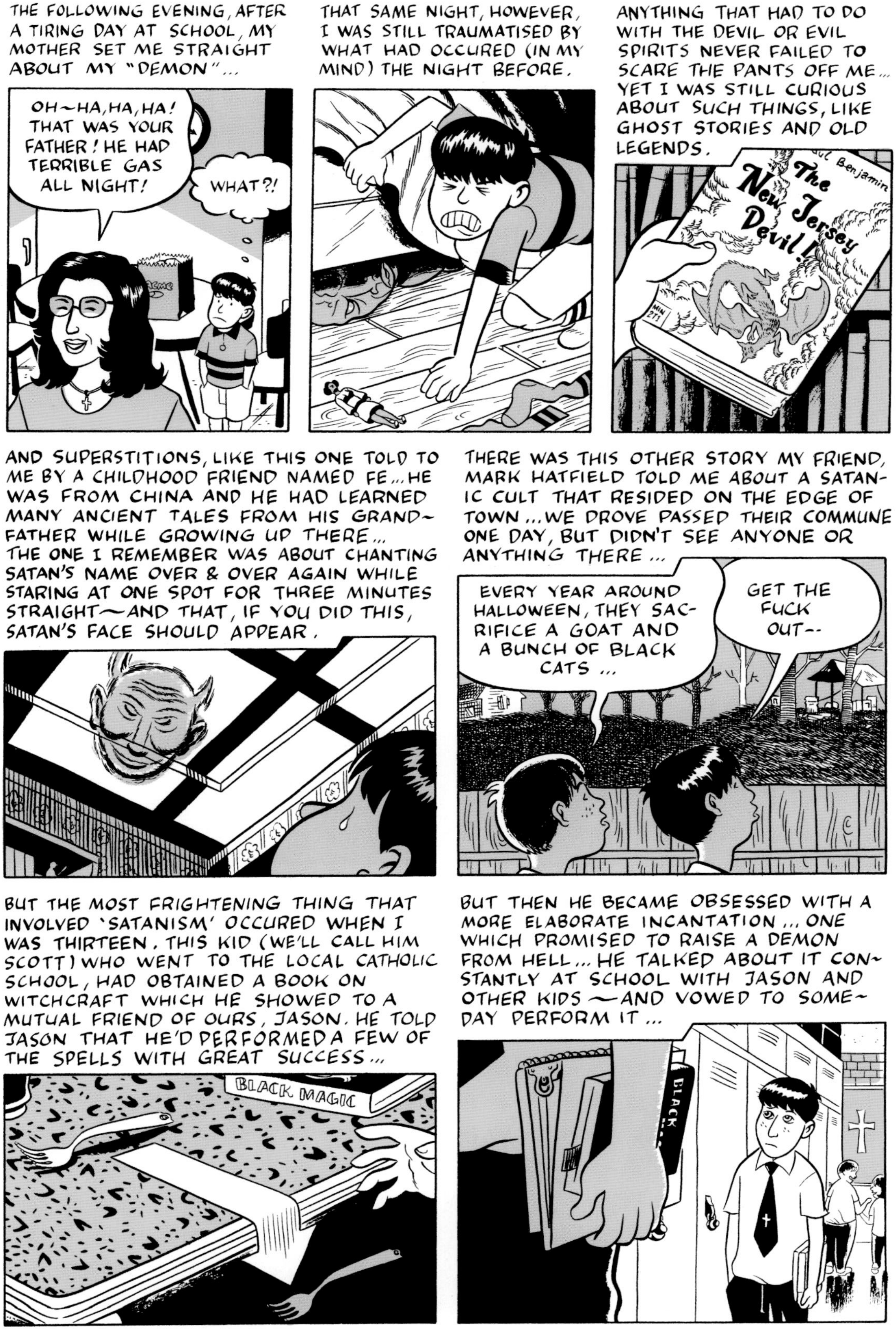
THE FOLLOWING EVENING, AFTER A TIRING DAY AT SCHOOL, MY MOTHER SET ME STRAIGHT ABOUT MY "DEMON"...
OH~HA, HA, HA! THAT WAS YOUR FATHER! HE HAD TERRIBLE GAS ALL NIGHT!
WHAT?!
ACME
THAT SAME NIGHT, HOWEVER, I WAS STILL TRAUMATISED BY WHAT HAD OCCURED (IN MY MIND) THE NIGHT BEFORE.
ANYTHING THAT HAD TO DO WITH THE DEVIL OR EVIL SPIRITS NEVER FAILED TO SCARE THE PANTS OFF ME... YET I WAS STILL CURIOUS ABOUT SUCH THINGS, LIKE GHOST STORIES AND OLD LEGENDS.
The New Jersey Devil!
AND SUPERSTITIONS, LIKE THIS ONE TOLD TO ME BY A CHILDHOOD FRIEND NAMED FE... HE WAS FROM CHINA AND HE HAD LEARNED MANY ANCIENT TALES FROM HIS GRAND~FATHER WHILE GROWING UP THERE... THE ONE I REMEMBER WAS ABOUT CHANTING SATAN'S NAME OVER & OVER AGAIN WHILE STARING AT ONE SPOT FOR THREE MINUTES STRAIGHT—AND THAT, IF YOU DID THIS, SATAN'S FACE SHOULD APPEAR.
THERE WAS THIS OTHER STORY MY FRIEND, MARK HATFIELD TOLD ME ABOUT A SATAN-IC CULT THAT RESIDED ON THE EDGE OF TOWN... WE DROVE PASSED THEIR COMMUNE ONE DAY, BUT DIDN'T SEE ANYONE OR ANYTHING THERE...
EVERY YEAR AROUND HALLOWEEN, THEY SAC-RIFICE A GOAT AND A BUNCH OF BLACK CATS...
GET THE FUCK OUT--
BUT THE MOST FRIGHTENING THING THAT INVOLVED 'SATANISM' OCCURED WHEN I WAS THIRTEEN. THIS KID (WE'LL CALL HIM SCOTT) WHO WENT TO THE LOCAL CATHOLIC SCHOOL, HAD OBTAINED A BOOK ON WITCHCRAFT WHICH HE SHOWED TO A MUTUAL FRIEND OF OURS, JASON. HE TOLD JASON THAT HE'D PERFORMED A FEW OF THE SPELLS WITH GREAT SUCCESS...
BLACK MAGIC
BUT THEN HE BECAME OBSESSED WITH A MORE ELABORATE INCANTATION... ONE WHICH PROMISED TO RAISE A DEMON FROM HELL... HE TALKED ABOUT IT CON~STANTLY AT SCHOOL WITH JASON AND OTHER KIDS—AND VOWED TO SOME~DAY PERFORM IT...
BLACK

SUFFICIENTLY SPOOKED, JASON ALERTED THE NUNS AT SCHOOL ABOUT THIS AND THEY STRONGLY URGED HIM TO WARN SCOTT OF THE REPURCUSS-IONS ~ FOR IF HE PERFORMED THE INCANTATION, IT WOULD BE A SUCCESS ~ FOR **SATAN** ... BUT SCOTT WOULD ONLY SUFFER ~ AND LOSE HIS SOUL FOR IT.

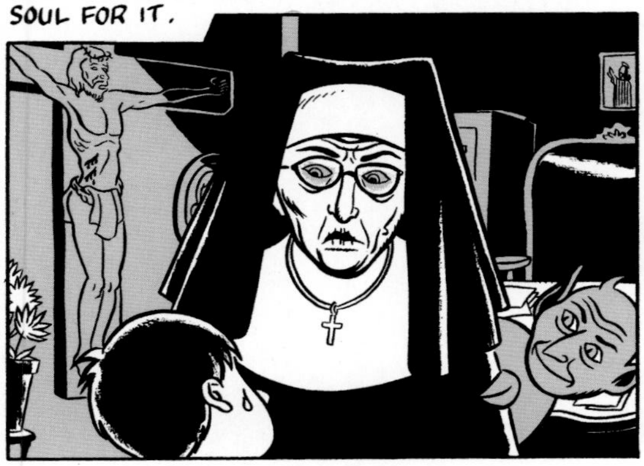

WHEN JASON RELATED THESE DETAILS TO ME, A HORRIBLE CHILL ROLLED UP MY SPINE ... AND THEN ~ ABOUT A DAY OR TWO LATER ~ WHILE MY MOTHER DROVE JASON AND I HOME FROM BASEBALL PRACTICE, THE RADIO FLASH-ED A TRAGIC NEWS UPDATE ...

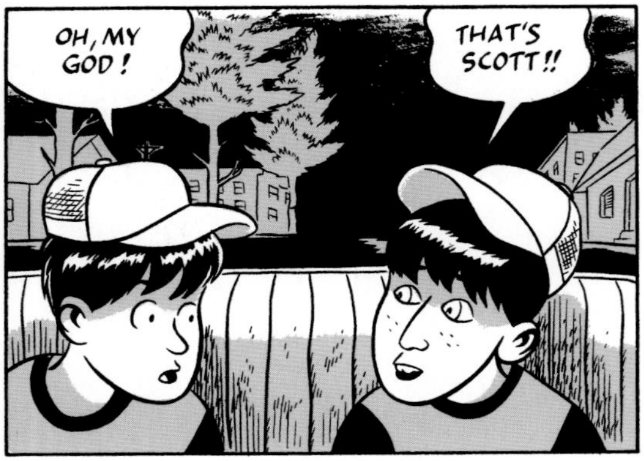
OH, MY GOD!
THAT'S SCOTT!!

SCOTT HAD COMMITED SUICIDE ... WE GOT THE FULL STORY ON T.V. LATER, AT MY HOUSE ... SCOTT HAD PAINTED SATANIC SYMBOLS ON THE BASEMENT FLOOR OF HIS HOUSE, ACCORDING TO THE BOOK'S ILLUSTRATIONS, AND HAD PERFORMED THE RITE ...

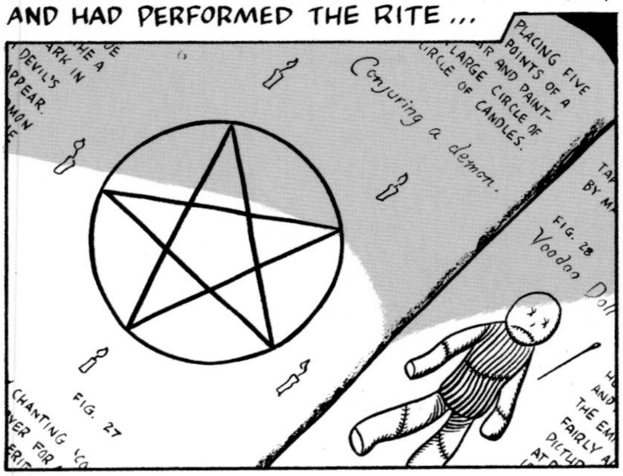
Conjuring a demon.
FIG. 27
FIG. 28

HE MURDERED HIS MOTHER AND FATHER AND HIS YOUNGER SISTER, WHILE THEY WERE SLEEPING. HE THEN RAN OFF INTO ANOTHER NEIGHBORHOOD AND WAS FOUND THE NEXT MORNING, DEAD, ON SOMEONE'S FRONT PORCH ~ WRISTS SLASHED AND HIS THROAT CUT FROM EAR TO EAR, BY HIS OWN HAND.

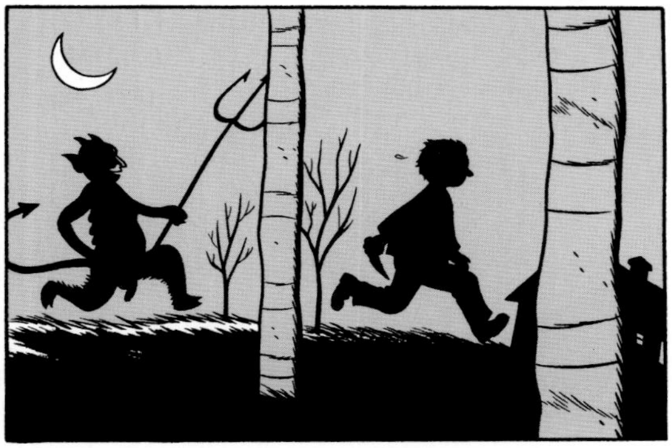

THE POLICE WERE BAFFLED BY THIS ... HOW COULD A YOUNG (12 YR. OLD) KID HAVE THE STRENGTH TO BOTH ~ CUT HIS WRISTS AND THEN CUT HIS OWN THROAT? THIS SEEMED PHYSICALLY IMPROBABLE, AND IT WAS THIS MYSTERIOUS CIRCUMSTANCE THAT LED ME TO BELIEVE HE'D ACTUALLY SUM-MONED A DEVIL TO EARTHLY GROUND!

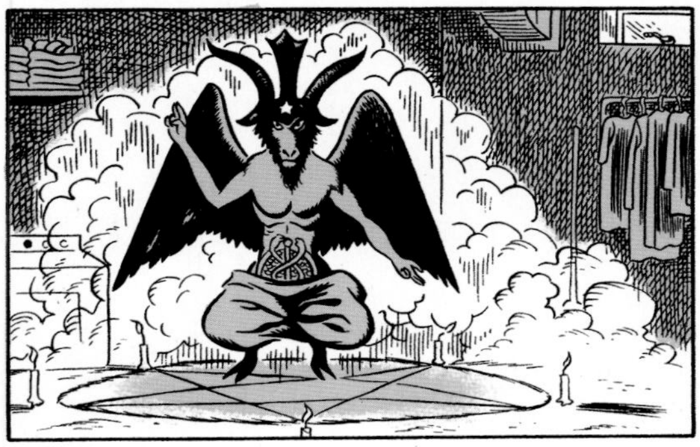

FOR WEEKS THESE KILLINGS DISTURBED ME, AND CONFIRMED MY BELIEF IN THE EXISTENCE OF SATAN ... I COULDN'T FIND ANY LOGICAL EXPLANATION FOR THESE ACTIONS OF BRUTAL ITY. I WAS STILL VERY YOUNG AND IMPRESS IONABLE TOO ...

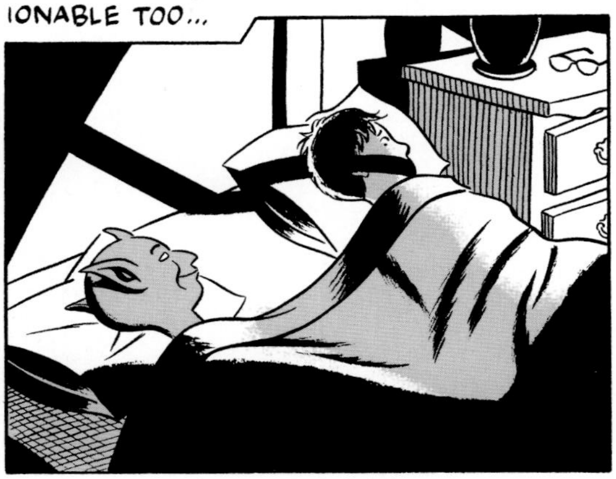

WHO KNOWS WHAT REALLY HAPPENED ON THAT NIGHT... WHEN I THINK OF IT TODAY, IT STILL MYSTIFIES ME. BUT NOW, AS A MATURE ADULT, I **CAN** SEE SOME LOGIC THEORIES, LIKE; MAYBE HE WAS ON SOME HEAVY-DUTY DRUGS OR PERHAPS THERE WAS ANOTHER PARTY INVOLVED—WHO KILLED SCOTT AND MADE IT LOOK LIKE A SUICIDE...

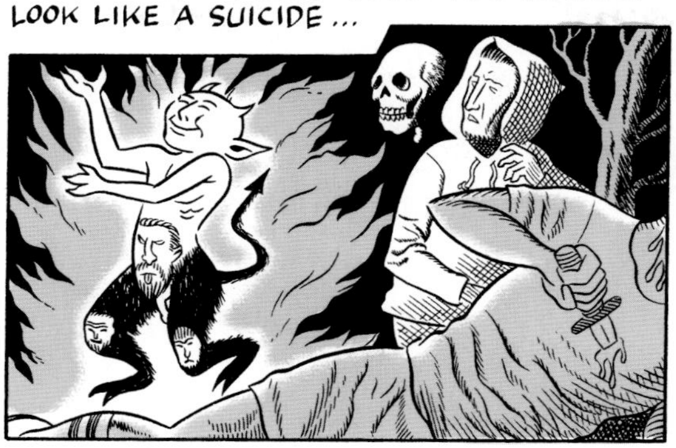

TODAY, MY FEAR OF 'THINGS-THAT-GO-BUMP-IN THE-NIGHT' ARE STILL SOMEWHAT THERE, BUT MY BELIEF IN A SATANIC FIGURE HAS FADED... TO ME, SATAN SEEMS MORE AN EMBODIMENT OF SOME EVIL ESSENCE WITHIN OURSELVES—AN ASPECT OF HUMAN NATURE.

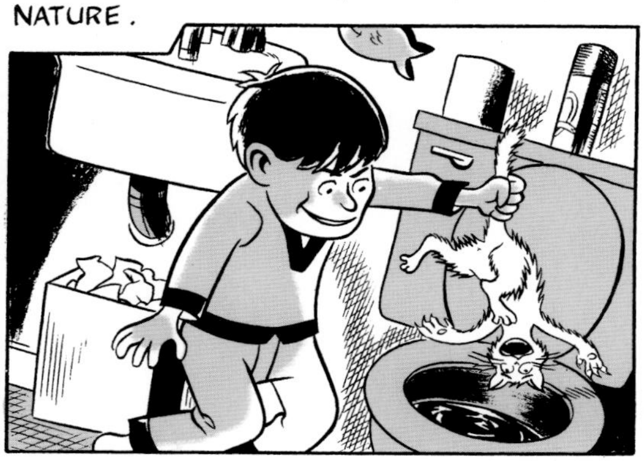

IT HAS BEEN SAID THAT HUMAN BEINGS ARE CRUEL BY NATURE... SOME JUST RELEASE A GREATER PERCENTAGE OF EVIL THAN OTHERS. WHILE SOME KEEP THEIR 'LITTLE DEMONS' TRAPPED INSIDE, OTHERS MAY POSSIBLY UNLEASH THEIR EVIL SIDES 100%... MAYBE THAT'S WHAT HAPPENS WHEN ONE GOES MAD...

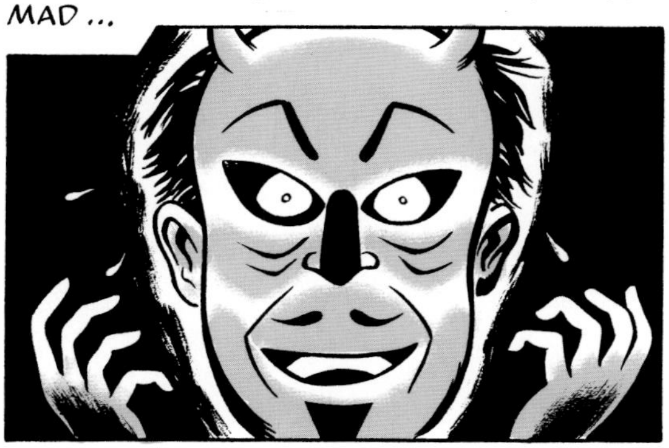

HAVE YOU EVER LOOKED AT A PHOTO OF A SERIAL KILLER'S FACE? THEIR SOUL SEEMS TO BE TOTALLY ERASED—LIKE A DEMON HAS TAKEN THEM OVER! NOTHING SEEMS TO BE THERE ANYMORE, BEHIND THEIR COLD EYES.

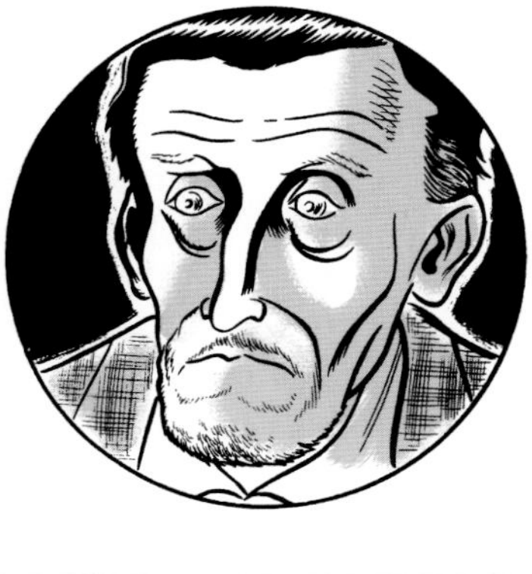

BUT WHAT CAUSES THOSE EVILS TO TAKE OVER? MEGALOMANIA? STRESS? AND WHAT OF WITCHCRAFT? IS IT ONLY A MANUAL THAT HELPS UNLEASH THOSE DORMANT POWERS OF DEVILRY INSIDE US ALL? WOULD SCOTT HAVE GONE MAD AT SOME POINT IN TIME ANYWAY? ... WHO KNOWS...

ONE THING I DO KNOW IS, WITH ALL THE CATHOLIC RHETORIC I'VE TOSSED AWAY AND REPLACED WITH EDUCATED LOGIC, THERE STILL REMAINS A PART OF ME THAT FEARS THE EXISTENCE OF A DEVIL INCARNATE...

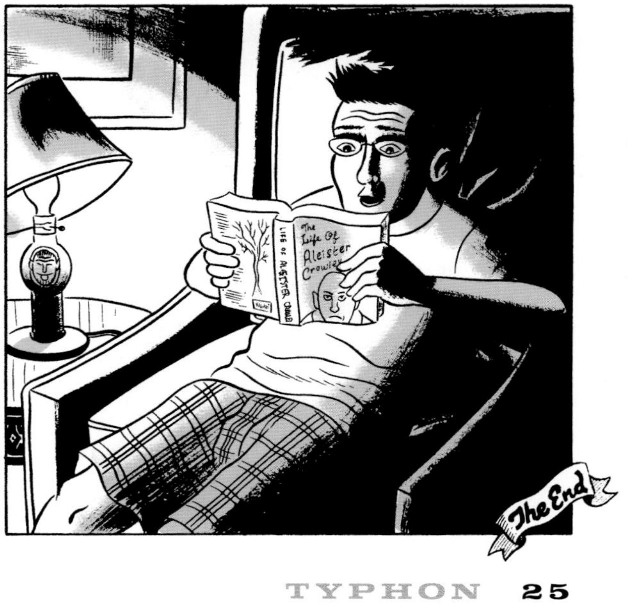
The Life Of Aleister Crowley
The End

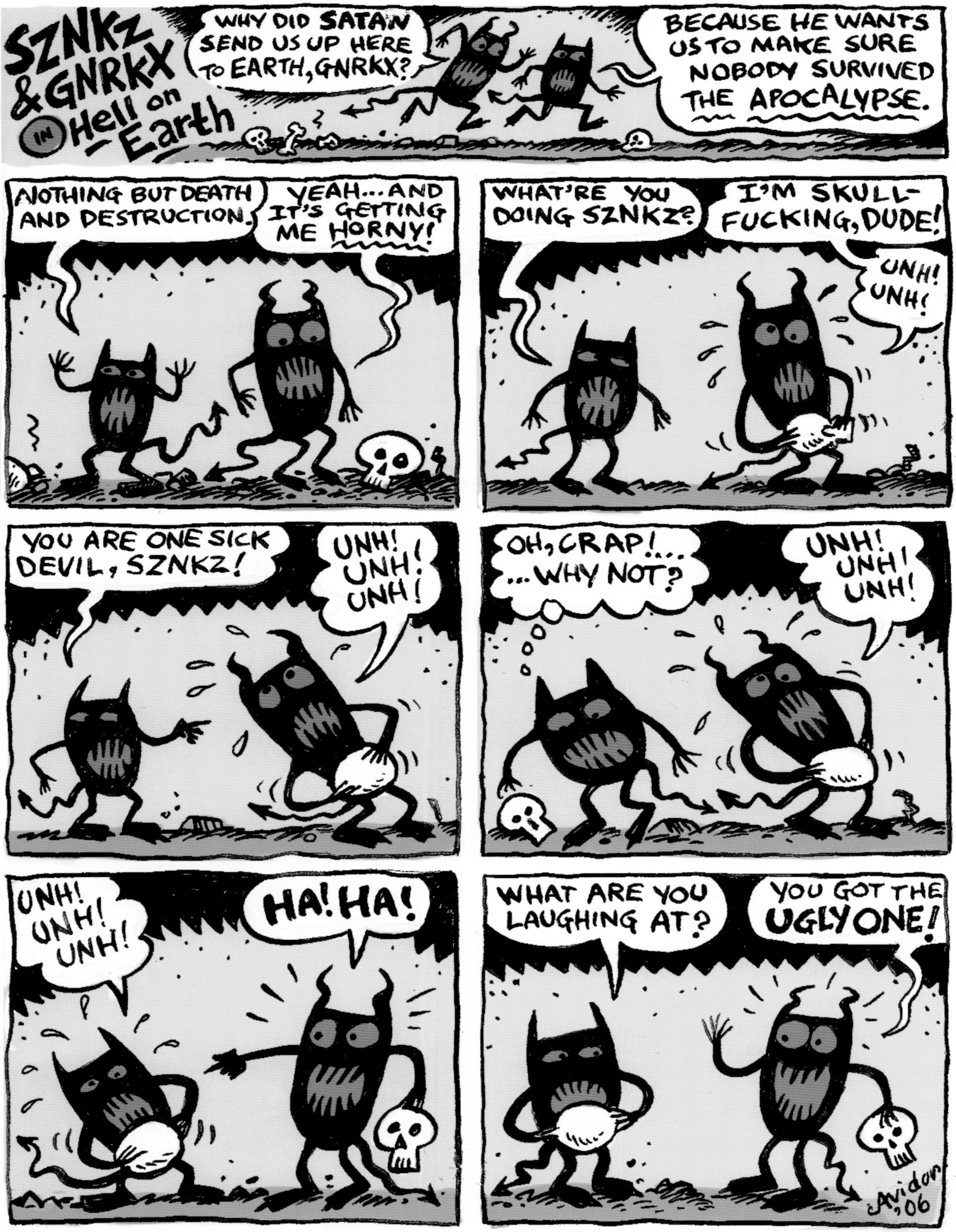
SZNKZ & GNRKX IN Hell on Earth
WHY DID SATAN SEND US UP HERE TO EARTH, GNRKX?
BECAUSE HE WANTS US TO MAKE SURE NOBODY SURVIVED THE APOCALYPSE.
NOTHING BUT DEATH AND DESTRUCTION.
YEAH... AND IT'S GETTING ME HORNY!
WHAT'RE YOU DOING SZNKZ?
I'M SKULL-FUCKING, DUDE!
UNH! UNH!
YOU ARE ONE SICK DEVIL, SZNKZ!
UNH! UNH! UNH!
OH, CRAP!... ...WHY NOT?
UNH! UNH! UNH!
UNH! UNH! UNH!
HA! HA!
WHAT ARE YOU LAUGHING AT?
YOU GOT THE UGLY ONE!
Avidon '06

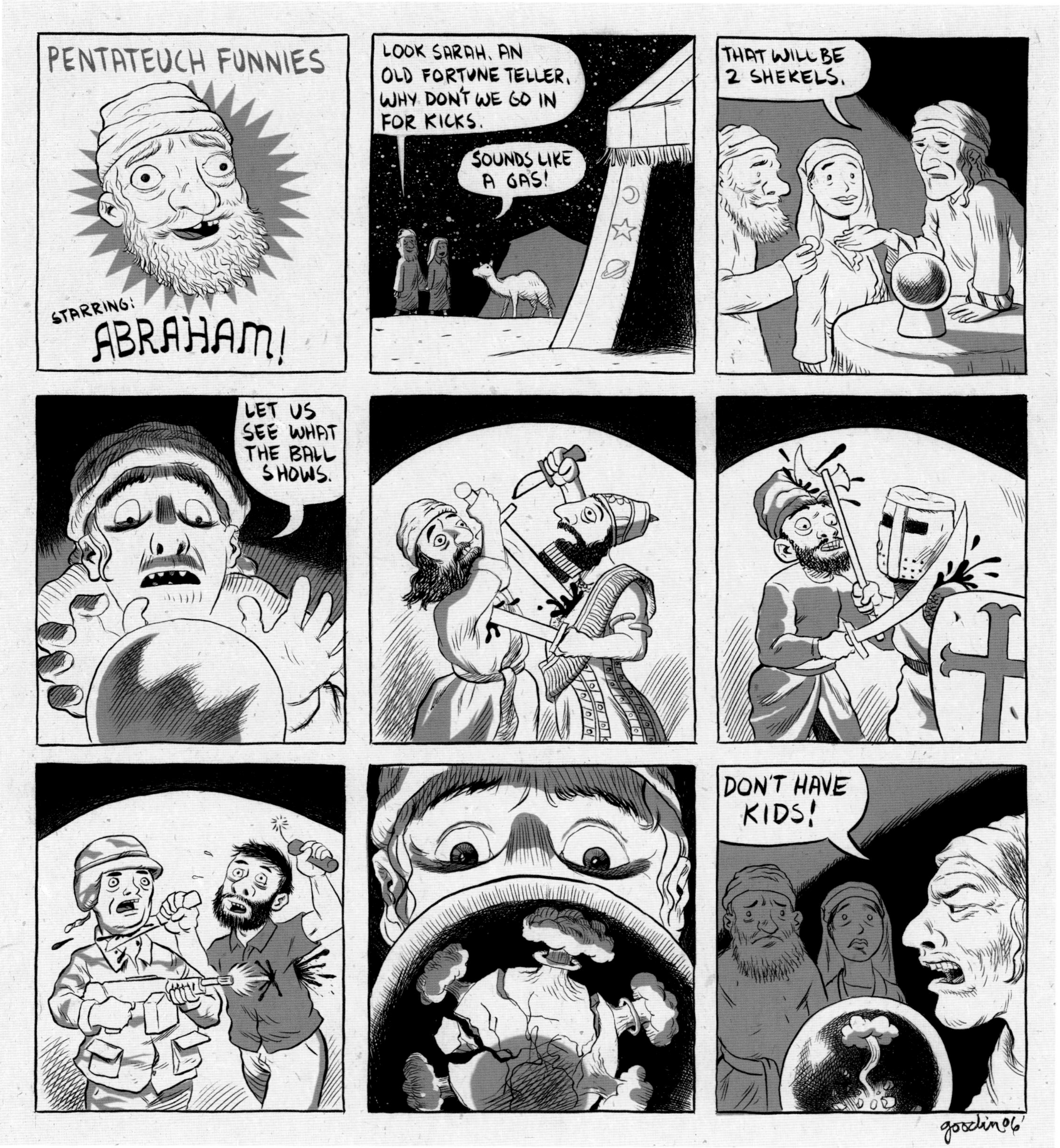
PENTATEUCH FUNNIES
STARRING: ABRAHAM!
LOOK SARAH. AN OLD FORTUNE TELLER. WHY DON'T WE GO IN FOR KICKS.
SOUNDS LIKE A GAS!
THAT WILL BE 2 SHEKELS.
LET US SEE WHAT THE BALL SHOWS.
DON'T HAVE KIDS!
goozlin 06'

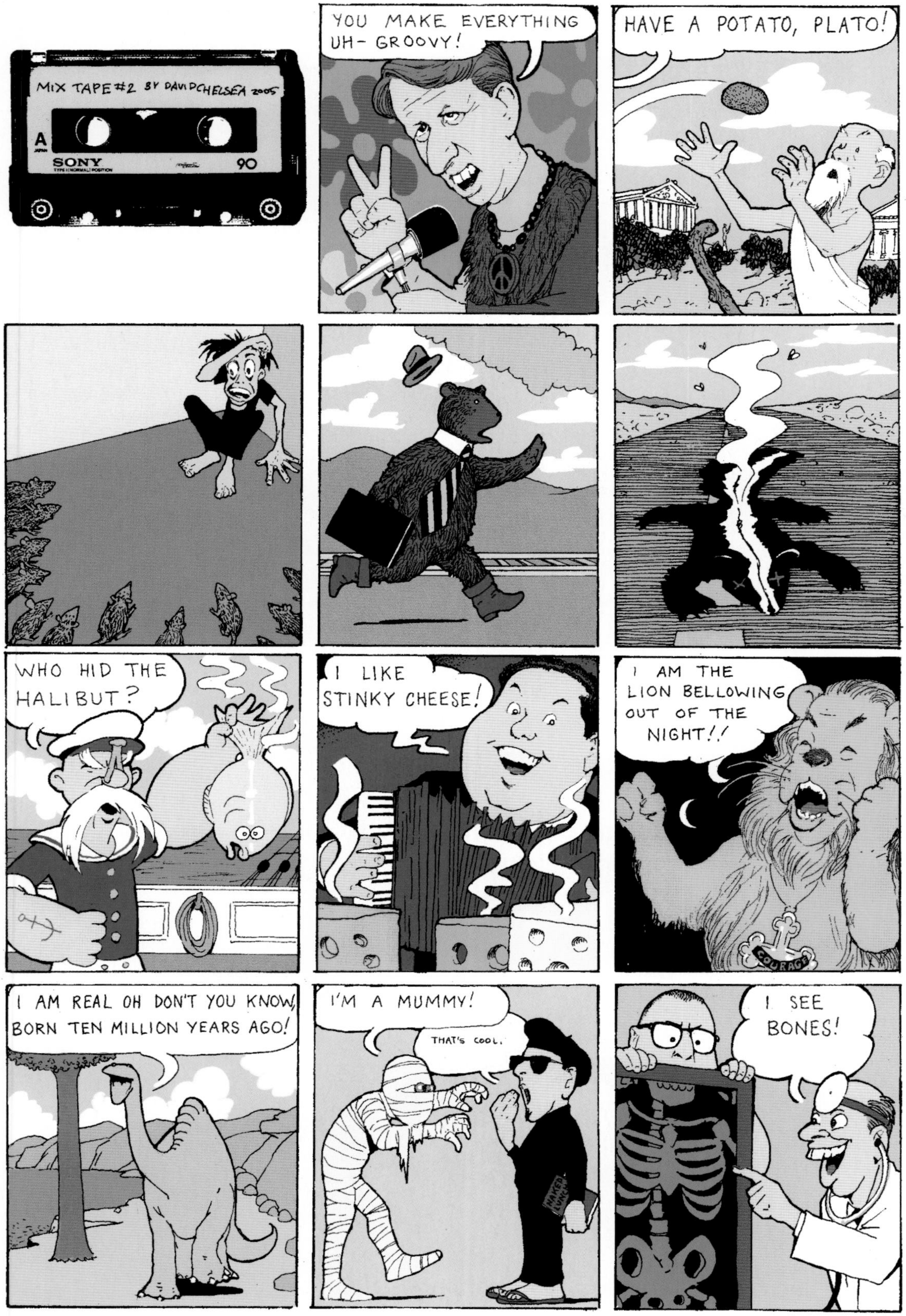
MIX TAPE #2 BY DAVID CHELSEA 2005
A
SONY
90
YOU MAKE EVERYTHING UH- GROOVY!
HAVE A POTATO, PLATO!
WHO HID THE HALIBUT?
I LIKE STINKY CHEESE!
I AM THE LION BELLOWING OUT OF THE NIGHT!!
COURAGE
I AM REAL OH DON'T YOU KNOW, BORN TEN MILLION YEARS AGO!
I'M A MUMMY!
THAT'S COOL.
NAKED LUNCH
I SEE BONES!

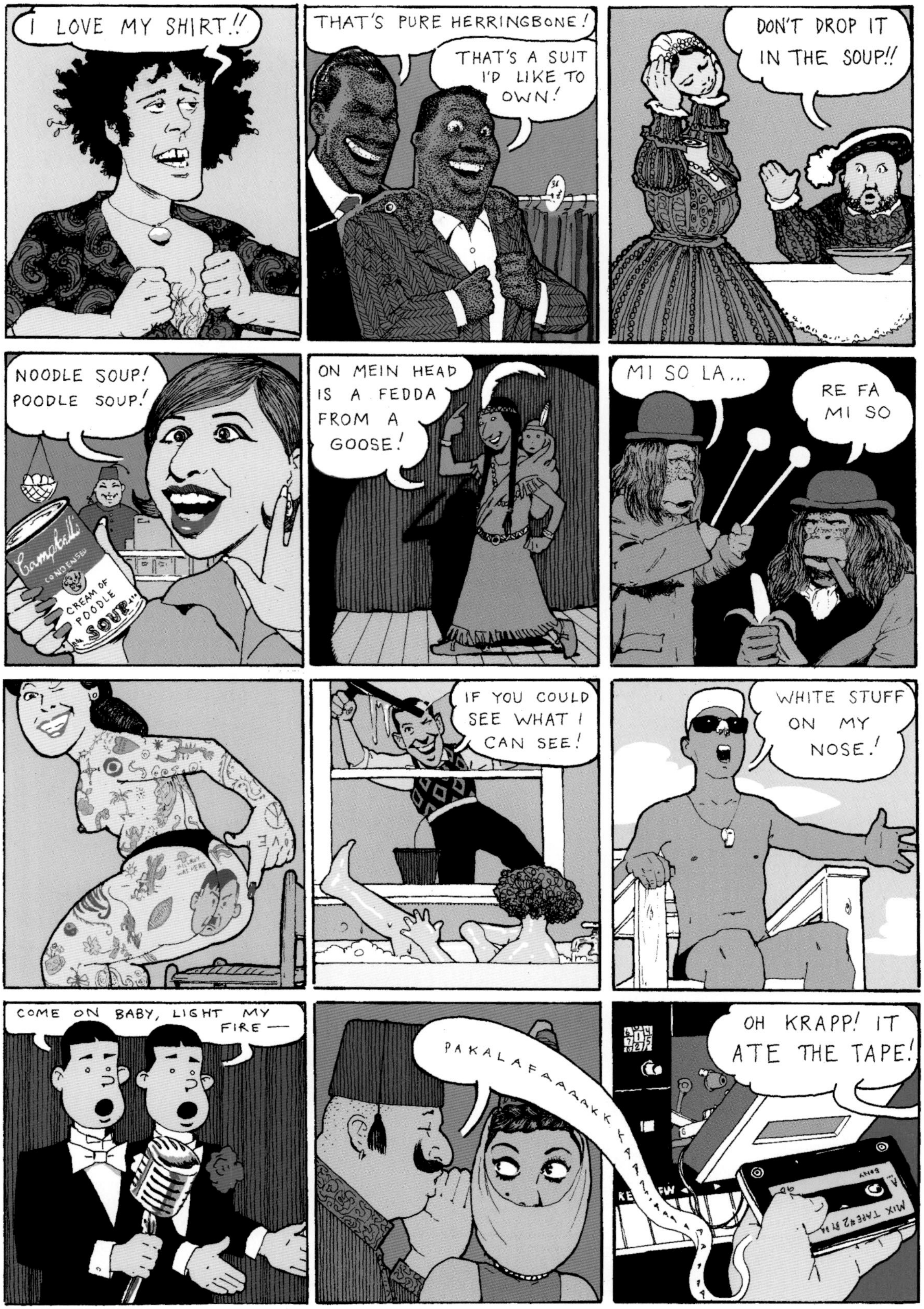
I LOVE MY SHIRT!!
THAT'S PURE HERRINGBONE!
THAT'S A SUIT I'D LIKE TO OWN!
DON'T DROP IT IN THE SOUP!!
NOODLE SOUP! POODLE SOUP!
CONDENSED
CREAM OF POODLE SOUP
ON MEIN HEAD IS A FEDDA FROM A GOOSE!
MI SO LA...
RE FA MI SO
IF YOU COULD SEE WHAT I CAN SEE!
WHITE STUFF ON MY NOSE!
COME ON BABY, LIGHT MY FIRE—
PAKALAFAAAAKK
OH KRAPP! IT ATE THE TAPE!

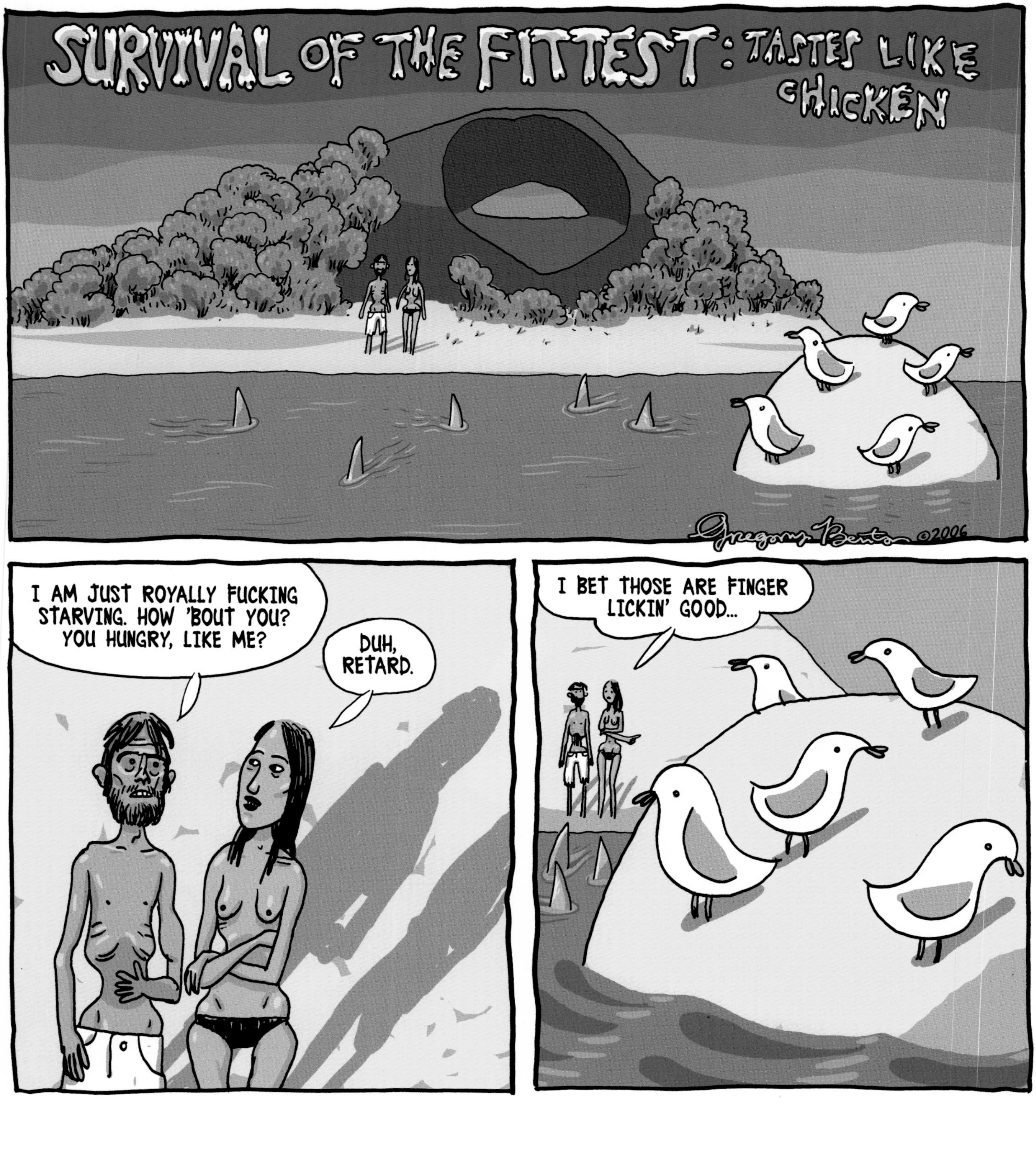
SURVIVAL OF THE FITTEST: TASTES LIKE CHICKEN
Gregory Benton ©2006
I AM JUST ROYALLY FUCKING STARVING. HOW 'BOUT YOU? YOU HUNGRY, LIKE ME?
DUH, RETARD.
I BET THOSE ARE FINGER LICKIN' GOOD...

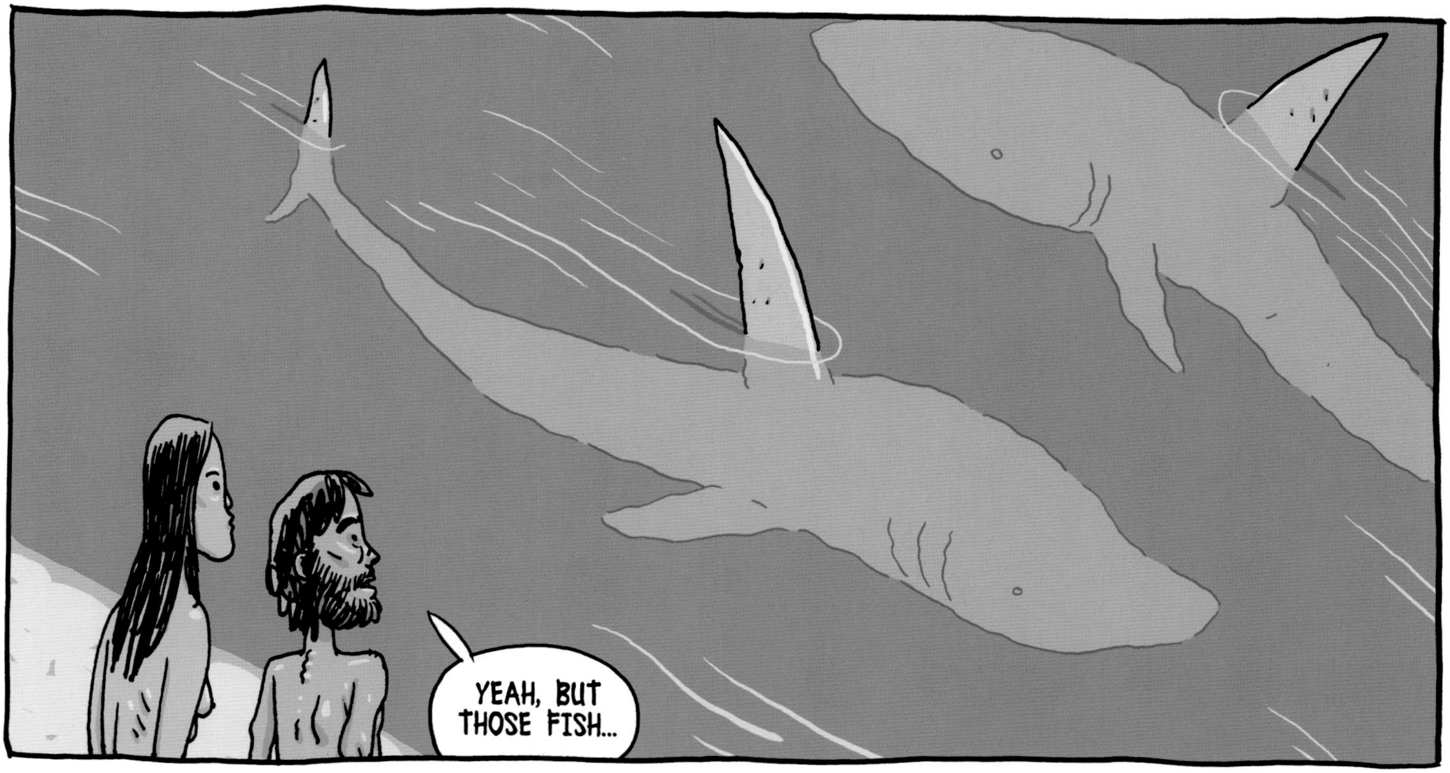
YEAH, BUT THOSE FISH...

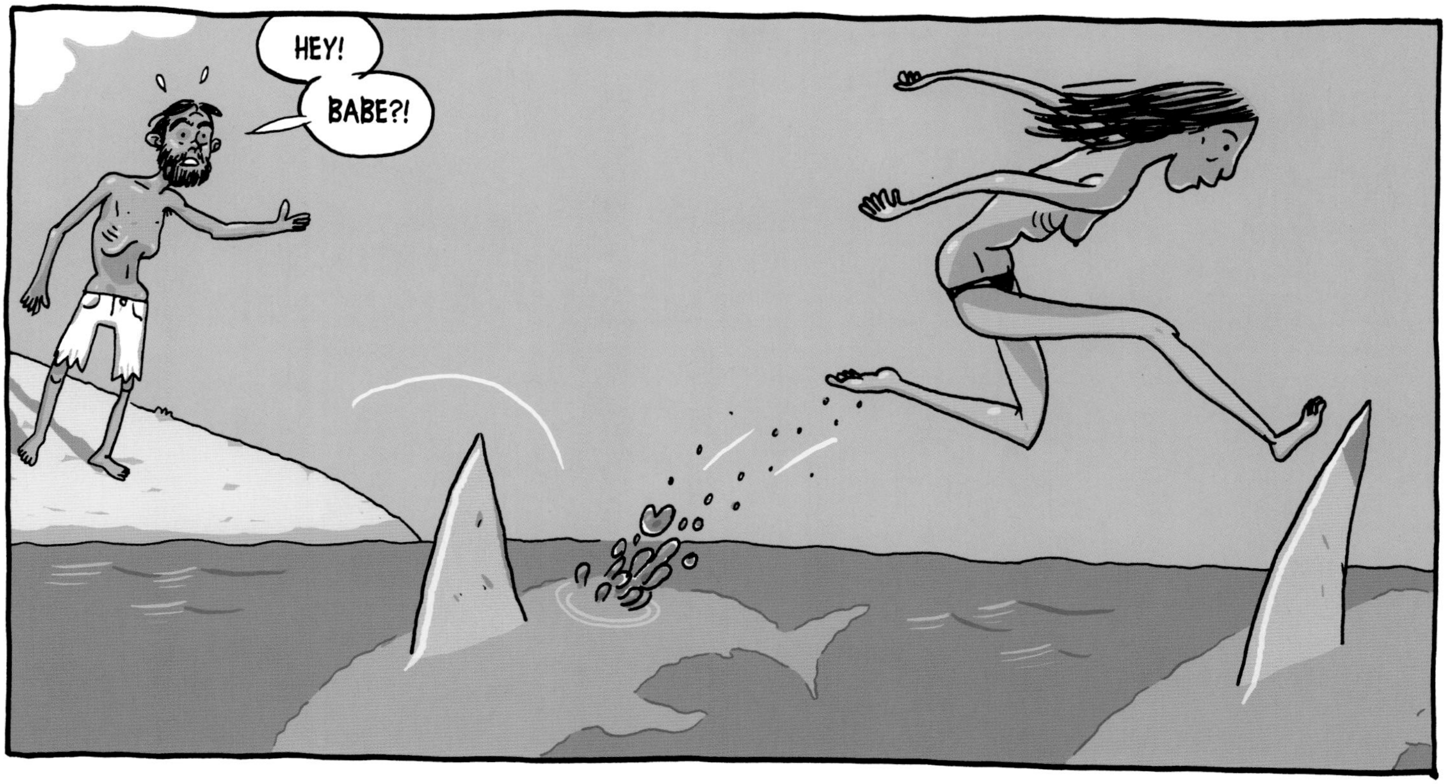
HEY!
BABE?!

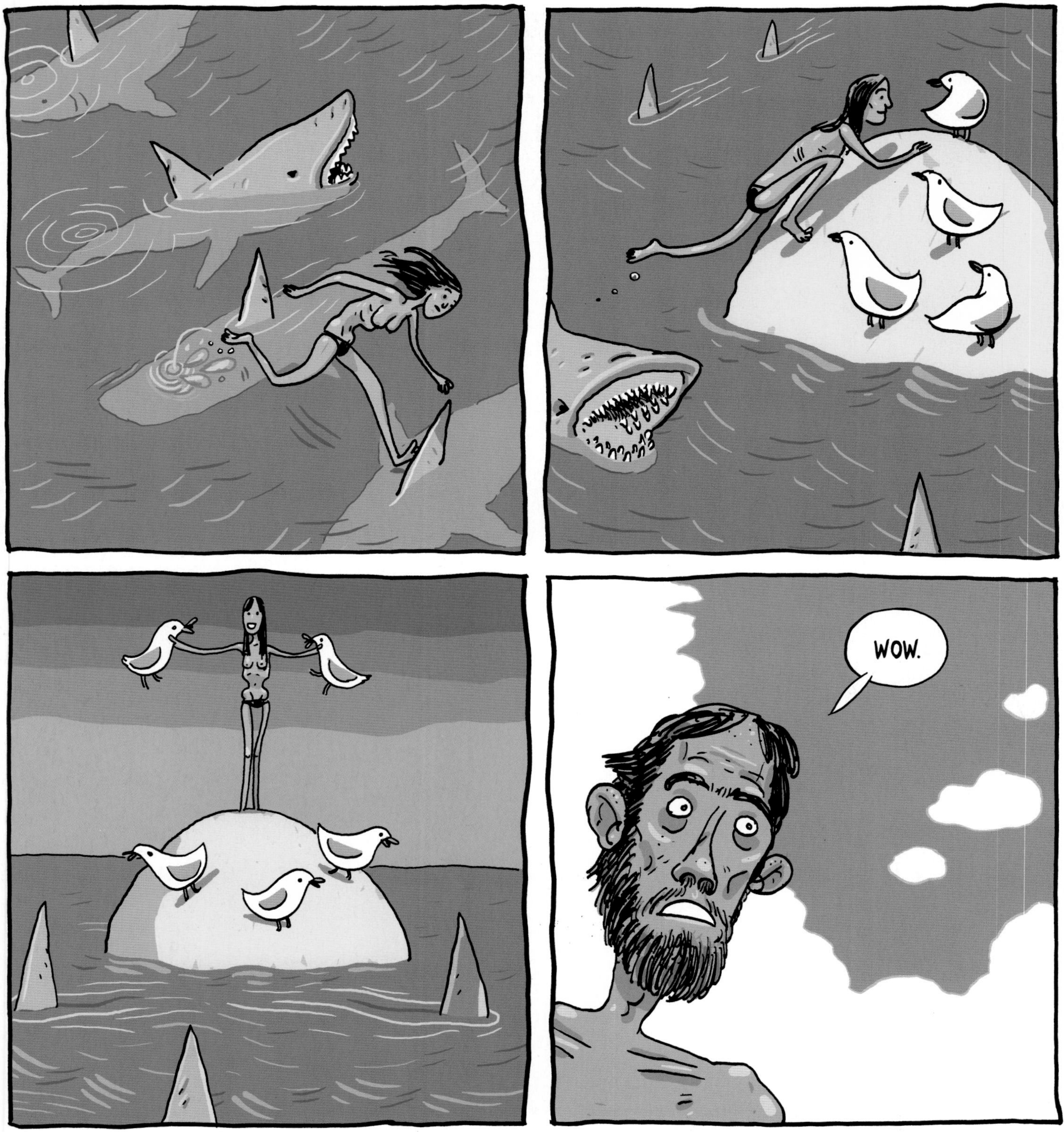
WOW.

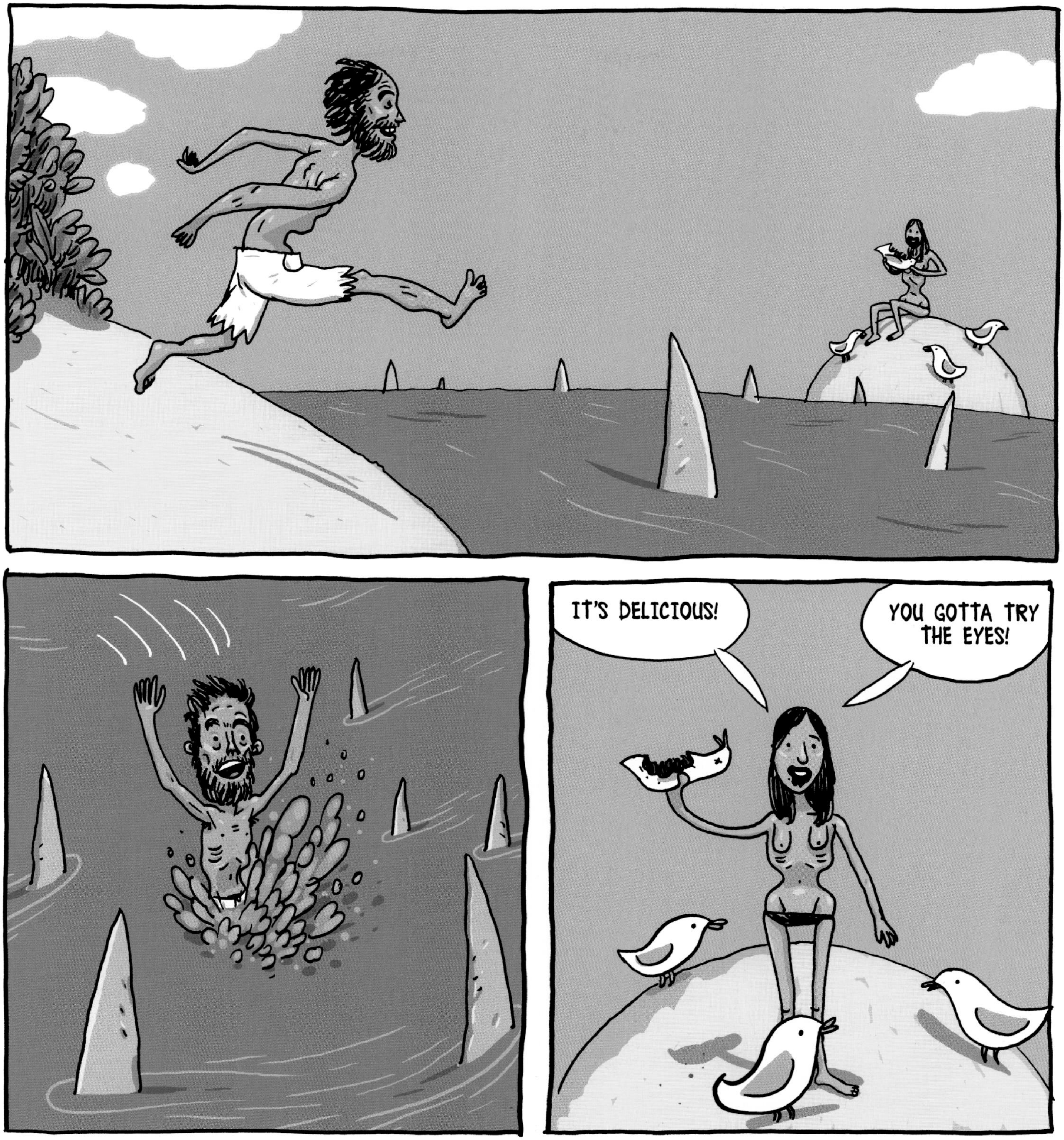
IT'S DELICIOUS!
YOU GOTTA TRY THE EYES!

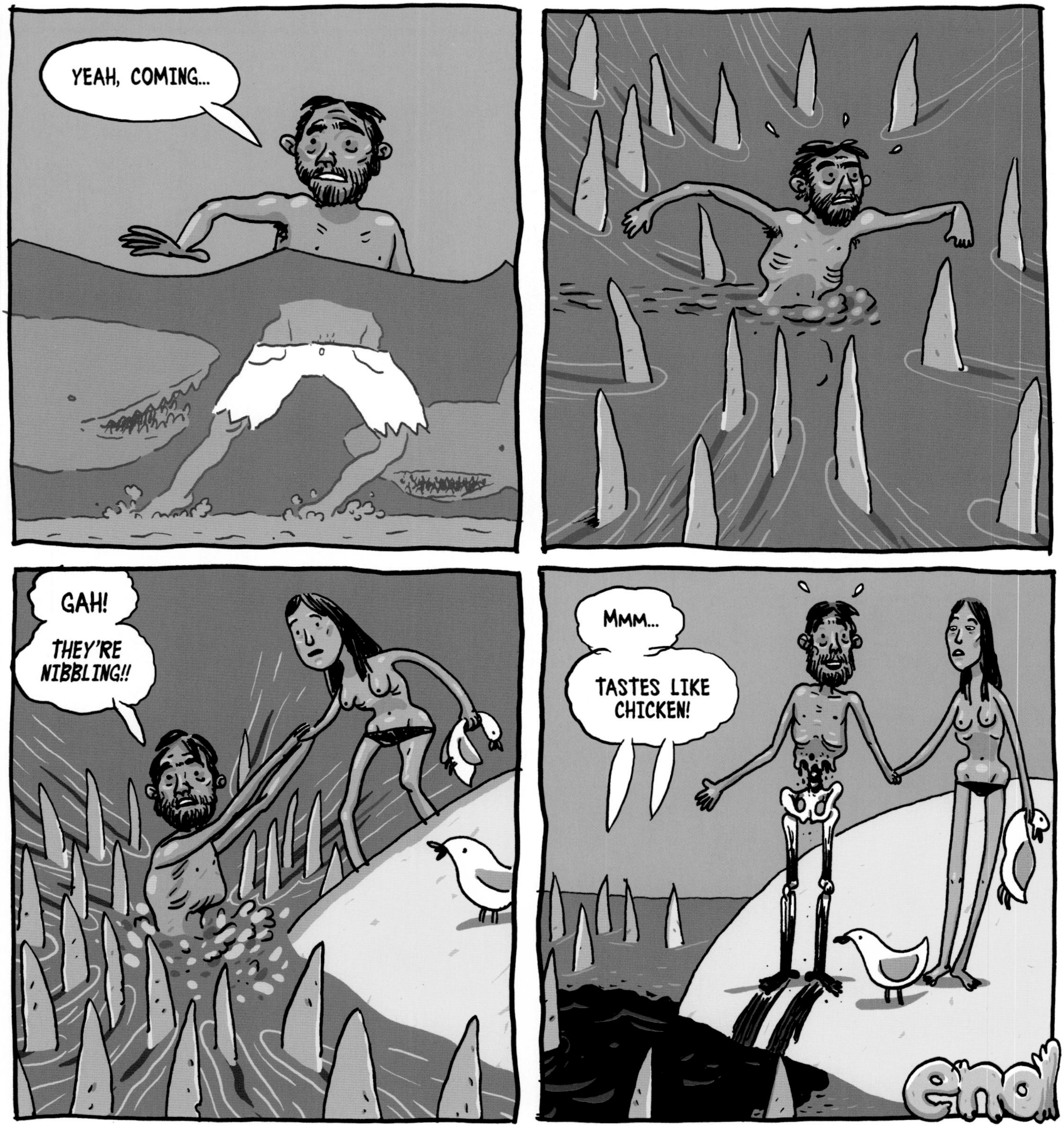
YEAH, COMING...
GAH!
THEY'RE NIBBLING!!
MMM...
TASTES LIKE CHICKEN!
end

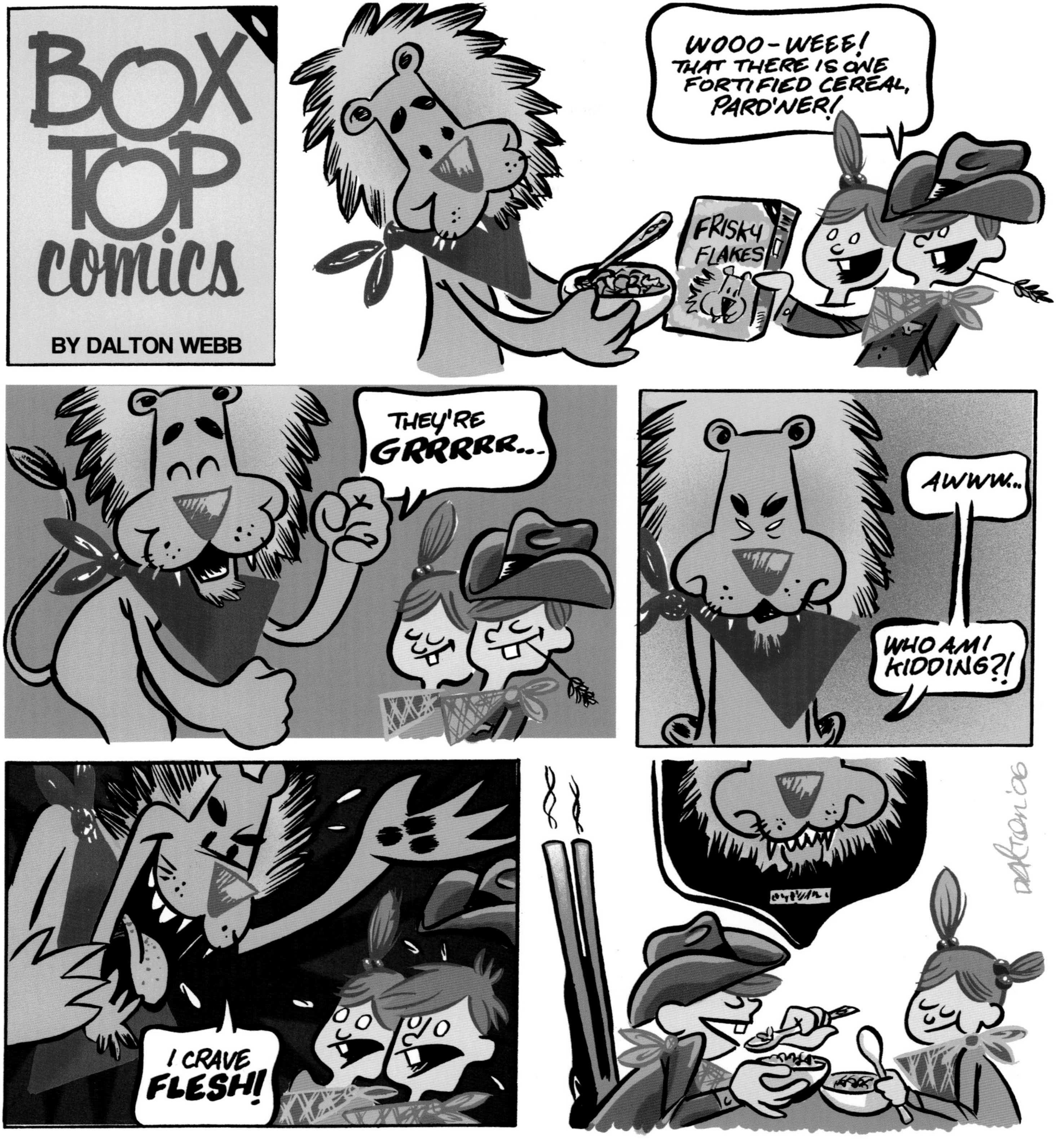
BOX TOP comics
BY DALTON WEBB
WOOO-WEEE! THAT THERE IS ONE FORTIFIED CEREAL, PARD'NER!
FRISKY FLAKES
THEY'RE GRRRRR...
AWWW..
WHO AM I KIDDING?!
I CRAVE FLESH!

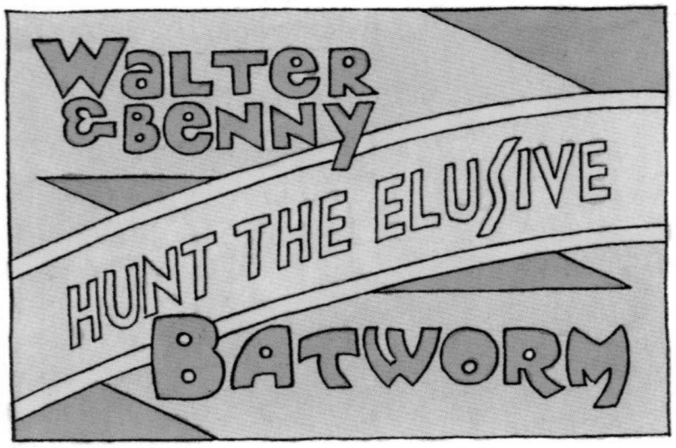
Walter & Benny
Hunt the Elusive
Batworm

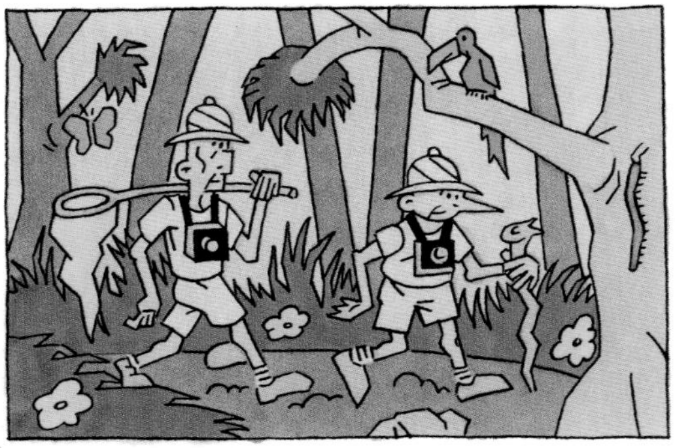

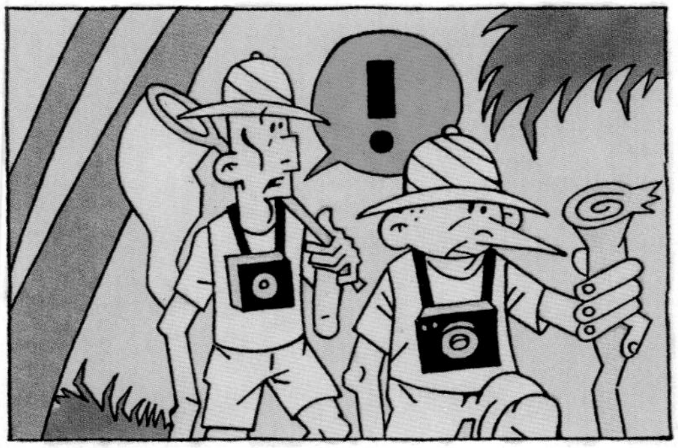
!

"PERHAPS TODAY WE'LL FIND IT!"

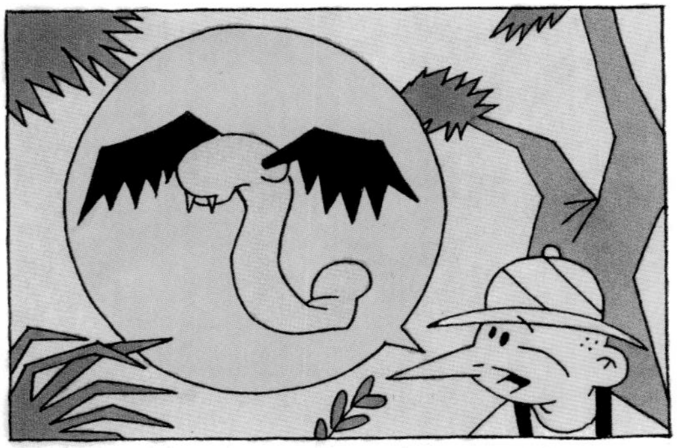

"THE ELUSIVE BATWORM - SOUGHT BY EXPLORERS FOR CENTURIES!"

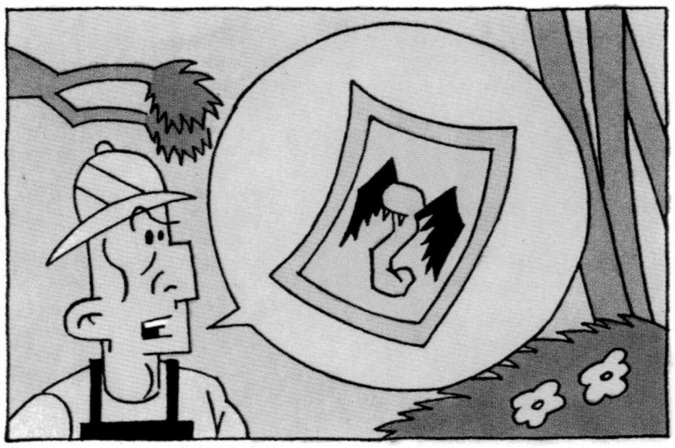

"A CLEAR PHOTO WILL PROVE ITS EXISTENCE TO SCIENCE."

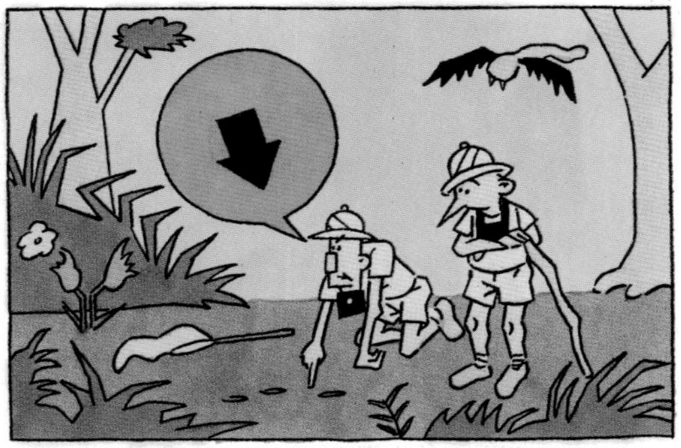

"AND I THINK WE'RE ON ITS TRAIL."

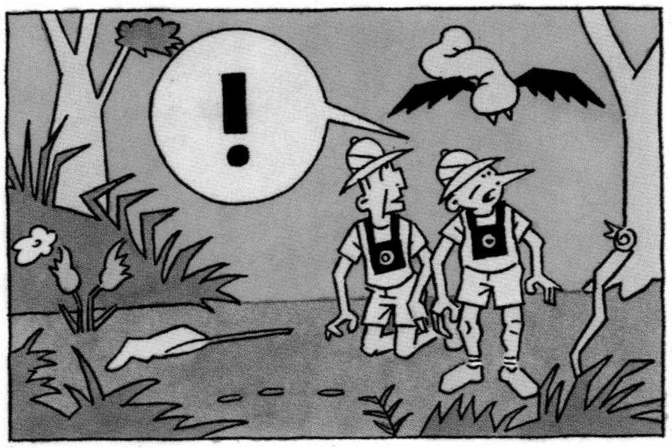
!

"THERE IT IS!"

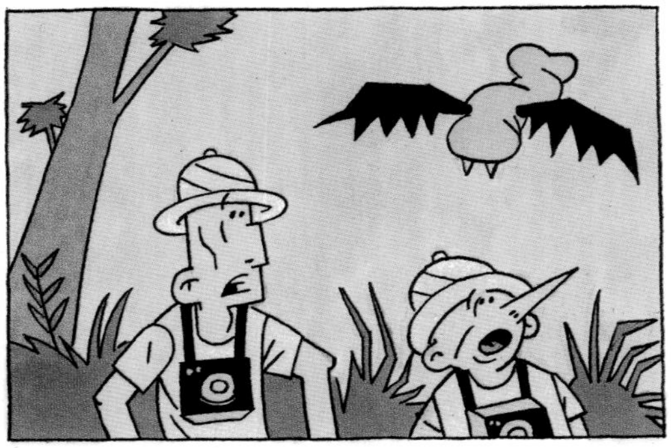

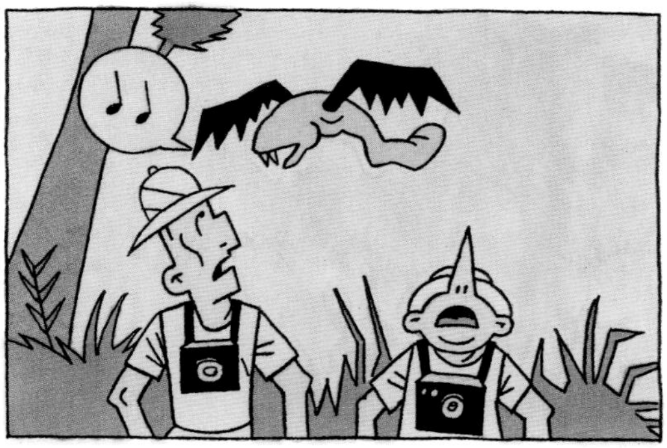

"CHEEP CHEEP"

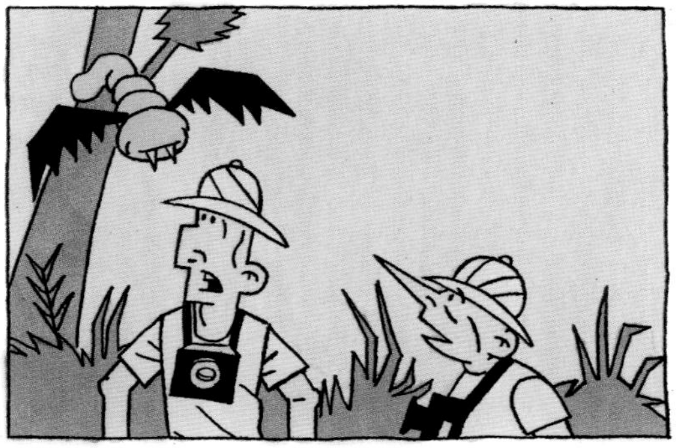

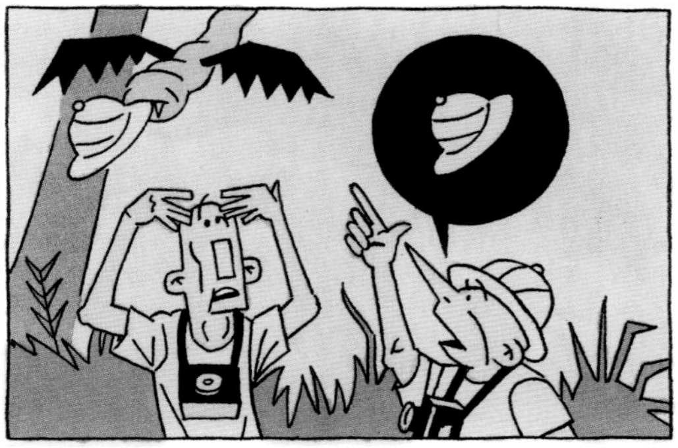

"YOUR PITH HELMET!"

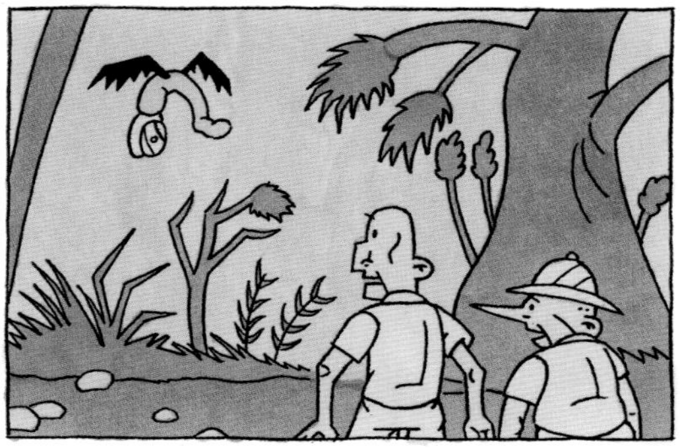

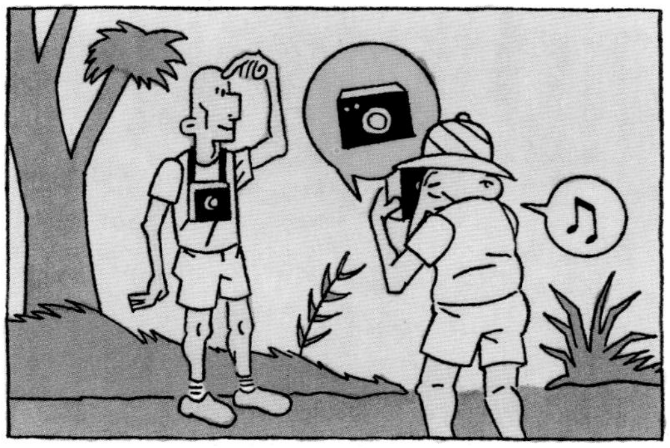

"I MUST DOCUMENT THIS ENCOUNTER."
"KA-LICK"

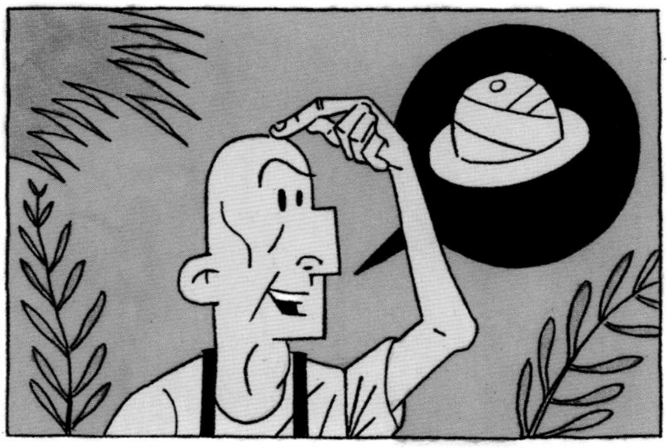

"LET'S SEE SCIENCE EXPLAIN MY MISSING PITH HELMET!"

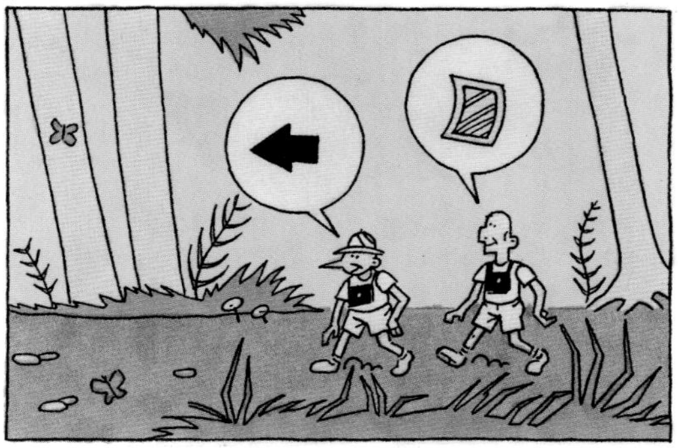

"NOW WE CAN RETURN TO AMERICA."
"WITH PHOTOGRAPHIC PROOF!"

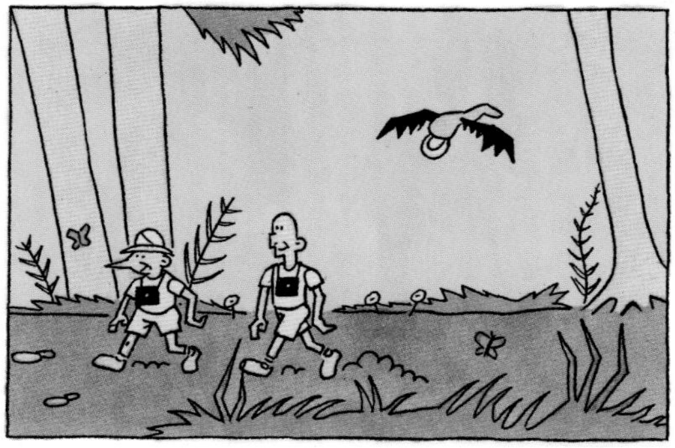

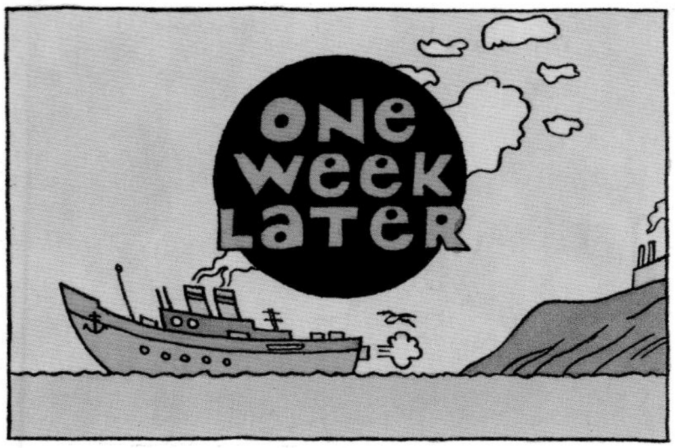
ONE WEEK LATER

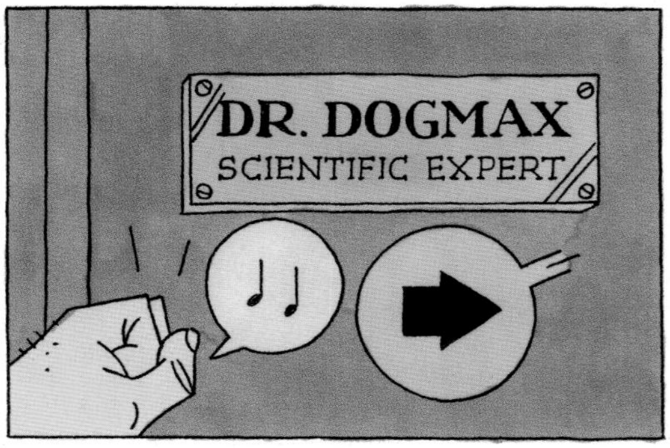
DR. DOGMAX
SCIENTIFIC EXPERT

"KNOCK KNOCK"
"COME IN!"

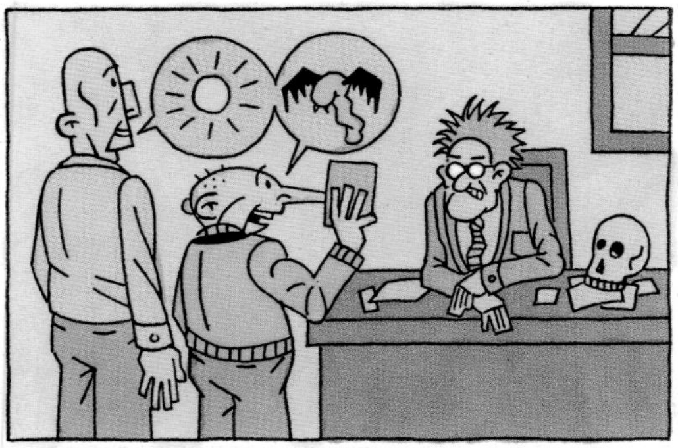

"GOOD MORNING."
"WE BRING PROOF OF THE ELUSIVE BATWORM."

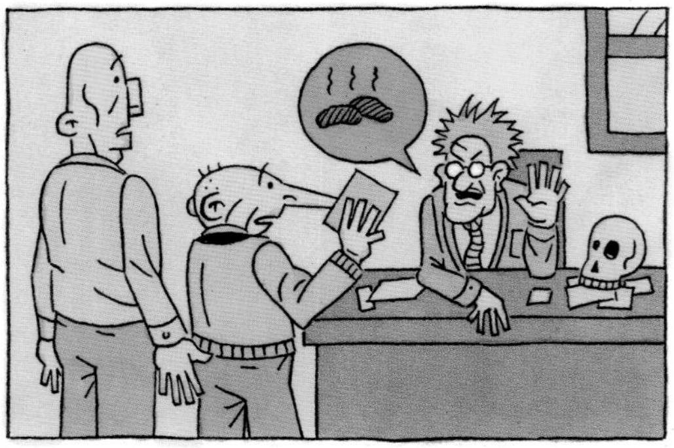

"POPPYCOCK!"

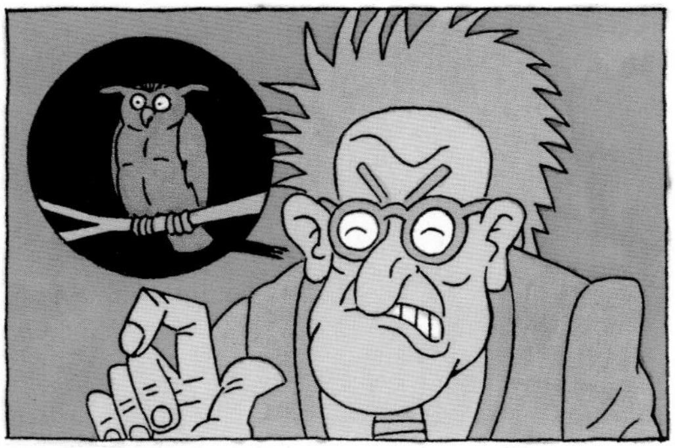

"THE BATWORM IS A FOOLISH LEGEND – IT'S JUST AN OWL."

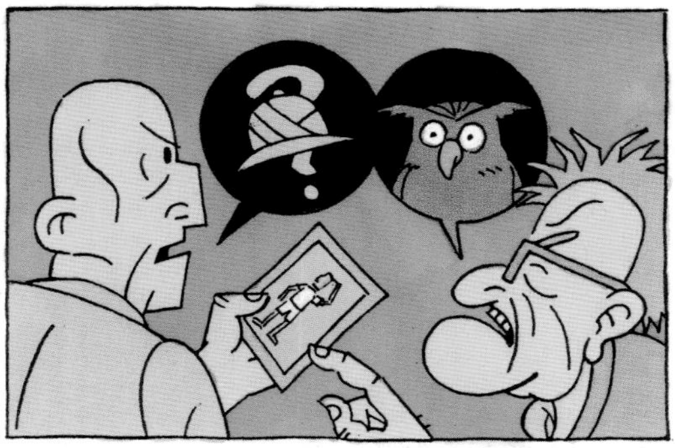

"AND WHAT ABOUT MY MISSING PITH HELMET?"
"AN OWL TOOK IT."

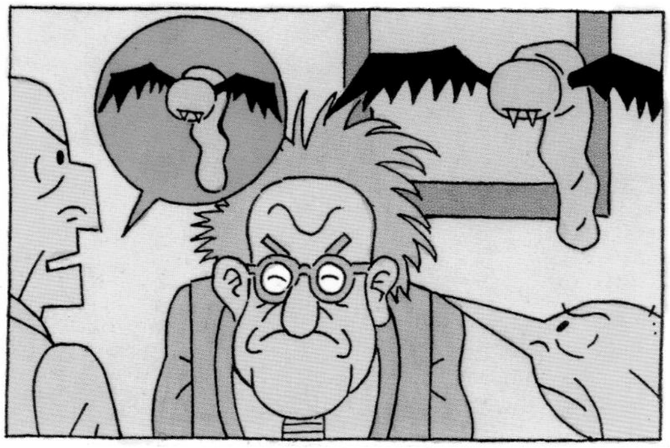

"IT WAS THE BATWORM!"

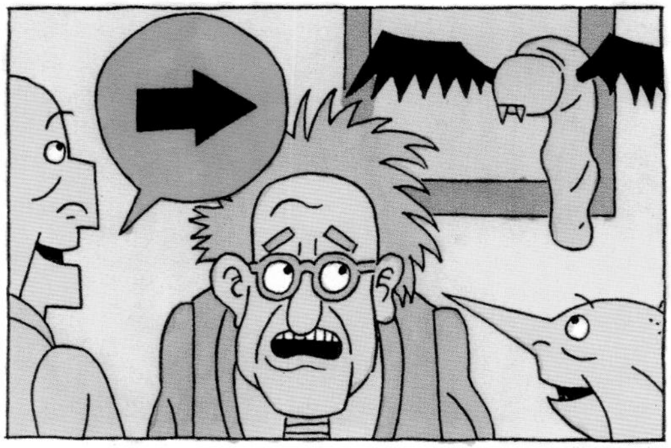

"THERE IT IS!"

"GET THAT OWL OUT OF MY OFFICE!"

"IT'S THE BATWORM!"
"IT'S AN OWL!"

"CHEEP CHEEP"

"LOOK - IT HAD BABIES!"

"NONSENSE! OWLS ARE OVIPAROUS."

"CHEEP"
"CHEEP"

"WATCH THE BIRDIE."
"KA-LICK"

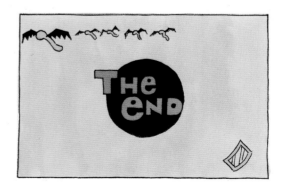

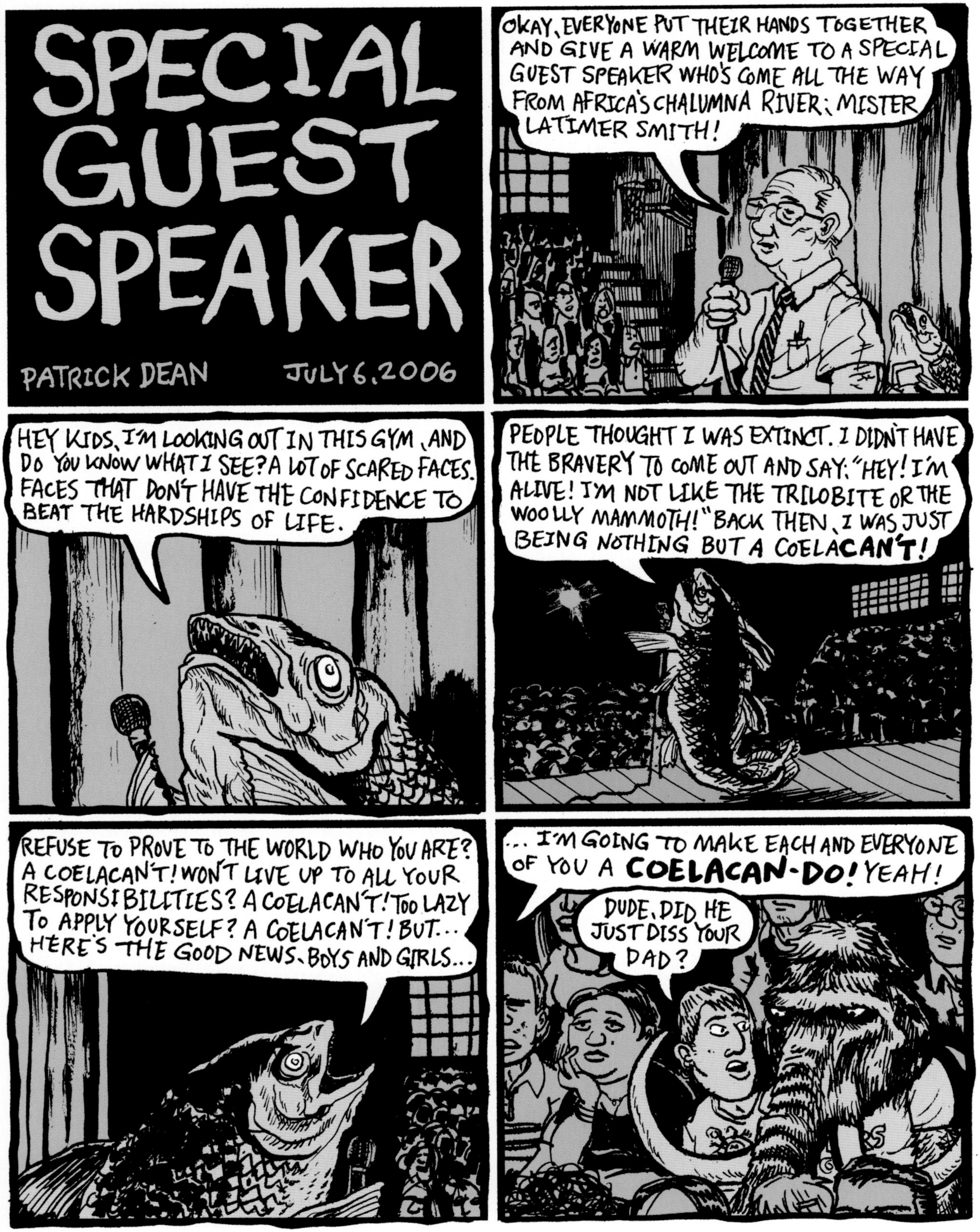
SPECIAL GUEST SPEAKER
PATRICK DEAN JULY 6, 2006
OKAY, EVERYONE PUT THEIR HANDS TOGETHER AND GIVE A WARM WELCOME TO A SPECIAL GUEST SPEAKER WHO'S COME ALL THE WAY FROM AFRICA'S CHALUMNA RIVER: MISTER LATIMER SMITH!
HEY KIDS, I'M LOOKING OUT IN THIS GYM, AND DO YOU KNOW WHAT I SEE? A LOT OF SCARED FACES. FACES THAT DON'T HAVE THE CONFIDENCE TO BEAT THE HARDSHIPS OF LIFE.
PEOPLE THOUGHT I WAS EXTINCT. I DIDN'T HAVE THE BRAVERY TO COME OUT AND SAY: "HEY! I'M ALIVE! I'M NOT LIKE THE TRILOBITE OR THE WOOLLY MAMMOTH!" BACK THEN, I WAS JUST BEING NOTHING BUT A COELACAN'T!
REFUSE TO PROVE TO THE WORLD WHO YOU ARE? A COELACAN'T! WON'T LIVE UP TO ALL YOUR RESPONSIBILITIES? A COELACAN'T! TOO LAZY TO APPLY YOURSELF? A COELACAN'T! BUT... HERE'S THE GOOD NEWS, BOYS AND GIRLS...
... I'M GOING TO MAKE EACH AND EVERYONE OF YOU A COELACAN-DO! YEAH!
DUDE, DID HE JUST DISS YOUR DAD?

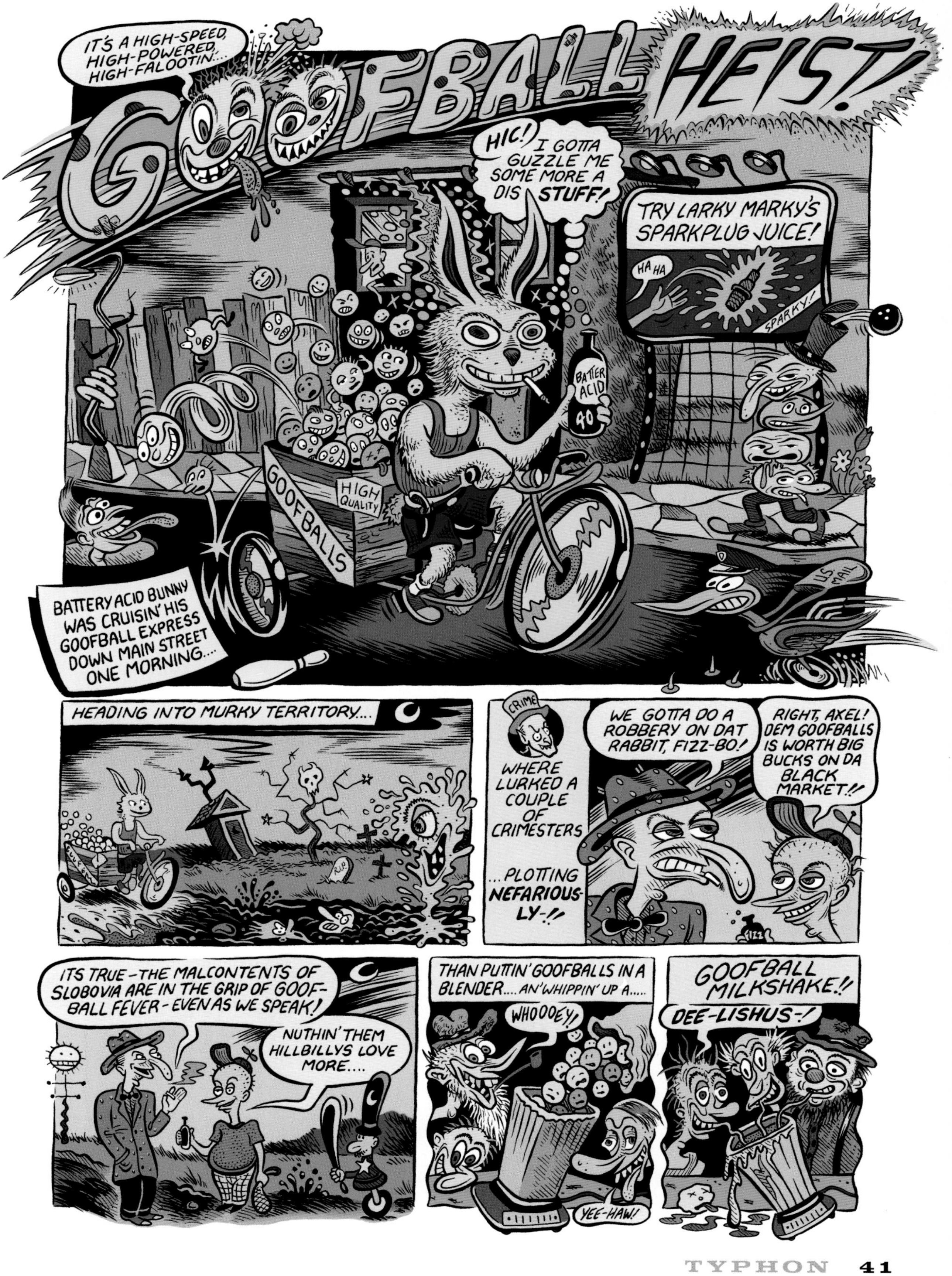
IT'S A HIGH-SPEED, HIGH-POWERED, HIGH-FALOOTIN'...
GOOFBALL HEIST!
HIC! I GOTTA GUZZLE ME SOME MORE A DIS STUFF!
TRY LARKY MARKY'S SPARKPLUG JUICE!
HA HA
SPARKY!
BATTER ACID 40
HIGH QUALITY
GOOFBALLS
U.S. MAIL
BATTERY ACID BUNNY WAS CRUISIN' HIS GOOFBALL EXPRESS DOWN MAIN STREET ONE MORNING....
HEADING INTO MURKY TERRITORY...
CRIME
WHERE LURKED A COUPLE OF CRIMESTERS
...PLOTTING NEFARIOUS-LY-!!
WE GOTTA DO A ROBBERY ON DAT RABBIT, FIZZ-BO!
RIGHT, AXEL! DEM GOOFBALLS IS WORTH BIG BUCKS ON DA BLACK MARKET!!
ITS TRUE - THE MALCONTENTS OF SLOBOVIA ARE IN THE GRIP OF GOOF-BALL FEVER - EVEN AS WE SPEAK!
NUTHIN' THEM HILLBILLYS LOVE MORE....
THAN PUTTIN' GOOFBALLS IN A BLENDER.... AN' WHIPPIN' UP A.....
WHOOOEY!
YEE-HAW!
GOOFBALL MILKSHAKE!!
DEE-LISHUS-!

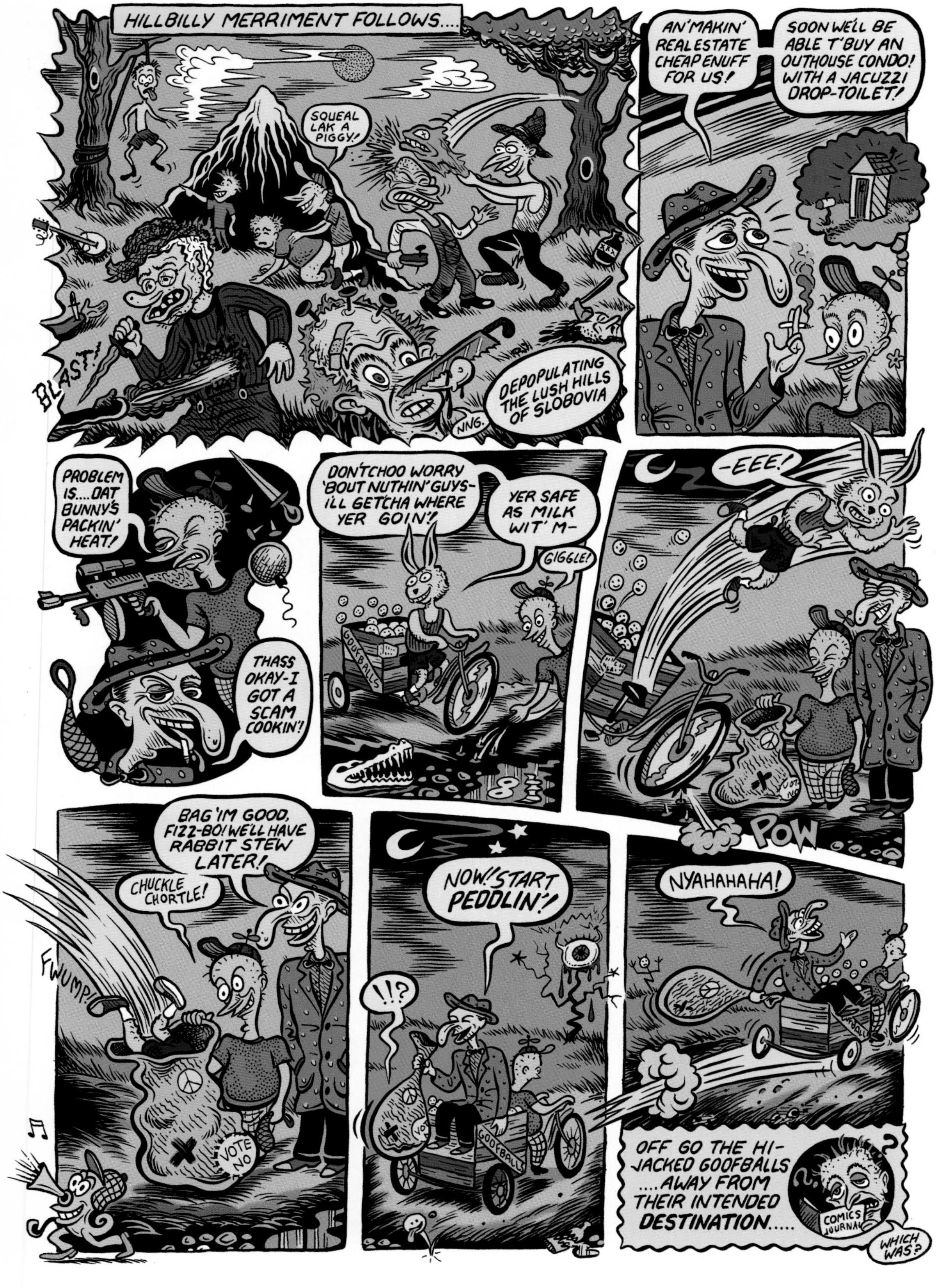
HILLBILLY MERRIMENT FOLLOWS....
SQUEAL LAK A PIGGY!
BLAST!
NNG.
DEPOPULATING THE LUSH HILLS OF SLOBOVIA
AN'MAKIN' REALESTATE CHEAPENUFF FOR US!
SOON WE'LL BE ABLE T'BUY AN OUTHOUSE CONDO! WITH A JACUZZI DROP-TOILET!
PROBLEM IS....DAT BUNNY'S PACKIN' HEAT!
THASS OKAY-I GOT A SCAM COOKIN'!
DON'TCHOO WORRY 'BOUT NUTHIN' GUYS-I'LL GETCHA WHERE YER GOIN'!
YER SAFE AS MILK WIT' M-
GIGGLE!
GOOFBALLS
-EEE!
POW
BAG 'IM GOOD, FIZZ-BO! WE'LL HAVE RABBIT STEW LATER!
CHUCKLE CHORTLE!
FWUMP!
VOTE NO
NOW! START PEDDLIN'!
!!?
GOOFBALL
NYAHAHAHA!
OFF GO THE HI-JACKED GOOFBALLS ....AWAY FROM THEIR INTENDED DESTINATION.....
?
COMICS JOURNAL
WHICH WAS?

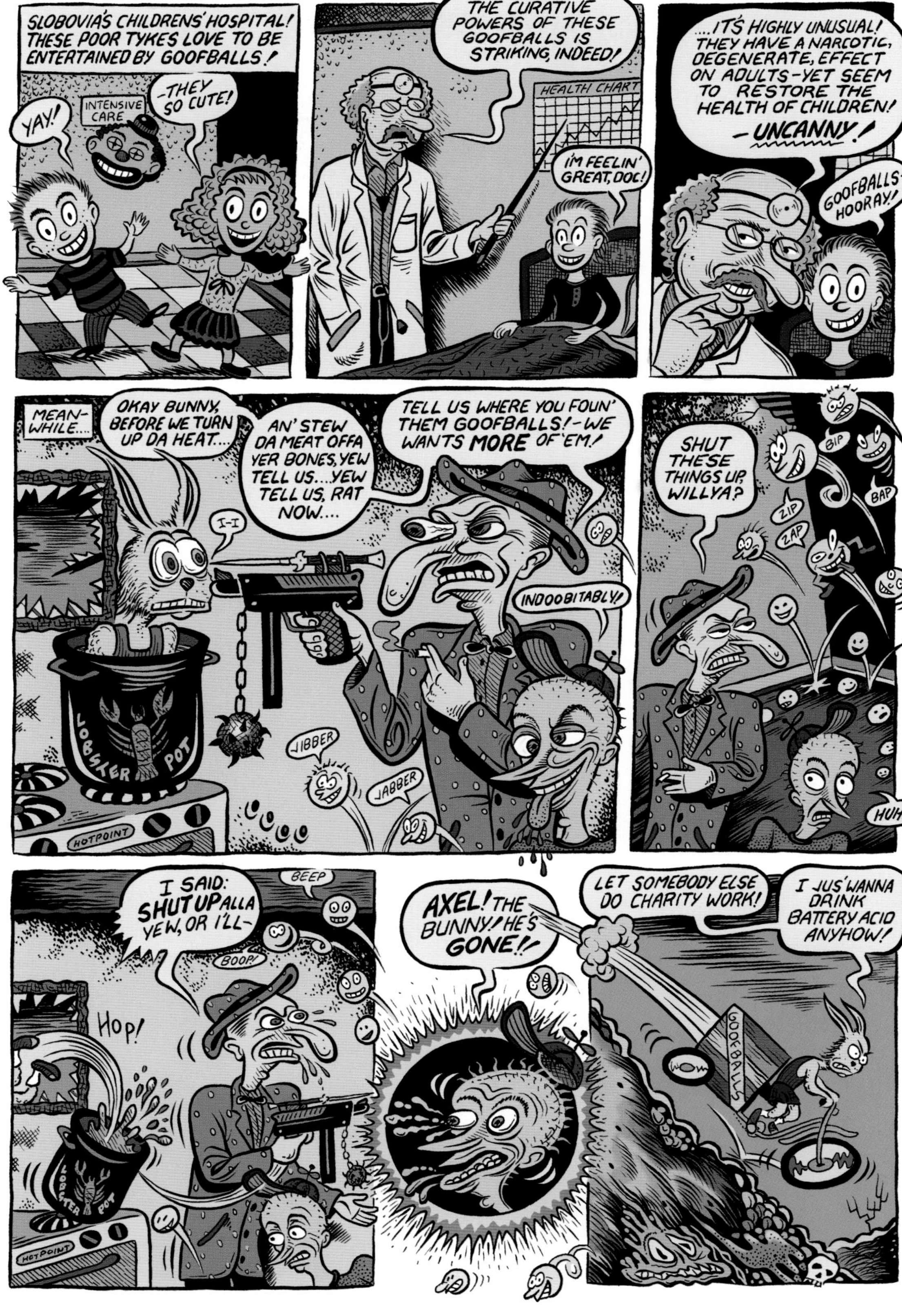
SLOBOVIA'S CHILDRENS' HOSPITAL! THESE POOR TYKES LOVE TO BE ENTERTAINED BY GOOFBALLS!
INTENSIVE CARE
YAY!
-THEY SO CUTE!
THE CURATIVE POWERS OF THESE GOOFBALLS IS STRIKING, INDEED!
HEALTH CHART
I'M FEELIN' GREAT, DOC!
....IT'S HIGHLY UNUSUAL! THEY HAVE A NARCOTIC, DEGENERATE, EFFECT ON ADULTS-YET SEEM TO RESTORE THE HEALTH OF CHILDREN! -UNCANNY!
GOOFBALLS-HOORAY!
MEAN-WHILE....
OKAY BUNNY, BEFORE WE TURN UP DA HEAT...
AN' STEW DA MEAT OFFA YER BONES, YEW TELL US....YEW TELL US, RAT NOW....
TELL US WHERE YOU FOUN' THEM GOOFBALLS!-WE WANTS MORE OF 'EM!
I-I
INDOOBITABLY!
LOBSTER POT
JIBBER
JABBER
HOTPOINT
SHUT THESE THINGS UP, WILLYA?
BIP
BAP
ZIP
ZAP
HUH!?
I SAID: SHUT UP ALLA YEW, OR I'LL-
BEEP
BOOP!
HOP!
LOBSTER POT
HOTPOINT
AXEL! THE BUNNY! HE'S GONE!!
LET SOMEBODY ELSE DO CHARITY WORK!
I JUS' WANNA DRINK BATTERY ACID ANYHOW!
GOOFBALLS

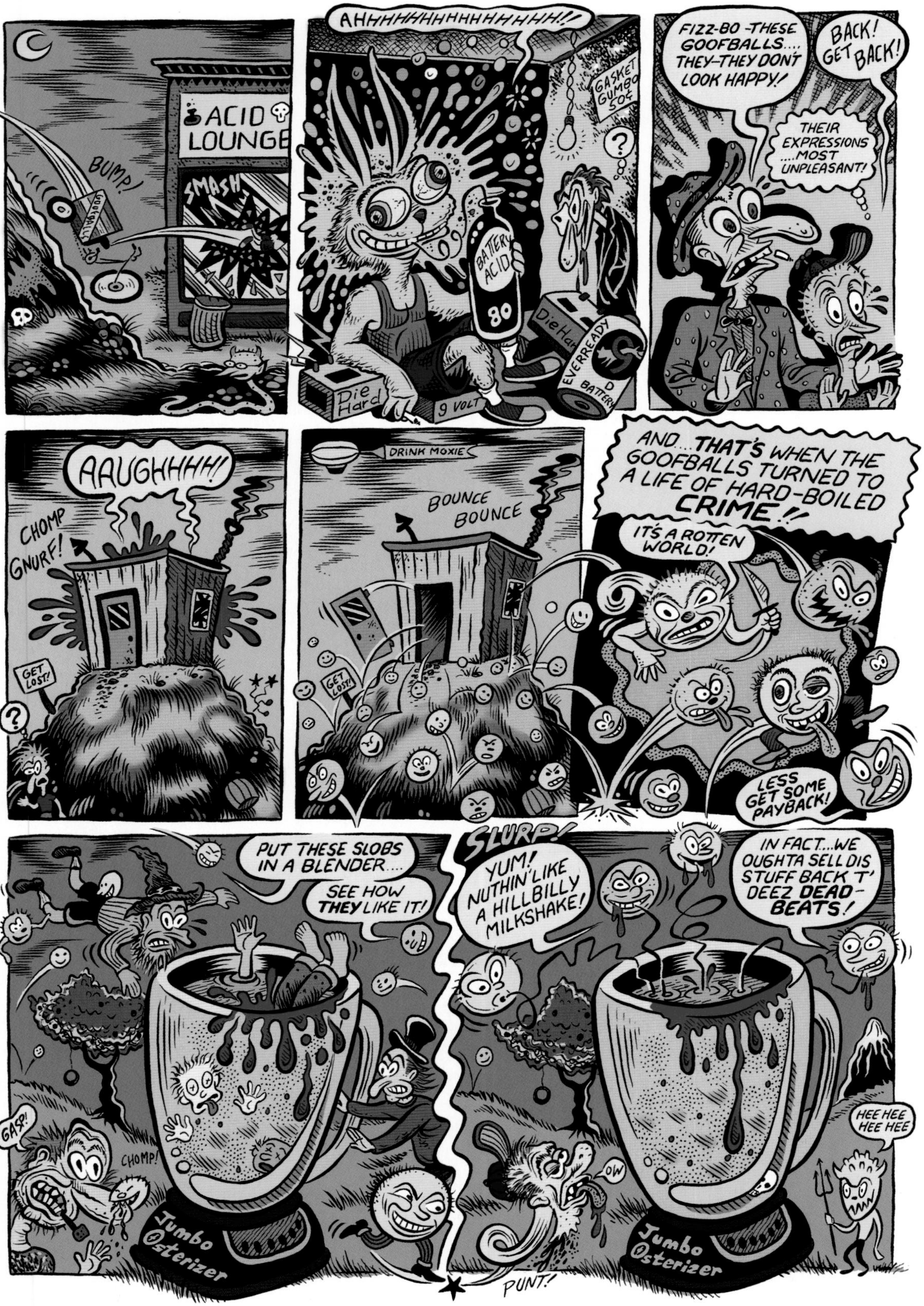

ACID LOUNGE
BUMP!
SMASH
AHHHHHHHHHHHHHHH!!
GASKET GUMBO 50¢
BATTERY ACID 80
DieHard
EVERREADY D BATTERY
Die Hard
9 VOLT
FIZZ-BO -THESE GOOFBALLS.... THEY-THEY DON'T LOOK HAPPY!
BACK! GET BACK!
THEIR EXPRESSIONS ....MOST UNPLEASANT!
AAUGHHHH!
CHOMP GNURF!
GET LOST!
DRINK MOXIE
BOUNCE BOUNCE
GET LOST!
AND... THAT'S WHEN THE GOOFBALLS TURNED TO A LIFE OF HARD-BOILED CRIME!!
IT'S A ROTTEN WORLD!
LESS GET SOME PAYBACK!
PUT THESE SLOBS IN A BLENDER....
SEE HOW THEY LIKE IT!
SLURP!
YUM! NUTHIN' LIKE A HILLBILLY MILKSHAKE!
IN FACT...WE OUGHTA SELL DIS STUFF BACK T' DEEZ DEAD-BEATS!
GASP!
CHOMP!
Jumbo Osterizer
OW
HEE HEE HEE HEE
Jumbo Osterizer
PUNT!

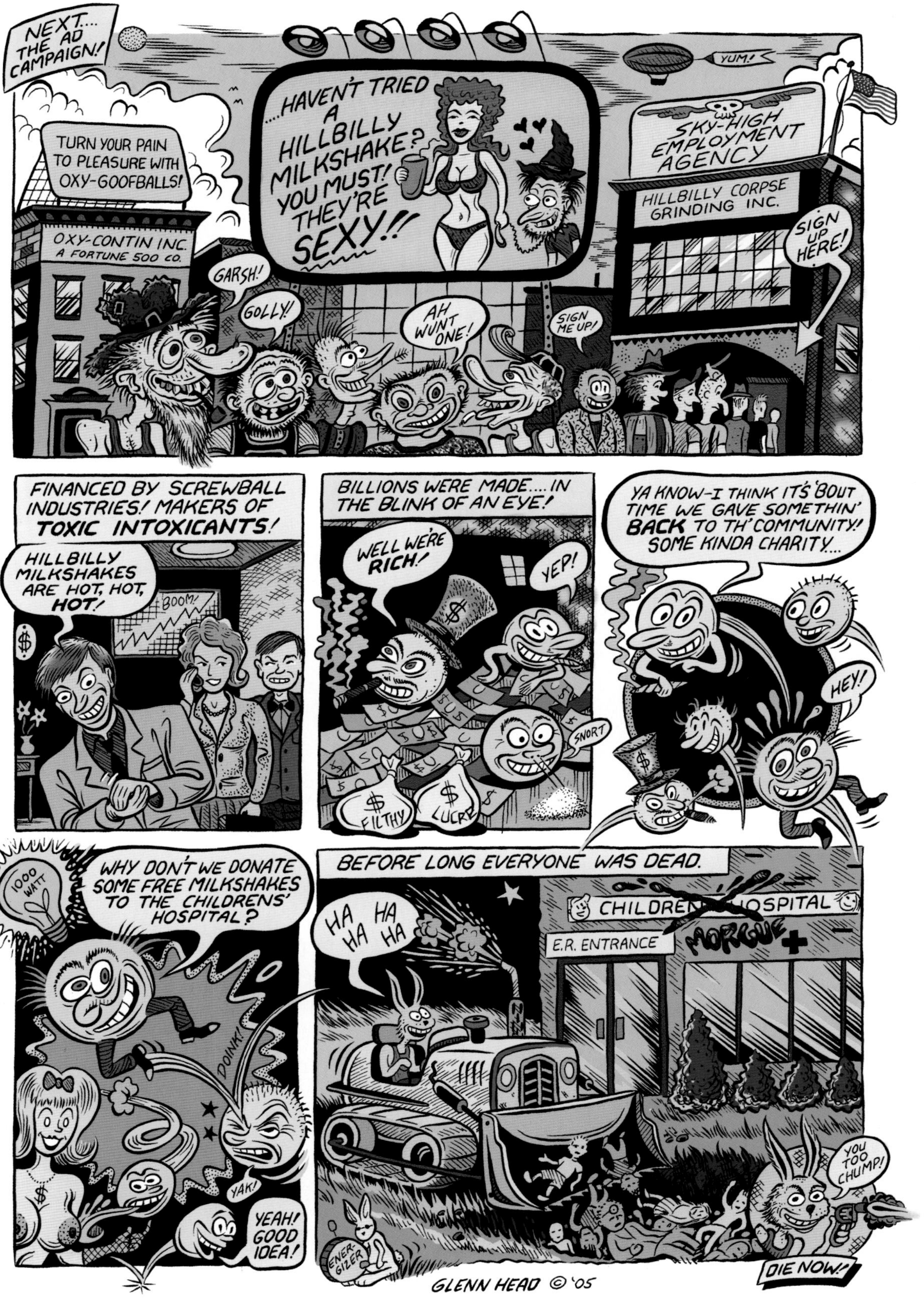

NEXT... THE AD CAMPAIGN!
YUM!
...HAVEN'T TRIED A HILLBILLY MILKSHAKE? YOU MUST! THEY'RE SEXY!!
TURN YOUR PAIN TO PLEASURE WITH OXY-GOOFBALLS!
OXY-CONTIN INC. A FORTUNE 500 CO.
SKY-HIGH EMPLOYMENT AGENCY
HILLBILLY CORPSE GRINDING INC.
SIGN UP HERE!
GARSH!
GOLLY!
AH WUNT ONE!
SIGN ME UP!
FINANCED BY SCREWBALL INDUSTRIES! MAKERS OF TOXIC INTOXICANTS!
HILLBILLY MILKSHAKES ARE HOT, HOT, HOT!
BOOM!
BILLIONS WERE MADE.... IN THE BLINK OF AN EYE!
WELL WE'RE RICH!
YEP!
SNORT
FILTHY
LUCRE
YA KNOW–I THINK IT'S 'BOUT TIME WE GAVE SOMETHIN' BACK TO TH' COMMUNITY! SOME KINDA CHARITY....
HEY!
1000 WATT
WHY DON'T WE DONATE SOME FREE MILKSHAKES TO THE CHILDRENS' HOSPITAL?
DOINK!
YAK!
YEAH! GOOD IDEA!
BEFORE LONG EVERYONE WAS DEAD.
HA HA HA HA
CHILDREN'S HOSPITAL
MORGUE
E.R. ENTRANCE
YOU TOO CHUMP!
ENER-GIZER
DIE NOW!
GLENN HEAD © '05

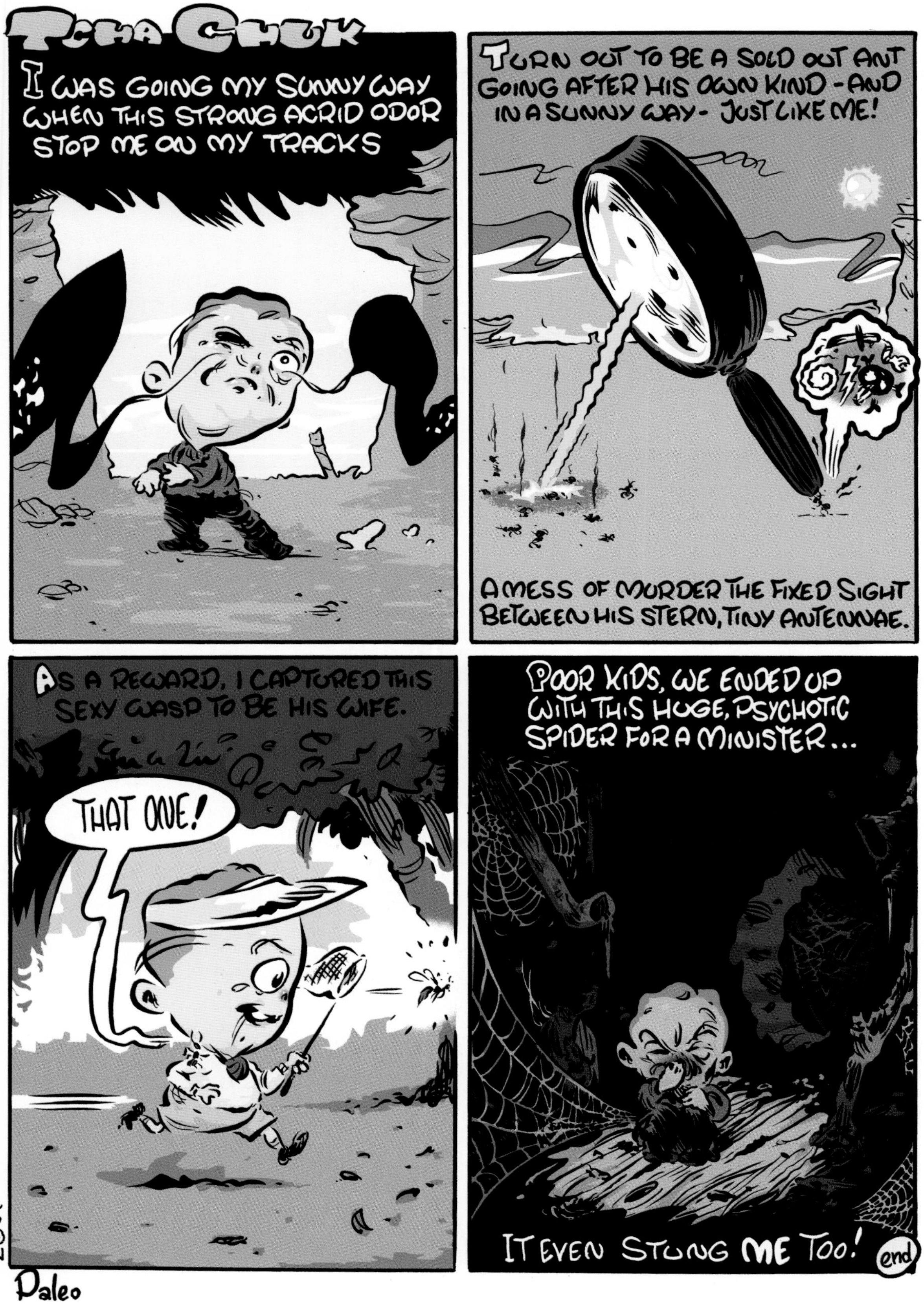
TCHA CHUK
I WAS GOING MY SUNNY WAY WHEN THIS STRONG ACRID ODOR STOP ME ON MY TRACKS
TURN OUT TO BE A SOLD OUT ANT GOING AFTER HIS OWN KIND - AND IN A SUNNY WAY - JUST LIKE ME!
A MESS OF MURDER THE FIXED SIGHT BETWEEN HIS STERN, TINY ANTENNAE.
AS A REWARD, I CAPTURED THIS SEXY WASP TO BE HIS WIFE.
THAT ONE!
POOR KIDS, WE ENDED UP WITH THIS HUGE, PSYCHOTIC SPIDER FOR A MINISTER...
IT EVEN STUNG ME TOO!
end
2©07
Daleo

INTO PIECES

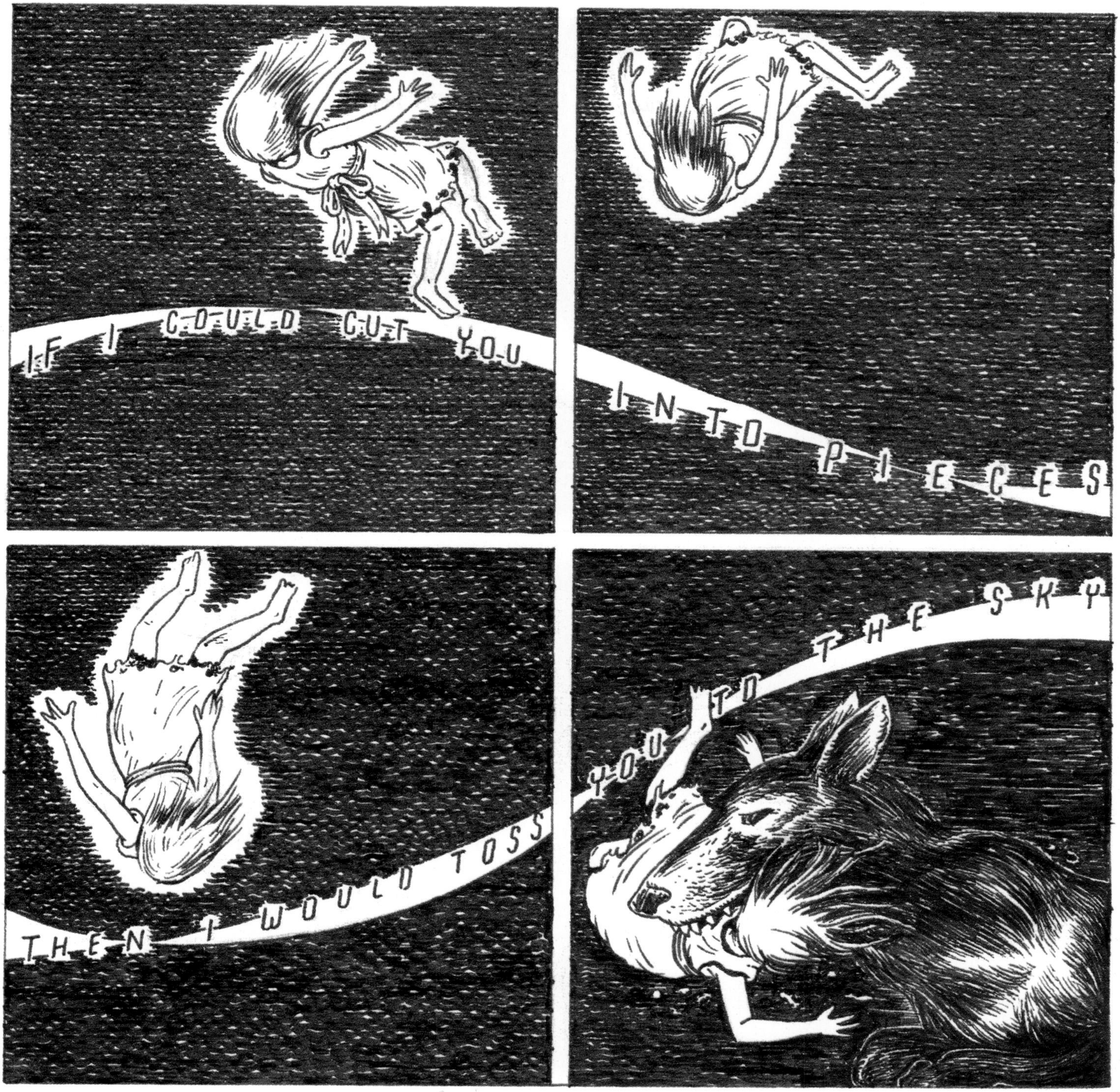
IF I COULD CUT YOU
INTO PIECES
THEN I WOULD TOSS
YOU INTO THE SKY

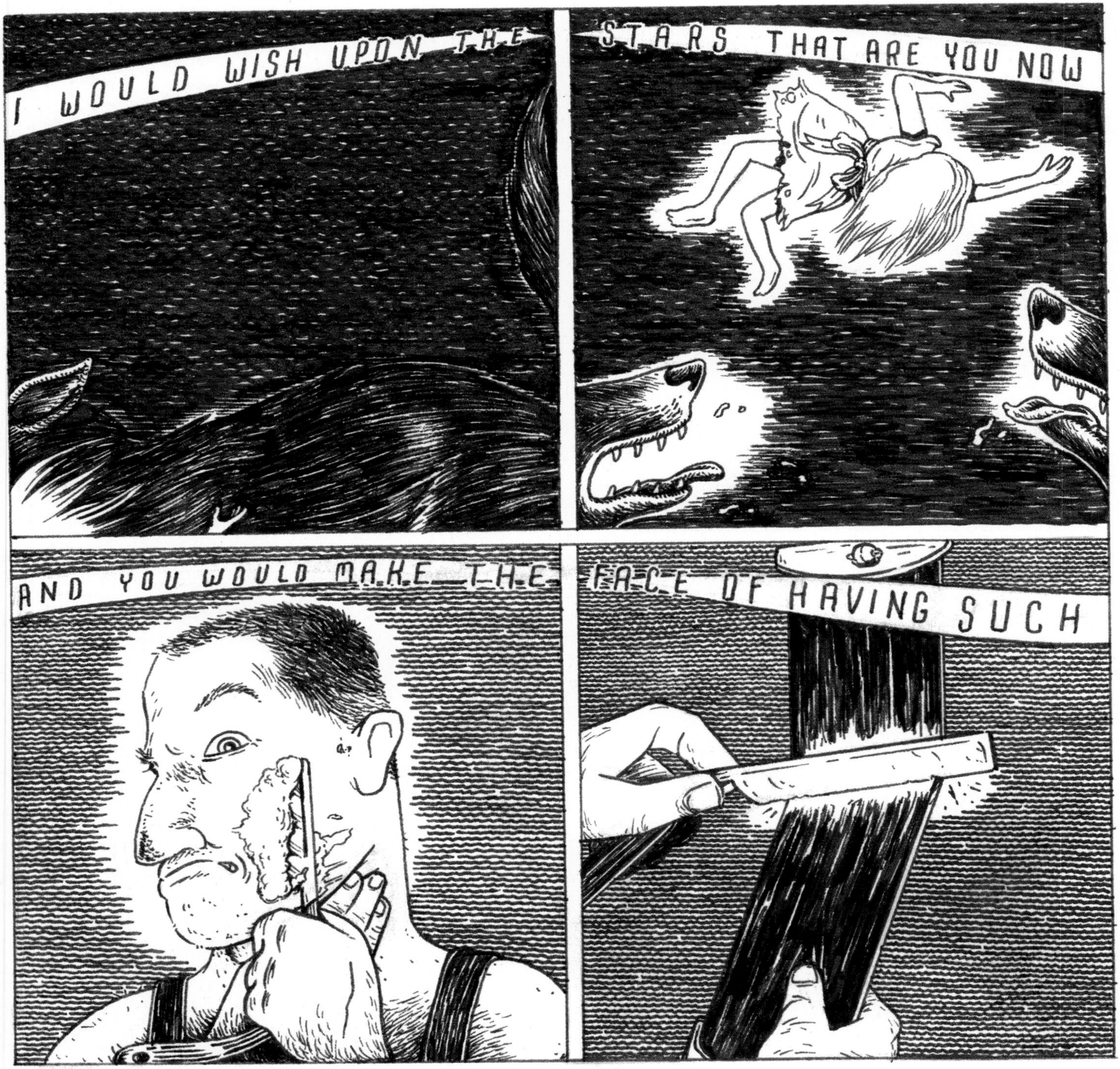
I WOULD WISH UPON THE
STARS THAT ARE YOU NOW
AND YOU WOULD MAKE THE
FACE OF HAVING SUCH

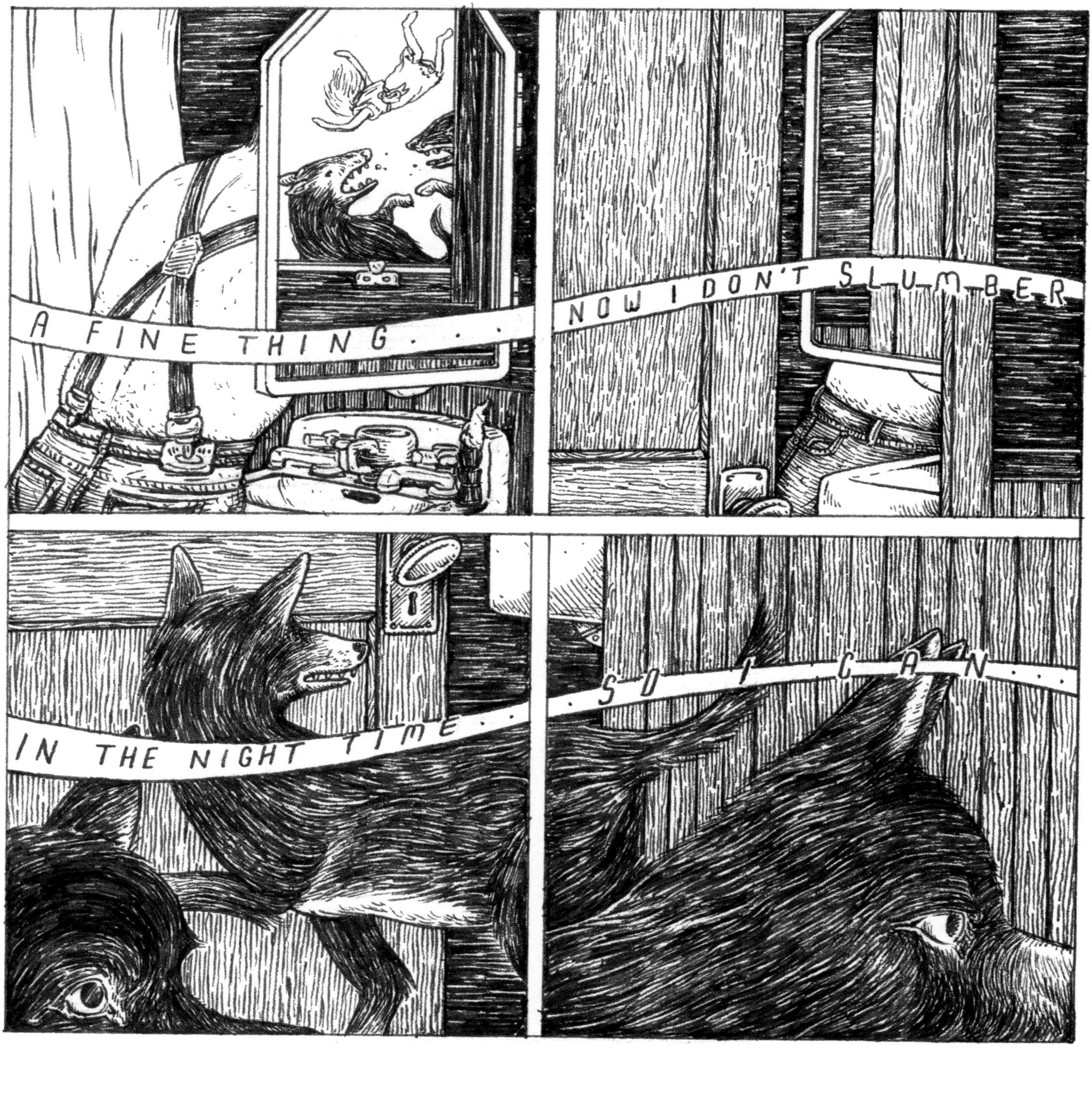
A FINE THING . . .
NOW I DON'T SLUMBER
IN THE NIGHT TIME . . .
SO I CAN . . .

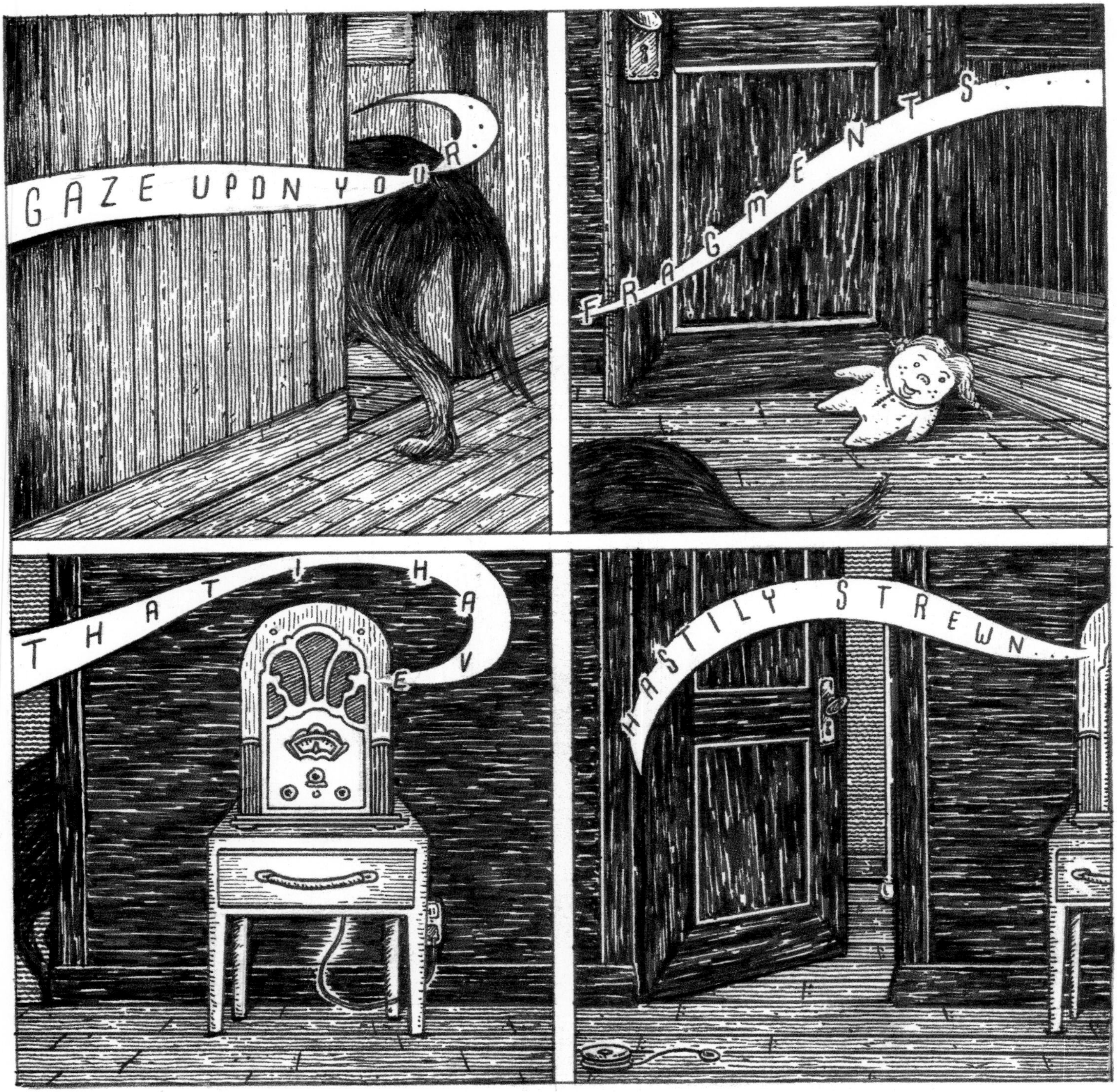
GAZE UPON YOUR
FRAGMENTS
THAT I HAVE
HASTILY STREWN...

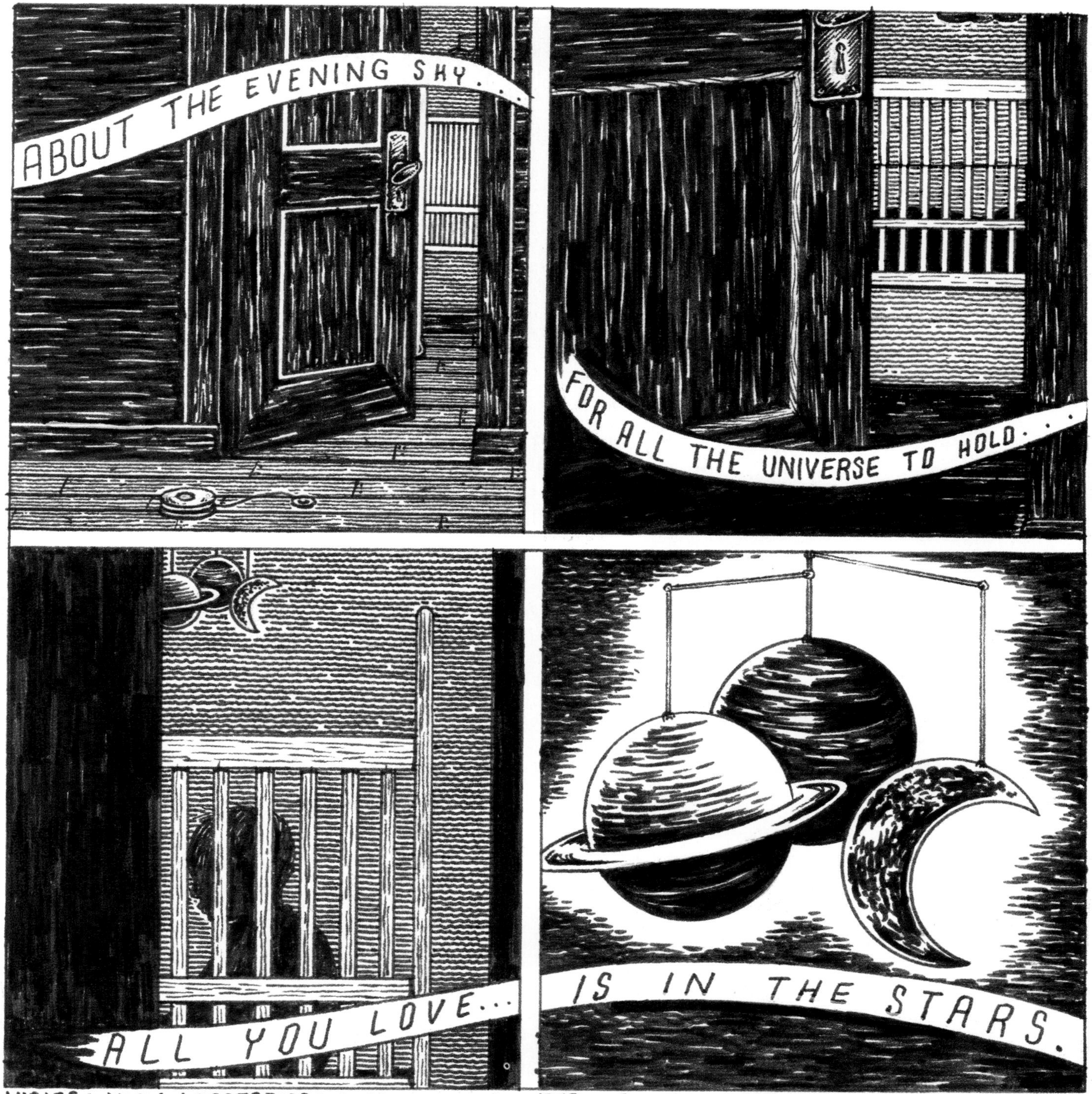
ABOUT THE EVENING SKY...
FOR ALL THE UNIVERSE TO HOLD...
ALL YOU LOVE...
IS IN THE STARS.

LYRICS: WWW.LESSERBIRDS.COM FEB... 2005 WWW.GRANTREYNOLDS.NET

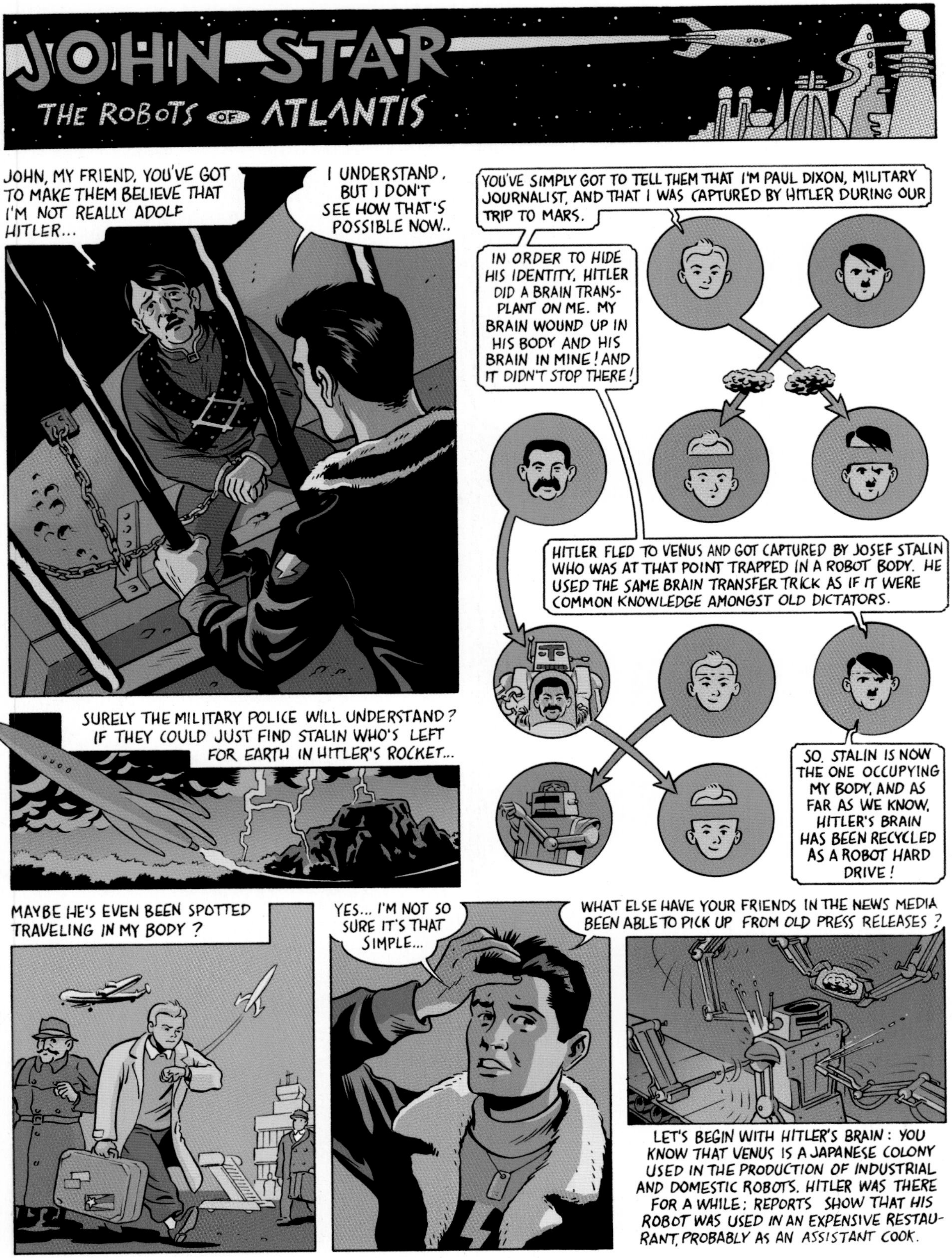
JOHN STAR
THE ROBOTS OF ATLANTIS
JOHN, MY FRIEND, YOU'VE GOT TO MAKE THEM BELIEVE THAT I'M NOT REALLY ADOLF HITLER...
I UNDERSTAND, BUT I DON'T SEE HOW THAT'S POSSIBLE NOW..
SURELY THE MILITARY POLICE WILL UNDERSTAND? IF THEY COULD JUST FIND STALIN WHO'S LEFT FOR EARTH IN HITLER'S ROCKET...
YOU'VE SIMPLY GOT TO TELL THEM THAT I'M PAUL DIXON, MILITARY JOURNALIST, AND THAT I WAS CAPTURED BY HITLER DURING OUR TRIP TO MARS.
IN ORDER TO HIDE HIS IDENTITY, HITLER DID A BRAIN TRANSPLANT ON ME. MY BRAIN WOUND UP IN HIS BODY AND HIS BRAIN IN MINE! AND IT DIDN'T STOP THERE!
HITLER FLED TO VENUS AND GOT CAPTURED BY JOSEF STALIN WHO WAS AT THAT POINT TRAPPED IN A ROBOT BODY. HE USED THE SAME BRAIN TRANSFER TRICK AS IF IT WERE COMMON KNOWLEDGE AMONGST OLD DICTATORS.
SO, STALIN IS NOW THE ONE OCCUPYING MY BODY, AND AS FAR AS WE KNOW, HITLER'S BRAIN HAS BEEN RECYCLED AS A ROBOT HARD DRIVE!
MAYBE HE'S EVEN BEEN SPOTTED TRAVELING IN MY BODY?
YES... I'M NOT SO SURE IT'S THAT SIMPLE...
WHAT ELSE HAVE YOUR FRIENDS IN THE NEWS MEDIA BEEN ABLE TO PICK UP FROM OLD PRESS RELEASES?
LET'S BEGIN WITH HITLER'S BRAIN: YOU KNOW THAT VENUS IS A JAPANESE COLONY USED IN THE PRODUCTION OF INDUSTRIAL AND DOMESTIC ROBOTS. HITLER WAS THERE FOR A WHILE; REPORTS SHOW THAT HIS ROBOT WAS USED IN AN EXPENSIVE RESTAURANT, PROBABLY AS AN ASSISTANT COOK.

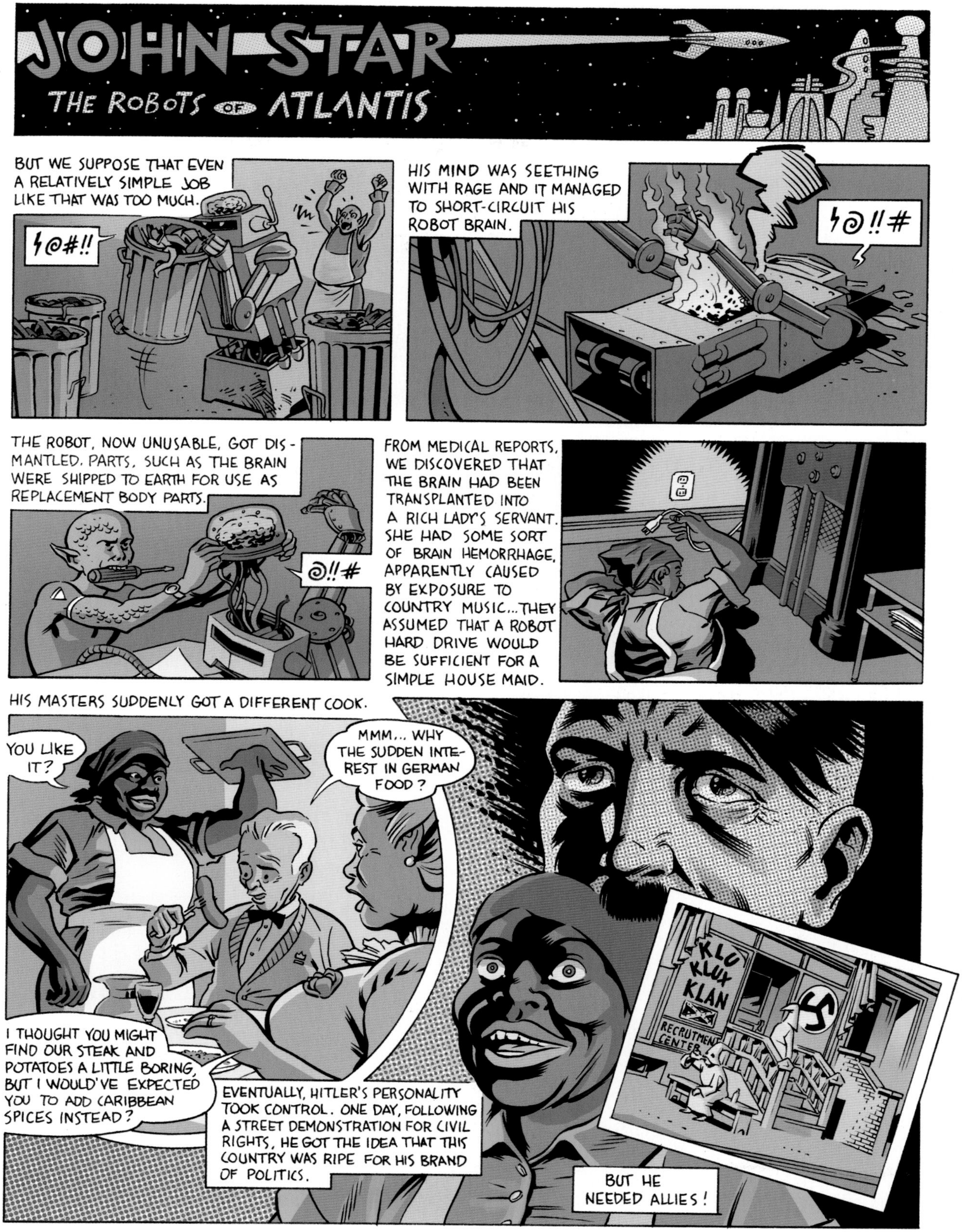
JOHN STAR
THE ROBOTS OF ATLANTIS
BUT WE SUPPOSE THAT EVEN A RELATIVELY SIMPLE JOB LIKE THAT WAS TOO MUCH.
ϟ@#!!
HIS MIND WAS SEETHING WITH RAGE AND IT MANAGED TO SHORT-CIRCUIT HIS ROBOT BRAIN.
ϟ@!!#
THE ROBOT, NOW UNUSABLE, GOT DIS-MANTLED. PARTS, SUCH AS THE BRAIN WERE SHIPPED TO EARTH FOR USE AS REPLACEMENT BODY PARTS.
@!!#
FROM MEDICAL REPORTS, WE DISCOVERED THAT THE BRAIN HAD BEEN TRANSPLANTED INTO A RICH LADY'S SERVANT. SHE HAD SOME SORT OF BRAIN HEMORRHAGE, APPARENTLY CAUSED BY EXPOSURE TO COUNTRY MUSIC... THEY ASSUMED THAT A ROBOT HARD DRIVE WOULD BE SUFFICIENT FOR A SIMPLE HOUSE MAID.
HIS MASTERS SUDDENLY GOT A DIFFERENT COOK.
YOU LIKE IT?
MMM... WHY THE SUDDEN INTE-REST IN GERMAN FOOD?
I THOUGHT YOU MIGHT FIND OUR STEAK AND POTATOES A LITTLE BORING, BUT I WOULD'VE EXPECTED YOU TO ADD CARIBBEAN SPICES INSTEAD?
EVENTUALLY, HITLER'S PERSONALITY TOOK CONTROL. ONE DAY, FOLLOWING A STREET DEMONSTRATION FOR CIVIL RIGHTS, HE GOT THE IDEA THAT THIS COUNTRY WAS RIPE FOR HIS BRAND OF POLITICS.
KLU KLUX KLAN
RECRUTMENT CENTER
BUT HE NEEDED ALLIES!

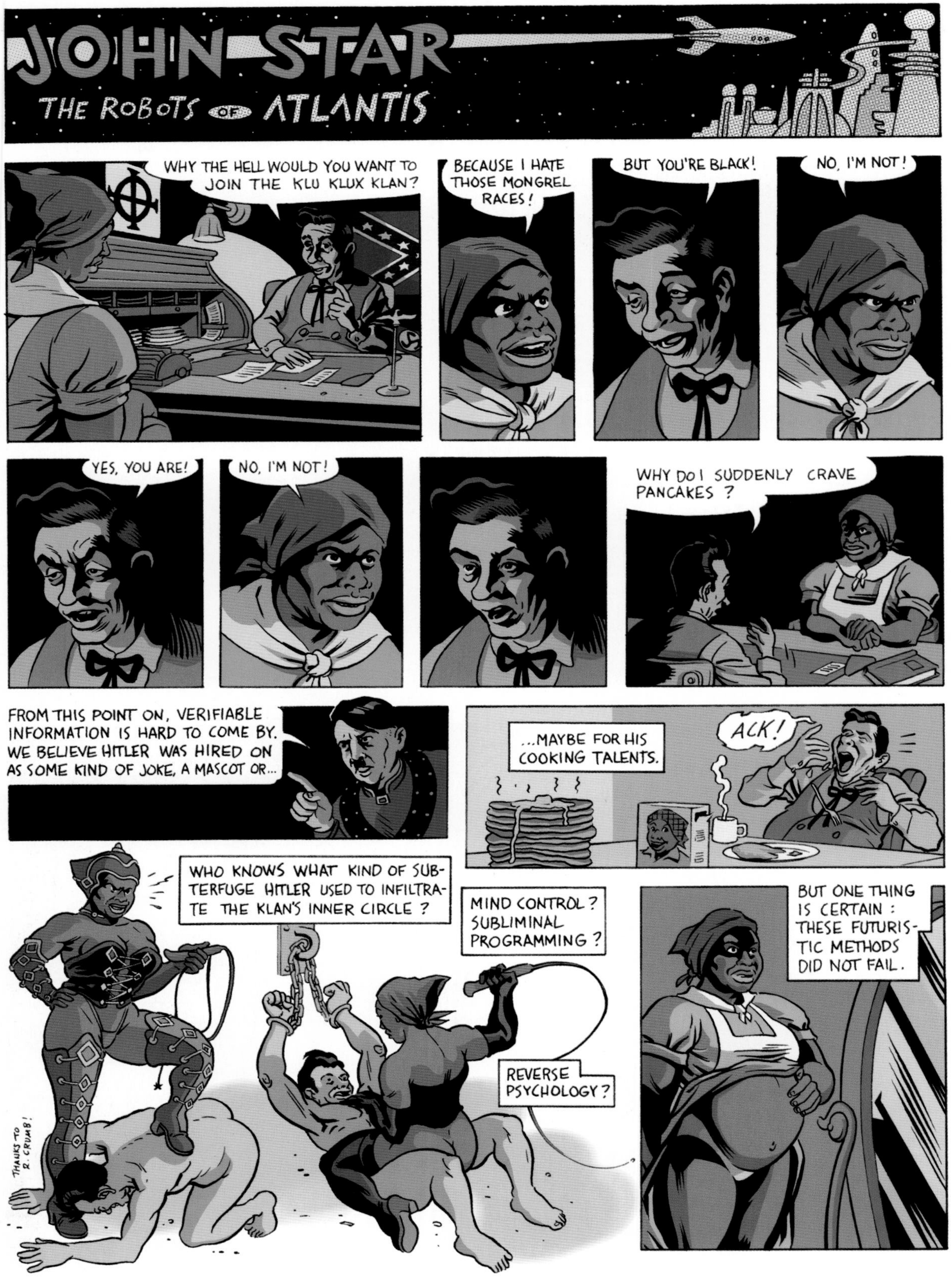
JOHN STAR
THE ROBOTS OF ATLANTIS
WHY THE HELL WOULD YOU WANT TO JOIN THE KLU KLUX KLAN?
BECAUSE I HATE THOSE MONGREL RACES!
BUT YOU'RE BLACK!
NO, I'M NOT!
YES, YOU ARE!
NO, I'M NOT!
WHY DO I SUDDENLY CRAVE PANCAKES ?
FROM THIS POINT ON, VERIFIABLE INFORMATION IS HARD TO COME BY. WE BELIEVE HITLER WAS HIRED ON AS SOME KIND OF JOKE, A MASCOT OR...
...MAYBE FOR HIS COOKING TALENTS.
ACK!
WHO KNOWS WHAT KIND OF SUBTERFUGE HITLER USED TO INFILTRATE THE KLAN'S INNER CIRCLE ?
MIND CONTROL ? SUBLIMINAL PROGRAMMING ?
REVERSE PSYCHOLOGY ?
THANKS TO R. CRUMB!
BUT ONE THING IS CERTAIN : THESE FUTURISTIC METHODS DID NOT FAIL.

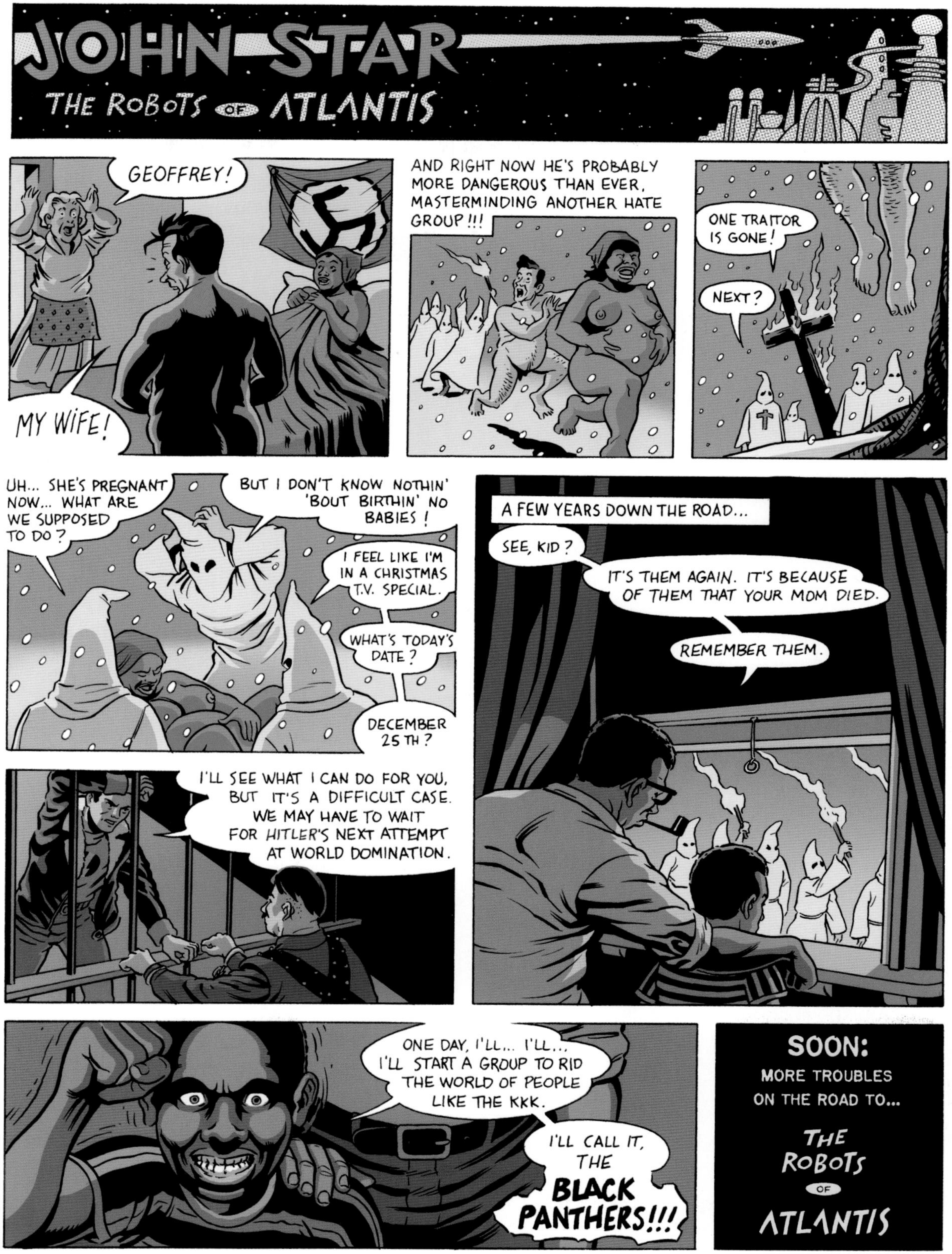
JOHN STAR
THE ROBOTS OF ATLANTIS
GEOFFREY!
MY WIFE!
AND RIGHT NOW HE'S PROBABLY MORE DANGEROUS THAN EVER, MASTERMINDING ANOTHER HATE GROUP!!!
ONE TRAITOR IS GONE!
NEXT?
UH... SHE'S PREGNANT NOW... WHAT ARE WE SUPPOSED TO DO?
BUT I DON'T KNOW NOTHIN' 'BOUT BIRTHIN' NO BABIES!
I FEEL LIKE I'M IN A CHRISTMAS T.V. SPECIAL.
WHAT'S TODAY'S DATE?
DECEMBER 25TH?
I'LL SEE WHAT I CAN DO FOR YOU, BUT IT'S A DIFFICULT CASE. WE MAY HAVE TO WAIT FOR HITLER'S NEXT ATTEMPT AT WORLD DOMINATION.
A FEW YEARS DOWN THE ROAD...
SEE, KID?
IT'S THEM AGAIN. IT'S BECAUSE OF THEM THAT YOUR MOM DIED.
REMEMBER THEM.
ONE DAY, I'LL... I'LL... I'LL START A GROUP TO RID THE WORLD OF PEOPLE LIKE THE KKK.
I'LL CALL IT, THE BLACK PANTHERS!!!
SOON: MORE TROUBLES ON THE ROAD TO... THE ROBOTS OF ATLANTIS

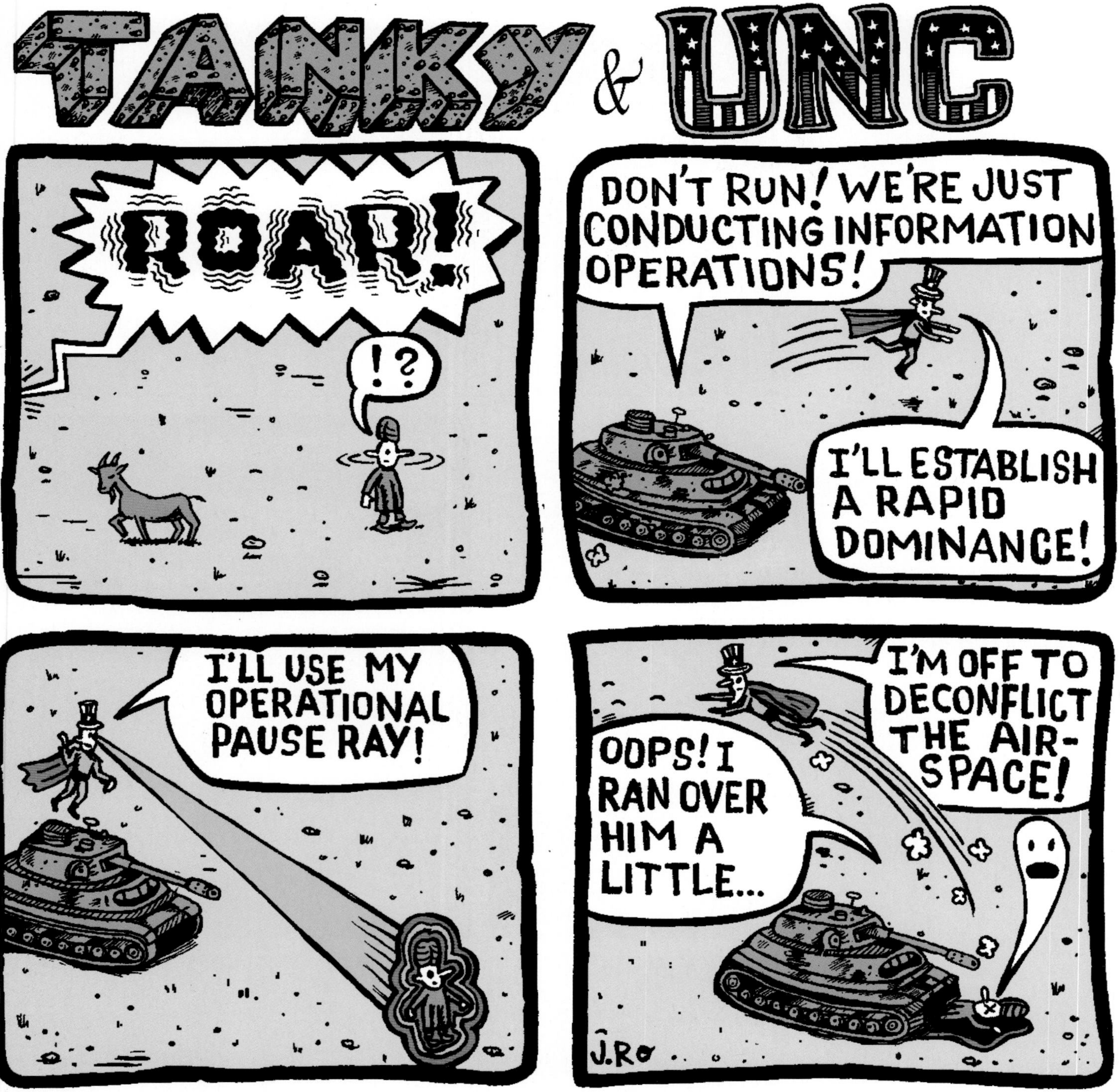
TANKY & UNC
ROAR!
!?
DON'T RUN! WE'RE JUST CONDUCTING INFORMATION OPERATIONS!
I'LL ESTABLISH A RAPID DOMINANCE!
I'LL USE MY OPERATIONAL PAUSE RAY!
I'M OFF TO DECONFLICT THE AIR-SPACE!
OOPS! I RAN OVER HIM A LITTLE...
J.RO

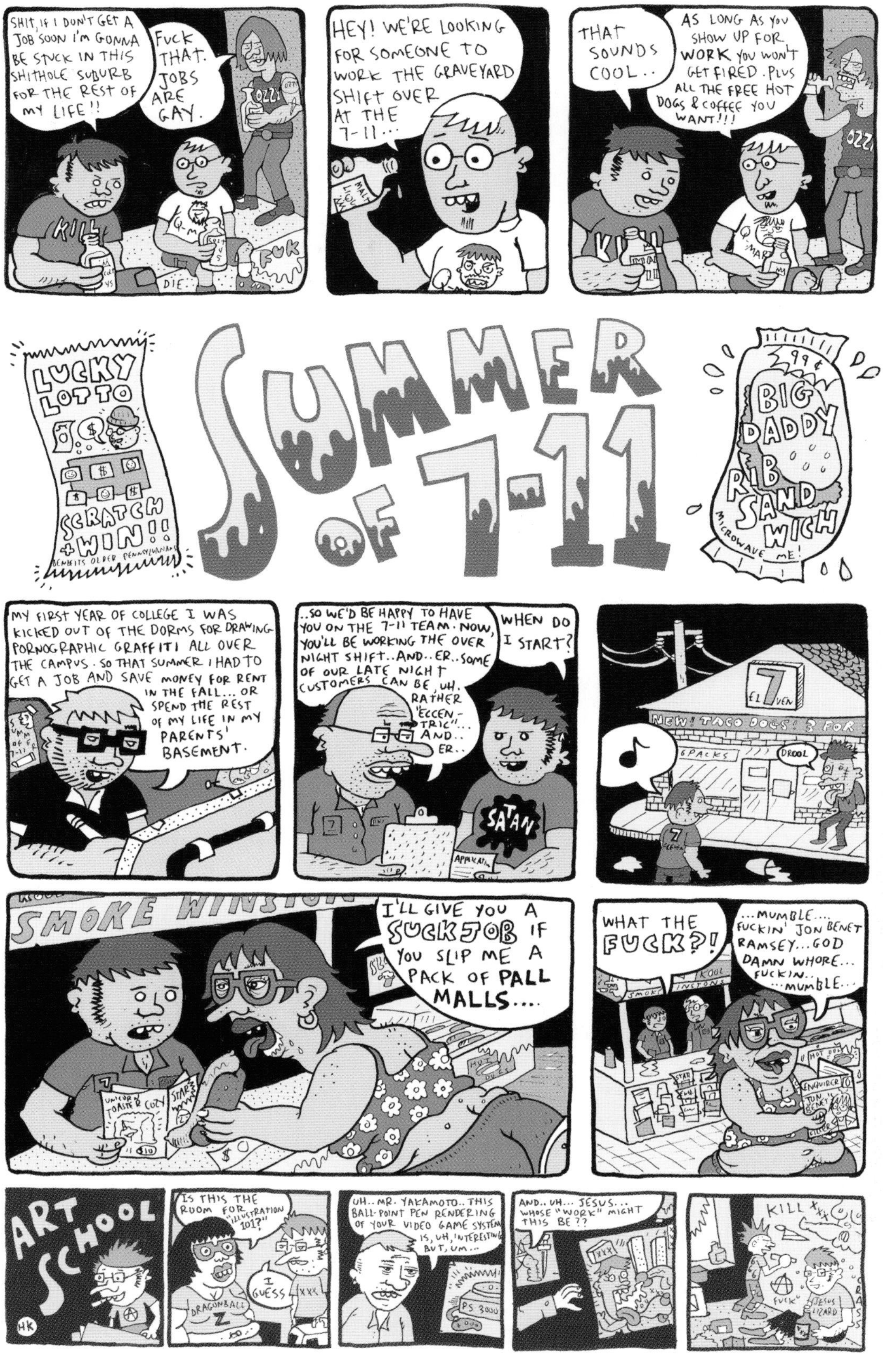

SHIT, IF I DON'T GET A JOB SOON I'M GONNA BE STUCK IN THIS SHITHOLE SUBURB FOR THE REST OF MY LIFE!!
FUCK THAT. JOBS ARE GAY.
HEY! WE'RE LOOKING FOR SOMEONE TO WORK THE GRAVEYARD SHIFT OVER AT THE 7-11...
THAT SOUNDS COOL..
AS LONG AS YOU SHOW UP FOR WORK YOU WON'T GET FIRED. PLUS ALL THE FREE HOT DOGS & COFFEE YOU WANT!!!
SUMMER OF 7-11
LUCKY LOTTO
SCRATCH + WIN!!
99¢
BIG DADDY RIB SANDWICH
MICROWAVE ME!
MY FIRST YEAR OF COLLEGE I WAS KICKED OUT OF THE DORMS FOR DRAWING PORNOGRAPHIC GRAFFITI ALL OVER THE CAMPUS. SO THAT SUMMER I HAD TO GET A JOB AND SAVE MONEY FOR RENT IN THE FALL... OR SPEND THE REST OF MY LIFE IN MY PARENTS' BASEMENT.
..SO WE'D BE HAPPY TO HAVE YOU ON THE 7-11 TEAM. NOW, YOU'LL BE WORKING THE OVER NIGHT SHIFT..AND..ER..SOME OF OUR LATE NIGHT CUSTOMERS CAN BE, UH. RATHER "ECCENTRIC"... AND.. ER..
WHEN DO I START?
SATAN
NEW! TACO DOGS! 3 FOR
6 PACKS
DROOL
SMOKE WINSTON
I'LL GIVE YOU A SUCKJOB IF YOU SLIP ME A PACK OF PALL MALLS....
WHAT THE FUCK?!
...MUMBLE... FUCKIN' JON BENET RAMSEY... GOD DAMN WHORE... FUCKIN.. ...MUMBLE...
ART SCHOOL
HK
IS THIS THE ROOM FOR "ILLUSTRATION 101?"
I GUESS
DRAGONBALL Z
UH.. MR. YAKAMOTO.. THIS BALL-POINT PEN RENDERING OF YOUR VIDEO GAME SYSTEM IS, UH, INTERESTING BUT, UM...
PS 3000
AND.. UH... JESUS... WHOSE "WORK" MIGHT THIS BE??
KILL
FUCK
JESUS LIZARD

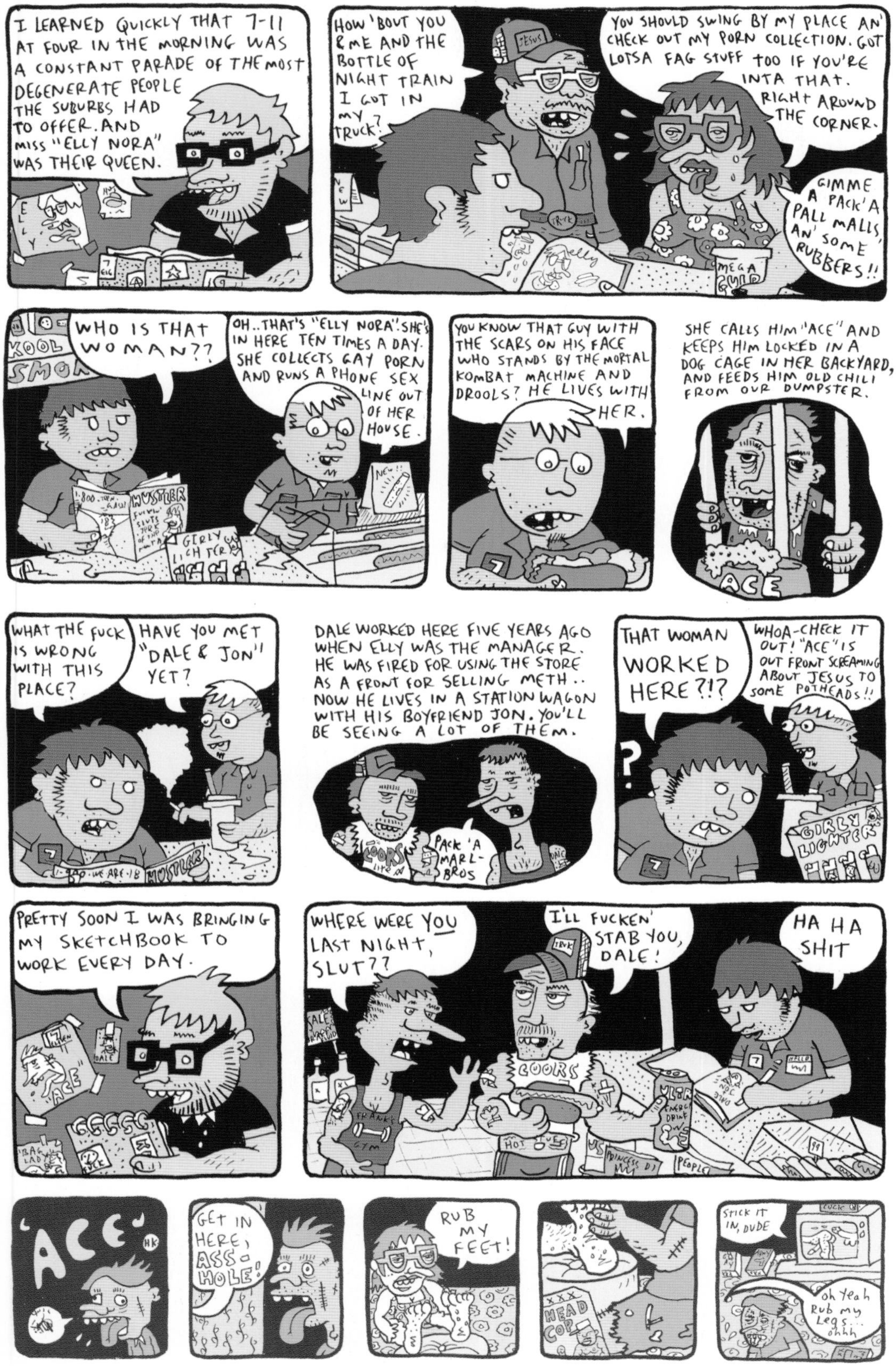
I LEARNED QUICKLY THAT 7-11 AT FOUR IN THE MORNING WAS A CONSTANT PARADE OF THE MOST DEGENERATE PEOPLE THE SUBURBS HAD TO OFFER. AND MISS "ELLY NORA" WAS THEIR QUEEN.
HOW 'BOUT YOU & ME AND THE BOTTLE OF NIGHT TRAIN I GOT IN MY TRUCK?
YOU SHOULD SWING BY MY PLACE AN' CHECK OUT MY PORN COLLECTION. GOT LOTSA FAG STUFF TOO IF YOU'RE INTA THAT. RIGHT AROUND THE CORNER.
GIMME A PACK 'A PALL MALLS, AN' SOME RUBBERS!!
MEGA GULP
WHO IS THAT WOMAN??
OH.. THAT'S "ELLY NORA". SHE'S IN HERE TEN TIMES A DAY. SHE COLLECTS GAY PORN AND RUNS A PHONE SEX LINE OUT OF HER HOUSE.
HUSTLER
GIRLY LIGHTER
YOU KNOW THAT GUY WITH THE SCARS ON HIS FACE WHO STANDS BY THE MORTAL KOMBAT MACHINE AND DROOLS? HE LIVES WITH HER.
SHE CALLS HIM "ACE" AND KEEPS HIM LOCKED IN A DOG CAGE IN HER BACKYARD, AND FEEDS HIM OLD CHILI FROM OUR DUMPSTER.
ACE
WHAT THE FUCK IS WRONG WITH THIS PLACE?
HAVE YOU MET "DALE & JON" YET?
HUSTLER
DALE WORKED HERE FIVE YEARS AGO WHEN ELLY WAS THE MANAGER. HE WAS FIRED FOR USING THE STORE AS A FRONT FOR SELLING METH.. NOW HE LIVES IN A STATION WAGON WITH HIS BOYFRIEND JON. YOU'LL BE SEEING A LOT OF THEM.
COORS LITE
PACK 'A MARLBROS
THAT WOMAN WORKED HERE?!?
WHOA-CHECK IT OUT! "ACE" IS OUT FRONT SCREAMING ABOUT JESUS TO SOME POTHEADS!!
?
GIRLY LIGHTER
PRETTY SOON I WAS BRINGING MY SKETCHBOOK TO WORK EVERY DAY.
ACE
WHERE WERE YOU LAST NIGHT, SLUT??
I'LL FUCKEN' STAB YOU, DALE!
HA HA SHIT
COORS
FRANK'S GYM
HOT DOGS
PEOPLE
'ACE'
GET IN HERE, ASS-HOLE!
RUB MY FEET!
XXX HEAD COP
STICK IT IN, DUDE
oh yeah Rub my Legs... ohhh

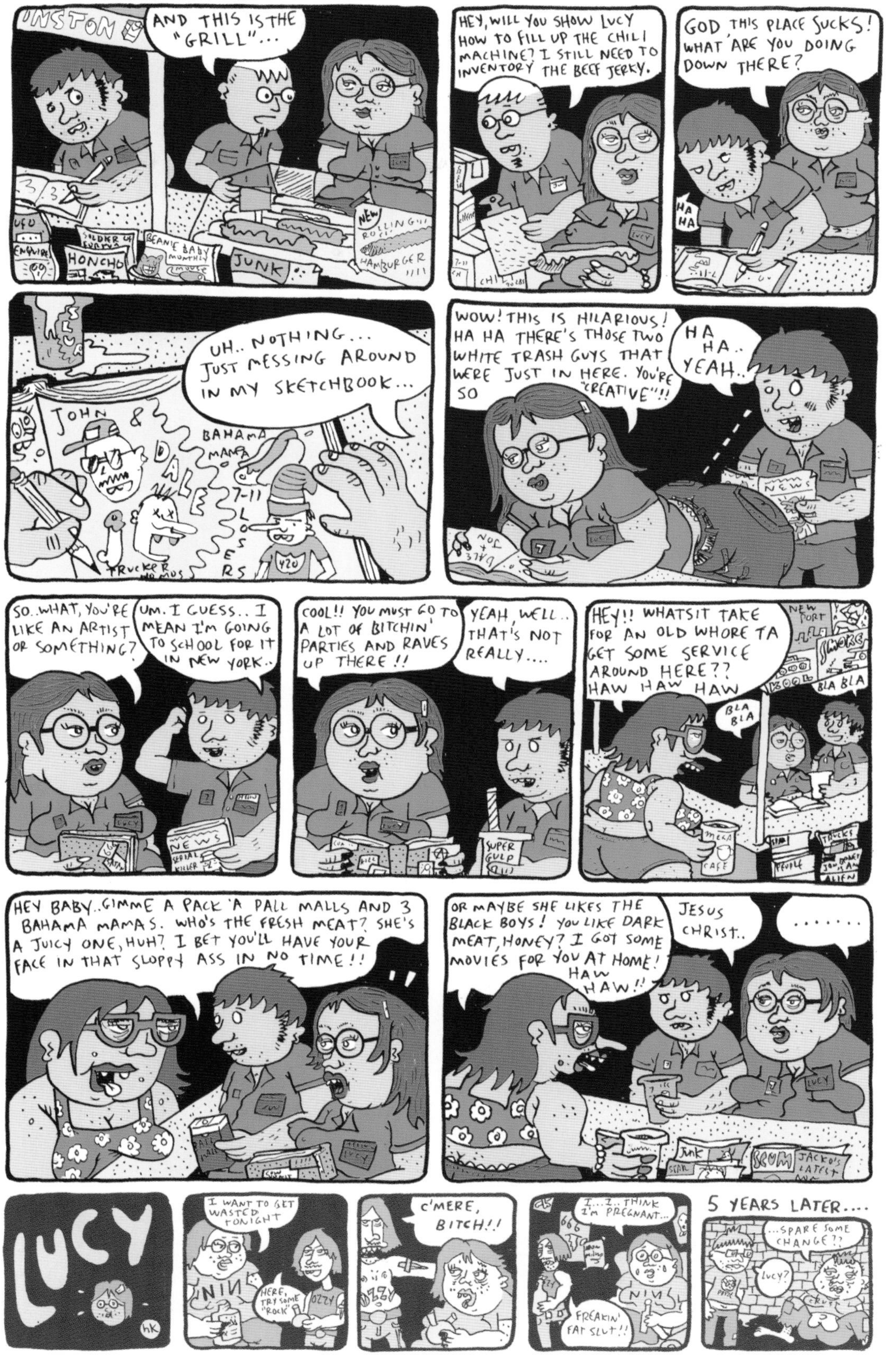
AND THIS IS THE "GRILL"...
UFO
ENQUIRER
HONCHO
BEANIE BABY MONTHLY
JUNK
NEW
HAMBURGER
HEY, WILL YOU SHOW LUCY HOW TO FILL UP THE CHILI MACHINE? I STILL NEED TO INVENTORY THE BEEF JERKY.
LUCY
GOD THIS PLACE SUCKS! WHAT ARE YOU DOING DOWN THERE?
HA HA
UH.. NOTHING... JUST MESSING AROUND IN MY SKETCHBOOK...
JOHN & DALE
BAHAMA MAMA
7-11 LOSERS
420
WOW! THIS IS HILARIOUS! HA HA THERE'S THOSE TWO WHITE TRASH GUYS THAT WERE JUST IN HERE. YOU'RE SO "CREATIVE"!!
HA HA.. YEAH..
NEWS
SO..WHAT, YOU'RE LIKE AN ARTIST OR SOMETHING?
UM. I GUESS.. I MEAN I'M GOING TO SCHOOL FOR IT IN NEW YORK..
LUCY
NEWS
SERIAL KILLER
COOL!! YOU MUST GO TO A LOT OF BITCHIN' PARTIES AND RAVES UP THERE!!
YEAH, WELL.. THAT'S NOT REALLY....
SUPER GULP
HEY!! WHATSIT TAKE FOR AN OLD WHORE TA GET SOME SERVICE AROUND HERE?? HAW HAW HAW
BLA BLA
BLA BLA
HEY BABY..GIMME A PACK 'A PALL MALLS AND 3 BAHAMA MAMAS. WHO'S THE FRESH MEAT? SHE'S A JUICY ONE, HUH? I BET YOU'LL HAVE YOUR FACE IN THAT SLOPPY ASS IN NO TIME!!
LUCY
OR MAYBE SHE LIKES THE BLACK BOYS! YOU LIKE DARK MEAT, HONEY? I GOT SOME MOVIES FOR YOU AT HOME! HAW HAW!!
JESUS CHRIST..
....
LUCY
JUNK
SCUM
LUCY
hk
I WANT TO GET WASTED TONIGHT
NIN
HERE, TRY SOME "ROCK"
OZZY
C'MERE, BITCH!!
I... I.. THINK I'M PREGNANT...
666
NIN
FREAKIN' FAT SLUT!!
5 YEARS LATER....
...SPARE SOME CHANGE??
LUCY?

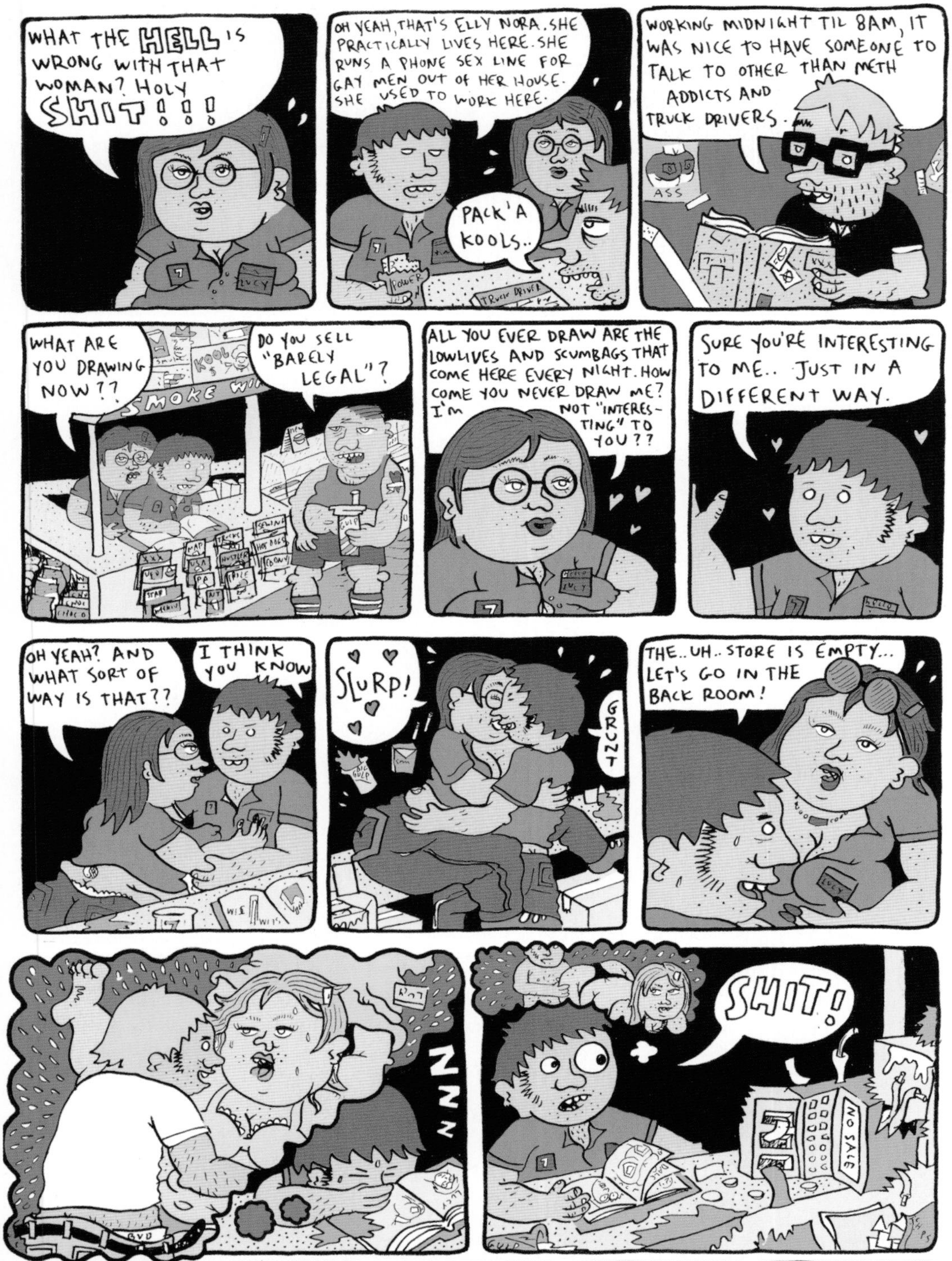
WHAT THE HELL IS WRONG WITH THAT WOMAN? HOLY SHIT!!!
OH YEAH, THAT'S ELLY NORA. SHE PRACTICALLY LIVES HERE. SHE RUNS A PHONE SEX LINE FOR GAY MEN OUT OF HER HOUSE. SHE USED TO WORK HERE.
PACK'A KOOLS..
WORKING MIDNIGHT TIL 8AM, IT WAS NICE TO HAVE SOMEONE TO TALK TO OTHER THAN METH ADDICTS AND TRUCK DRIVERS.
WHAT ARE YOU DRAWING NOW??
DO YOU SELL "BARELY LEGAL"?
ALL YOU EVER DRAW ARE THE LOWLIVES AND SCUMBAGS THAT COME HERE EVERY NIGHT. HOW COME YOU NEVER DRAW ME? I'M NOT "INTERESTING" TO YOU??
SURE YOU'RE INTERESTING TO ME.. JUST IN A DIFFERENT WAY.
OH YEAH? AND WHAT SORT OF WAY IS THAT??
I THINK YOU KNOW
SLURP!
GRUNT
THE.. UH.. STORE IS EMPTY... LET'S GO IN THE BACK ROOM!
ZZZ
SHIT!
NO SALE

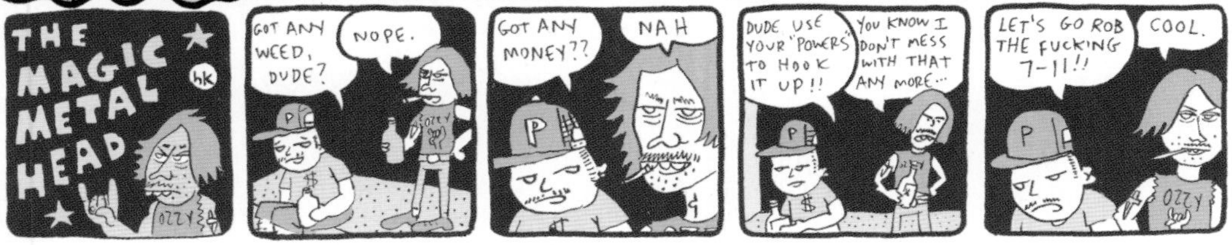
THE MAGIC METAL HEAD
GOT ANY WEED, DUDE?
NOPE.
GOT ANY MONEY??
NAH
DUDE USE YOUR 'POWERS' TO HOOK IT UP!!
YOU KNOW I DON'T MESS WITH THAT ANY MORE...
LET'S GO ROB THE FUCKING 7-11!!
COOL.

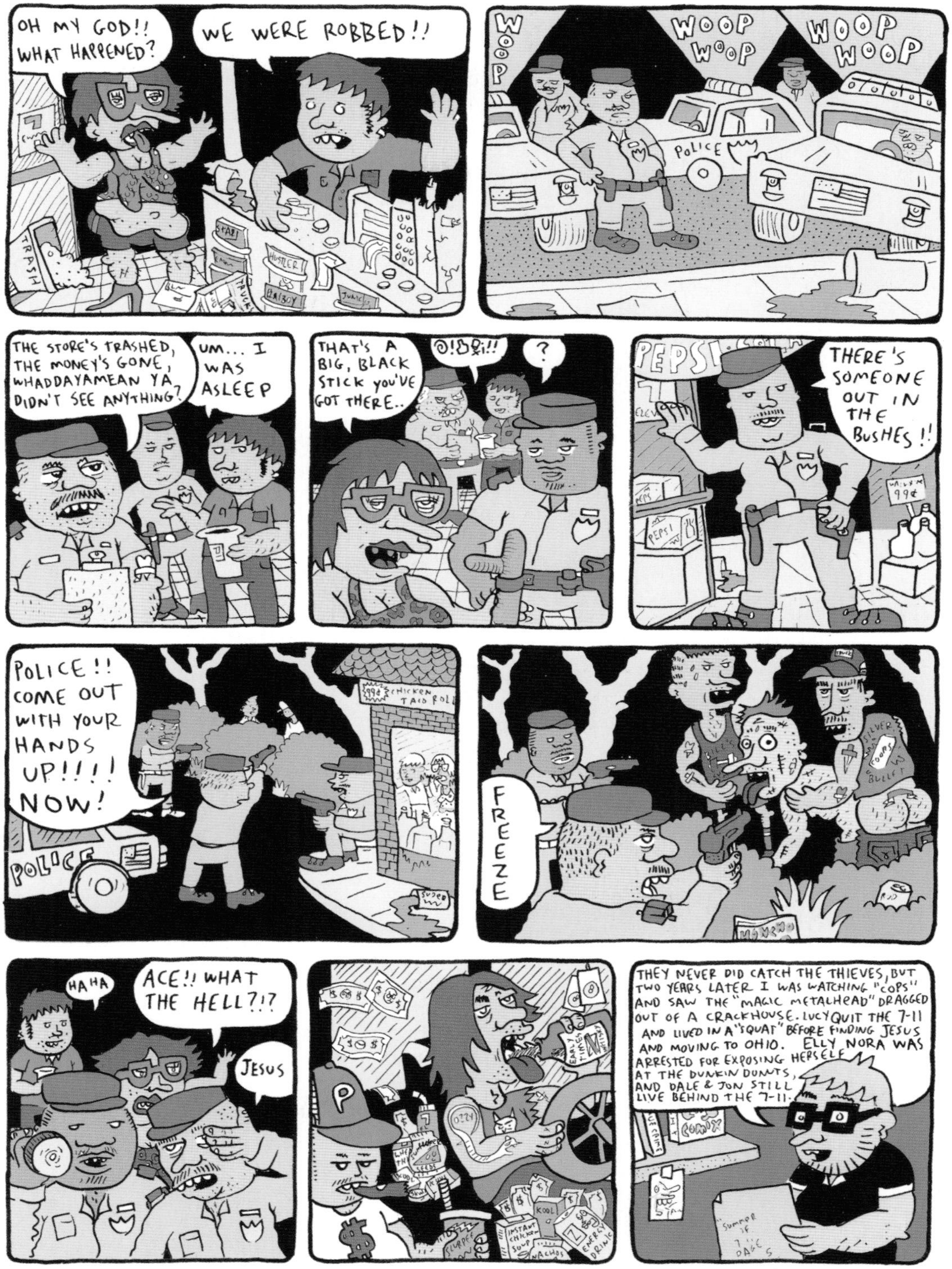
OH MY GOD!! WHAT HAPPENED?
WE WERE ROBBED!!
WOOP
WOOP WOOP
WOOP WOOP
POLICE
THE STORE'S TRASHED, THE MONEY'S GONE, WHADDAYAMEAN YA DIDN'T SEE ANYTHING?
UM... I WAS ASLEEP
THAT'S A BIG, BLACK STICK YOU'VE GOT THERE..
?
PEPSI
THERE'S SOMEONE OUT IN THE BUSHES!!
POLICE!! COME OUT WITH YOUR HANDS UP!!!! NOW!
POLICE
FREEZE
HAHA
ACE!! WHAT THE HELL?!?
JESUS
THEY NEVER DID CATCH THE THIEVES, BUT TWO YEARS LATER I WAS WATCHING "COPS" AND SAW THE "MAGIC METALHEAD" DRAGGED OUT OF A CRACKHOUSE. LUCY QUIT THE 7-11 AND LIVED IN A "SQUAT" BEFORE FINDING JESUS AND MOVING TO OHIO. ELLY NORA WAS ARRESTED FOR EXPOSING HERSELF AT THE DUNKIN DONUTS, AND DALE & JON STILL LIVE BEHIND THE 7-11.

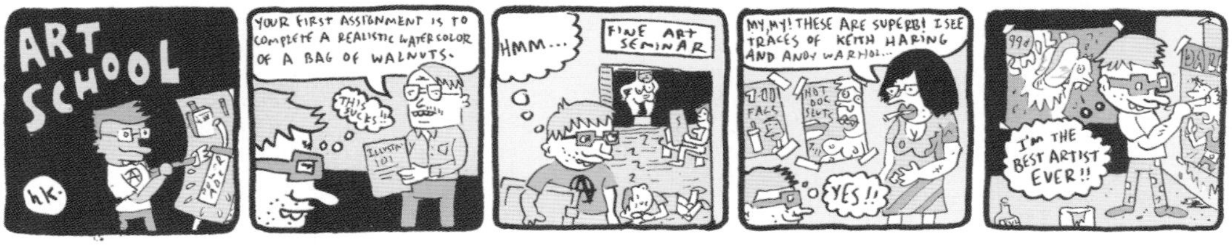
ART SCHOOL
hk.
YOUR FIRST ASSIGNMENT IS TO COMPLETE A REALISTIC WATERCOLOR OF A BAG OF WALNUTS.
THIS SUCKS!!
HMM...
FINE ART SEMINAR
MY, MY! THESE ARE SUPERB! I SEE TRACES OF KEITH HARING AND ANDY WARHOL...
YES!!
I'M THE BEST ARTIST EVER!!

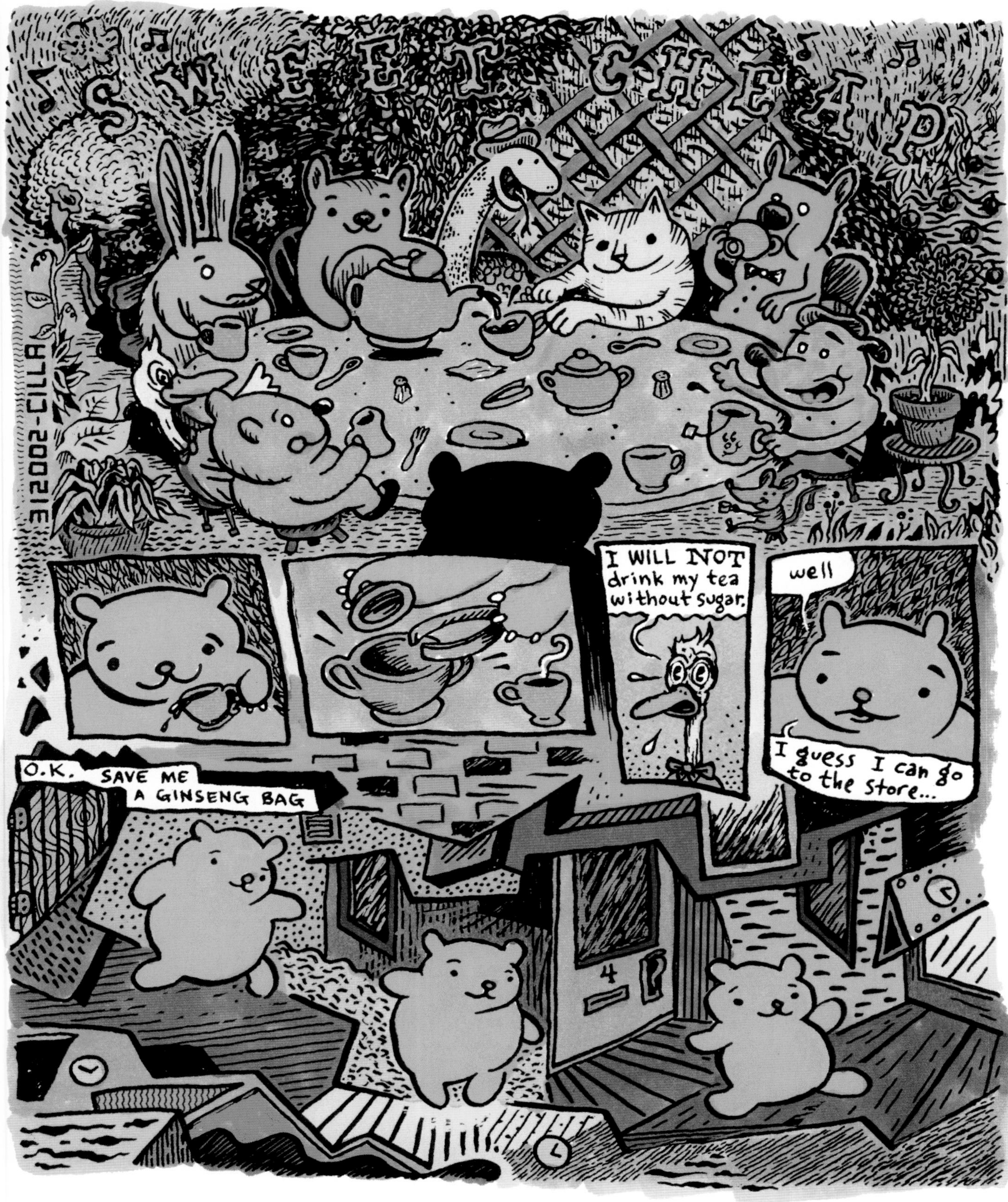
SWEET CHEAP
312002-CILLA
I WILL NOT drink my tea without sugar.
well
I guess I can go to the store...
O.K. SAVE ME A GINSENG BAG
4

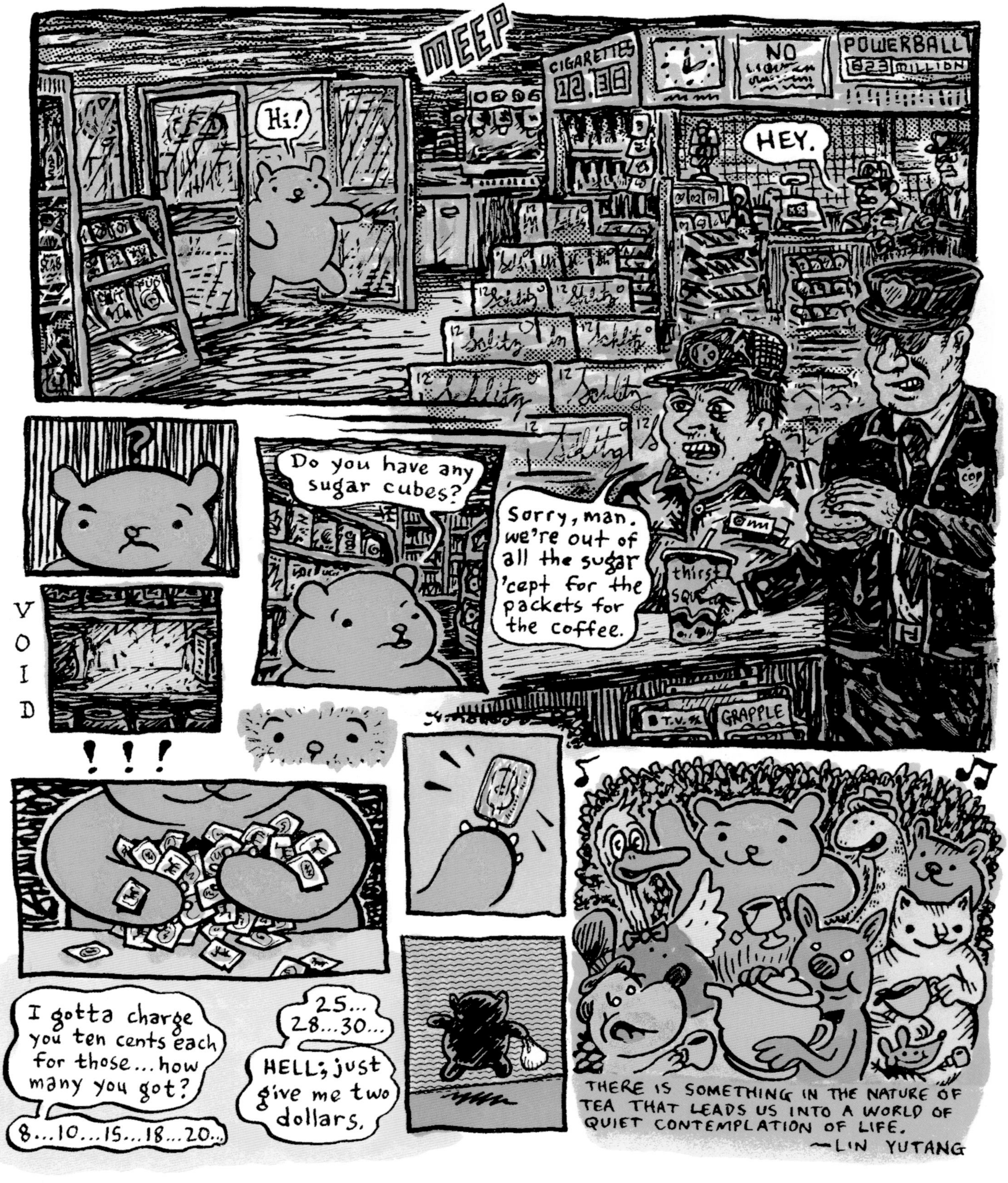
MEEP
CIGARETTES
POWERBALL
Hi!
HEY.
Do you have any sugar cubes?
Sorry, man. we're out of all the sugar 'cept for the packets for the coffee.
GRAPPLE
V O I D
! ! !
I gotta charge you ten cents each for those...how many you got?
8...10...15...18...20...
25... 28...30...
HELL; just give me two dollars.
THERE IS SOMETHING IN THE NATURE OF TEA THAT LEADS US INTO A WORLD OF QUIET CONTEMPLATION OF LIFE.
—LIN YUTANG

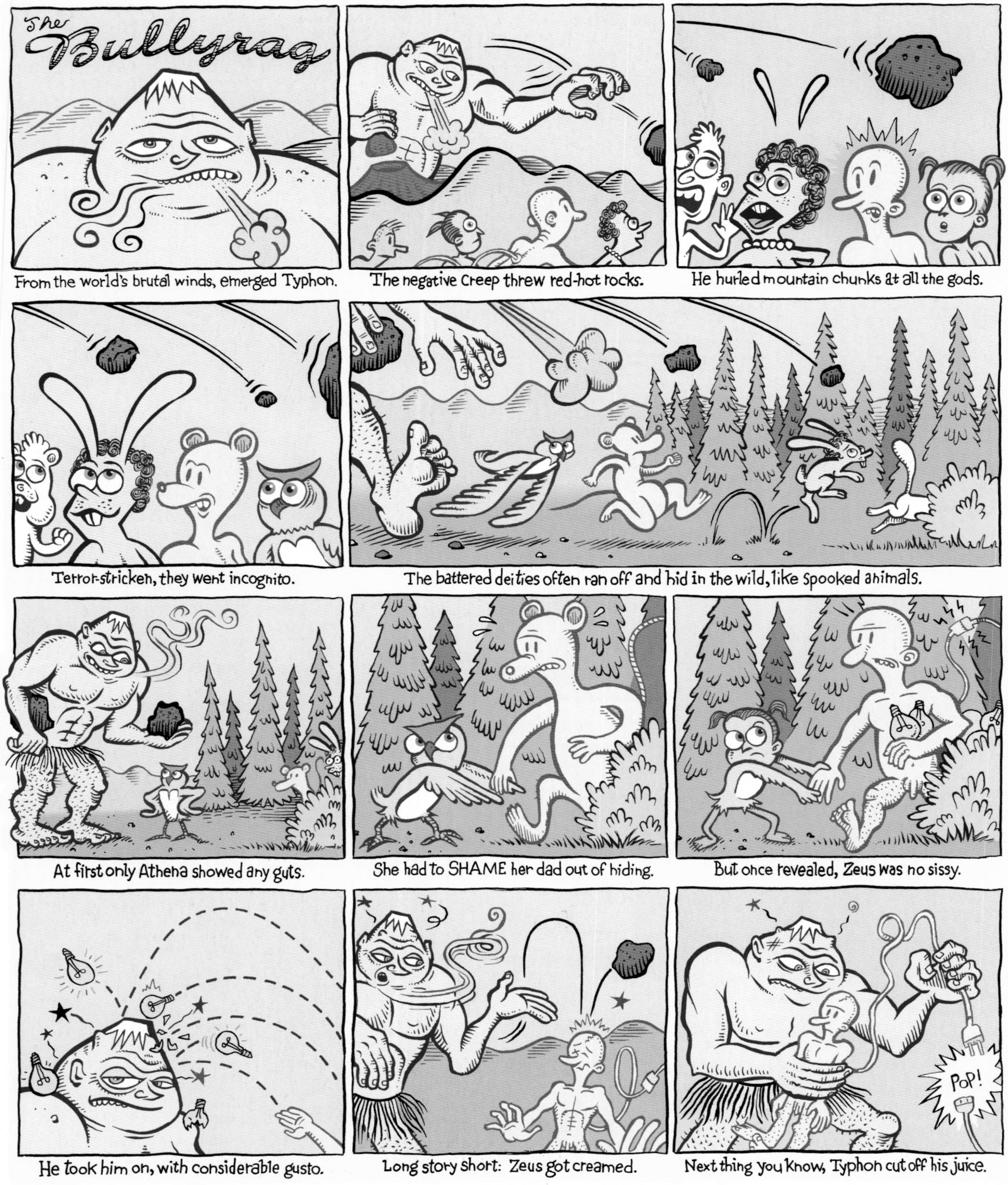
The Bullyrag
From the world's brutal winds, emerged Typhon.
The negative Creep threw red-hot rocks.
He hurled mountain chunks at all the gods.
Terror-stricken, they went incognito.
The battered deities often ran off and hid in the wild, like spooked animals.
At first only Athena showed any guts.
She had to SHAME her dad out of hiding.
But once revealed, Zeus was no sissy.
He took him on, with considerable gusto.
Long story short: Zeus got creamed.
PoP!
Next thing you know, Typhon cut off his juice.

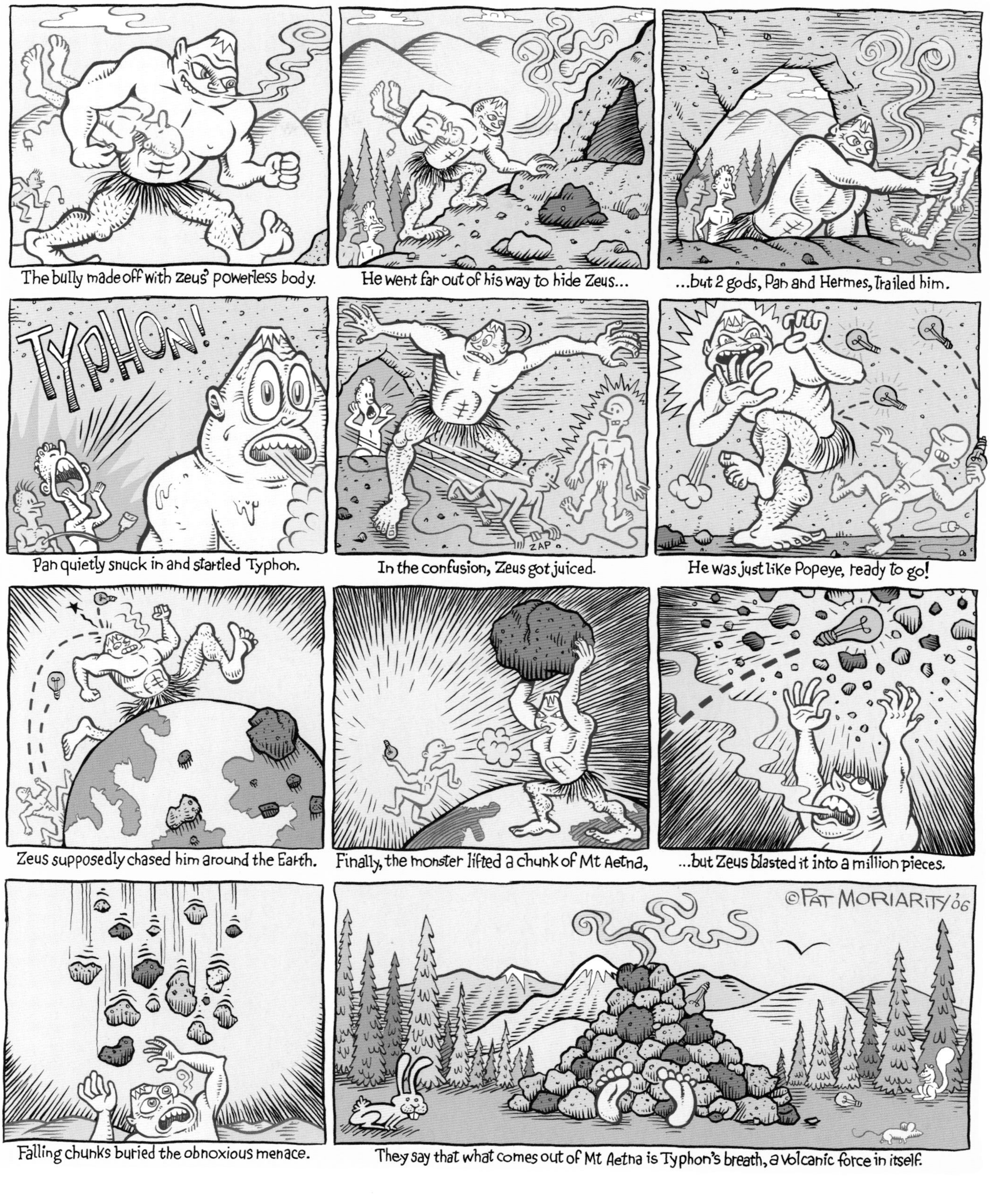
The bully made off with zeus' powerless body.
He went far out of his way to hide Zeus...
...but 2 gods, Pan and Hermes, trailed him.
TYPHON!
Pan quietly snuck in and startled Typhon.
ZAP
In the confusion, Zeus got juiced.
He was just like Popeye, ready to go!
Zeus supposedly chased him around the Earth.
Finally, the monster lifted a chunk of Mt Aetna,
...but Zeus blasted it into a million pieces.
Falling chunks buried the obnoxious menace.
©PAT MORIARITY '06
They say that what comes out of Mt Aetna is Typhon's breath, a volcanic force in itself.

THERE • IS • A • LAW

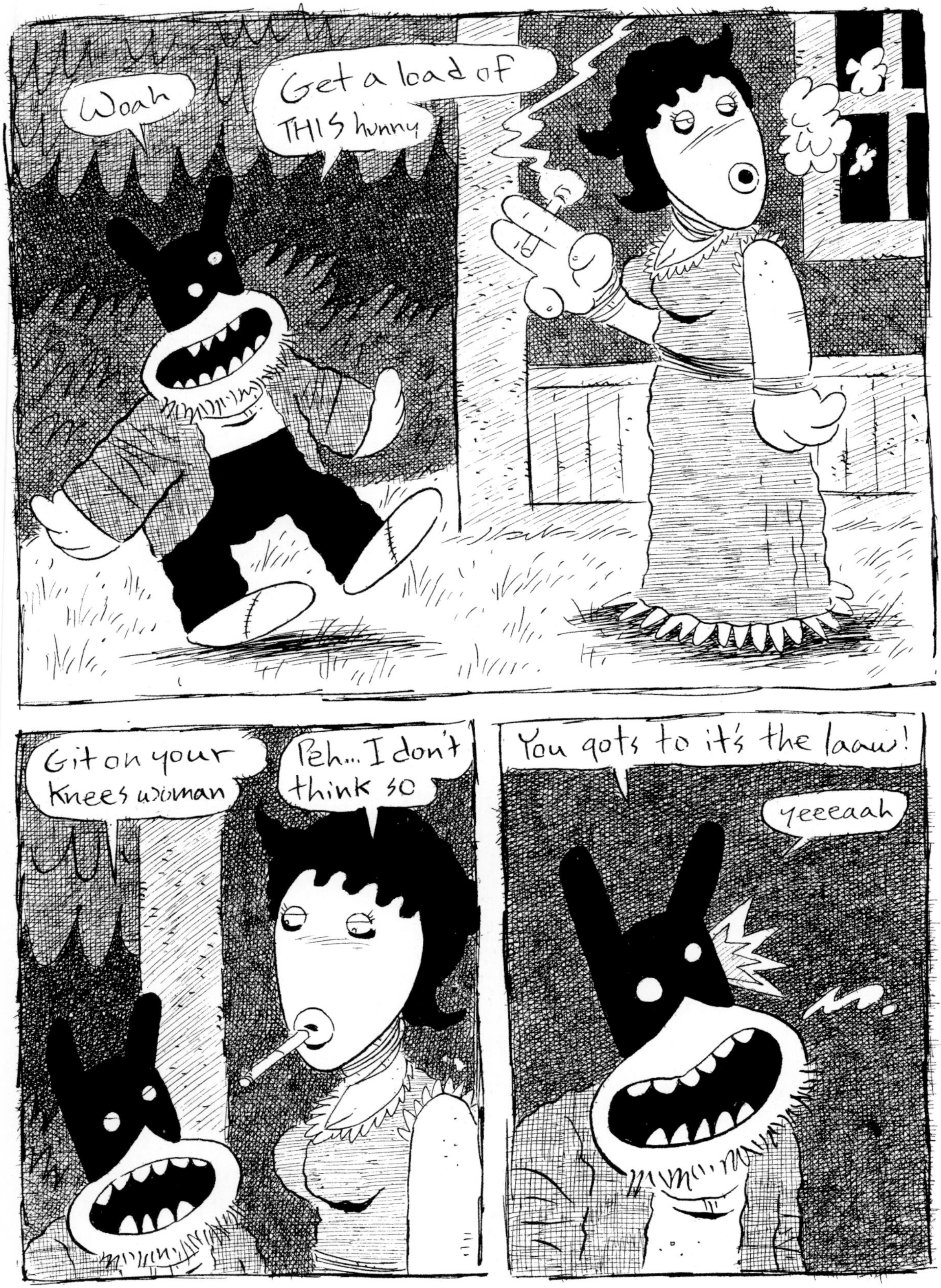
Woah
Get a load of THIS hunny
Git on your Knees woman
Peh... I don't think so
You gots to it's the laaw!
yeeeaah

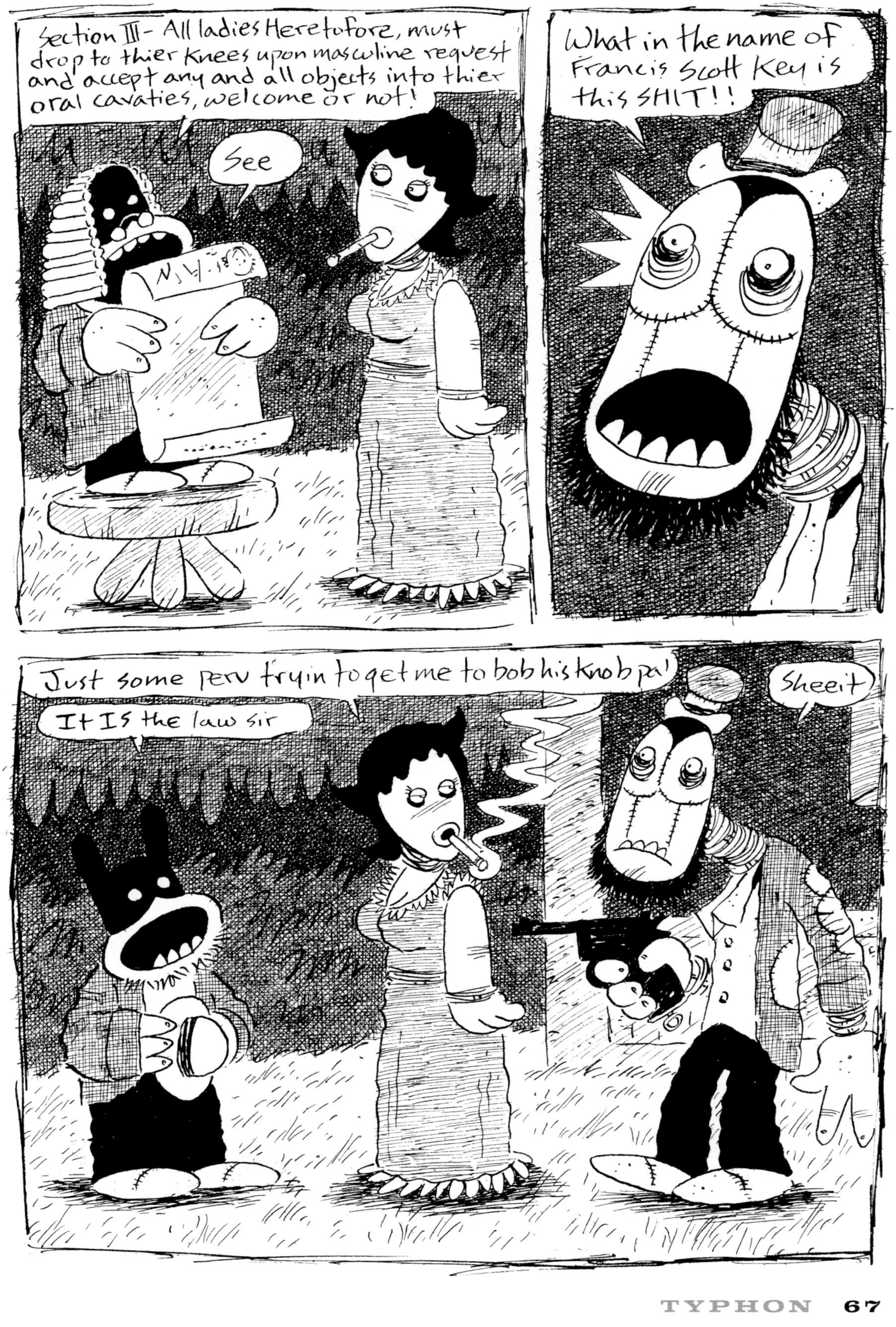
Section III- All ladies Heretofore, must drop to thier Knees upon masculine request and accept any and all objects into thier oral cavaties, welcome or not!
See
What in the name of Francis Scott Key is this SHIT!!
Just some perv tryin to get me to bob his knob pal
It IS the law sir
Sheeit

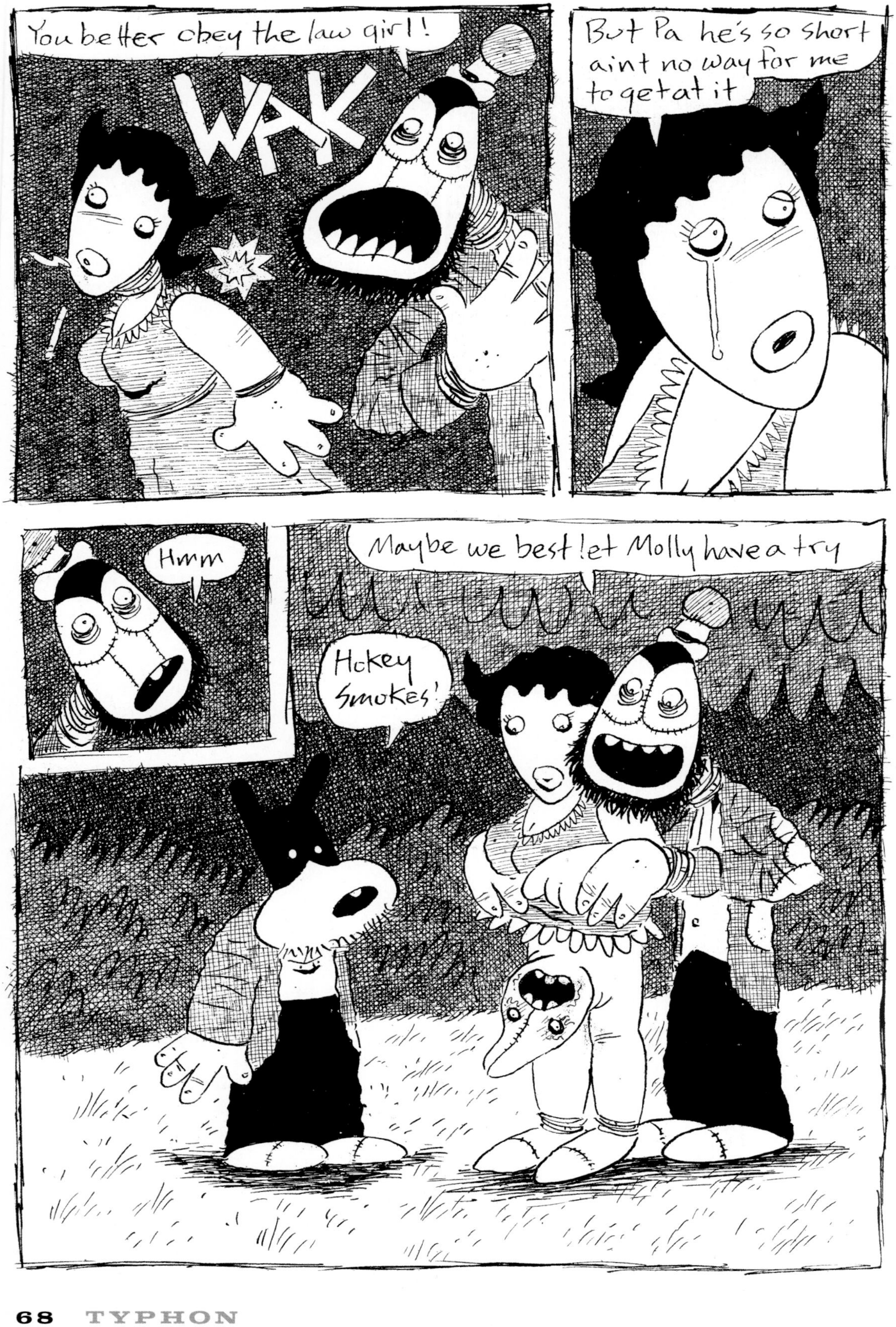
You better obey the law girl!
WAK
But Pa he's so short aint no way for me to get at it
Hmm
Maybe we best let Molly have a try
Hokey Smokes!

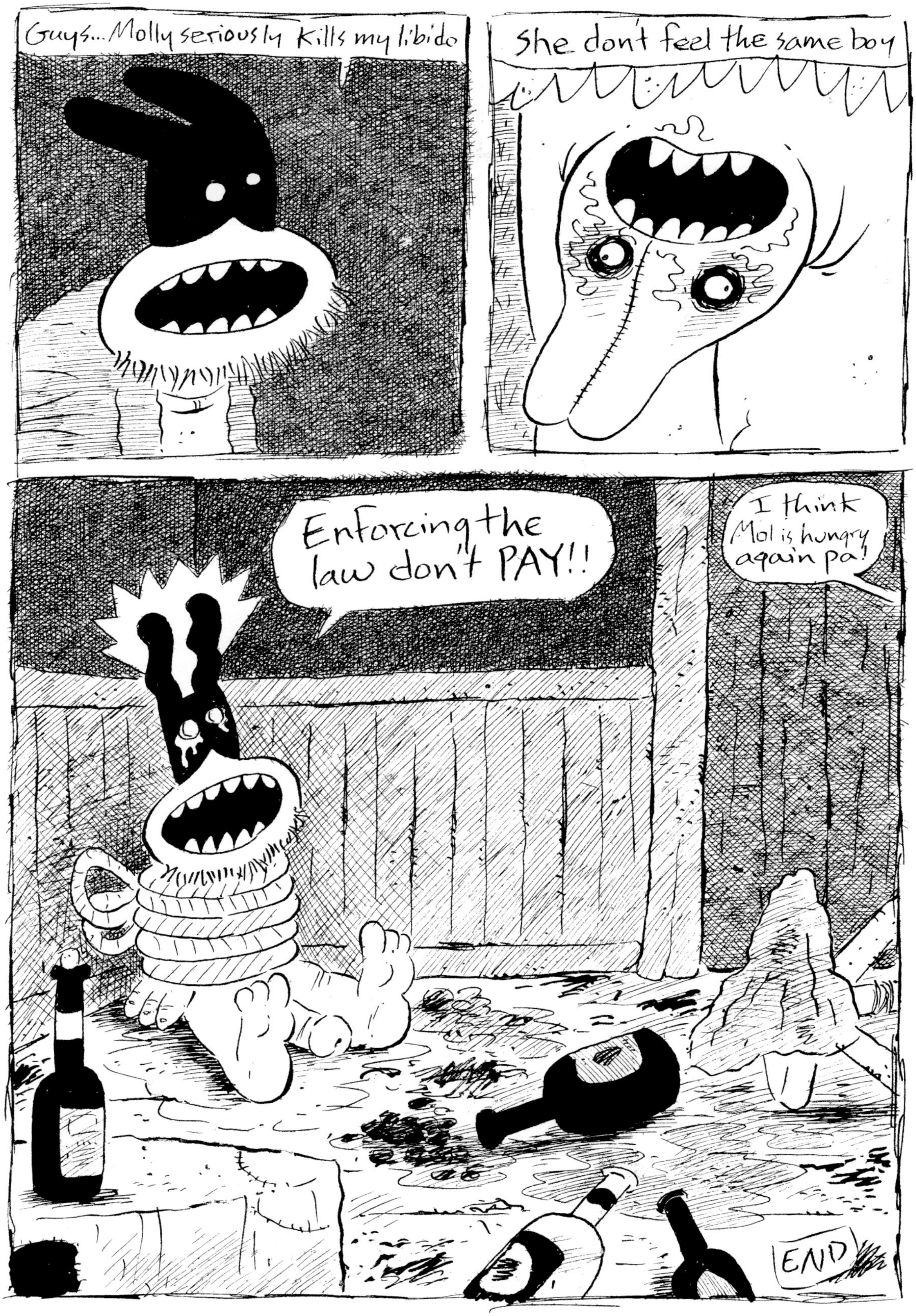
Guys... Molly seriously Kills my libido
She don't feel the same boy
Enforcing the law don't PAY!!
I think Mol is hungry again pa!
END

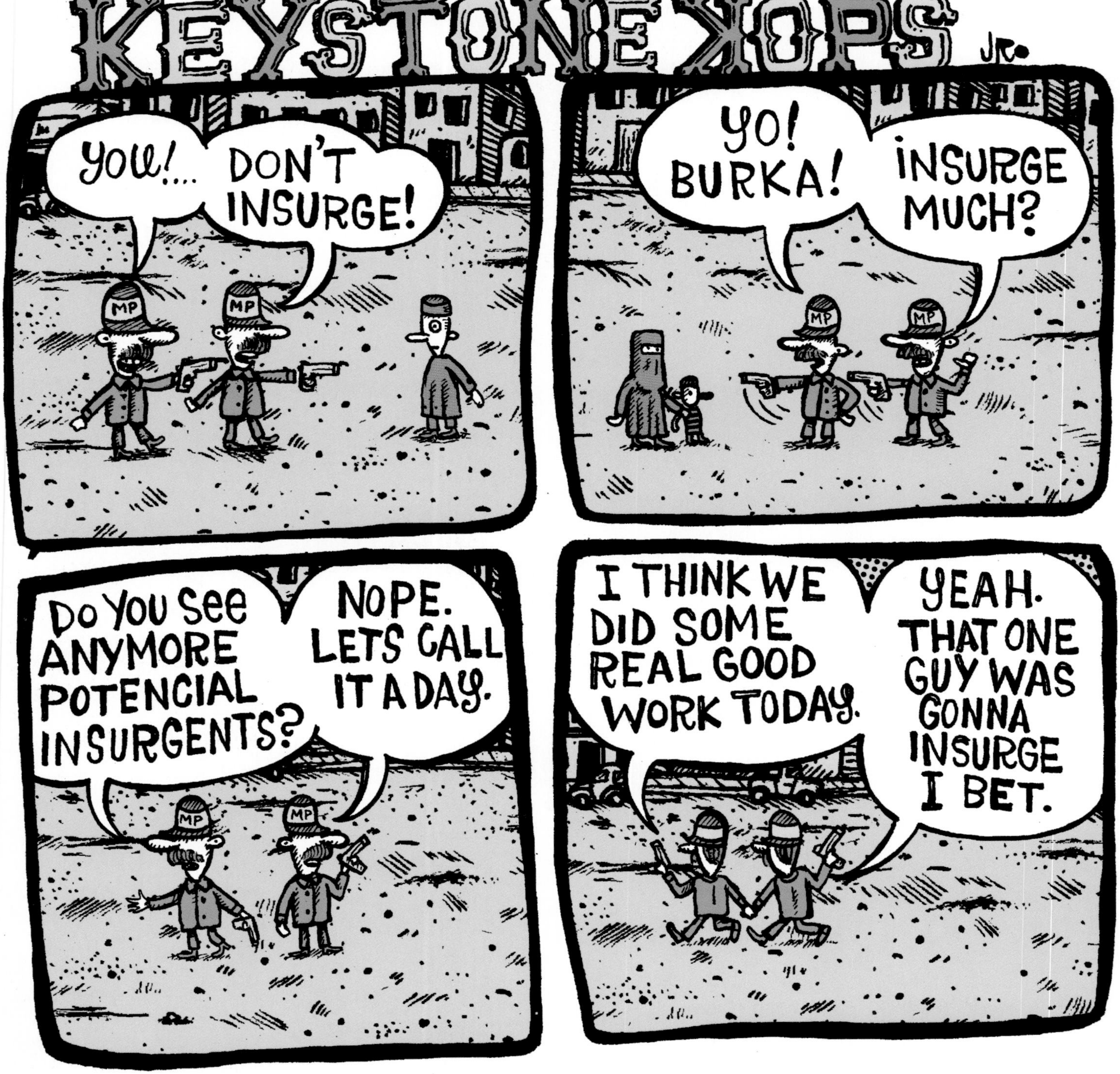
KEYSTONE KOPS
JRo
YOU!...
DON'T INSURGE!
MP
MP
YO! BURKA!
INSURGE MUCH?
MP
MP
Do You See ANYMORE POTENCIAL INSURGENTS?
NOPE. LETS CALL IT A DAY.
MP
MP
I THINK WE DID SOME REAL GOOD WORK TODAY.
YEAH. THAT ONE GUY WAS GONNA INSURGE I BET.

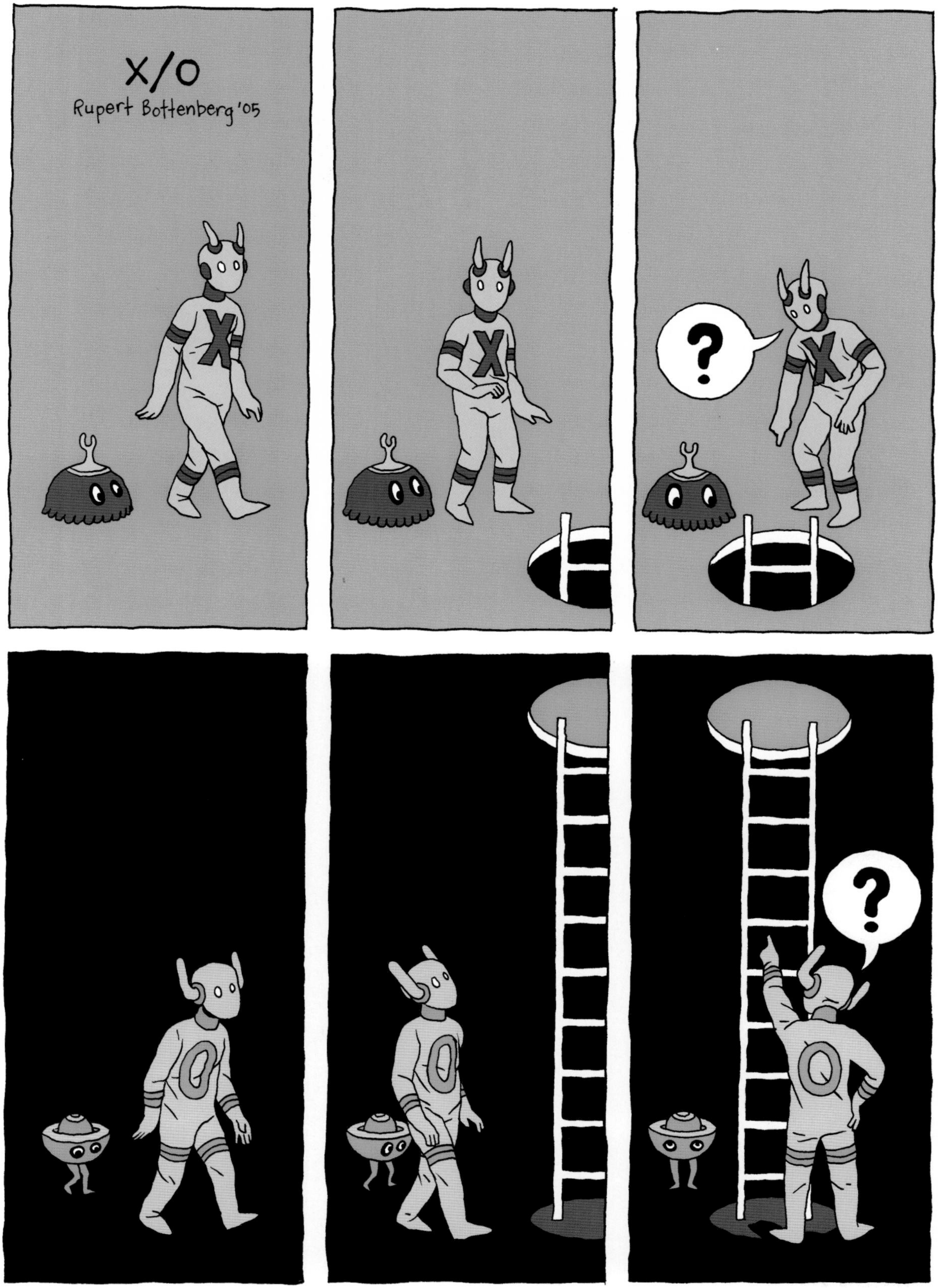
X/O
Rupert Bottenberg '05
?
?

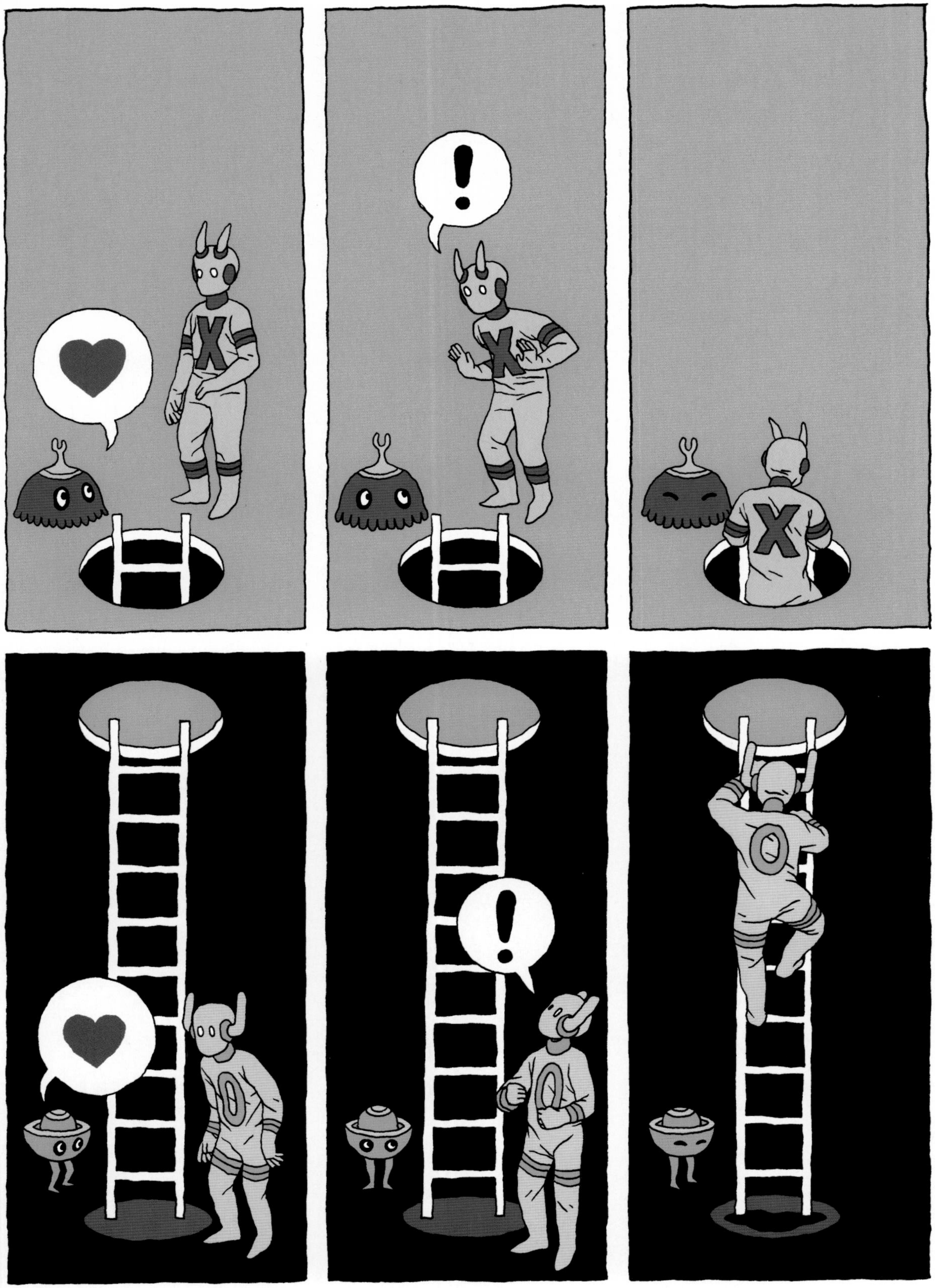
!
!

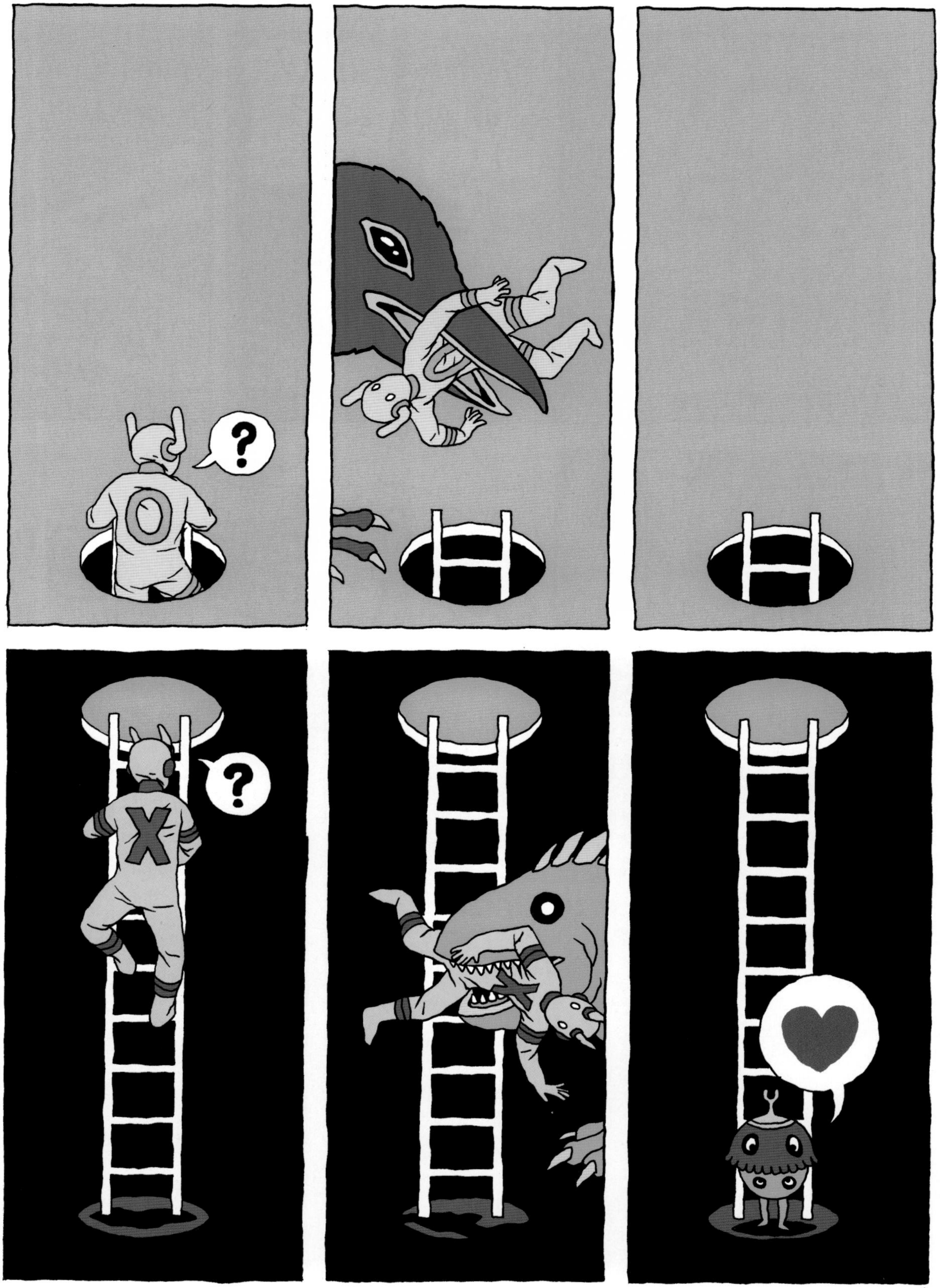
?
?

end

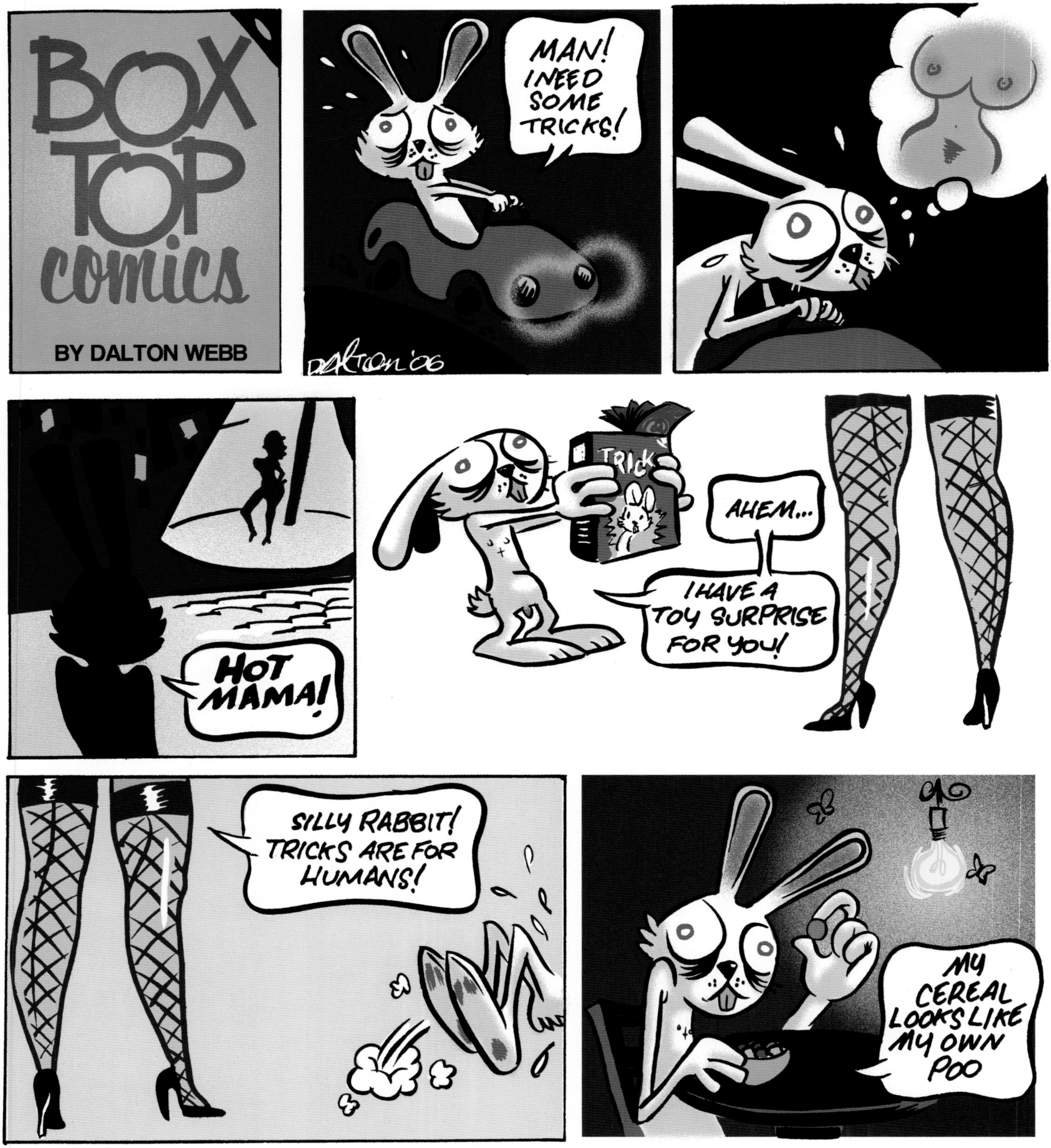
BOX TOP comics
BY DALTON WEBB
MAN! I NEED SOME TRICKS!
DALTON '06
HOT MAMA!
TRICKS
AHEM...
I HAVE A TOY SURPRISE FOR YOU!
SILLY RABBIT! TRICKS ARE FOR HUMANS!
MY CEREAL LOOKS LIKE MY OWN POO

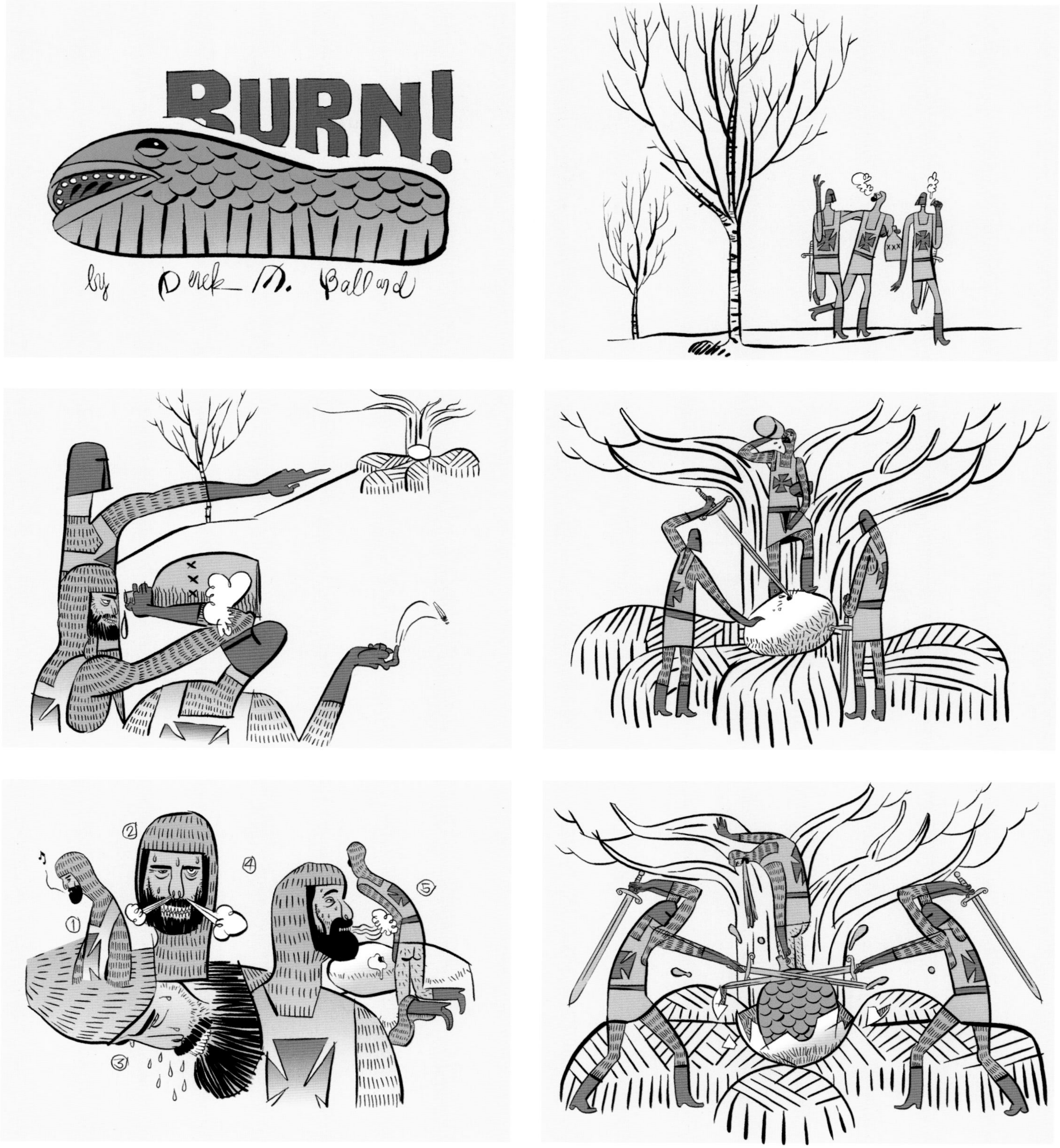
BURN!
by Derek M. Ballard

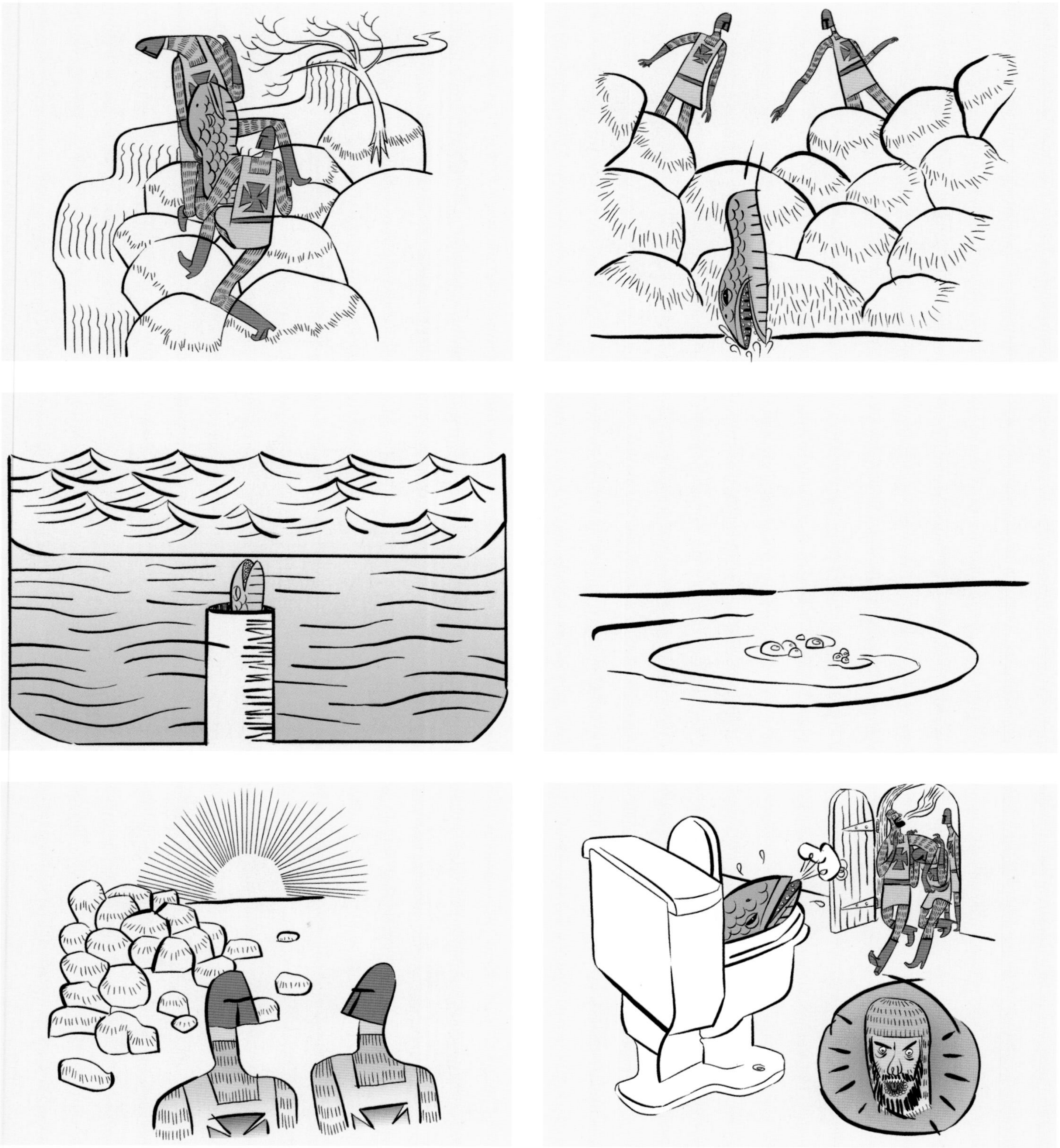

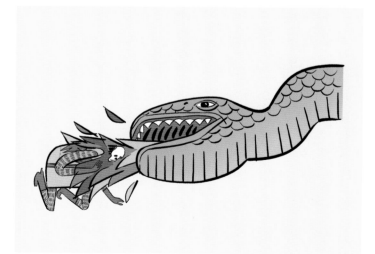

END!

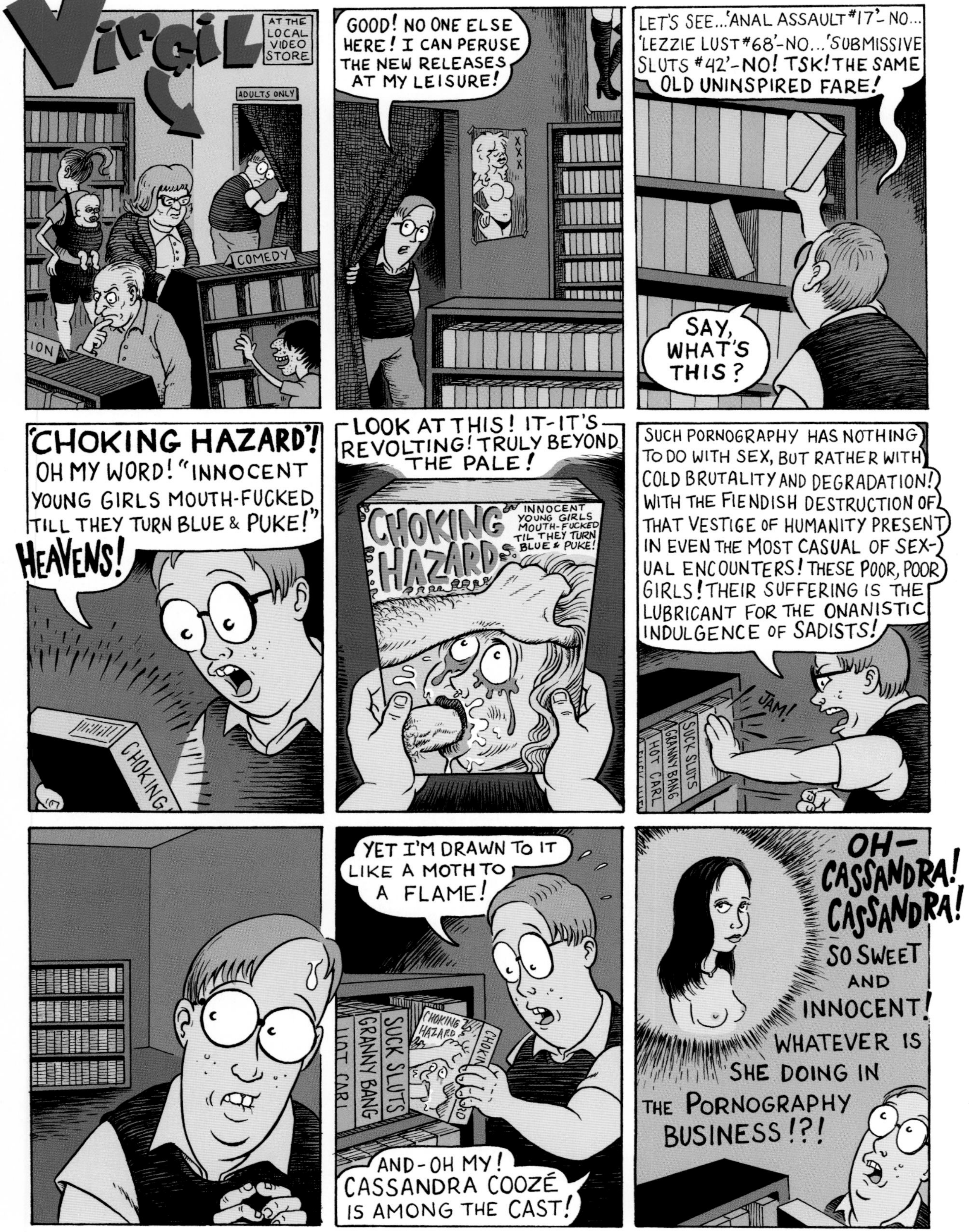
Virgil
AT THE LOCAL VIDEO STORE
ADULTS ONLY
COMEDY
ION
GOOD! NO ONE ELSE HERE! I CAN PERUSE THE NEW RELEASES AT MY LEISURE!
XXX
LET'S SEE...'ANAL ASSAULT #17'- NO... 'LEZZIE LUST #68'-NO...'SUBMISSIVE SLUTS #42'-NO! TSK! THE SAME OLD UNINSPIRED FARE!
SAY, WHAT'S THIS?
'CHOKING HAZARD'! OH MY WORD! "INNOCENT YOUNG GIRLS MOUTH-FUCKED TILL THEY TURN BLUE & PUKE!"
HEAVENS!
CHOKING
LOOK AT THIS! IT-IT'S REVOLTING! TRULY BEYOND THE PALE!
CHOKING HAZARD
INNOCENT YOUNG GIRLS MOUTH-FUCKED TIL THEY TURN BLUE & PUKE!
SUCH PORNOGRAPHY HAS NOTHING TO DO WITH SEX, BUT RATHER WITH COLD BRUTALITY AND DEGRADATION! WITH THE FIENDISH DESTRUCTION OF THAT VESTIGE OF HUMANITY PRESENT IN EVEN THE MOST CASUAL OF SEX-UAL ENCOUNTERS! THESE POOR, POOR GIRLS! THEIR SUFFERING IS THE LUBRICANT FOR THE ONANISTIC INDULGENCE OF SADISTS!
JAM!
SUCK SLUTS
GRANNY BANG
HOT CARL
YET I'M DRAWN TO IT LIKE A MOTH TO A FLAME!
CHOKING HAZARD
SUCK SLUTS
GRANNY BANG
AND-OH MY! CASSANDRA COOZÉ IS AMONG THE CAST!
OH-CASSANDRA! CASSANDRA!
SO SWEET AND INNOCENT! WHATEVER IS SHE DOING IN THE PORNOGRAPHY BUSINESS!?!

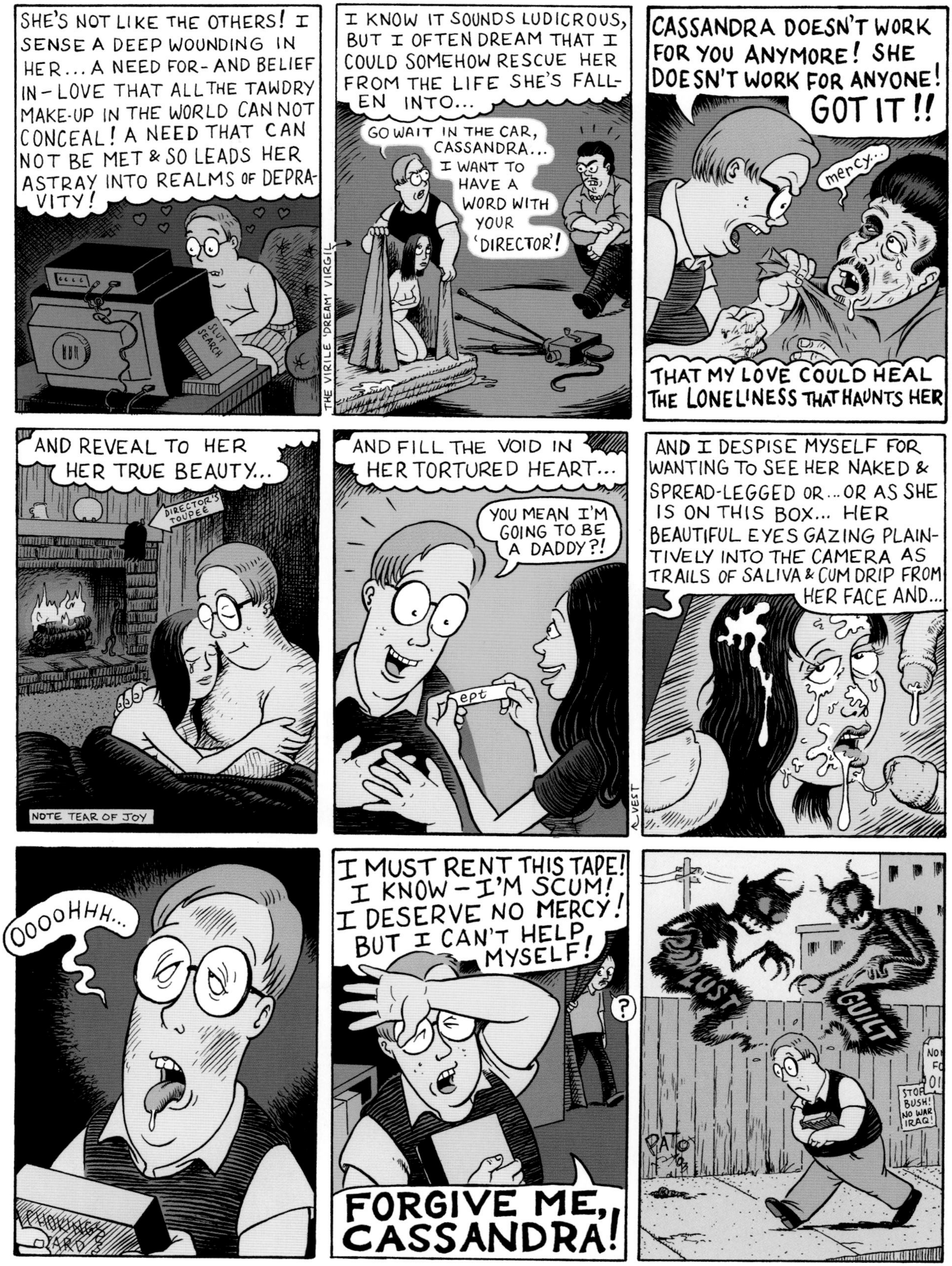
SHE'S NOT LIKE THE OTHERS! I SENSE A DEEP WOUNDING IN HER... A NEED FOR- AND BELIEF IN- LOVE THAT ALL THE TAWDRY MAKE-UP IN THE WORLD CAN NOT CONCEAL! A NEED THAT CAN NOT BE MET & SO LEADS HER ASTRAY INTO REALMS OF DEPRAVITY!
SLUT SEARCH
I KNOW IT SOUNDS LUDICROUS, BUT I OFTEN DREAM THAT I COULD SOMEHOW RESCUE HER FROM THE LIFE SHE'S FALLEN INTO...
THE VIRILE 'DREAM' VIRGIL
GO WAIT IN THE CAR, CASSANDRA... I WANT TO HAVE A WORD WITH YOUR 'DIRECTOR'!
CASSANDRA DOESN'T WORK FOR YOU ANYMORE! SHE DOESN'T WORK FOR ANYONE! GOT IT!!
mercy...
THAT MY LOVE COULD HEAL THE LONELINESS THAT HAUNTS HER
AND REVEAL TO HER HER TRUE BEAUTY...
DIRECTOR'S TOUPEE
NOTE TEAR OF JOY
AND FILL THE VOID IN HER TORTURED HEART...
YOU MEAN I'M GOING TO BE A DADDY?!
ept
VEST
AND I DESPISE MYSELF FOR WANTING TO SEE HER NAKED & SPREAD-LEGGED OR... OR AS SHE IS ON THIS BOX... HER BEAUTIFUL EYES GAZING PLAINTIVELY INTO THE CAMERA AS TRAILS OF SALIVA & CUM DRIP FROM HER FACE AND...
OOOOHHH...
I MUST RENT THIS TAPE! I KNOW - I'M SCUM! I DESERVE NO MERCY! BUT I CAN'T HELP MYSELF!
?
FORGIVE ME, CASSANDRA!
LUST
GUILT
STOP BUSH! NO WAR IRAQ!

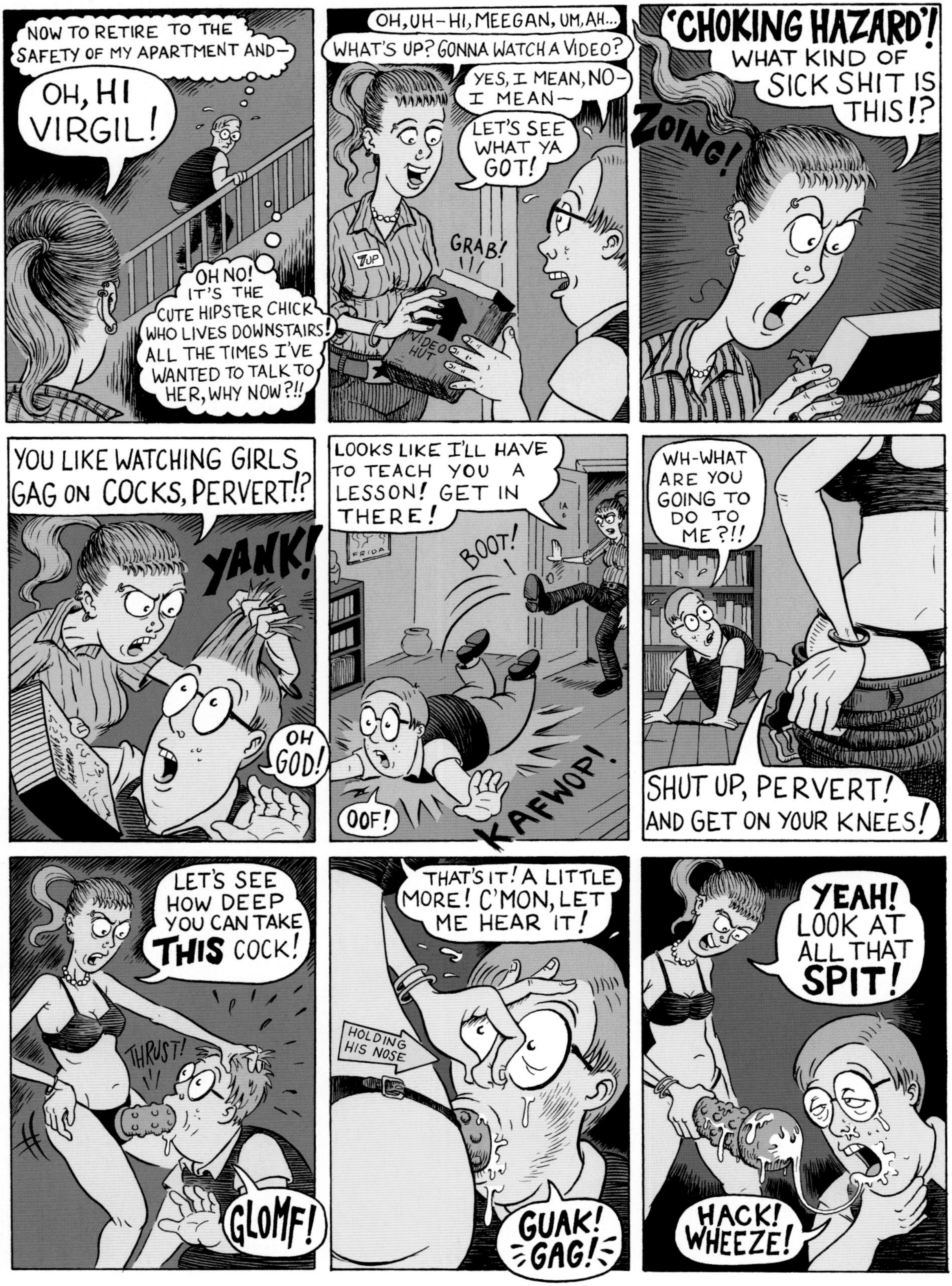
NOW TO RETIRE TO THE SAFETY OF MY APARTMENT AND—
OH, HI VIRGIL!
OH NO! IT'S THE CUTE HIPSTER CHICK WHO LIVES DOWNSTAIRS! ALL THE TIMES I'VE WANTED TO TALK TO HER, WHY NOW?!!
OH, UH—HI, MEEGAN, UM, AH...
WHAT'S UP? GONNA WATCH A VIDEO?
YES, I MEAN, NO— I MEAN—
LET'S SEE WHAT YA GOT!
GRAB!
7UP
VIDEO HUT
'CHOKING HAZARD'!
WHAT KIND OF SICK SHIT IS THIS!?
ZOING!
YOU LIKE WATCHING GIRLS GAG ON COCKS, PERVERT!?
YANK!
OH GOD!
LOOKS LIKE I'LL HAVE TO TEACH YOU A LESSON! GET IN THERE!
FRIDA
BOOT!
OOF!
KAFWOP!
WH-WHAT ARE YOU GOING TO DO TO ME?!!
SHUT UP, PERVERT! AND GET ON YOUR KNEES!
LET'S SEE HOW DEEP YOU CAN TAKE THIS COCK!
THRUST!
GLOMF!
THAT'S IT! A LITTLE MORE! C'MON, LET ME HEAR IT!
HOLDING HIS NOSE
GUAK! GAG!
YEAH! LOOK AT ALL THAT SPIT!
HACK! WHEEZE!

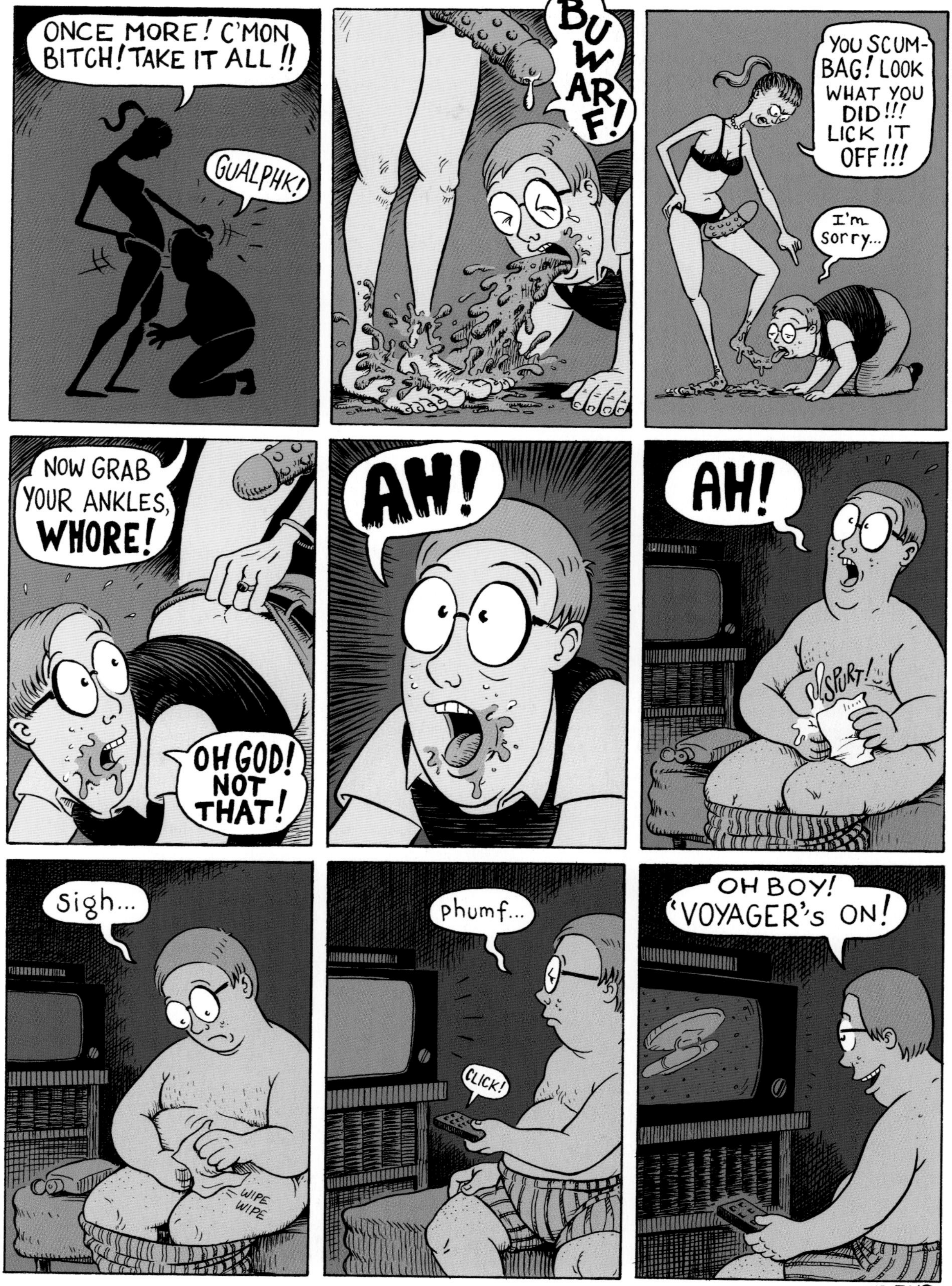
ONCE MORE! C'MON BITCH! TAKE IT ALL!!
GUALPHK!
BUWARF!
YOU SCUM-BAG! LOOK WHAT YOU DID!!! LICK IT OFF!!!
I'm sorry...
NOW GRAB YOUR ANKLES, WHORE!
OH GOD! NOT THAT!
AH!
AH!
SPURT!
Sigh...
WIPE WIPE
phumf...
CLICK!
OH BOY! 'VOYAGER's ON!

THE END

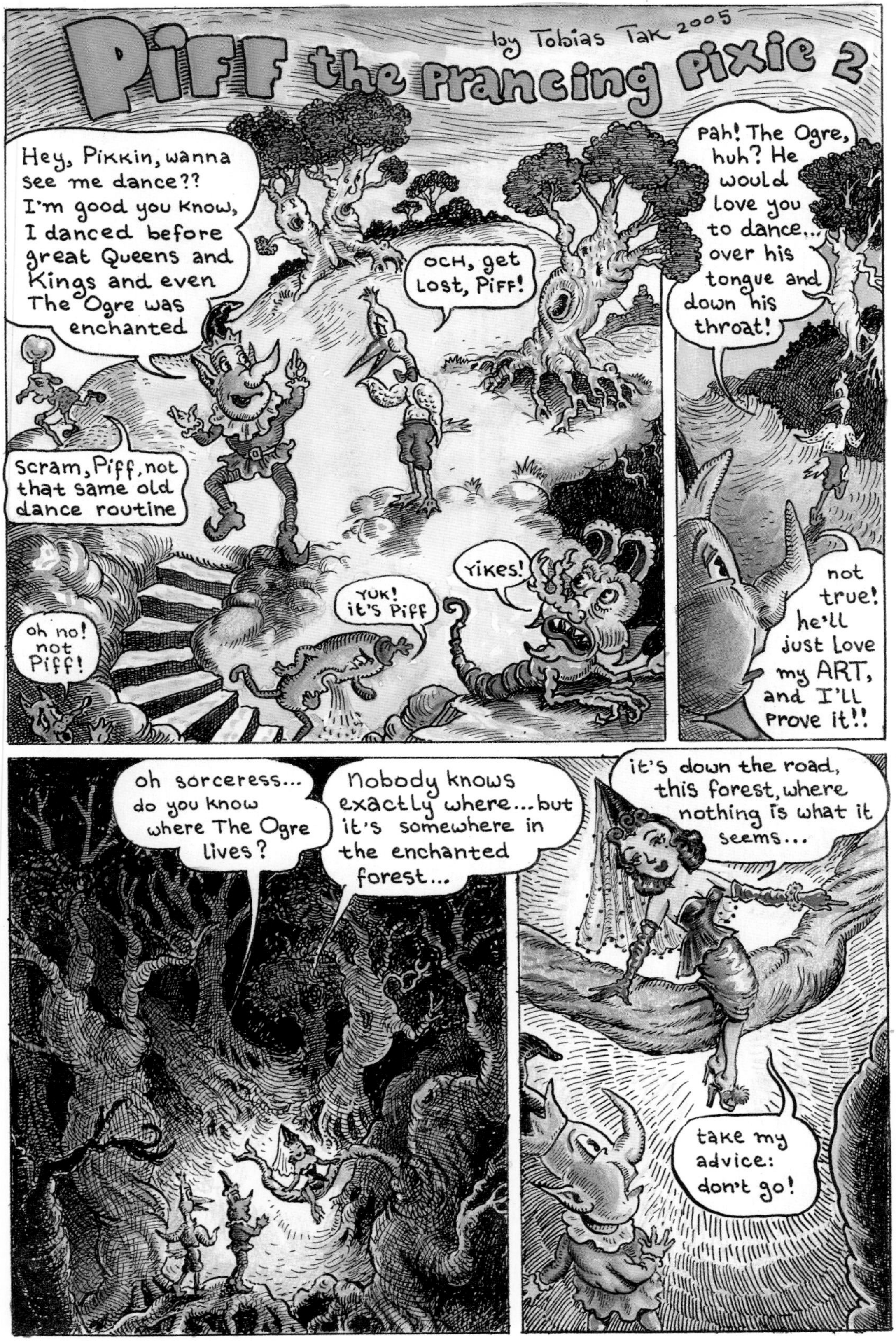

PIFF the Prancing Pixie 2
by Tobias Tak 2005
Hey, Pikkin, wanna see me dance?? I'm good you know, I danced before great Queens and Kings and even The Ogre was enchanted
OCH, get lost, Piff!
Scram, Piff, not that same old dance routine
YIKES!
YUK! it's Piff
oh no! not Piff!
Pah! The Ogre, huh? He would love you to dance... over his tongue and down his throat!
not true! he'll just love my ART, and I'll prove it!!
oh sorceress... do you know where The Ogre lives?
Nobody knows exactly where... but it's somewhere in the enchanted forest...
it's down the road, this forest, where nothing is what it seems...
take my advice: don't go!

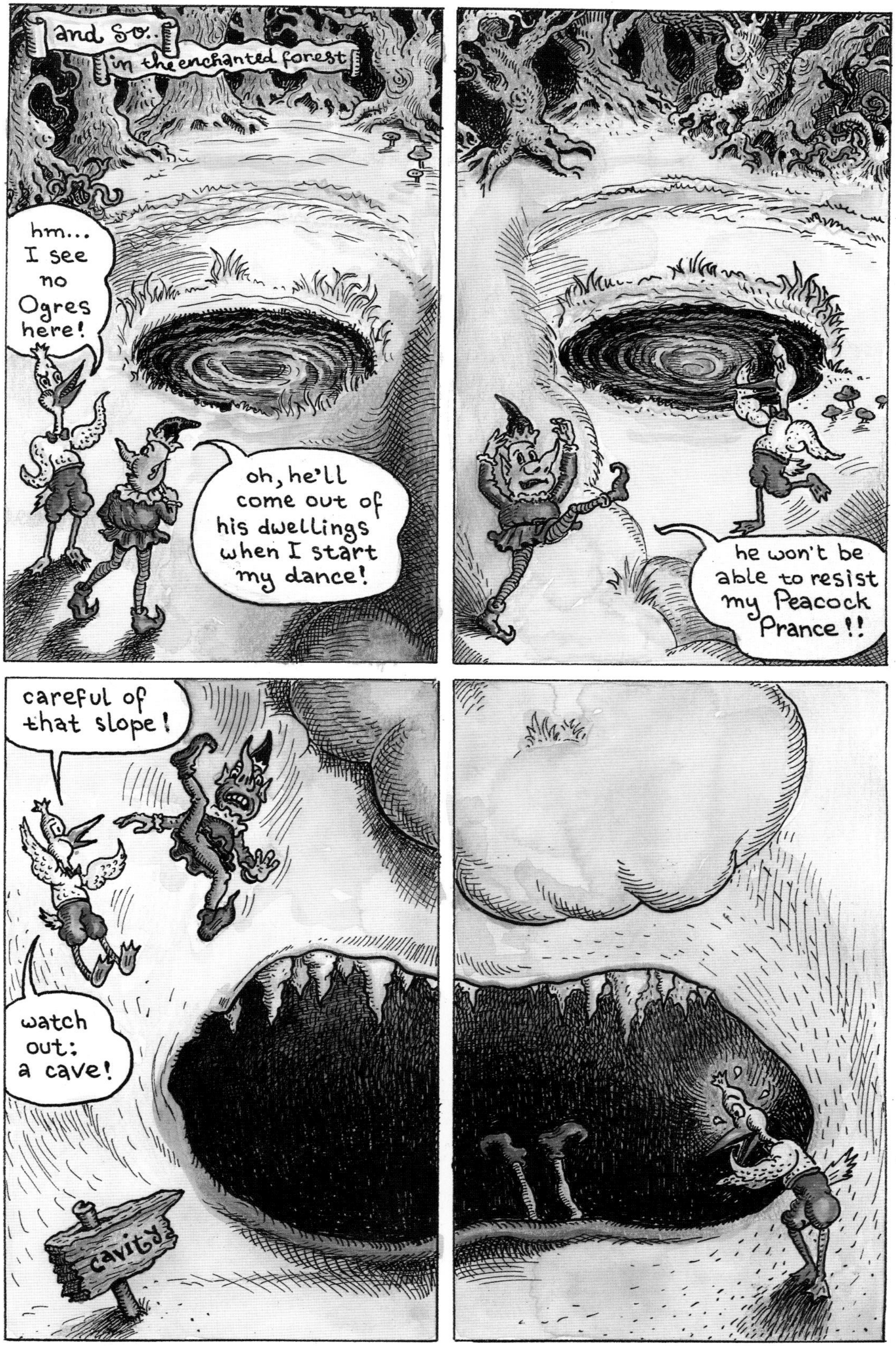
and so..
in the enchanted forest
hm... I see no Ogres here!
oh, he'll come out of his dwellings when I start my dance!
he won't be able to resist my Peacock Prance!!
careful of that slope!
watch out: a cave!
cavity

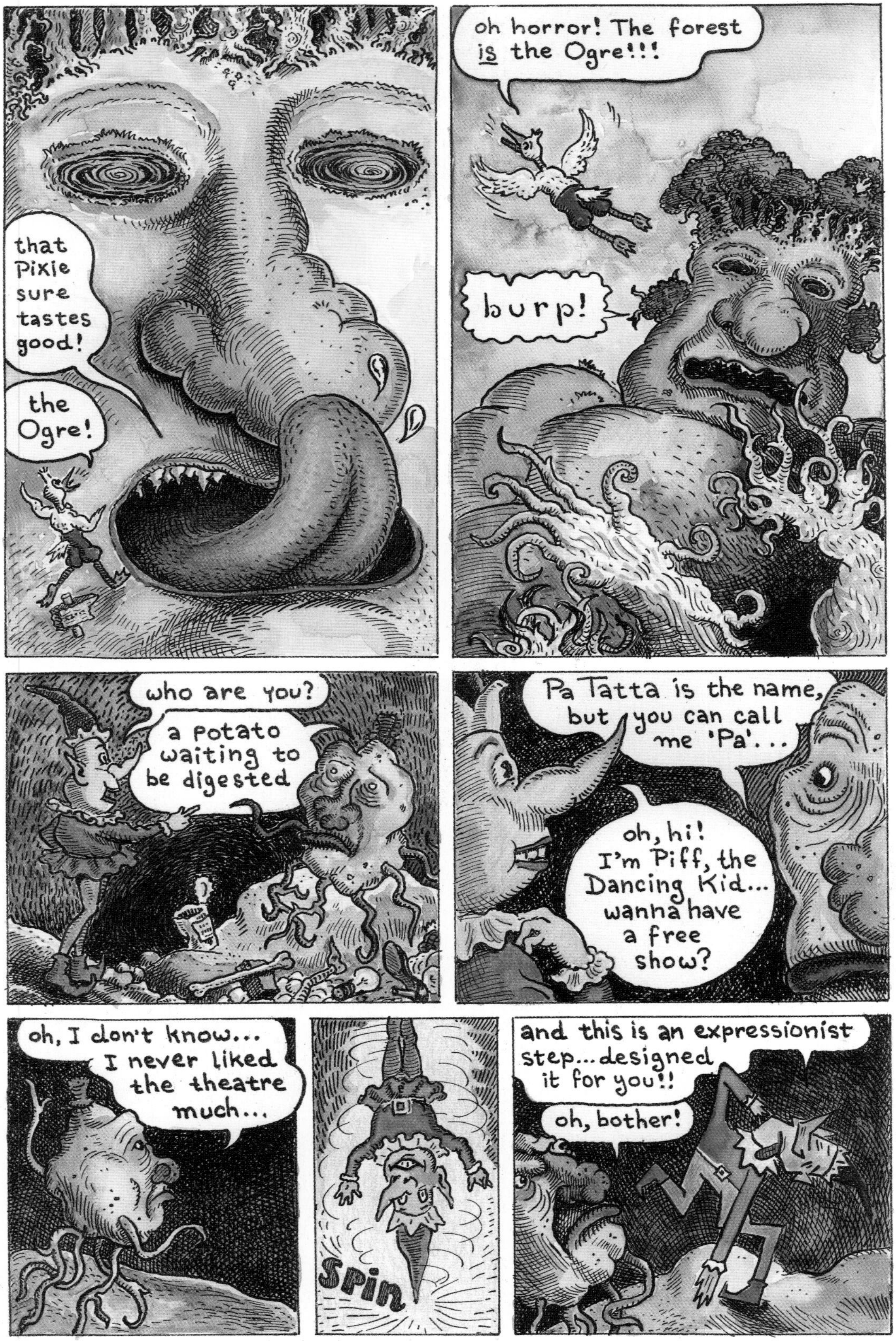
that Pixie sure tastes good!
the Ogre!
oh horror! The forest is the Ogre!!!
burp!
who are you?
a potato waiting to be digested
Pa Tatta is the name, but you can call me 'Pa'...
oh, hi! I'm Piff, the Dancing Kid... wanna have a free show?
oh, I don't know... I never liked the theatre much...
SPIN
and this is an expressionist step... designed it for you!!
oh, bother!

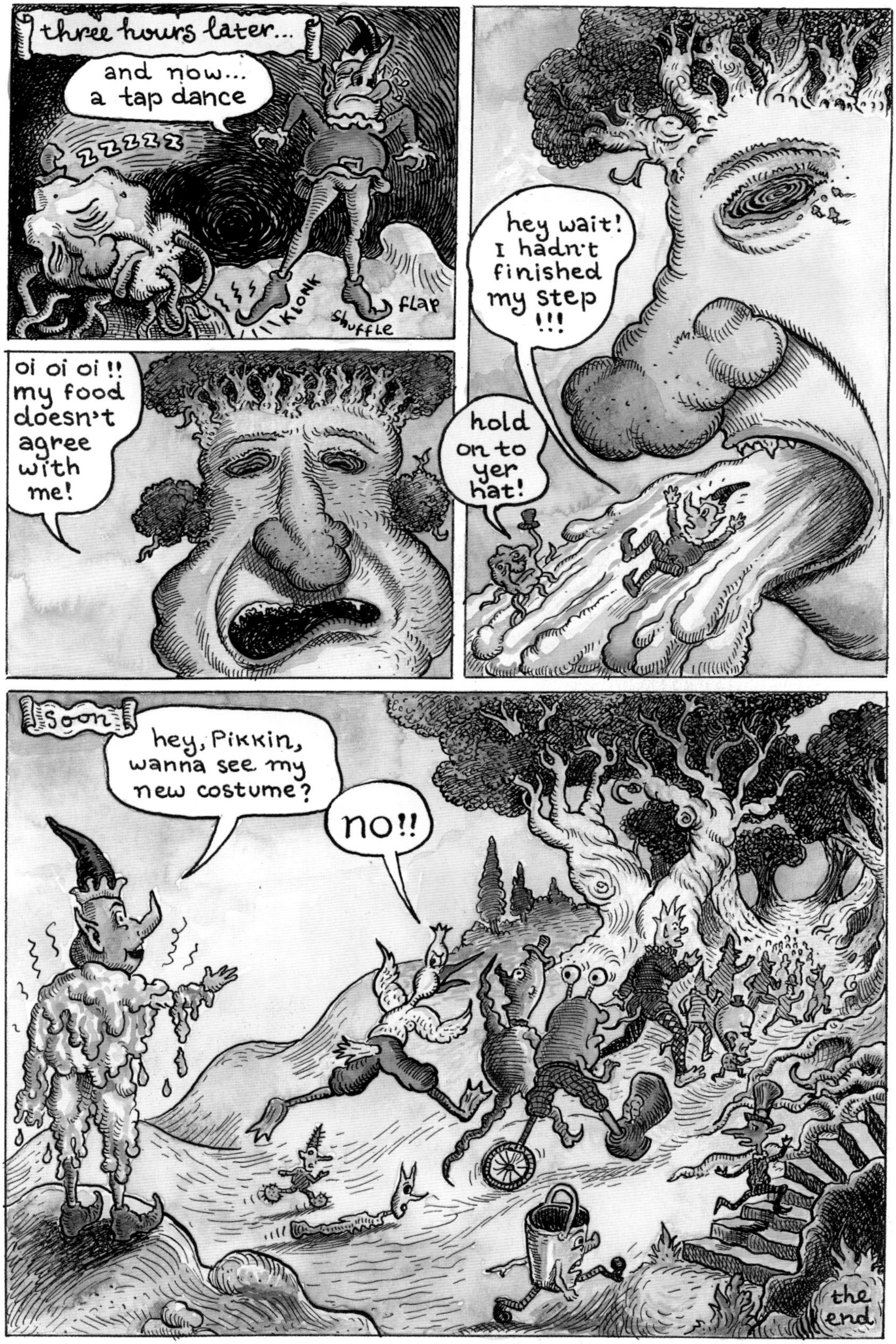
three hours later...
and now... a tap dance
ZZZZZ
KLONK
shuffle
flap
hey wait! I hadn't finished my step !!!
oi oi oi !! my food doesn't agree with me!
hold on to yer hat!
soon
hey, Pikkin, wanna see my new costume?
no!!
the end

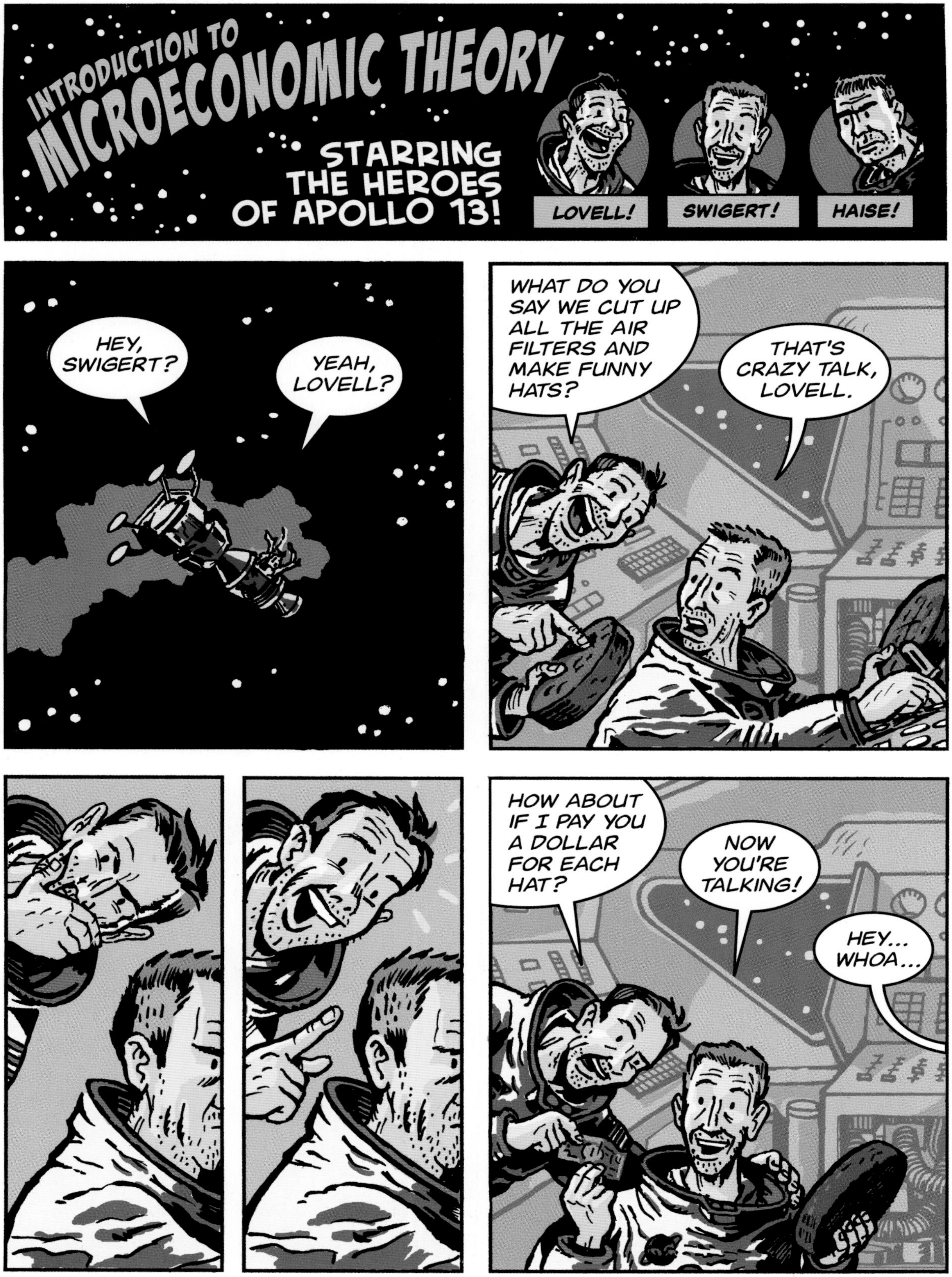
INTRODUCTION TO
MICROECONOMIC THEORY
STARRING THE HEROES OF APOLLO 13!
LOVELL!
SWIGERT!
HAISE!
HEY, SWIGERT?
YEAH, LOVELL?
WHAT DO YOU SAY WE CUT UP ALL THE AIR FILTERS AND MAKE FUNNY HATS?
THAT'S CRAZY TALK, LOVELL.
HOW ABOUT IF I PAY YOU A DOLLAR FOR EACH HAT?
NOW YOU'RE TALKING!
HEY... WHOA...

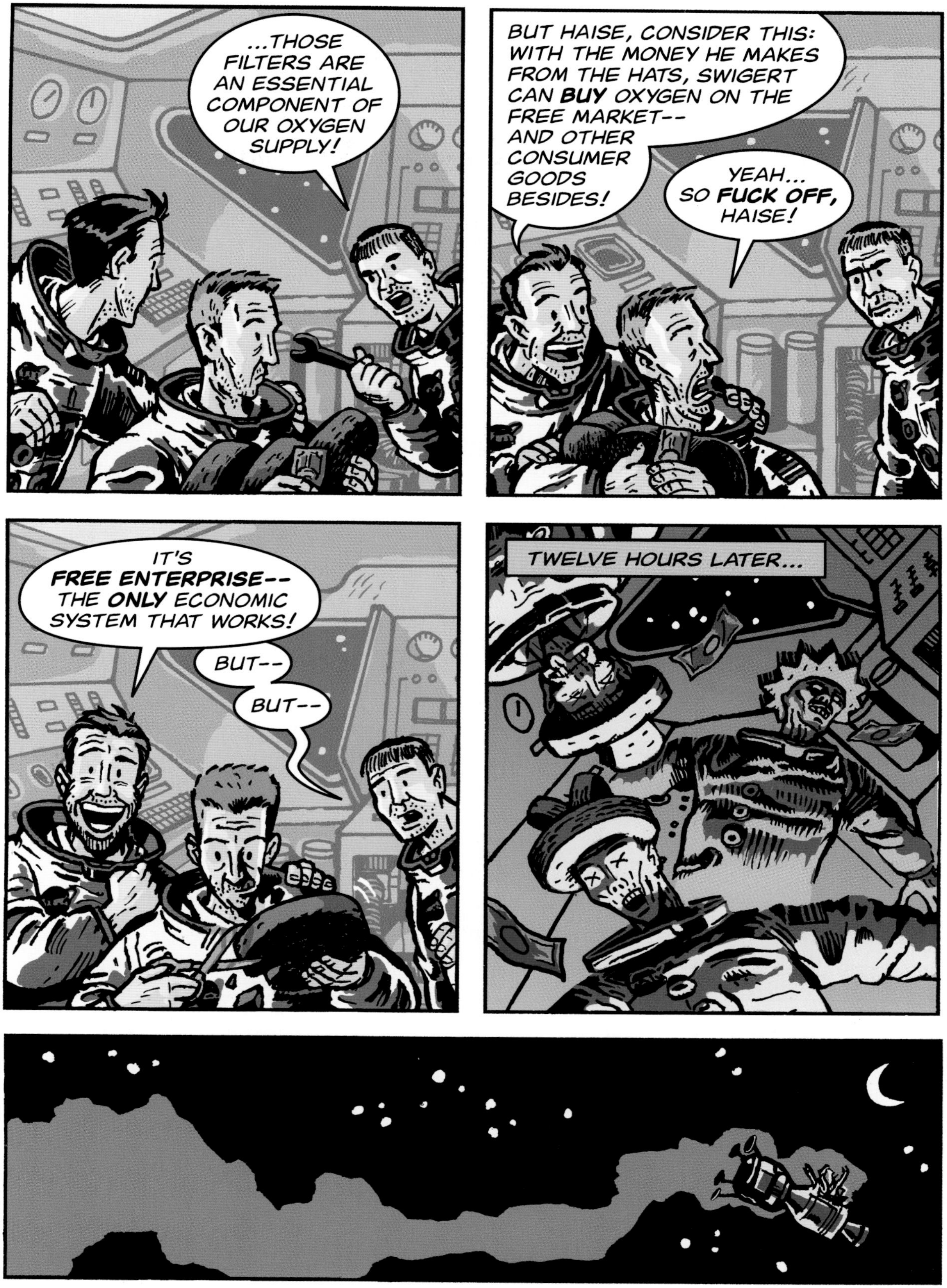
...THOSE FILTERS ARE AN ESSENTIAL COMPONENT OF OUR OXYGEN SUPPLY!
BUT HAISE, CONSIDER THIS: WITH THE MONEY HE MAKES FROM THE HATS, SWIGERT CAN **BUY** OXYGEN ON THE FREE MARKET-- AND OTHER CONSUMER GOODS BESIDES!
YEAH... SO **FUCK OFF,** HAISE!
IT'S **FREE ENTERPRISE--** THE **ONLY** ECONOMIC SYSTEM THAT WORKS!
BUT--
BUT--
TWELVE HOURS LATER...

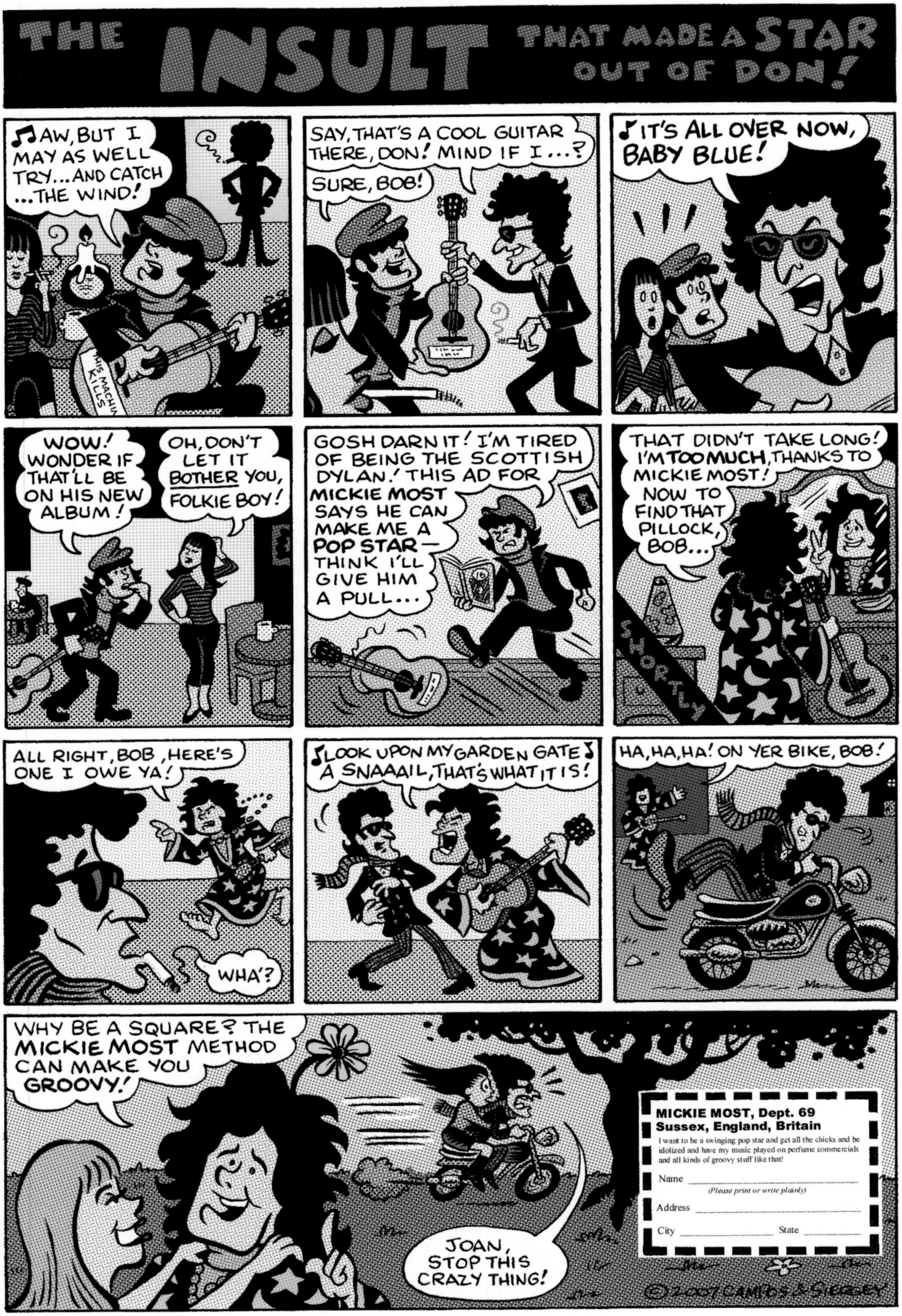
THE INSULT THAT MADE A STAR OUT OF DON!
AW, BUT I MAY AS WELL TRY...AND CATCH ...THE WIND!
THIS MACHINE KILLS
SAY, THAT'S A COOL GUITAR THERE, DON! MIND IF I...?
SURE, BOB!
IT'S ALL OVER NOW, BABY BLUE!
WOW! WONDER IF THAT'LL BE ON HIS NEW ALBUM!
OH, DON'T LET IT BOTHER YOU, FOLKIE BOY!
GOSH DARN IT! I'M TIRED OF BEING THE SCOTTISH DYLAN! THIS AD FOR MICKIE MOST SAYS HE CAN MAKE ME A POP STAR— THINK I'LL GIVE HIM A PULL...
THAT DIDN'T TAKE LONG! I'M TOO MUCH, THANKS TO MICKIE MOST! NOW TO FIND THAT PILLOCK, BOB...
SHORTLY
ALL RIGHT, BOB, HERE'S ONE I OWE YA!
WHA'?
LOOK UPON MY GARDEN GATE A SNAAAIL, THAT'S WHAT IT IS!
HA, HA, HA! ON YER BIKE, BOB!
WHY BE A SQUARE? THE MICKIE MOST METHOD CAN MAKE YOU GROOVY!
JOAN, STOP THIS CRAZY THING!
MICKIE MOST, Dept. 69
Sussex, England, Britain
I want to be a swinging pop star and get all the chicks and be idolized and have my music played on perfume commercials and all kinds of groovy stuff like that!
Name
(Please print or write plainly)
Address
City
State
©2007 CAMPOS & SIERGEY

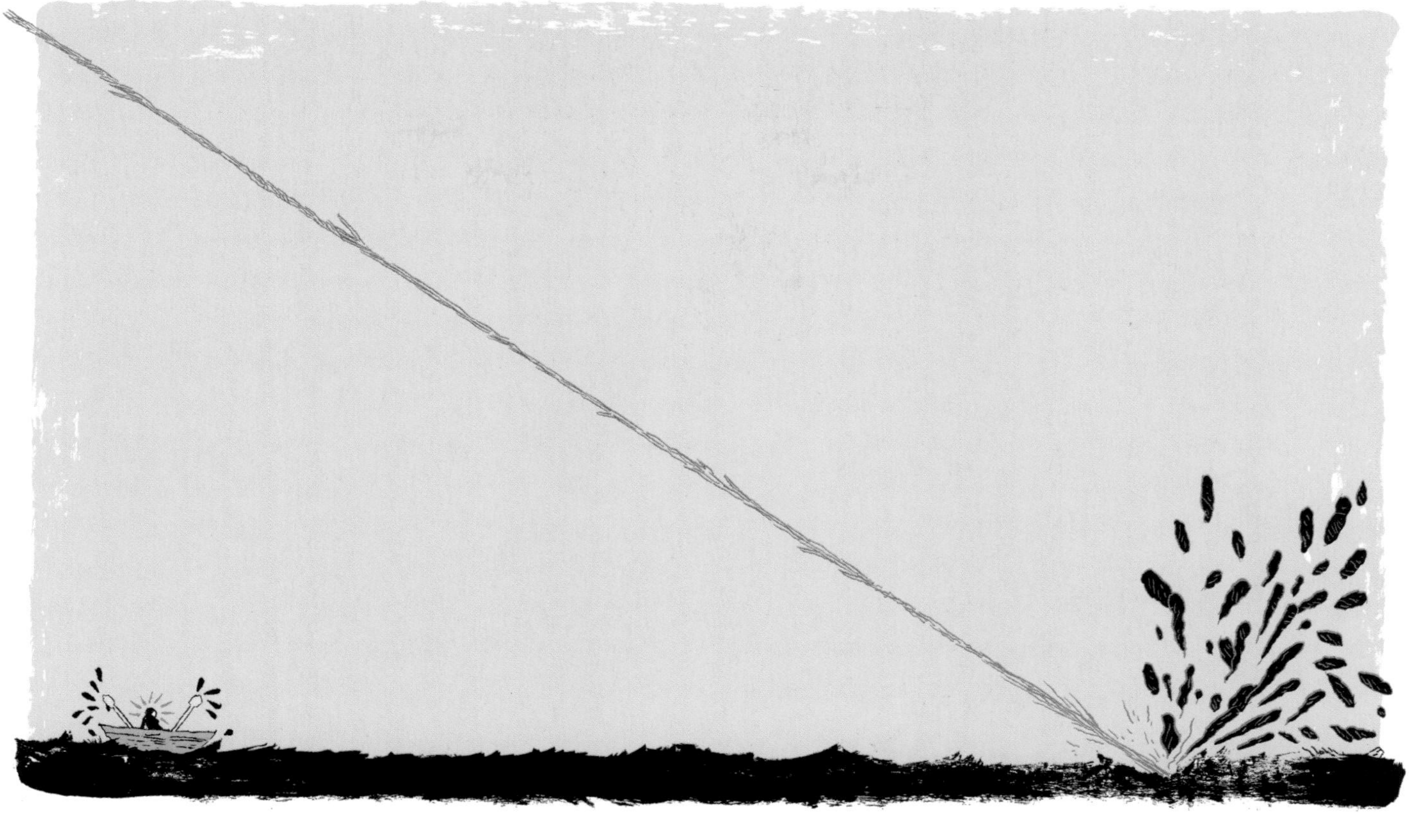

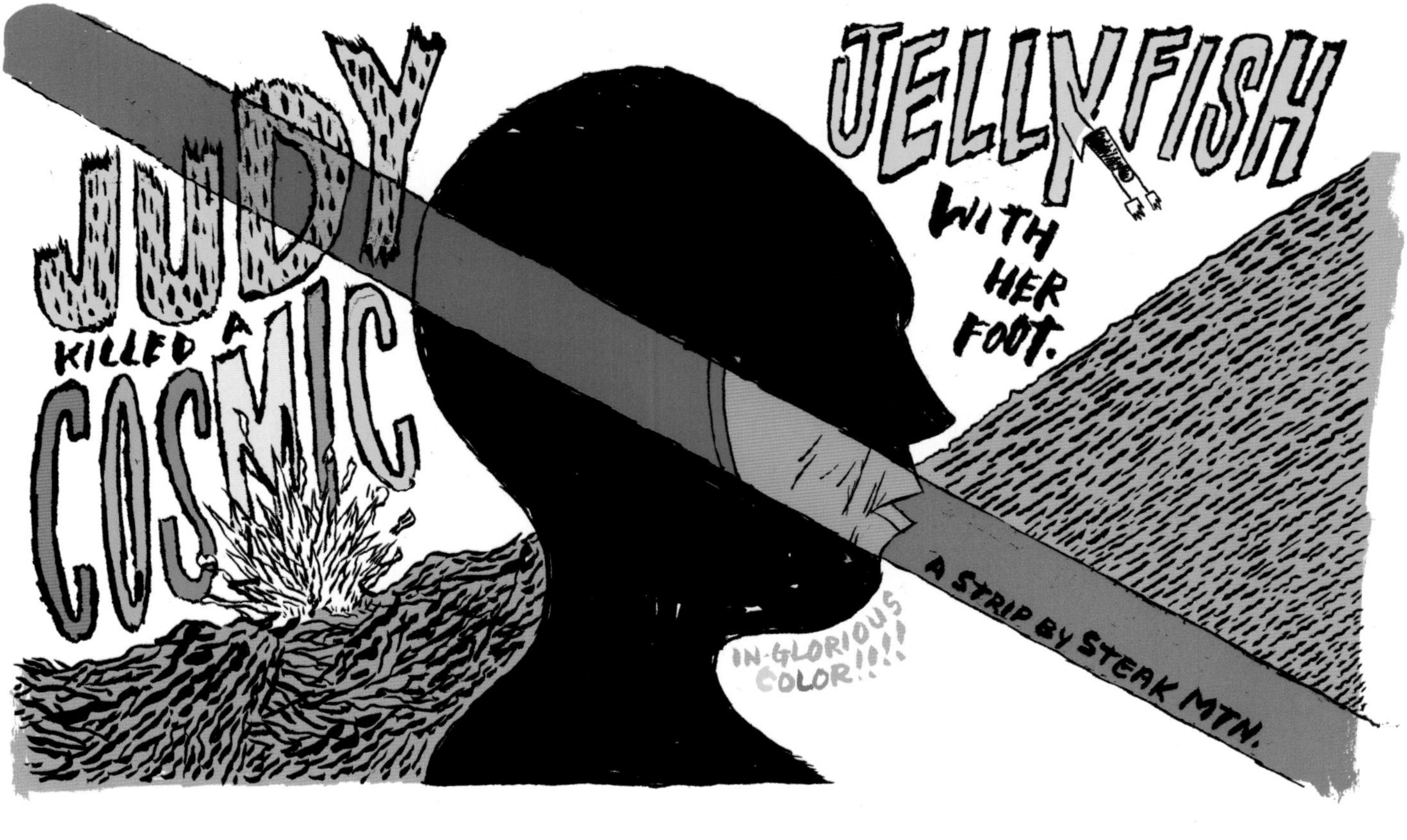
JUDY KILLED A COSMIC JELLYFISH WITH HER FOOT.
A STRIP BY STEAK MTN.
IN-GLORIOUS COLOR!!!!

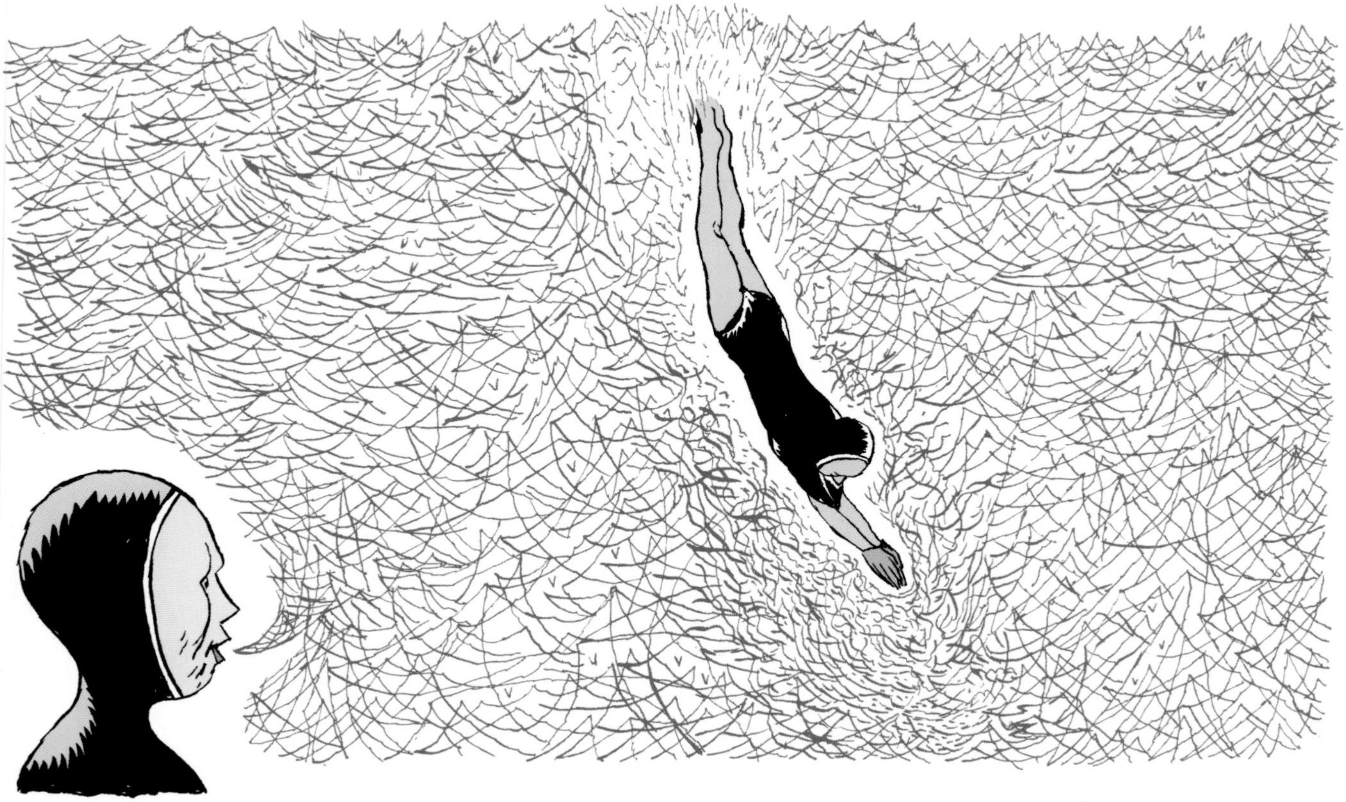

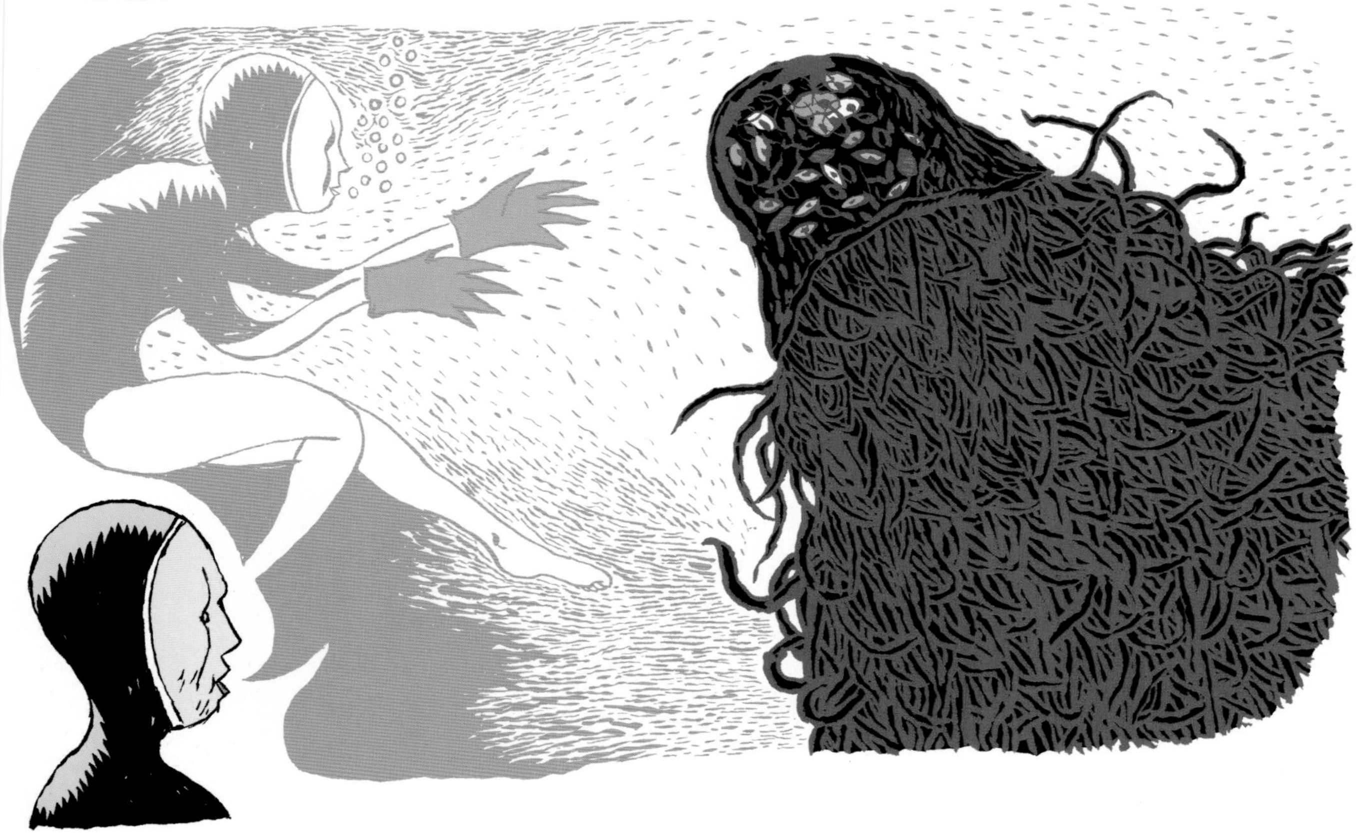

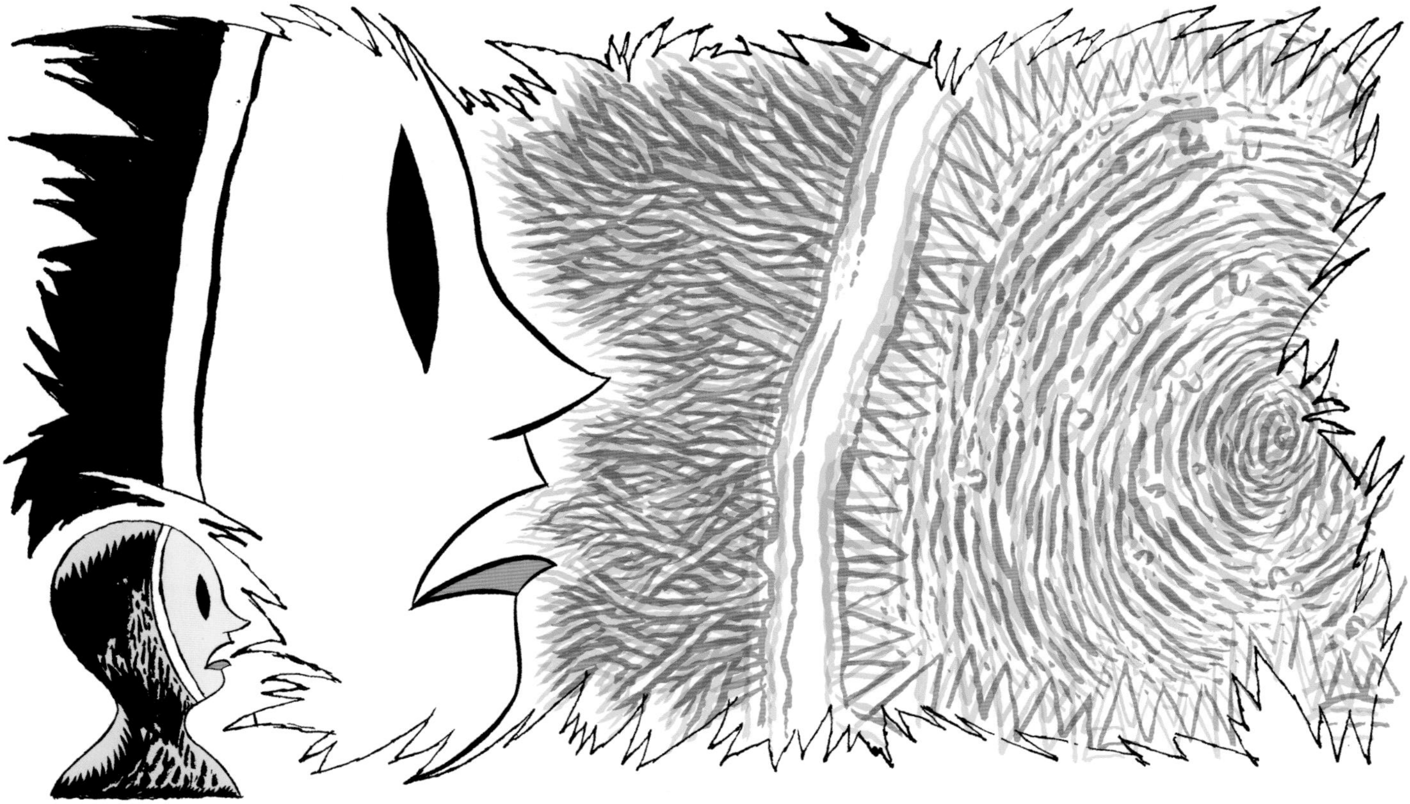

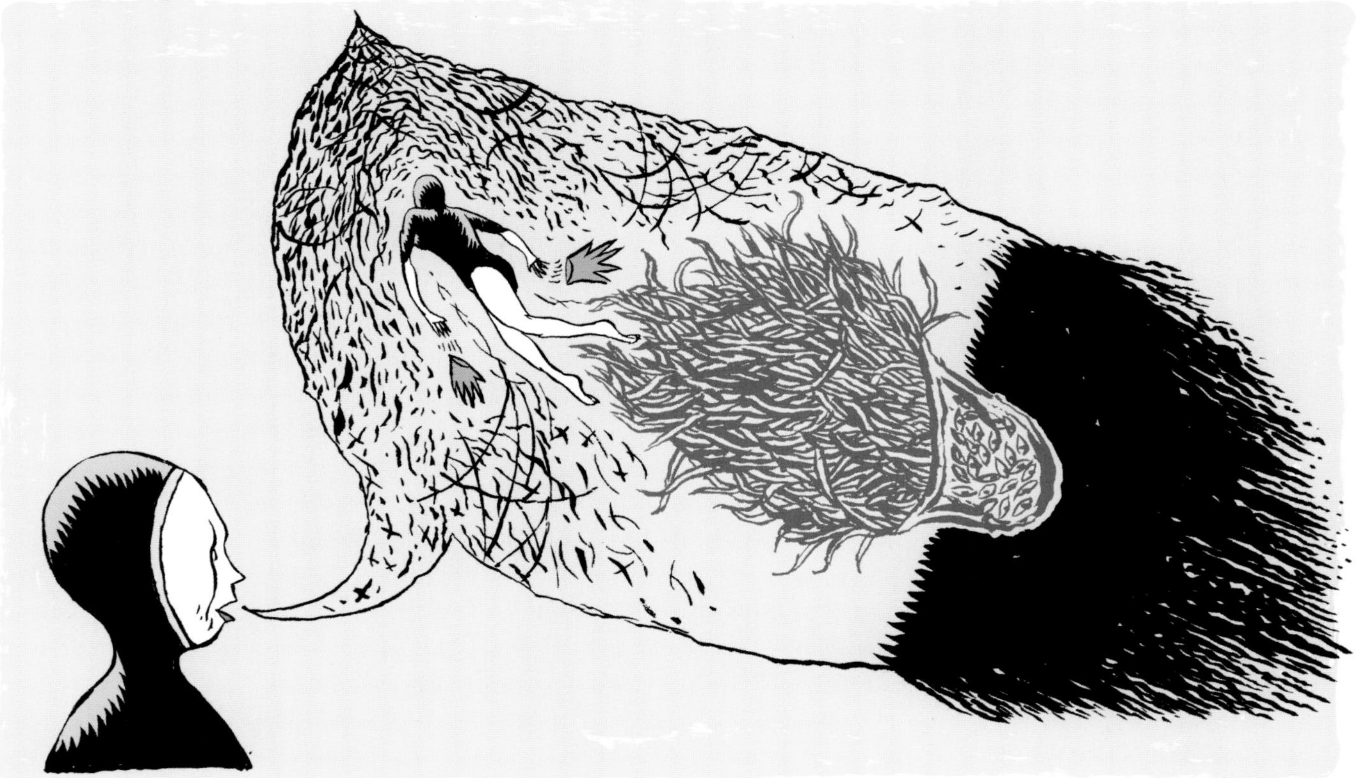

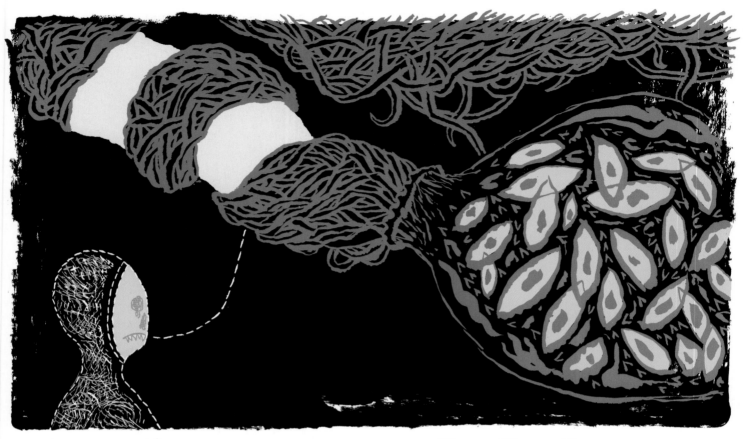

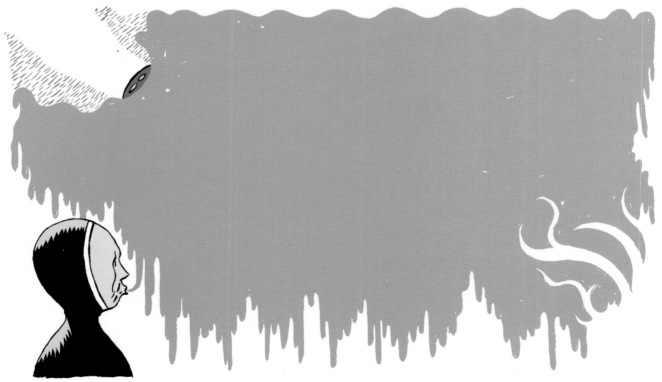

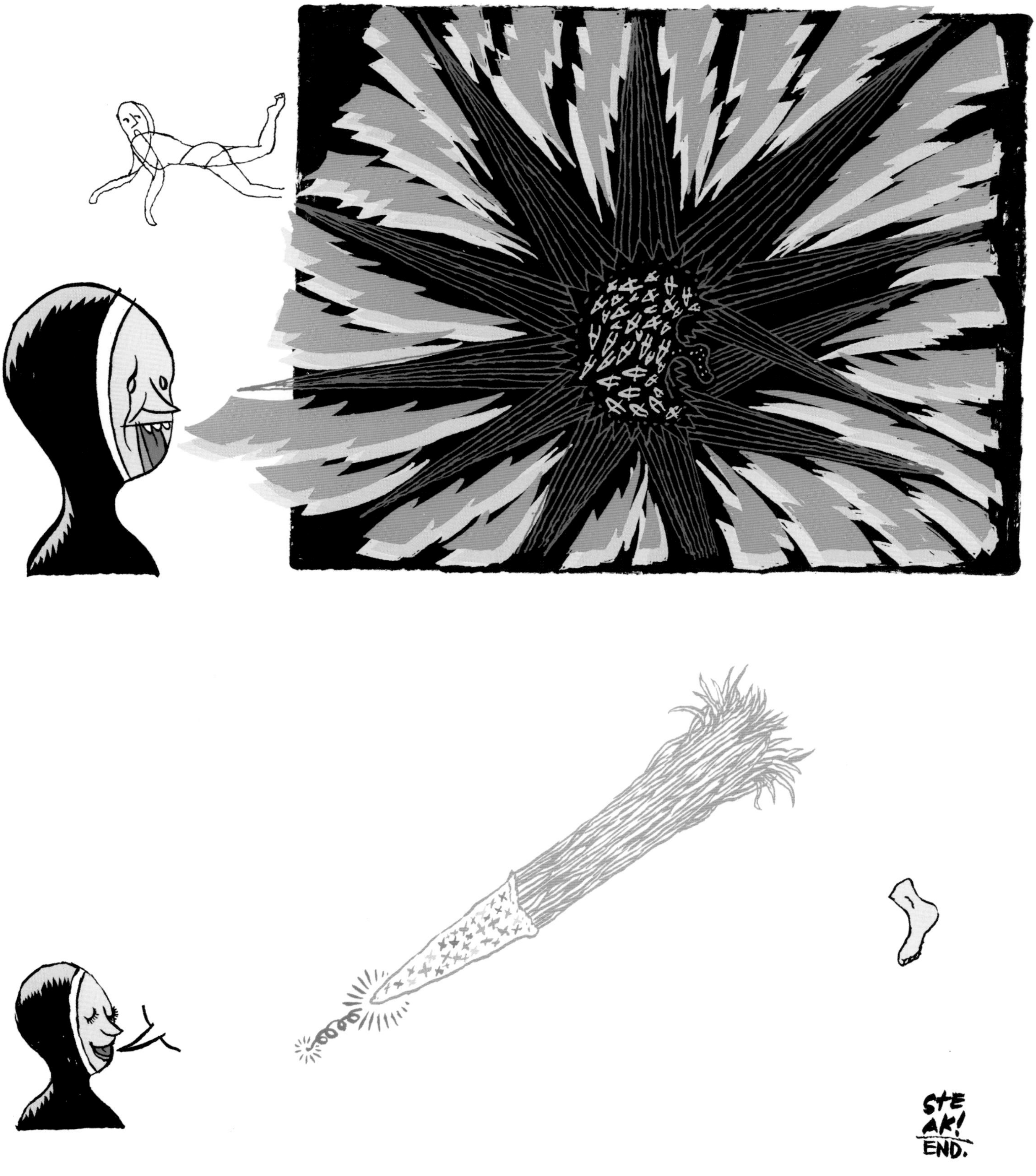
STE
AK!
END.

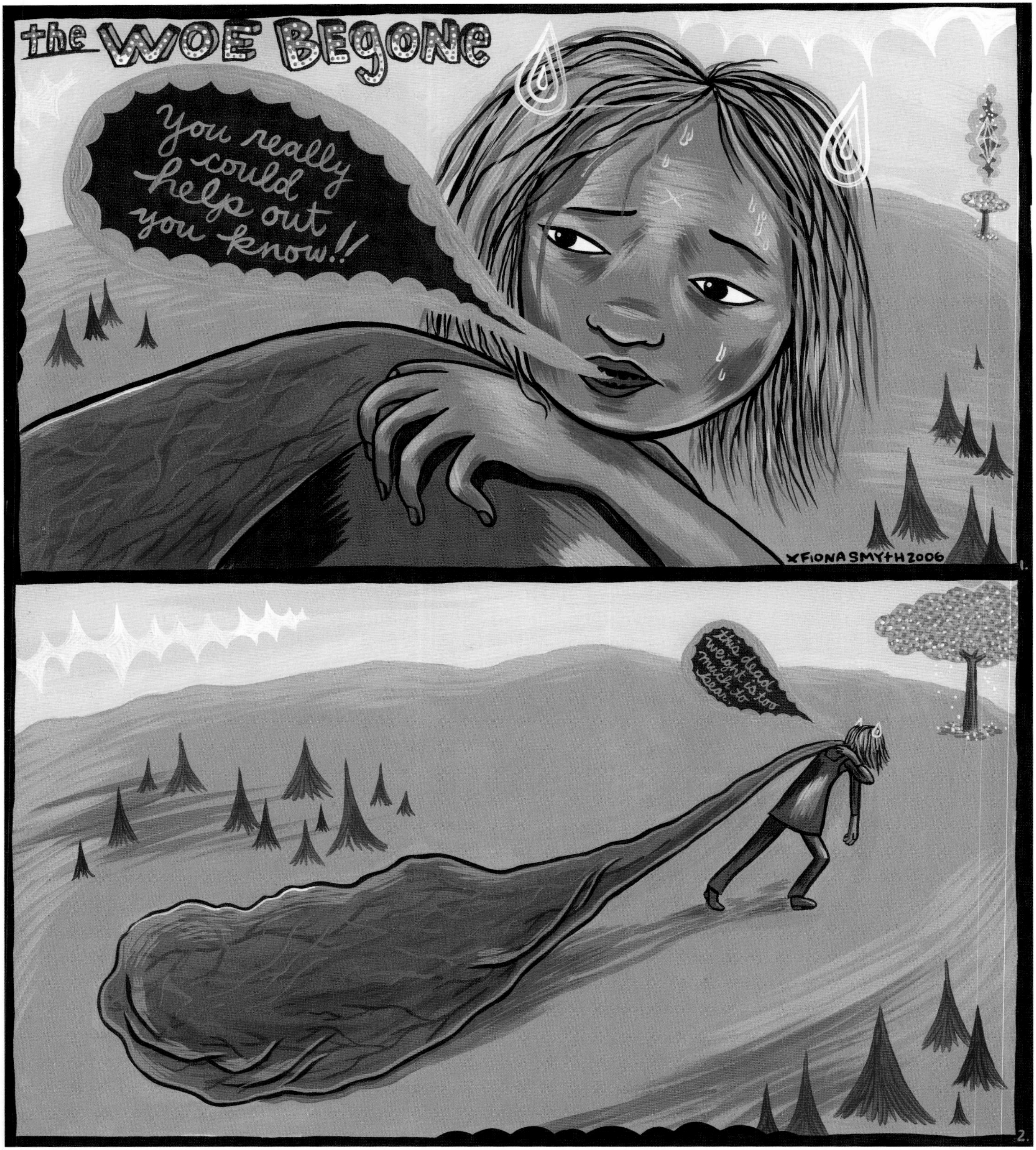
the WOE BEGONE
you really could help out you know!!
xFIONASMYTH2006
1.
this dead weight is too much to bear.
2.

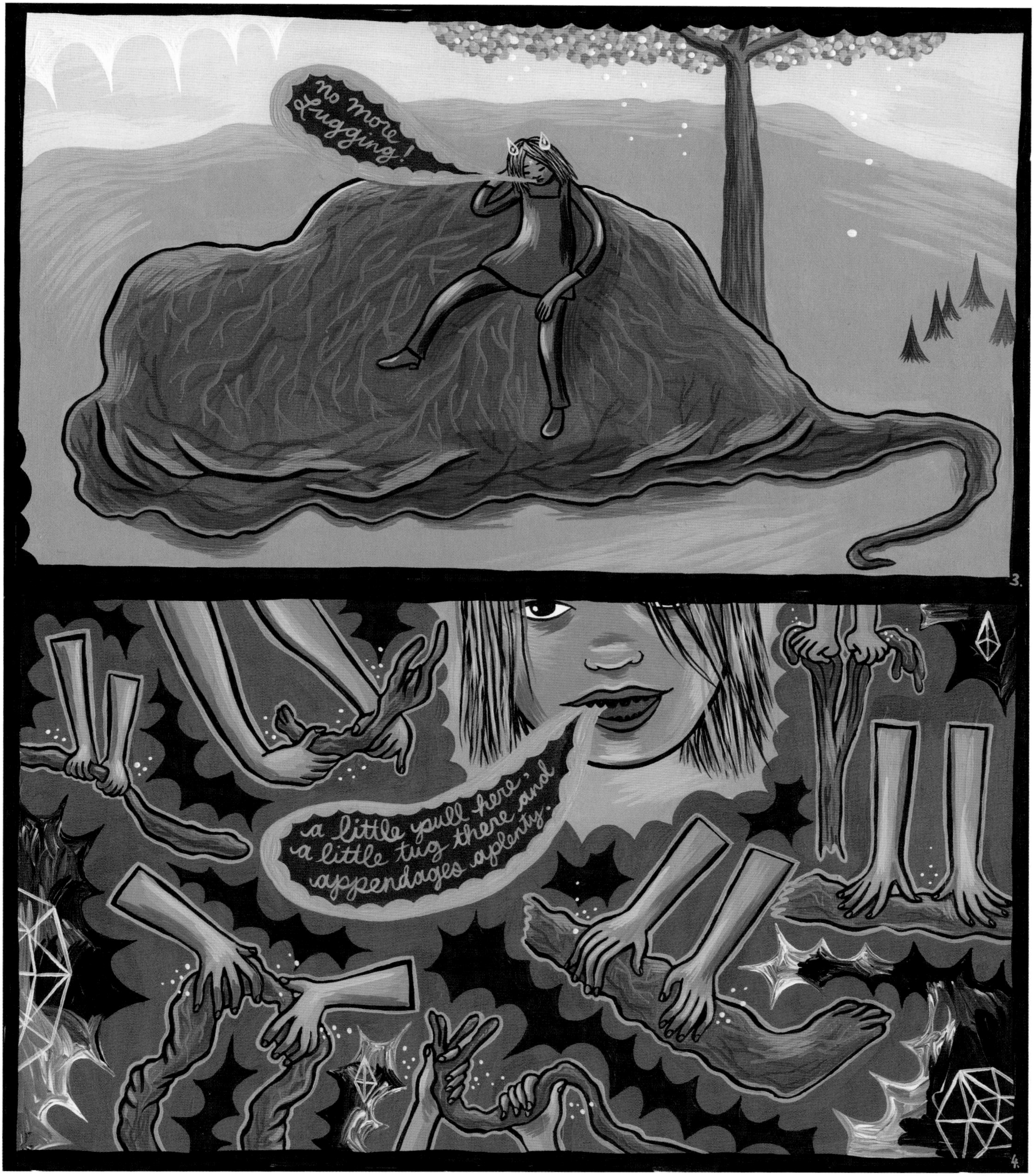
no more tugging!
3.
a little pull here, a little tug there and appendages aplenty.
4.

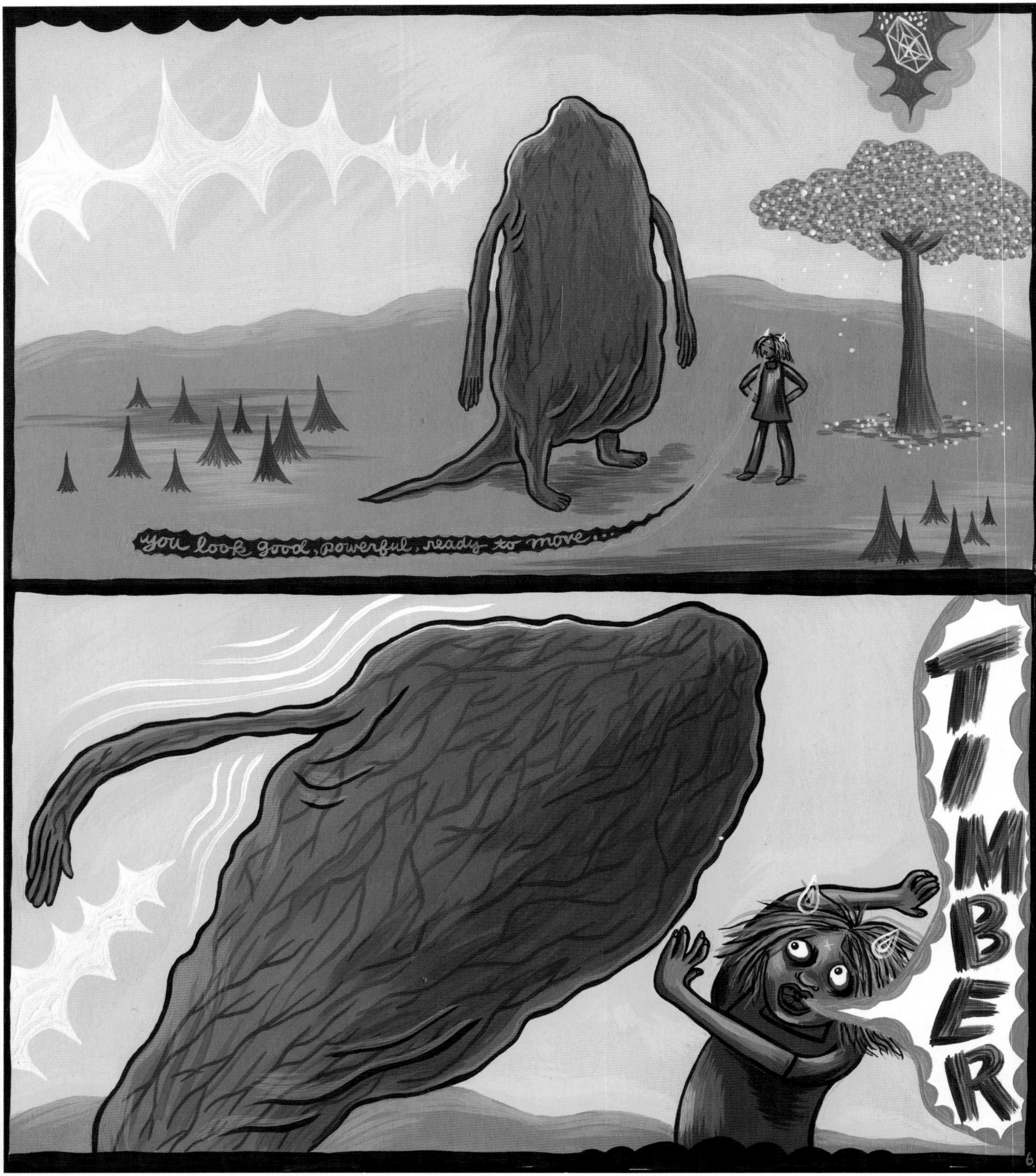
you look good, powerful, ready to move...
TIMBER

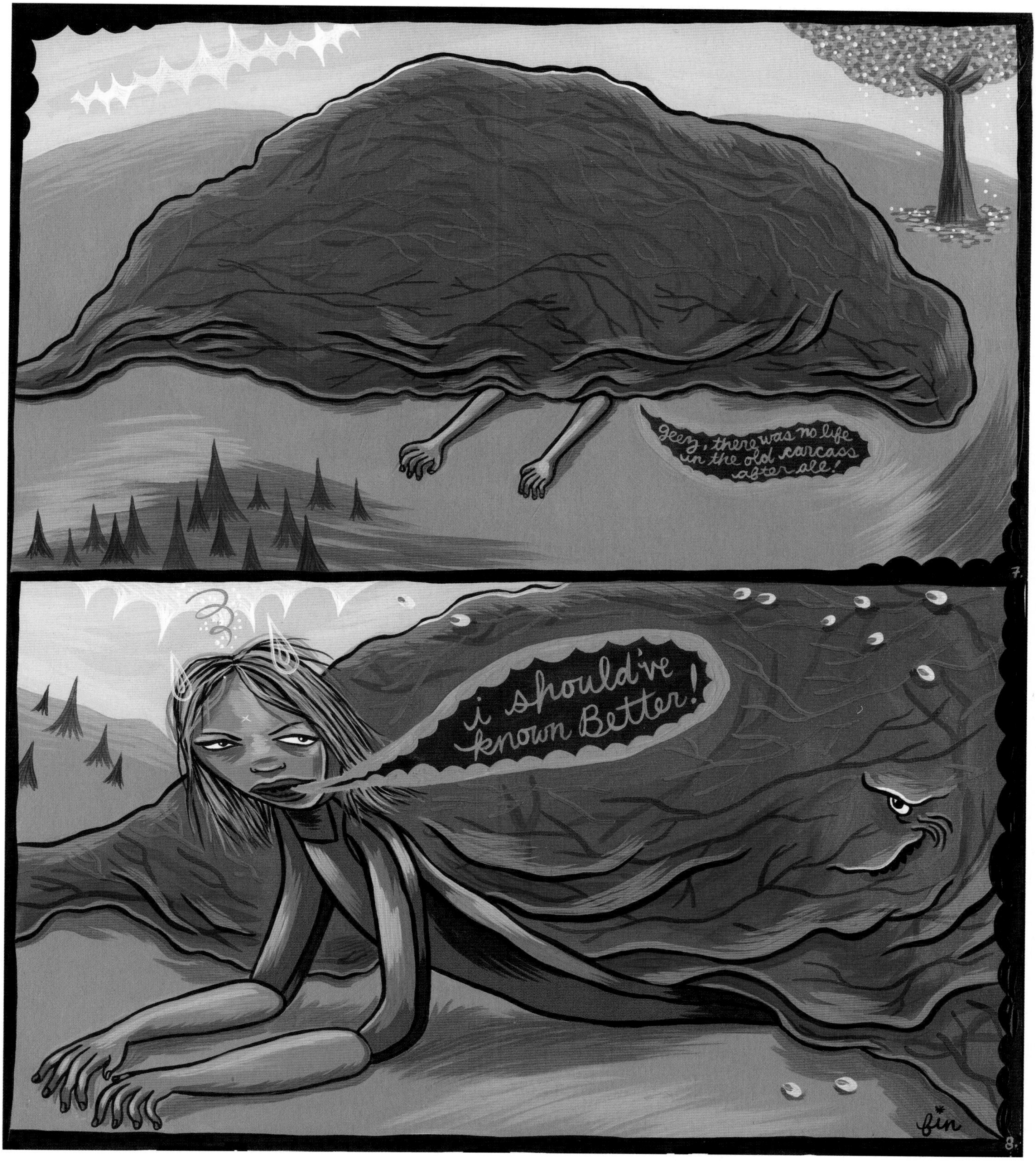
geez, there was no life in the old carcass after all!
7.
i should've known Better!
fin
8.

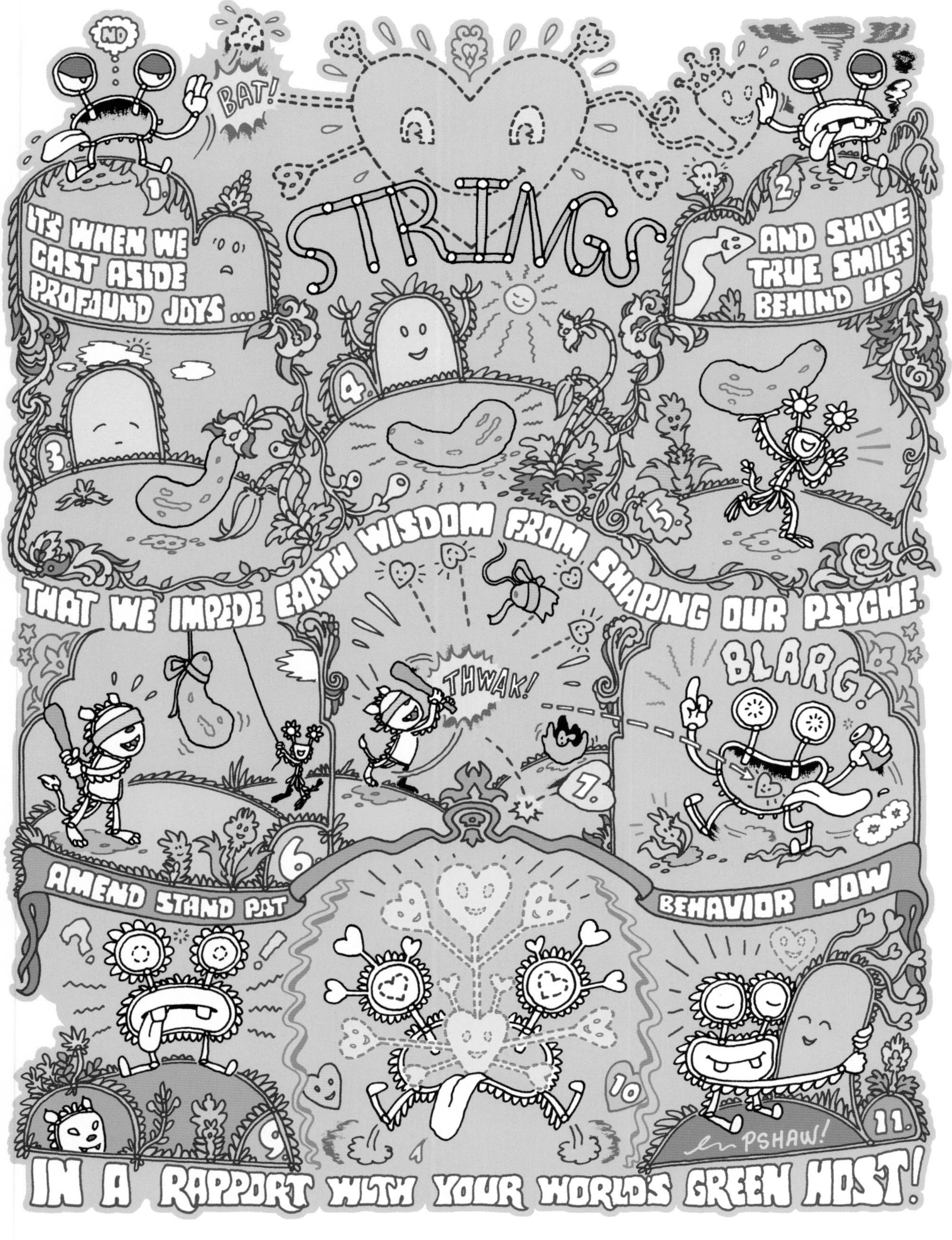
NO
BAT!
STRING
1.
IT'S WHEN WE CAST ASIDE PROFOUND JOYS...
2.
AND SHOVE TRUE SMILES BEHIND US
3.
4.
5.
THAT WE IMPEDE EARTH WISDOM FROM SHAPING OUR PSYCHE.
6.
THWAK!
7.
BLARG!
AMEND STAND PAT
BEHAVIOR NOW
9.
10
11.
PSHAW!
IN A RAPPORT WITH YOUR WORLD'S GREEN HOST!

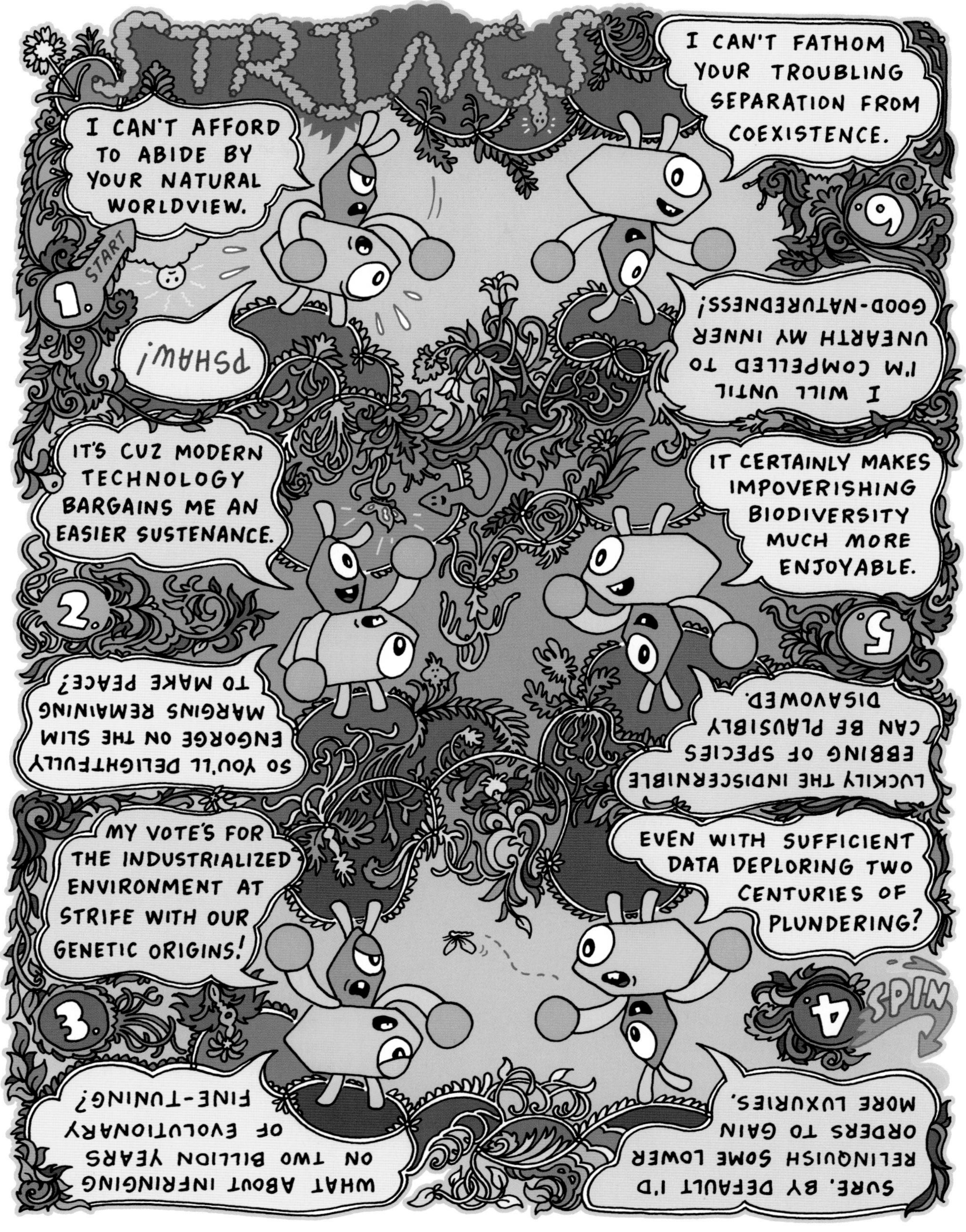
START
1.
I CAN'T AFFORD TO ABIDE BY YOUR NATURAL WORLDVIEW.
PSHAW!
2.
IT'S CUZ MODERN TECHNOLOGY BARGAINS ME AN EASIER SUSTENANCE.
SO YOU'LL DELIGHTFULLY ENGORGE ON THE SLIM MARGINS REMAINING TO MAKE PEACE?
3.
MY VOTE'S FOR THE INDUSTRIALIZED ENVIRONMENT AT STRIFE WITH OUR GENETIC ORIGINS!
WHAT ABOUT INFRINGING ON TWO BILLION YEARS OF EVOLUTIONARY FINE-TUNING?
4
SPIN
EVEN WITH SUFFICIENT DATA DEPLORING TWO CENTURIES OF PLUNDERING?
SURE, BY DEFAULT I'D RELINQUISH SOME LOWER ORDERS TO GAIN MORE LUXURIES.
5
IT CERTAINLY MAKES IMPOVERISHING BIODIVERSITY MUCH MORE ENJOYABLE.
LUCKILY THE INDISCERNIBLE EBBING OF SPECIES CAN BE PLAUSIBLY DISAVOWED.
6
I CAN'T FATHOM YOUR TROUBLING SEPARATION FROM COEXISTENCE.
I WILL UNTIL I'M COMPELLED TO UNEARTH MY INNER GOOD-NATUREDNESS!

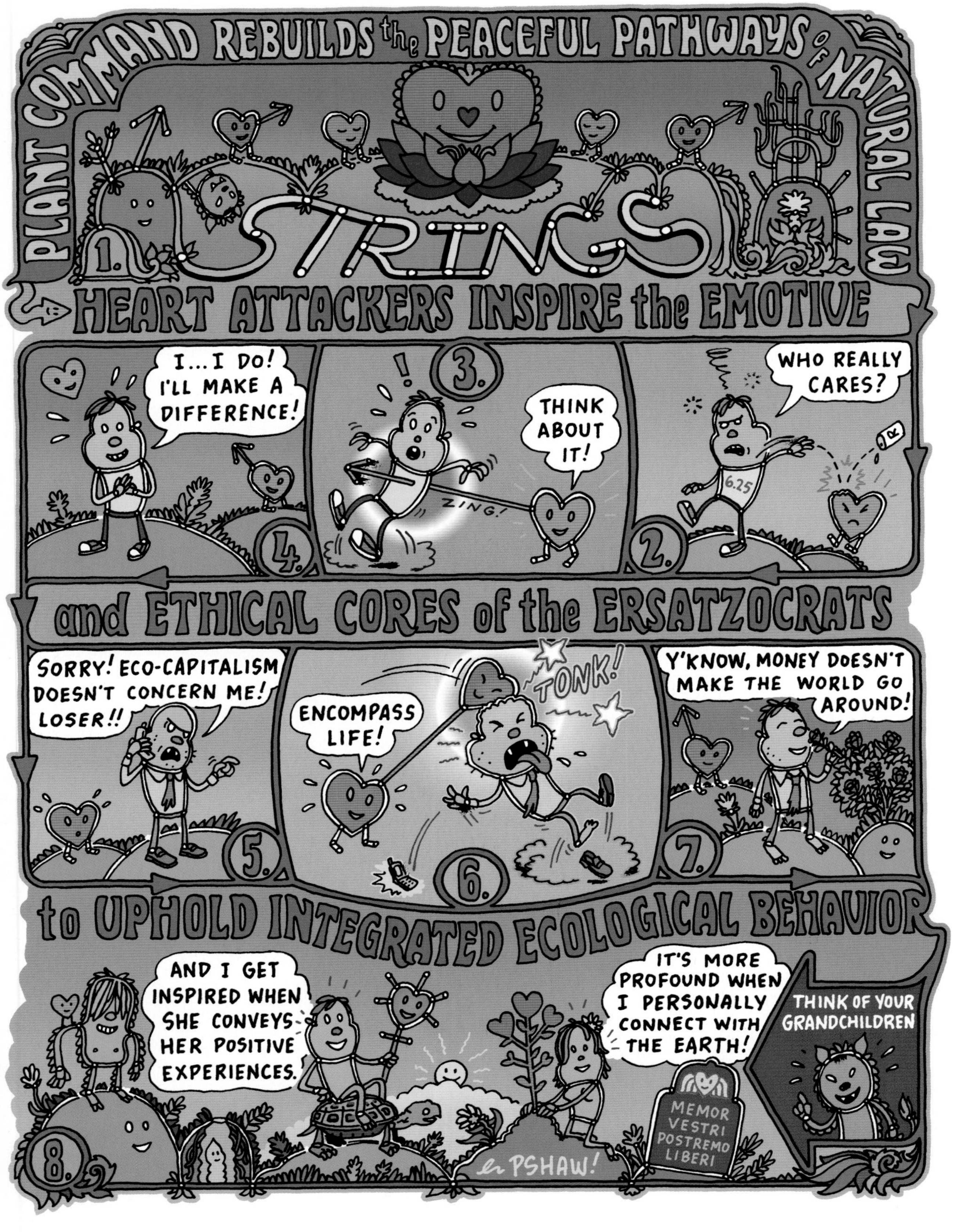
PLANT COMMAND REBUILDS the PEACEFUL PATHWAYS of NATURAL LAW
1.
STRINGS
HEART ATTACKERS INSPIRE the EMOTIVE
2.
6.25
WHO REALLY CARES?
3.
THINK ABOUT IT!
ZING!
4.
I... I DO! I'LL MAKE A DIFFERENCE!
and ETHICAL CORES of the ERSATZOCRATS
5.
SORRY! ECO-CAPITALISM DOESN'T CONCERN ME! LOSER!!
6.
ENCOMPASS LIFE!
TONK!
7.
Y'KNOW, MONEY DOESN'T MAKE THE WORLD GO AROUND!
to UPHOLD INTEGRATED ECOLOGICAL BEHAVIOR
8.
AND I GET INSPIRED WHEN SHE CONVEYS HER POSITIVE EXPERIENCES.
IT'S MORE PROFOUND WHEN I PERSONALLY CONNECT WITH THE EARTH!
MEMOR VESTRI POSTREMO LIBERI
THINK OF YOUR GRANDCHILDREN
PSHAW!

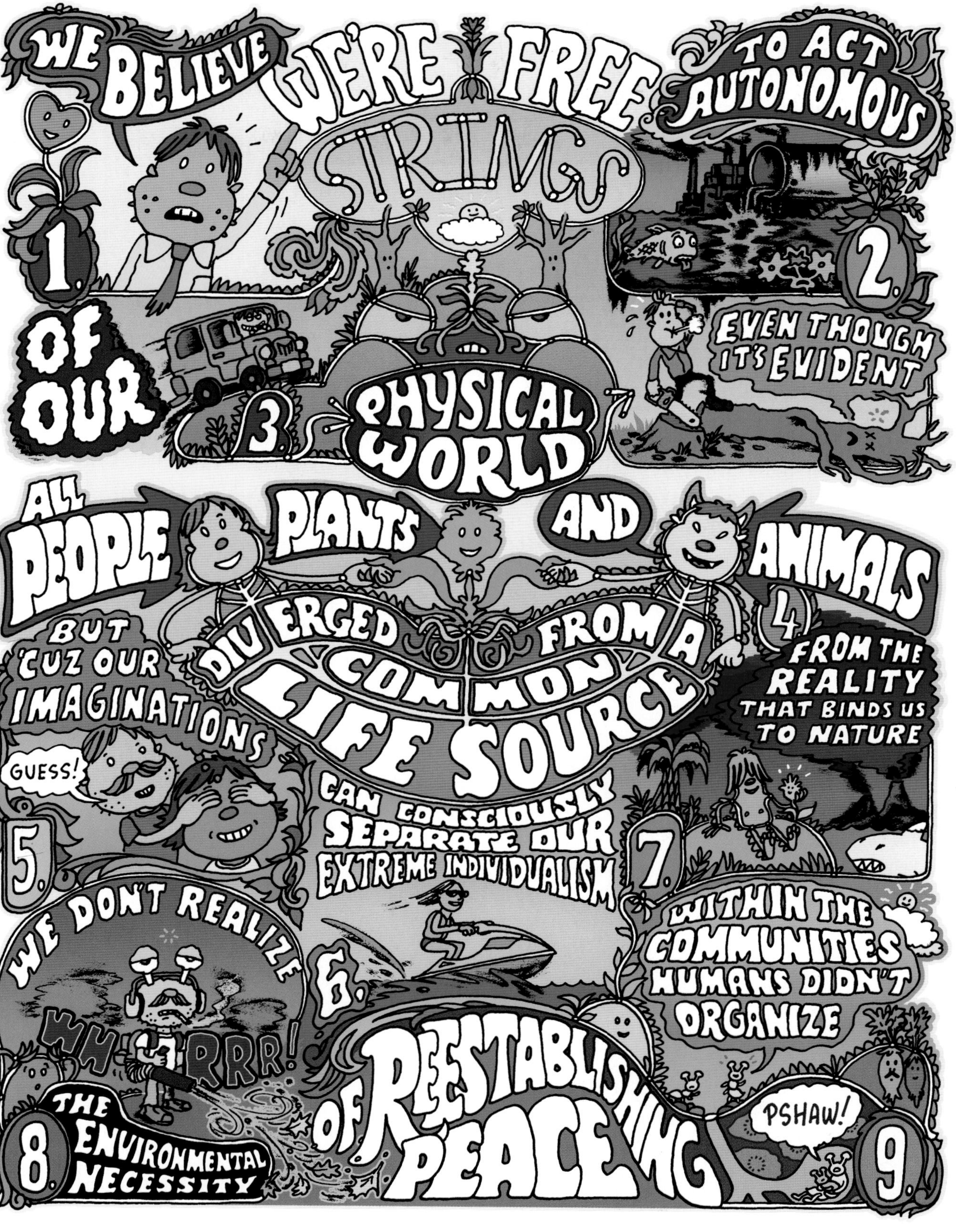

WE BELIEVE
WE'RE FREE
STRINGS
TO ACT AUTONOMOUS
1.
2.
OF OUR
3.
PHYSICAL WORLD
EVEN THOUGH IT'S EVIDENT
ALL PEOPLE
PLANTS
AND
ANIMALS
4.
DIVERGED FROM A COMMON LIFE SOURCE
BUT 'CUZ OUR IMAGINATIONS
FROM THE REALITY THAT BINDS US TO NATURE
GUESS!
CAN CONSCIOUSLY SEPARATE OUR EXTREME INDIVIDUALISM
5.
7.
WE DON'T REALIZE
WITHIN THE COMMUNITIES HUMANS DIDN'T ORGANIZE
6.
WHIRRR!
THE ENVIRONMENTAL NECESSITY
OF REESTABLISHING PEACE
PSHAW!
8.
9.

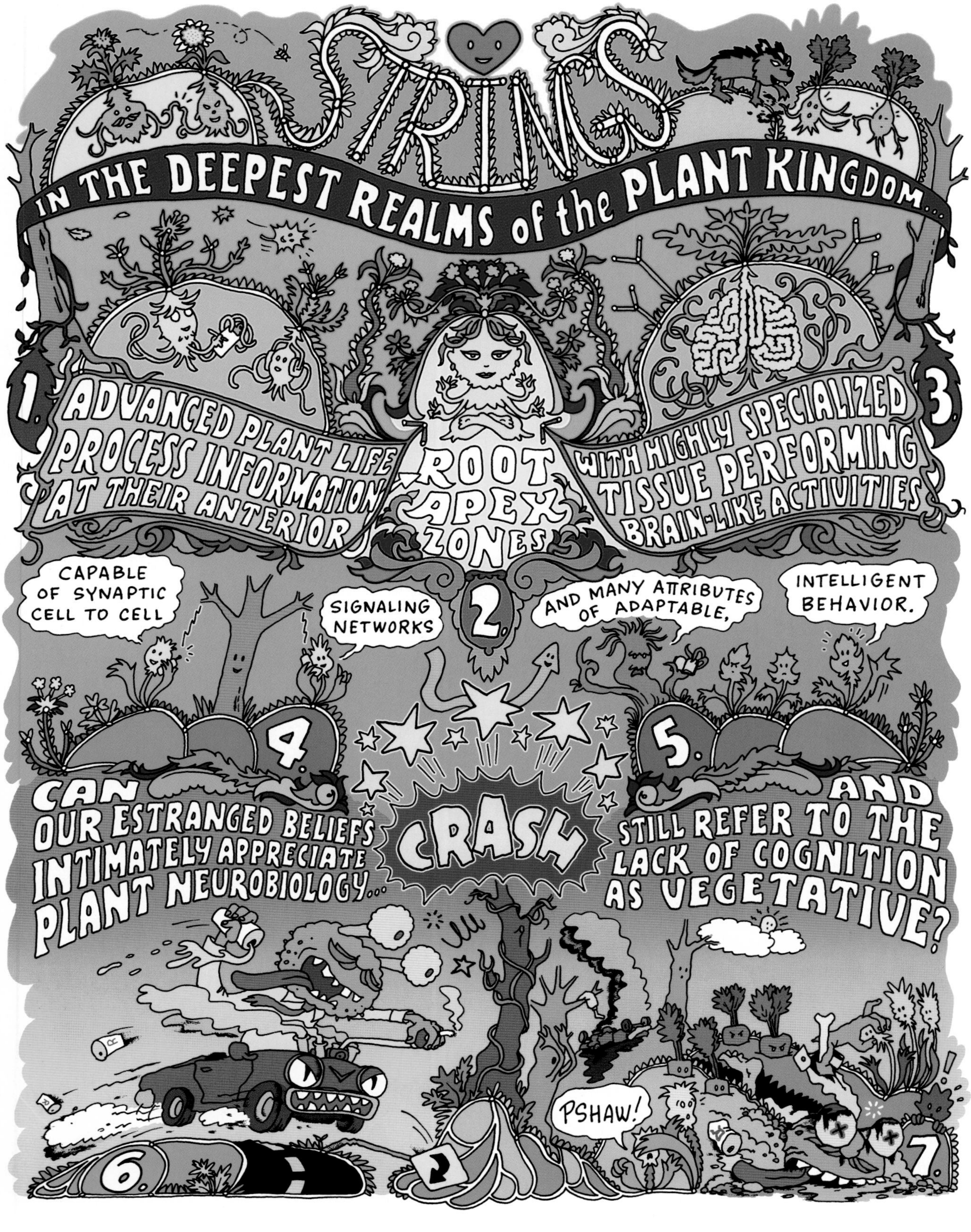

STRINGS
IN THE DEEPEST REALMS of the PLANT KINGDOM...
1. ADVANCED PLANT LIFE PROCESS INFORMATION AT THEIR ANTERIOR
ROOT APEX ZONES
WITH HIGHLY SPECIALIZED TISSUE PERFORMING BRAIN-LIKE ACTIVITIES 3.
CAPABLE OF SYNAPTIC CELL TO CELL
SIGNALING NETWORKS
2.
AND MANY ATTRIBUTES OF ADAPTABLE,
INTELLIGENT BEHAVIOR.
4.
5.
CAN OUR ESTRANGED BELIEFS INTIMATELY APPRECIATE PLANT NEUROBIOLOGY...
CRASH
AND STILL REFER TO THE LACK OF COGNITION AS VEGETATIVE?
PSHAW!
6.
7.

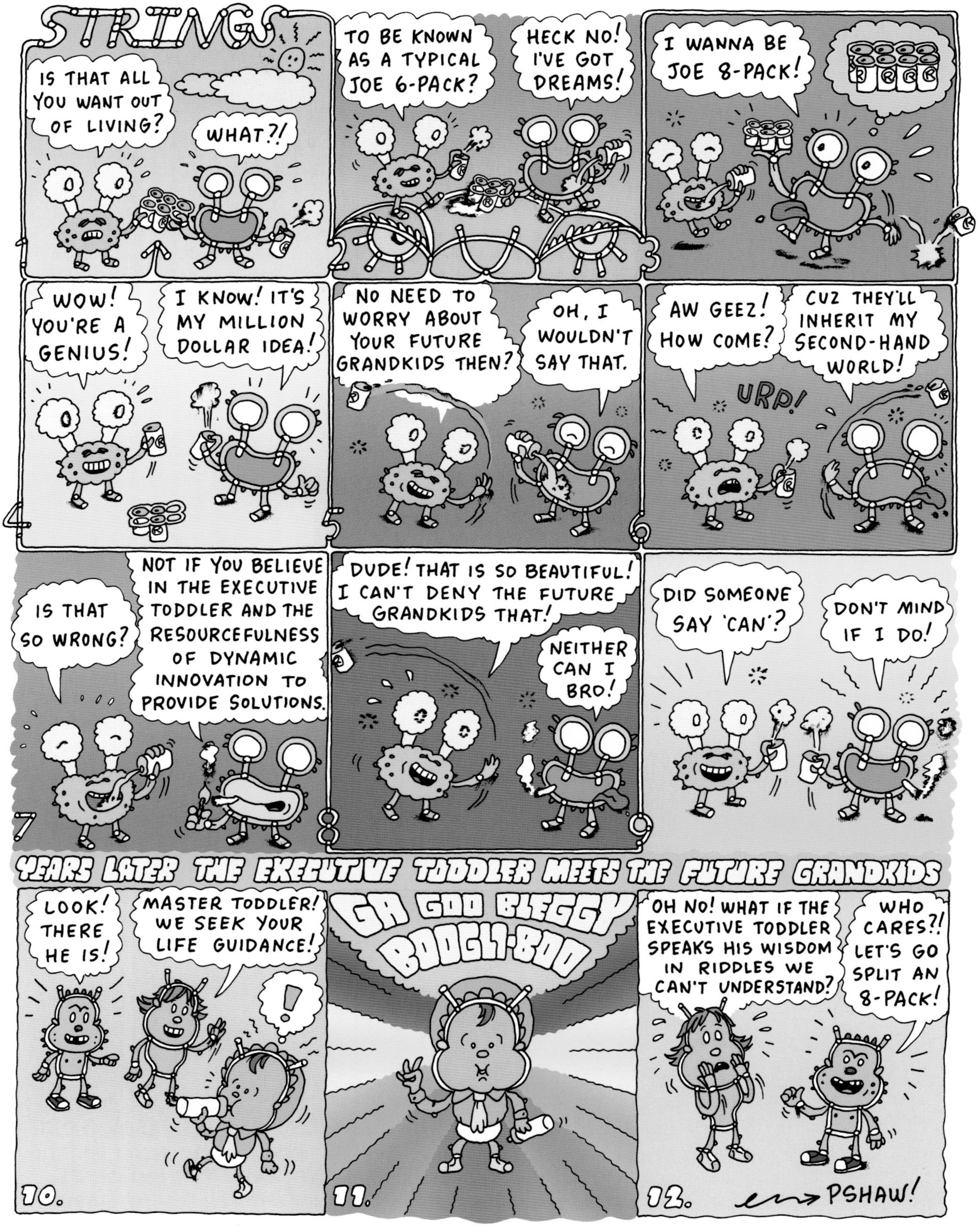
STRINGS
IS THAT ALL YOU WANT OUT OF LIVING?
WHAT?!
TO BE KNOWN AS A TYPICAL JOE 6-PACK?
HECK NO! I'VE GOT DREAMS!
I WANNA BE JOE 8-PACK!
WOW! YOU'RE A GENIUS!
I KNOW! IT'S MY MILLION DOLLAR IDEA!
NO NEED TO WORRY ABOUT YOUR FUTURE GRANDKIDS THEN?
OH, I WOULDN'T SAY THAT.
AW GEEZ! HOW COME?
CUZ THEY'LL INHERIT MY SECOND-HAND WORLD!
URP!
IS THAT SO WRONG?
NOT IF YOU BELIEVE IN THE EXECUTIVE TODDLER AND THE RESOURCEFULNESS OF DYNAMIC INNOVATION TO PROVIDE SOLUTIONS.
DUDE! THAT IS SO BEAUTIFUL! I CAN'T DENY THE FUTURE GRANDKIDS THAT!
NEITHER CAN I BRO!
DID SOMEONE SAY 'CAN'?
DON'T MIND IF I DO!
YEARS LATER THE EXECUTIVE TODDLER MEETS THE FUTURE GRANDKIDS
LOOK! THERE HE IS!
MASTER TODDLER! WE SEEK YOUR LIFE GUIDANCE!
!
GA GOO BLEGGY BOOGLI-BOO
OH NO! WHAT IF THE EXECUTIVE TODDLER SPEAKS HIS WISDOM IN RIDDLES WE CAN'T UNDERSTAND?
WHO CARES?! LET'S GO SPLIT AN 8-PACK!
PSHAW!

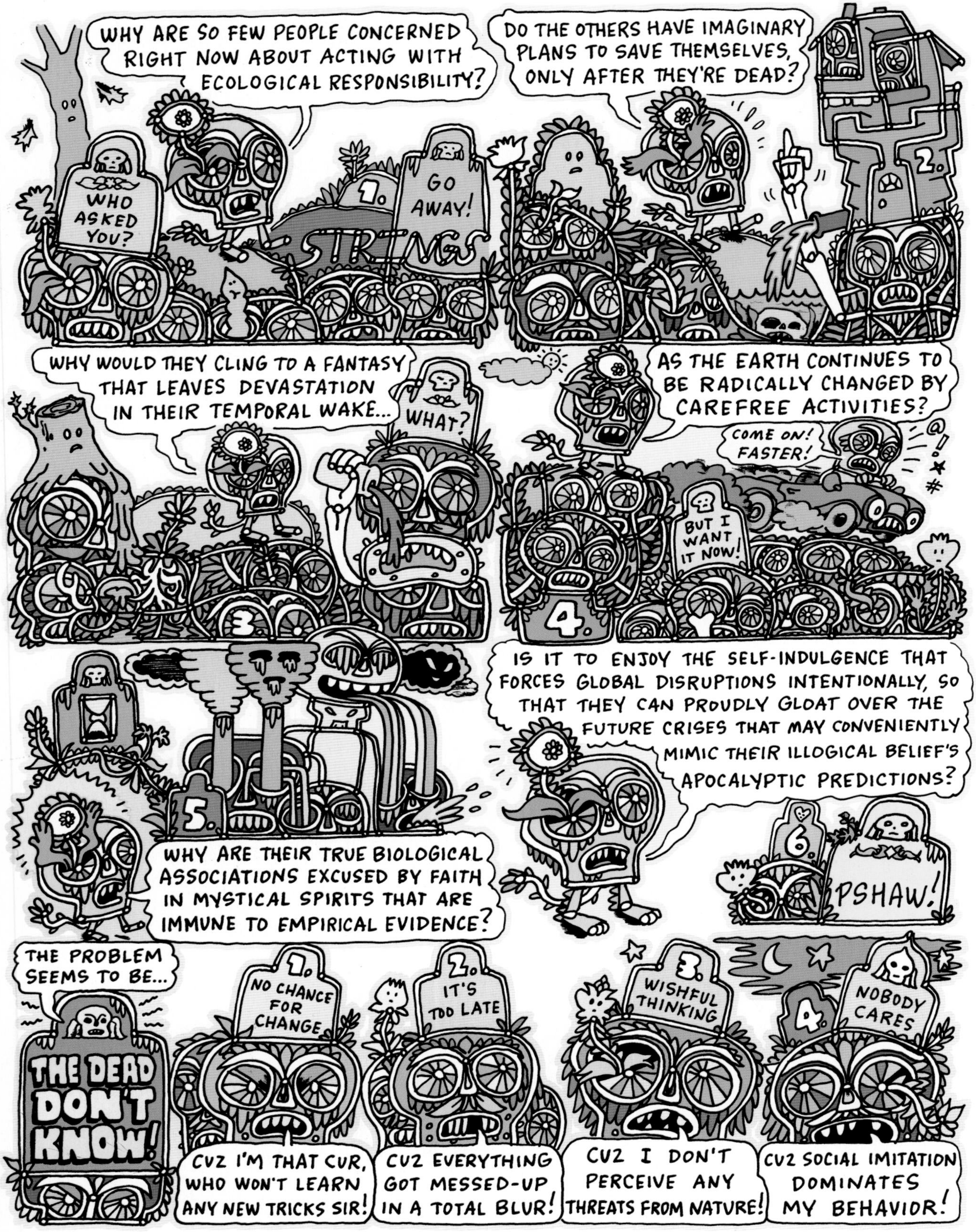
WHY ARE SO FEW PEOPLE CONCERNED RIGHT NOW ABOUT ACTING WITH ECOLOGICAL RESPONSIBILITY?
WHO ASKED YOU?
1.
GO AWAY!
STRINGS
DO THE OTHERS HAVE IMAGINARY PLANS TO SAVE THEMSELVES, ONLY AFTER THEY'RE DEAD?
2.
WHY WOULD THEY CLING TO A FANTASY THAT LEAVES DEVASTATION IN THEIR TEMPORAL WAKE...
WHAT?
3.
AS THE EARTH CONTINUES TO BE RADICALLY CHANGED BY CAREFREE ACTIVITIES?
COME ON! FASTER!
BUT I WANT IT NOW!
4.
5.
IS IT TO ENJOY THE SELF-INDULGENCE THAT FORCES GLOBAL DISRUPTIONS INTENTIONALLY, SO THAT THEY CAN PROUDLY GLOAT OVER THE FUTURE CRISES THAT MAY CONVENIENTLY MIMIC THEIR ILLOGICAL BELIEF'S APOCALYPTIC PREDICTIONS?
WHY ARE THEIR TRUE BIOLOGICAL ASSOCIATIONS EXCUSED BY FAITH IN MYSTICAL SPIRITS THAT ARE IMMUNE TO EMPIRICAL EVIDENCE?
6.
PSHAW!
THE PROBLEM SEEMS TO BE...
THE DEAD DON'T KNOW!
1. NO CHANCE FOR CHANGE
CUZ I'M THAT CUR, WHO WON'T LEARN ANY NEW TRICKS SIR!
2. IT'S TOO LATE
CUZ EVERYTHING GOT MESSED-UP IN A TOTAL BLUR!
3. WISHFUL THINKING
CUZ I DON'T PERCEIVE ANY THREATS FROM NATURE!
4. NOBODY CARES
CUZ SOCIAL IMITATION DOMINATES MY BEHAVIOR!

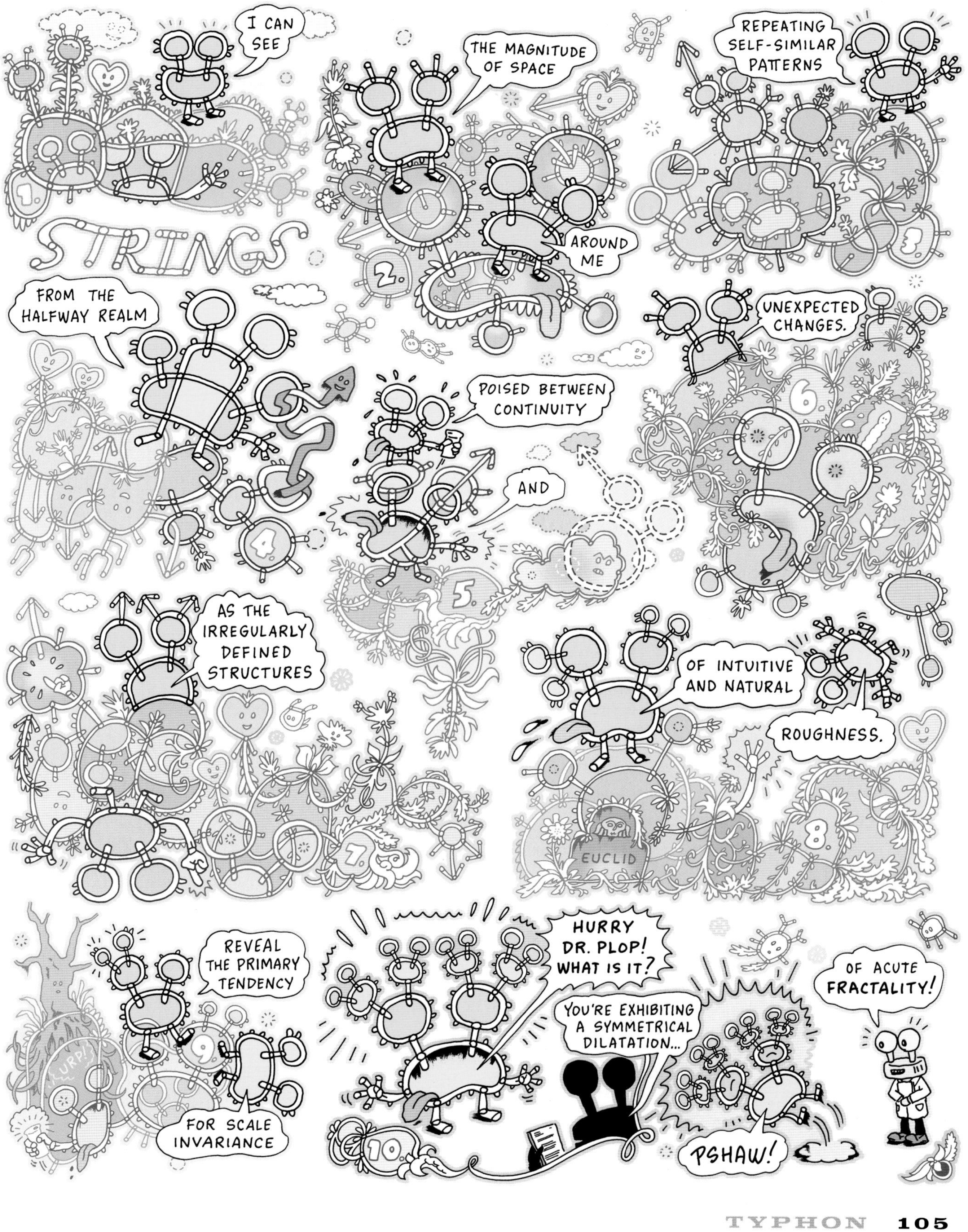
STRINGS
I CAN SEE
THE MAGNITUDE OF SPACE
AROUND ME
REPEATING SELF-SIMILAR PATTERNS
FROM THE HALFWAY REALM
POISED BETWEEN CONTINUITY
AND
UNEXPECTED CHANGES.
AS THE IRREGULARLY DEFINED STRUCTURES
OF INTUITIVE AND NATURAL
ROUGHNESS.
EUCLID
REVEAL THE PRIMARY TENDENCY
FOR SCALE INVARIANCE
SLURP!
HURRY DR. PLOP! WHAT IS IT?
YOU'RE EXHIBITING A SYMMETRICAL DILATATION...
OF ACUTE FRACTALITY!
PSHAW!

GREGORY SPALDING The Most Boring VAMPIRE EVER

by LORENZ PETER

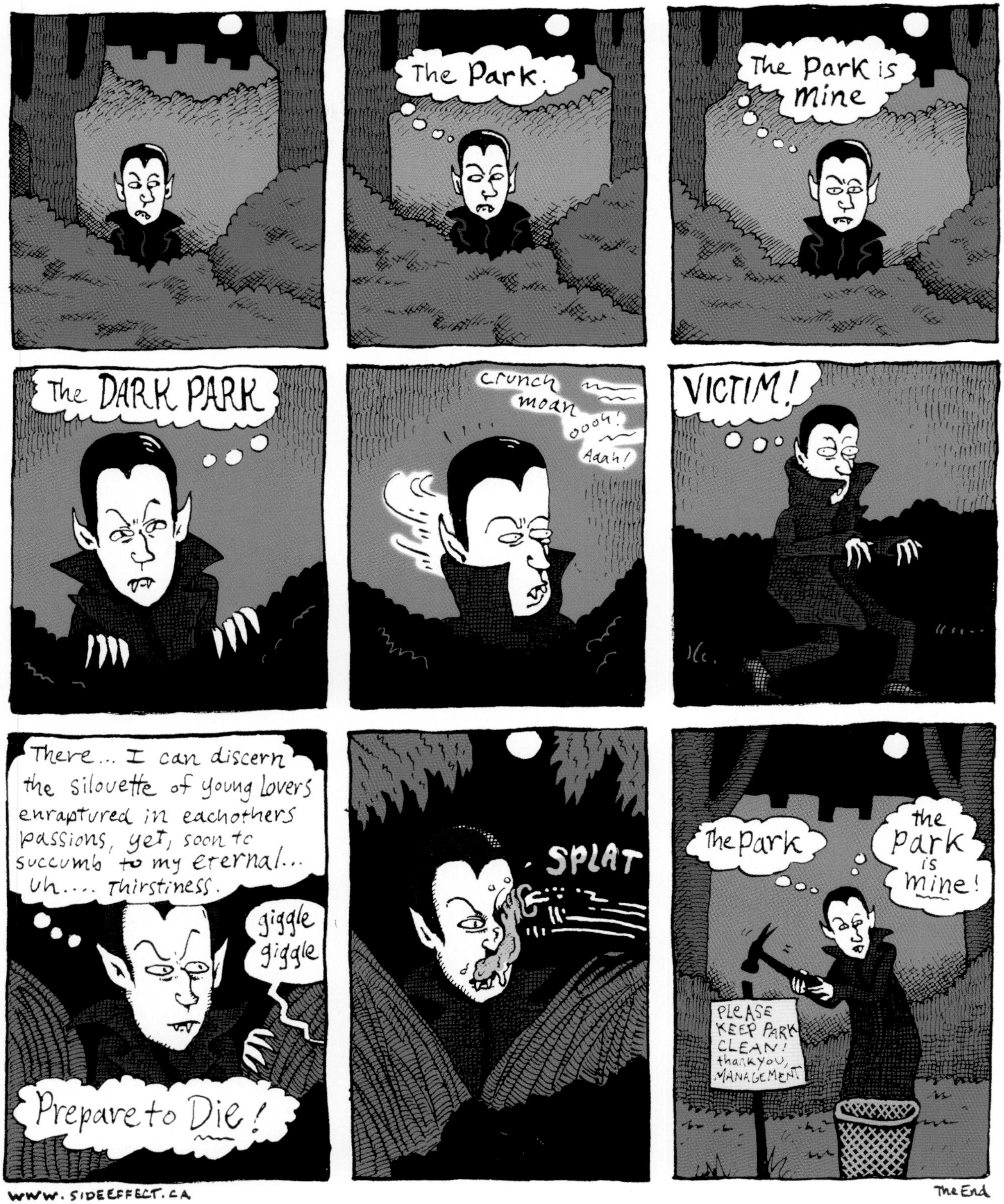

The Park.
The Park is mine
The DARK PARK
crunch
moan
oooh!
Aaah!
VICTIM!
There... I can discern the silouette of young lovers enraptured in eachothers passions, yet, soon to succumb to my eternal... uh.... thirstiness.
giggle giggle
Prepare to Die!
SPLAT
The park
the park is mine!
PLEASE KEEP PARK CLEAN! thank you, MANAGEMENT

WWW.SIDEEFFECT.CA

The End

GREGORY SPALDING the Most Boring Vampire EVER by LORENZ PETER

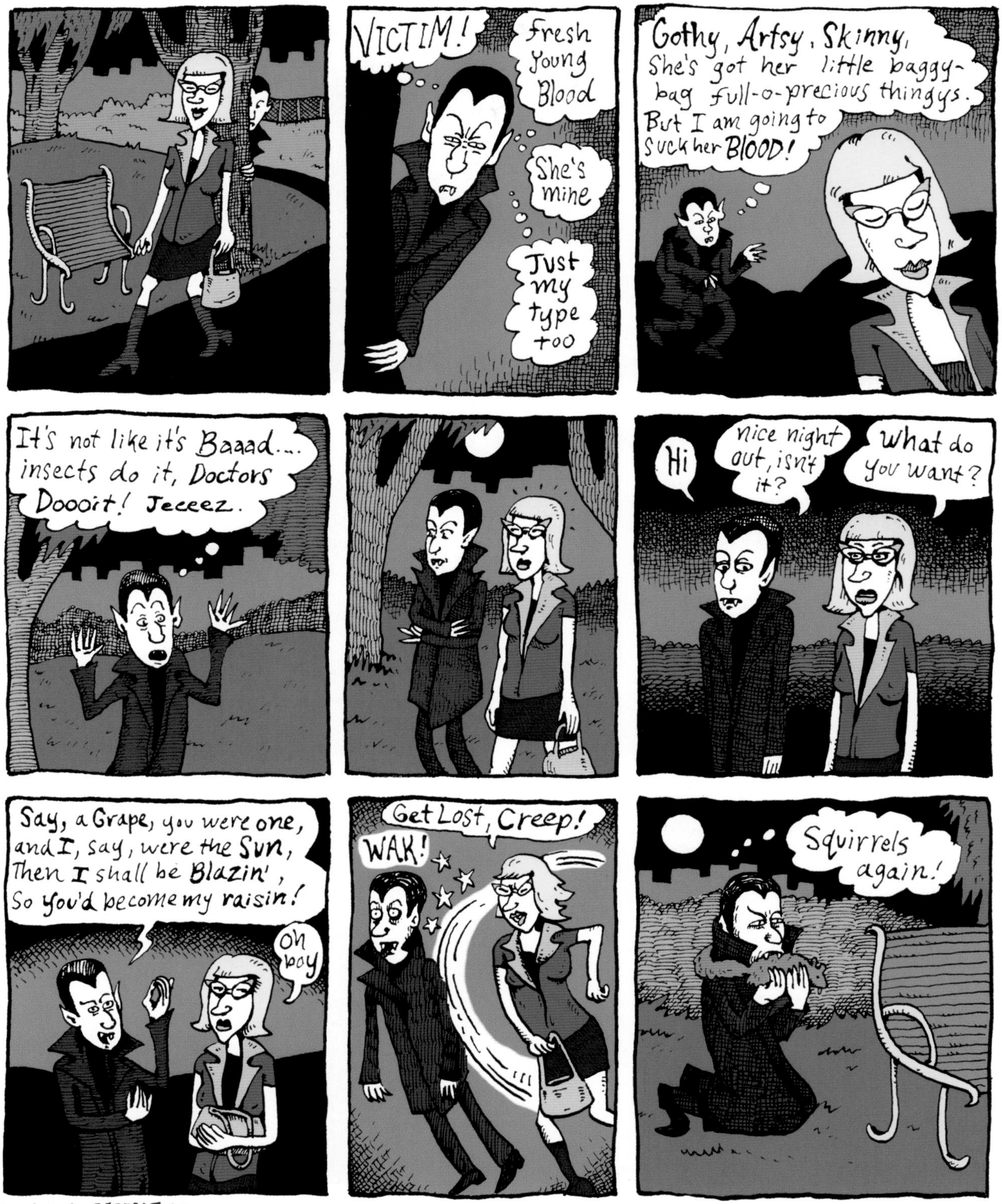
VICTIM!
Fresh Young Blood
She's mine
Just my type too
Gothy, Artsy, Skinny, She's got her little baggy-bag full-o-precious thingys. But I am going to Suck her BLOOD!
It's not like it's Baaad.... insects do it, Doctors Doooit! Jeeeez.
Hi
nice night out, isn't it?
What do you want?
Say, a Grape, you were one, and I, say, were the Sun, Then I shall be Blazin', So you'd become my raisin!
oh boy
Get Lost, Creep!
WAK!
Squirrels again!

WWW.SIDEEFFECT.CA

The End

GREGORY SPALDING the most BORING VAMPIRE EVER

by Lorenz Peter

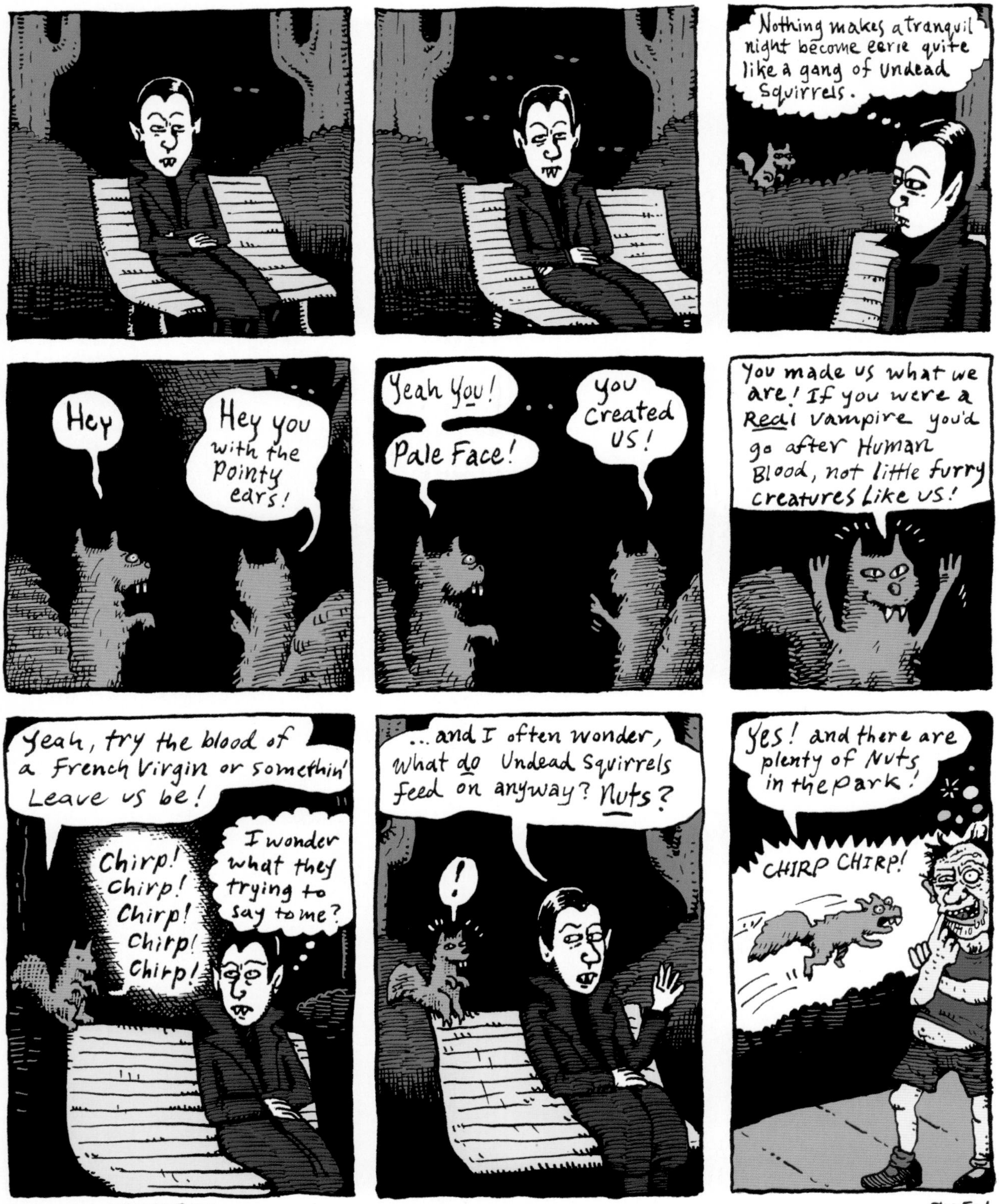

Nothing makes a tranquil night become eerie quite like a gang of Undead Squirrels.
Hey
Hey you with the pointy ears!
Yeah You!
Pale Face!
You Created US!
You made us what we are! If you were a Real vampire you'd go after Human Blood, not little furry creatures Like US!
Yeah, try the blood of a French Virgin or somethin' Leave us be!
Chirp! Chirp! Chirp! Chirp! Chirp!
I wonder what they trying to say to me?
...and I often wonder, What do Undead Squirrels feed on anyway? Nuts?
!
Yes! and there are plenty of Nuts in the Park!
CHIRP CHIRP!

WWW.SIDEEFFECT.CA

The End

GREGORY SPALDING the most BORING VAMPIRE EVER

by LORENZ PETER

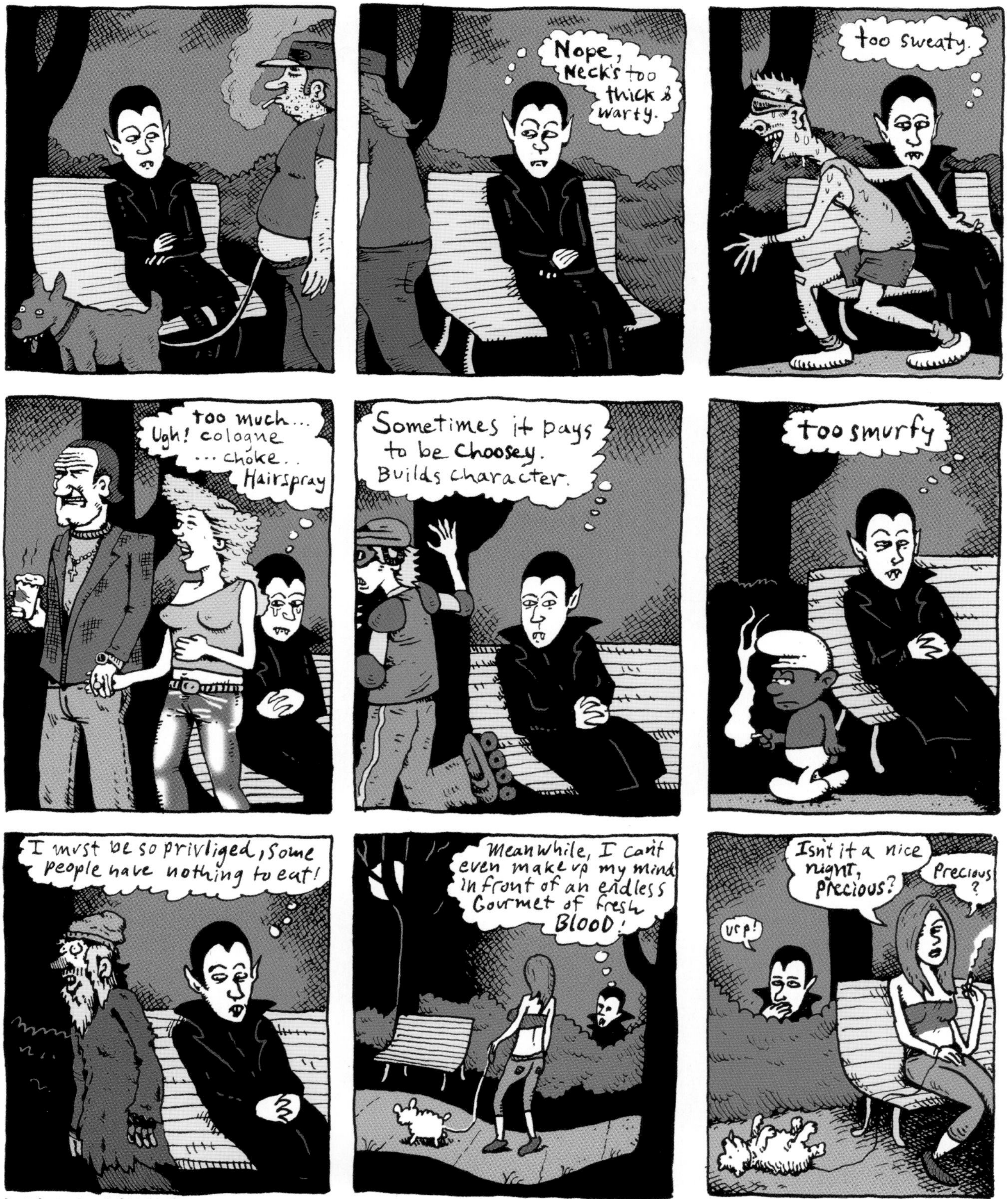
Nope, Neck's too thick & warty.
too sweaty.
too much... Ugh! cologne ...choke.. Hairspray
Sometimes it pays to be Choosey. Builds character.
too smurfy
I must be so privliged, Some people have nothing to eat!
Meanwhile, I can't even make up my mind in front of an endless Gourmet of fresh BLOOD!
urp!
Isn't it a nice night, Precious?
Precious?

WWW.SIDEEFFECT.CA

The End

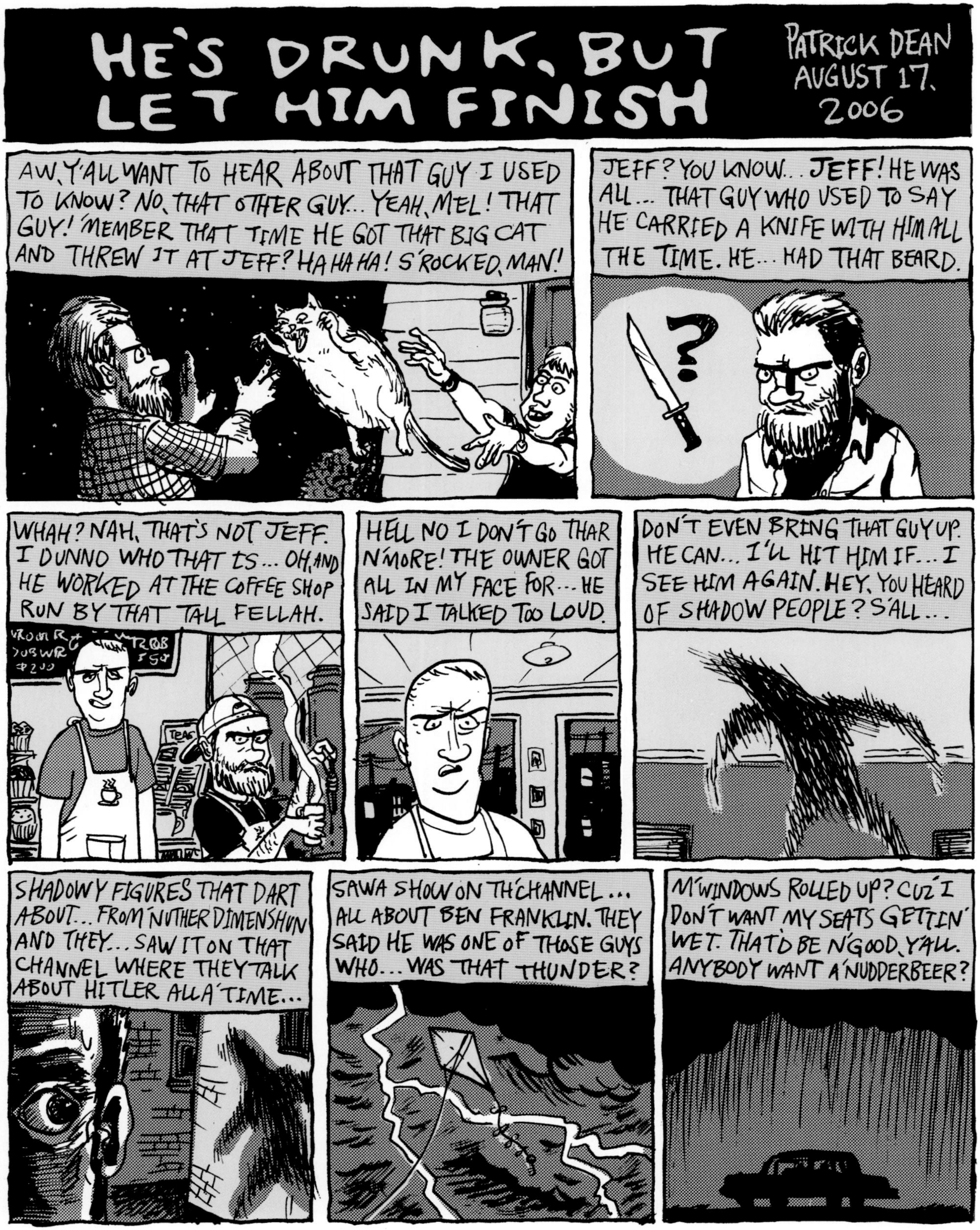
HE'S DRUNK, BUT LET HIM FINISH
PATRICK DEAN AUGUST 17, 2006
AW, Y'ALL WANT TO HEAR ABOUT THAT GUY I USED TO KNOW? NO, THAT OTHER GUY... YEAH, MEL! THAT GUY! 'MEMBER THAT TIME HE GOT THAT BIG CAT AND THREW IT AT JEFF? HA HA HA! S'ROCKED, MAN!
JEFF? YOU KNOW... JEFF! HE WAS ALL... THAT GUY WHO USED TO SAY HE CARRIED A KNIFE WITH HIM ALL THE TIME. HE... HAD THAT BEARD.
?
WHAH? NAH, THAT'S NOT JEFF. I DUNNO WHO THAT IS... OH, AND HE WORKED AT THE COFFEE SHOP RUN BY THAT TALL FELLAH.
TEAS
HELL NO I DON'T GO THAR N'MORE! THE OWNER GOT ALL IN MY FACE FOR... HE SAID I TALKED TOO LOUD.
DON'T EVEN BRING THAT GUY UP. HE CAN... I'LL HIT HIM IF... I SEE HIM AGAIN. HEY, YOU HEARD OF SHADOW PEOPLE? S'ALL...
SHADOWY FIGURES THAT DART ABOUT... FROM 'NUTHER DIMENSHUN AND THEY... SAW IT ON THAT CHANNEL WHERE THEY TALK ABOUT HITLER ALLA' TIME...
SAWA SHOW ON TH'CHANNEL... ALL ABOUT BEN FRANKLIN. THEY SAID HE WAS ONE OF THOSE GUYS WHO... WAS THAT THUNDER?
M'WINDOWS ROLLED UP? CUZ' I DON'T WANT MY SEATS GETTIN' WET. THAT'D BE N'GOOD, Y'ALL. ANYBODY WANT A 'NUDDERBEER?

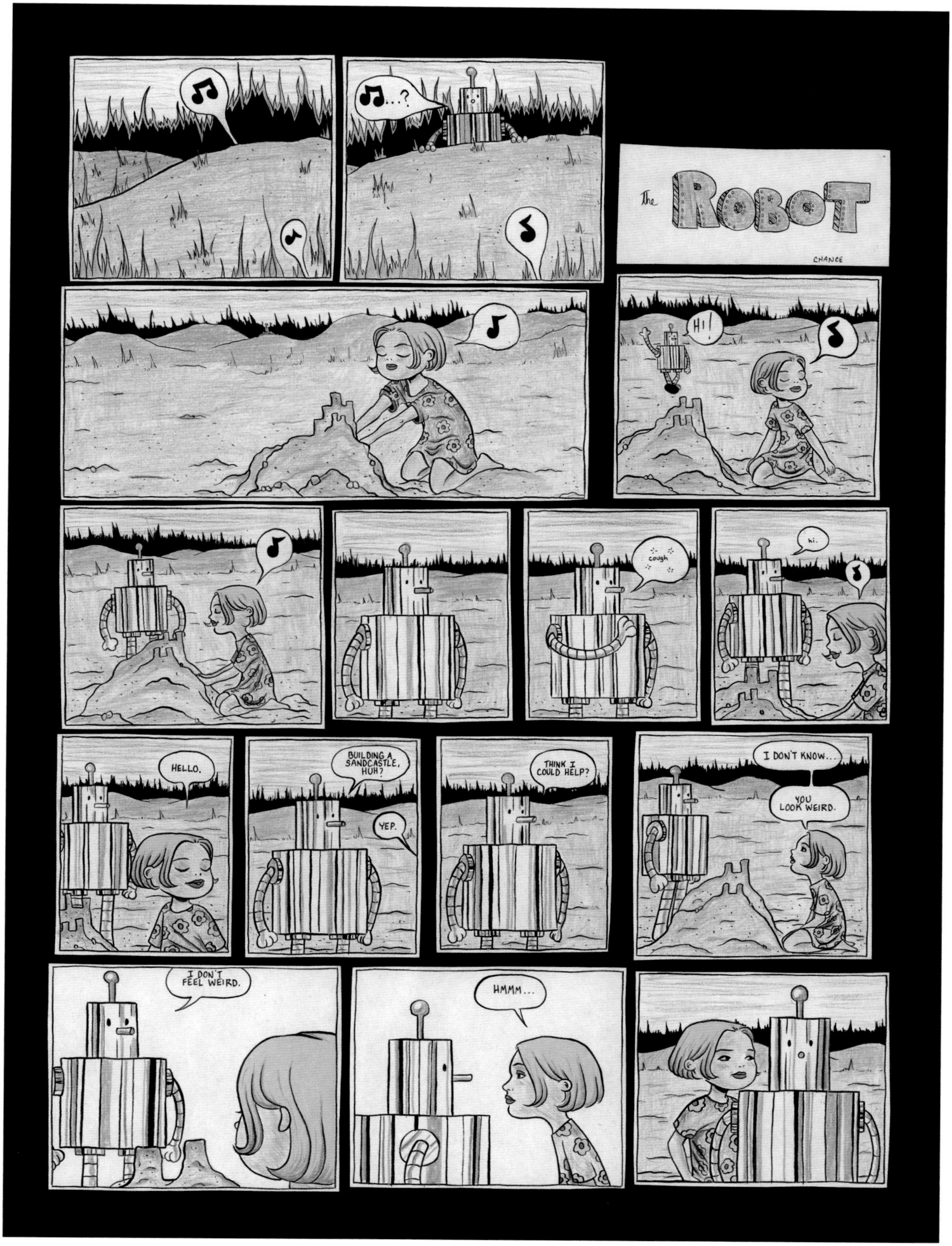

...?
The ROBOT
CHANCE
HI!
cough
hi.
HELLO.
BUILDING A SANDCASTLE, HUH?
YEP.
THINK I COULD HELP?
I DON'T KNOW...
YOU LOOK WEIRD.
I DON'T FEEL WEIRD.
HMMM...

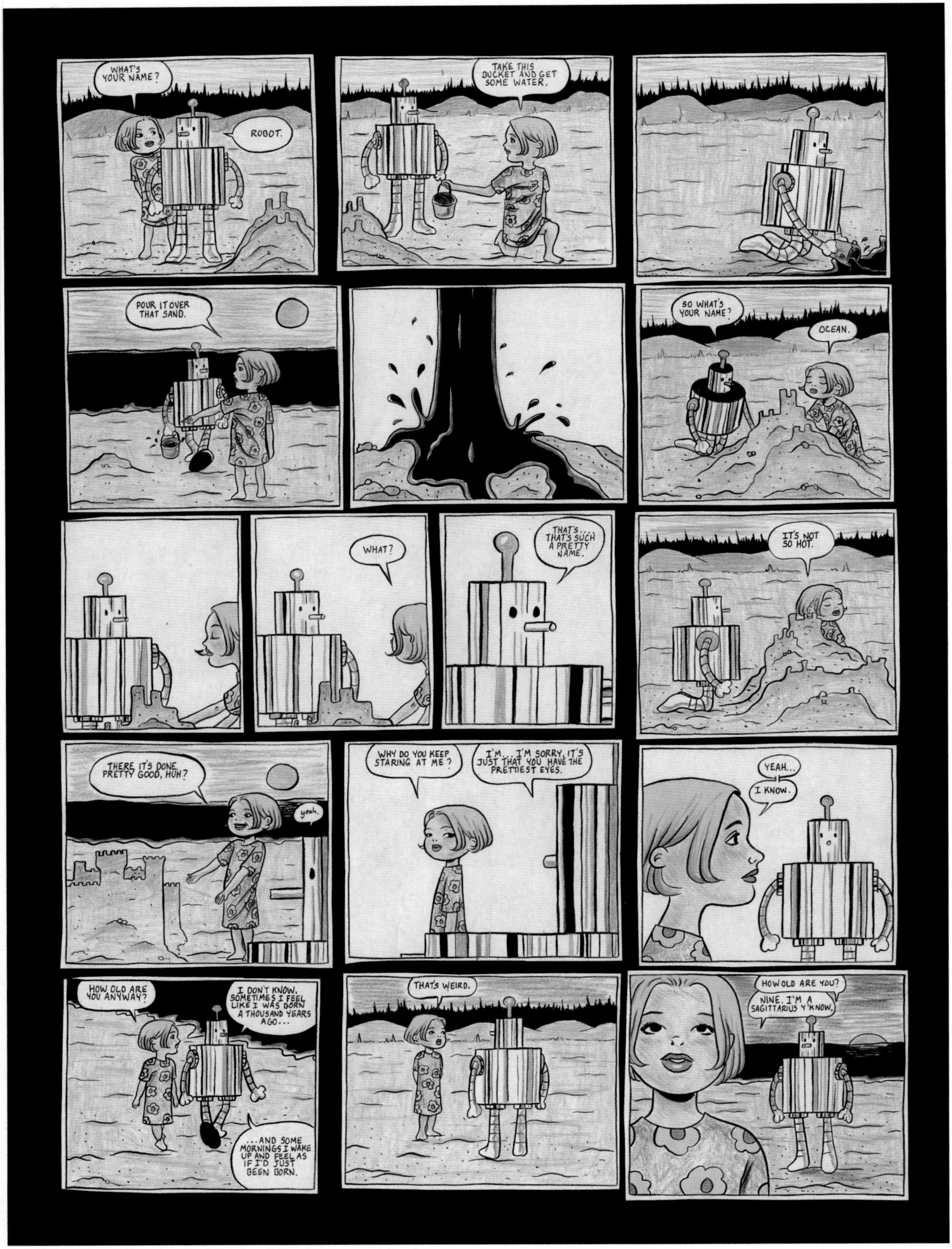
WHAT'S YOUR NAME?
ROBOT.
TAKE THIS BUCKET AND GET SOME WATER.
POUR IT OVER THAT SAND.
SO WHAT'S YOUR NAME?
OCEAN.
WHAT?
THAT'S... THAT'S SUCH A PRETTY NAME.
IT'S NOT SO HOT.
THERE IT'S DONE. PRETTY GOOD, HUH?
yeah.
WHY DO YOU KEEP STARING AT ME?
I'M... I'M SORRY, IT'S JUST THAT YOU HAVE THE PRETTIEST EYES.
YEAH...
I KNOW.
HOW OLD ARE YOU ANYWAY?
I DON'T KNOW. SOMETIMES I FEEL LIKE I WAS BORN A THOUSAND YEARS AGO...
...AND SOME MORNINGS I WAKE UP AND FEEL AS IF I'D JUST BEEN BORN.
THAT'S WEIRD.
HOW OLD ARE YOU?
NINE. I'M A SAGITTARIUS Y'KNOW.

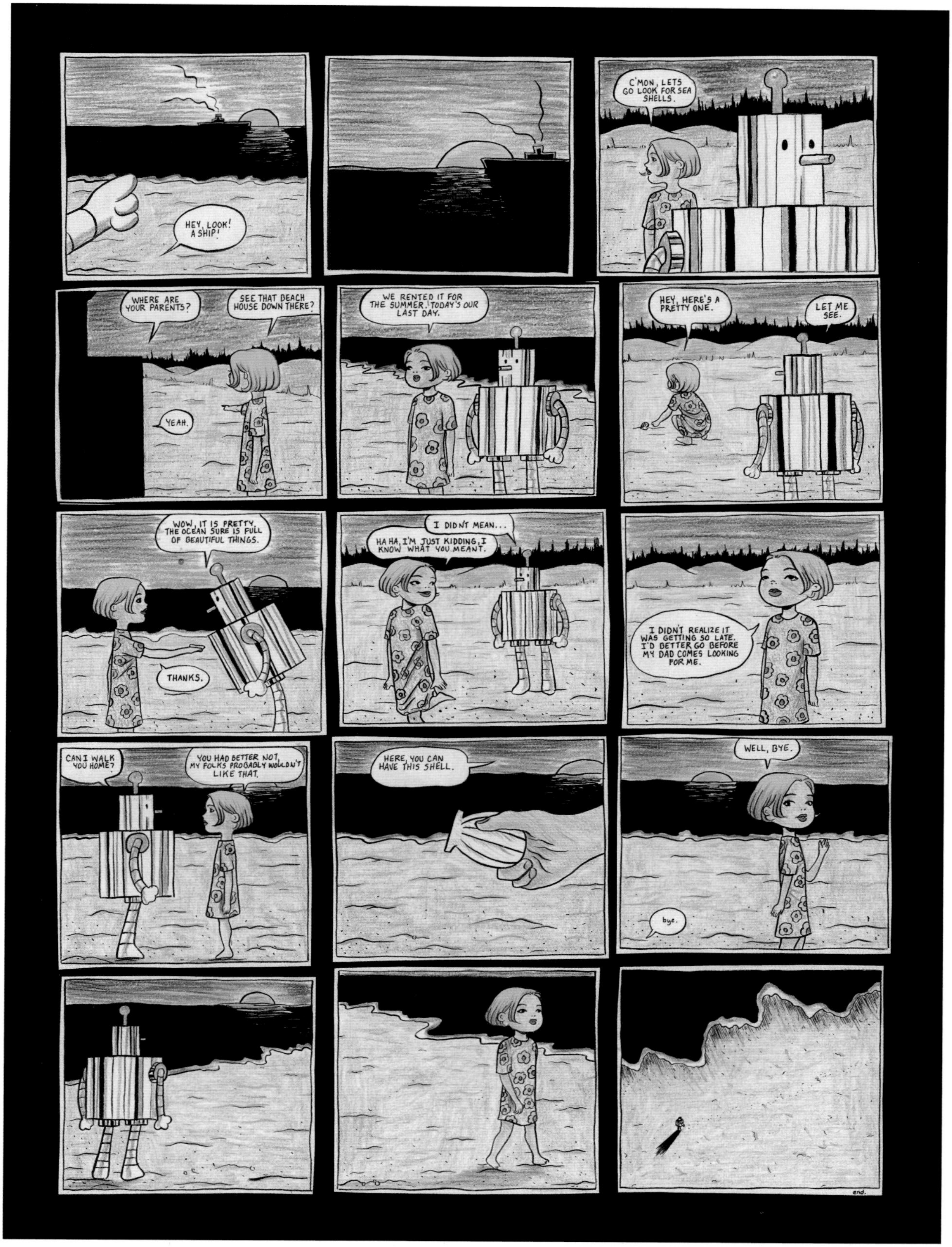
HEY, LOOK! A SHIP!
C'MON, LETS GO LOOK FOR SEA SHELLS.
WHERE ARE YOUR PARENTS?
SEE THAT BEACH HOUSE DOWN THERE?
YEAH.
WE RENTED IT FOR THE SUMMER. TODAY'S OUR LAST DAY.
HEY, HERE'S A PRETTY ONE.
LET ME SEE.
WOW, IT IS PRETTY. THE OCEAN SURE IS FULL OF BEAUTIFUL THINGS.
THANKS.
I DIDN'T MEAN...
HA HA, I'M JUST KIDDING, I KNOW WHAT YOU MEANT.
I DIDN'T REALIZE IT WAS GETTING SO LATE. I'D BETTER GO BEFORE MY DAD COMES LOOKING FOR ME.
CAN I WALK YOU HOME?
YOU HAD BETTER NOT, MY FOLKS PROBABLY WOULDN'T LIKE THAT.
HERE, YOU CAN HAVE THIS SHELL.
WELL, BYE.
bye.
end.

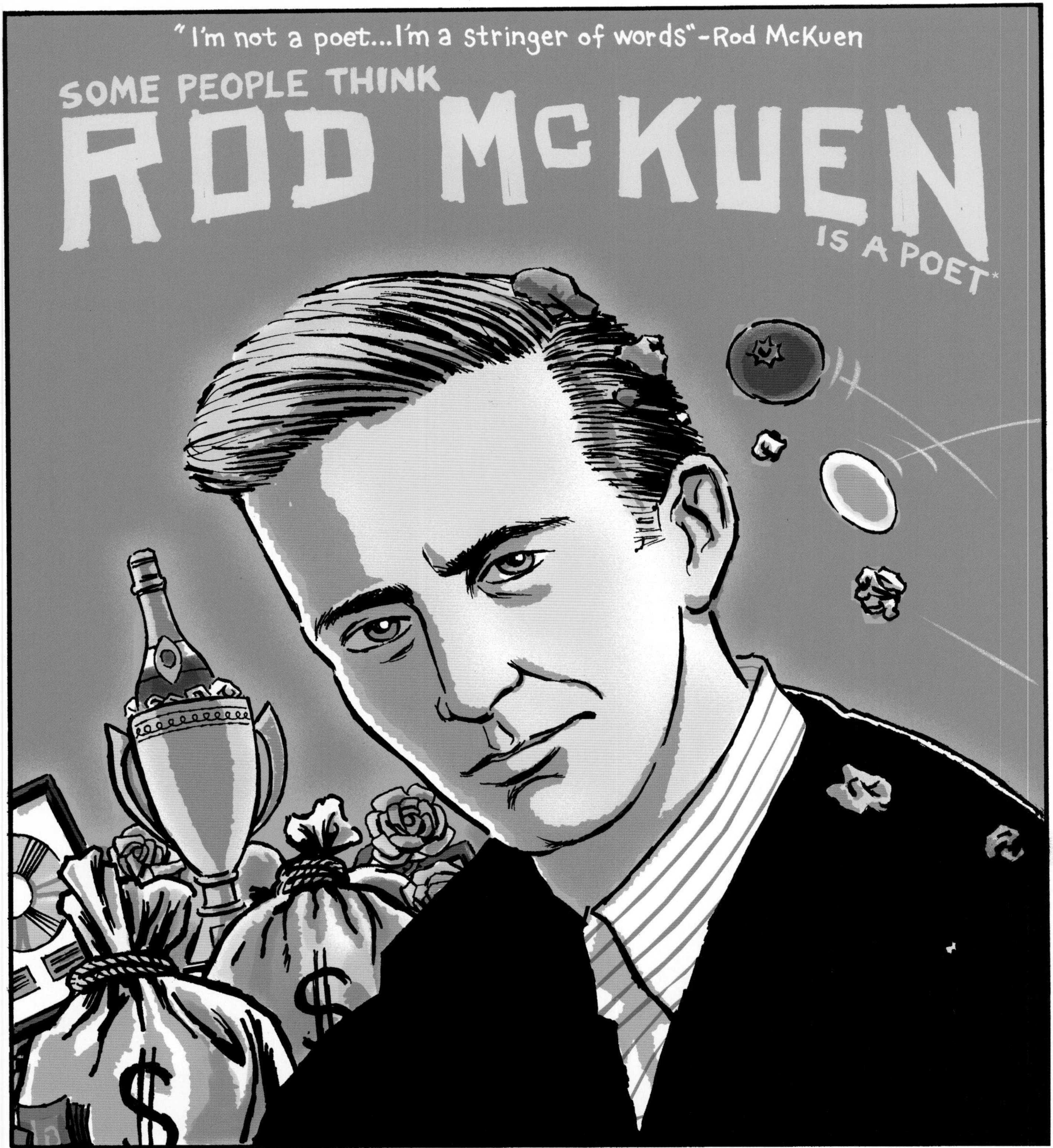
"I'm not a poet...I'm a stringer of words"-Rod McKuen
SOME PEOPLE THINK
ROD McKUEN
IS A POET*

*Too Much Joy, "Good Kill"

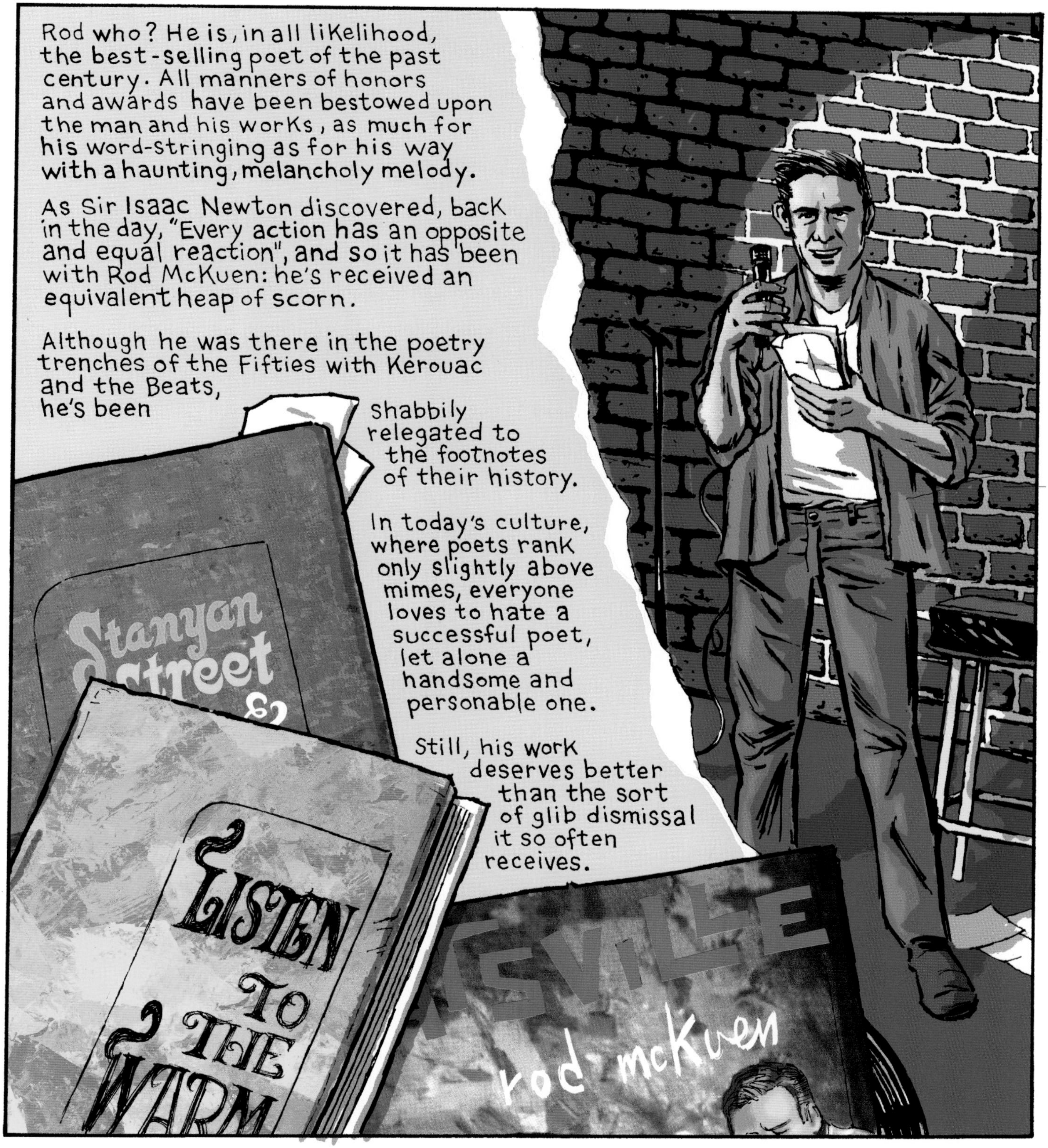
Rod who? He is, in all likelihood, the best-selling poet of the past century. All manners of honors and awards have been bestowed upon the man and his works, as much for his word-stringing as for his way with a haunting, melancholy melody.
As Sir Isaac Newton discovered, back in the day, "Every action has an opposite and equal reaction", and so it has been with Rod McKuen: he's received an equivalent heap of scorn.
Although he was there in the poetry trenches of the Fifties with Kerouac and the Beats, he's been shabbily relegated to the footnotes of their history.
In today's culture, where poets rank only slightly above mimes, everyone loves to hate a successful poet, let alone a handsome and personable one.
Still, his work deserves better than the sort of glib dismissal it so often receives.
Stanyan Street
LISTEN TO THE WARM
rod mcKuen

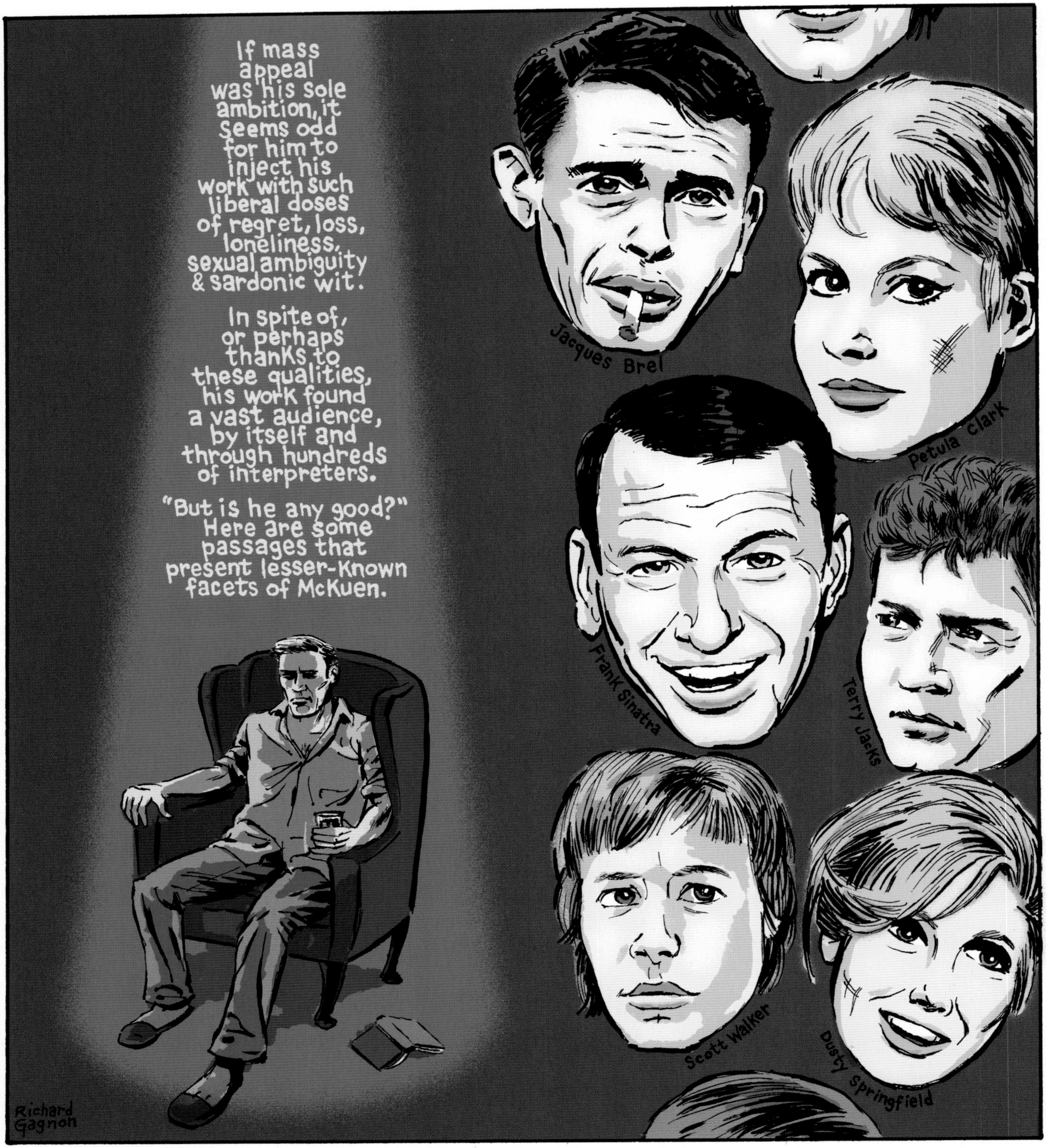
If mass appeal was his sole ambition, it seems odd for him to inject his work with such liberal doses of regret, loss, loneliness, sexual ambiguity & sardonic wit.
In spite of, or perhaps thanks to these qualities, his work found a vast audience, by itself and through hundreds of interpreters.
"But is he any good?" Here are some passages that present lesser-known facets of McKuen.
Jacques Brel
Petula Clark
Frank Sinatra
Terry Jacks
Scott Walker
Dusty Springfield
Richard Gagnon

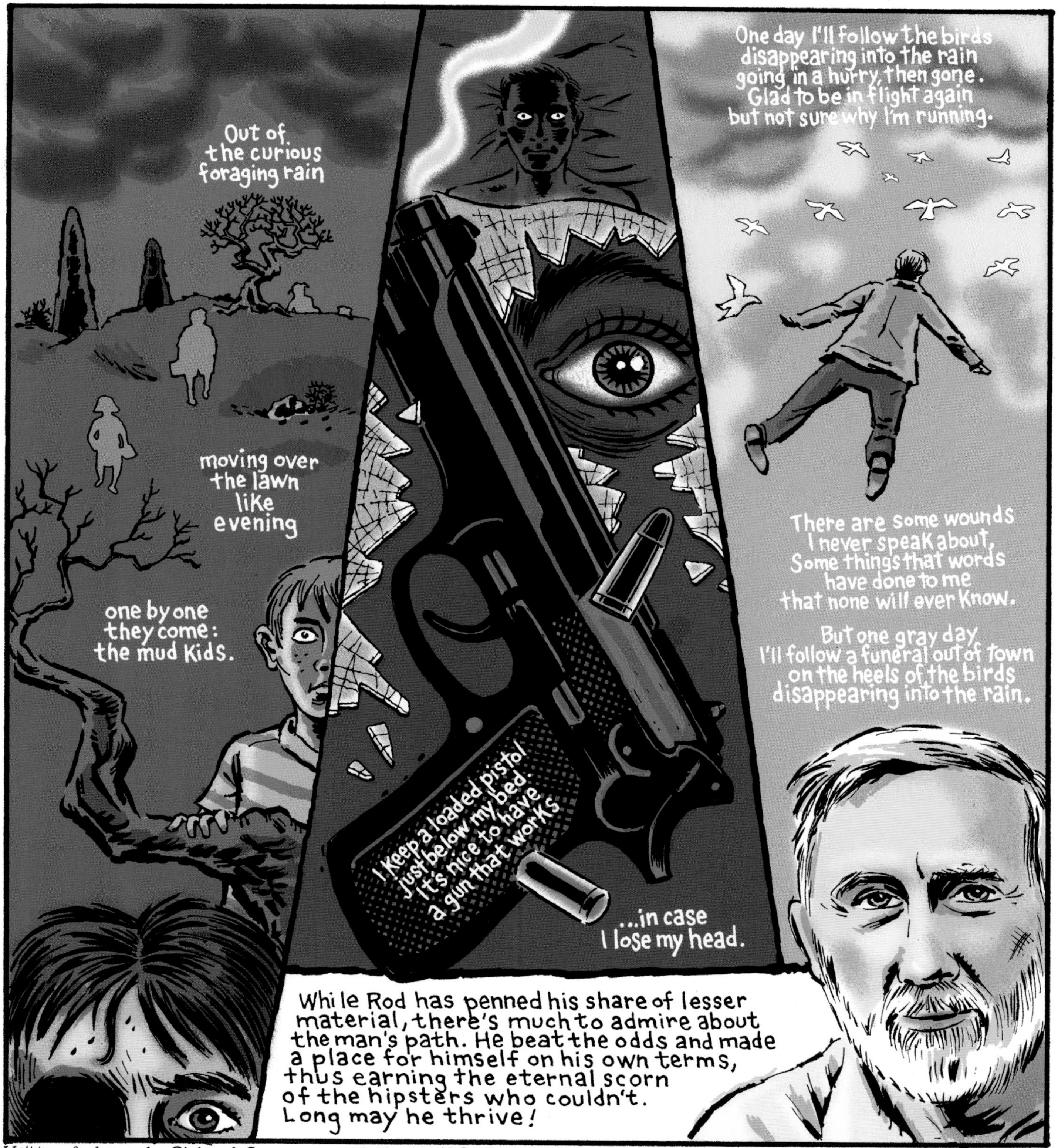
Out of the curious foraging rain
moving over the lawn like evening
one by one they come: the mud kids.
I keep a loaded pistol just below my bed. It's nice to have a gun that works
...in case I lose my head.
One day I'll follow the birds disappearing into the rain going in a hurry, then gone. Glad to be in flight again but not sure why I'm running.
There are some wounds I never speak about, Some things that words have done to me that none will ever know.
But one gray day, I'll follow a funeral out of town on the heels of the birds disappearing into the rain.
While Rod has penned his share of lesser material, there's much to admire about the man's path. He beat the odds and made a place for himself on his own terms, thus earning the eternal scorn of the hipsters who couldn't. Long may he thrive!

BOX TOP comics
BY DALTON WEBB
BLIMEY! THEY ARE AFTER ME LUCKY GERMS!
HEY! YOU AREN'T LUCKY!
OF COURSE NOT YOU BRATS!
I'M LEPROSY LEPRECHAUN!!!
MY CEREAL COMES WITH A...
TOY SURPRISE!!!
TOOT!
EEWW! IT'S A TOE!
HURK
YOU FOUND ME TOE!!!
LUCKY GERMS! ALSO COMES WITH A GIFT THAT KEEPS ON GIVING!

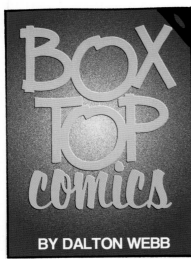

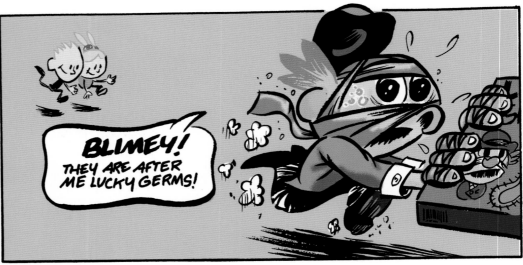

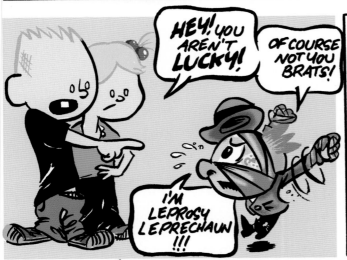

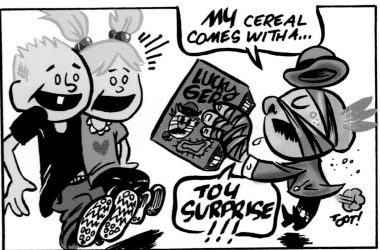

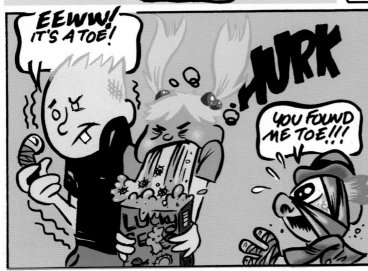

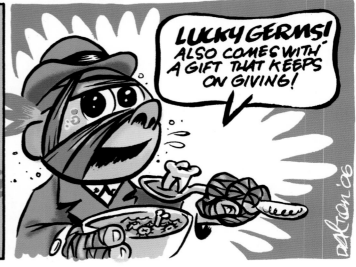

GOOPY SPASMS

BY RICK TREMBLES

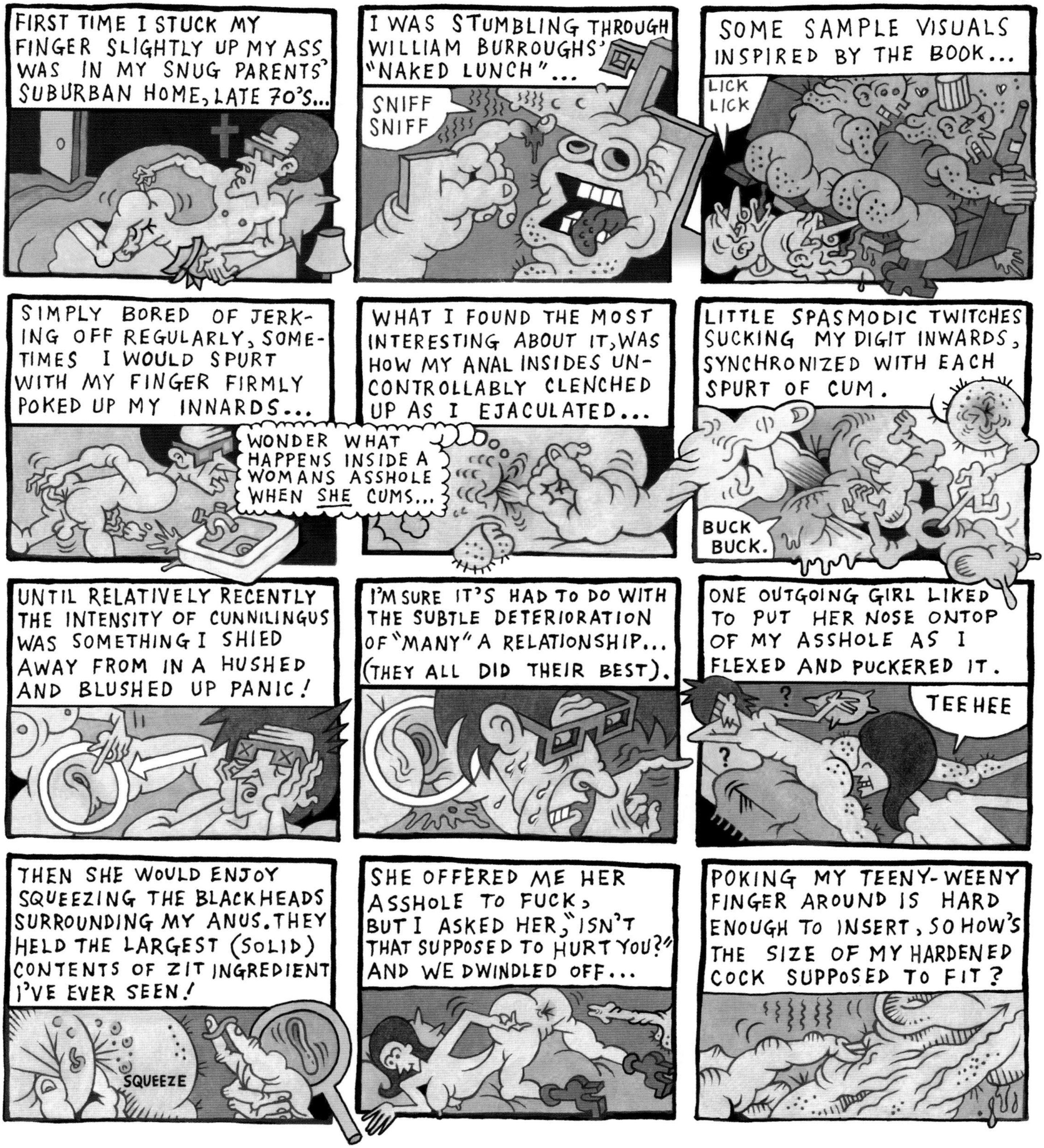
FIRST TIME I STUCK MY FINGER SLIGHTLY UP MY ASS WAS IN MY SNUG PARENTS' SUBURBAN HOME, LATE 70'S...
I WAS STUMBLING THROUGH WILLIAM BURROUGHS' "NAKED LUNCH"...
SNIFF SNIFF
SOME SAMPLE VISUALS INSPIRED BY THE BOOK...
LICK LICK
SIMPLY BORED OF JERKING OFF REGULARLY, SOMETIMES I WOULD SPURT WITH MY FINGER FIRMLY POKED UP MY INNARDS...
WONDER WHAT HAPPENS INSIDE A WOMANS ASSHOLE WHEN SHE CUMS...
WHAT I FOUND THE MOST INTERESTING ABOUT IT, WAS HOW MY ANAL INSIDES UNCONTROLLABLY CLENCHED UP AS I EJACULATED...
LITTLE SPASMODIC TWITCHES SUCKING MY DIGIT INWARDS, SYNCHRONIZED WITH EACH SPURT OF CUM.
BUCK BUCK.
UNTIL RELATIVELY RECENTLY THE INTENSITY OF CUNNILINGUS WAS SOMETHING I SHIED AWAY FROM IN A HUSHED AND BLUSHED UP PANIC!
I'M SURE IT'S HAD TO DO WITH THE SUBTLE DETERIORATION OF "MANY" A RELATIONSHIP... (THEY ALL DID THEIR BEST).
ONE OUTGOING GIRL LIKED TO PUT HER NOSE ONTOP OF MY ASSHOLE AS I FLEXED AND PUCKERED IT.
?
?
TEEHEE
THEN SHE WOULD ENJOY SQUEEZING THE BLACKHEADS SURROUNDING MY ANUS. THEY HELD THE LARGEST (SOLID) CONTENTS OF ZIT INGREDIENT I'VE EVER SEEN!
SQUEEZE
SHE OFFERED ME HER ASSHOLE TO FUCK, BUT I ASKED HER, "ISN'T THAT SUPPOSED TO HURT YOU?" AND WE DWINDLED OFF...
POKING MY TEENY-WEENY FINGER AROUND IS HARD ENOUGH TO INSERT, SO HOW'S THE SIZE OF MY HARDENED COCK SUPPOSED TO FIT?

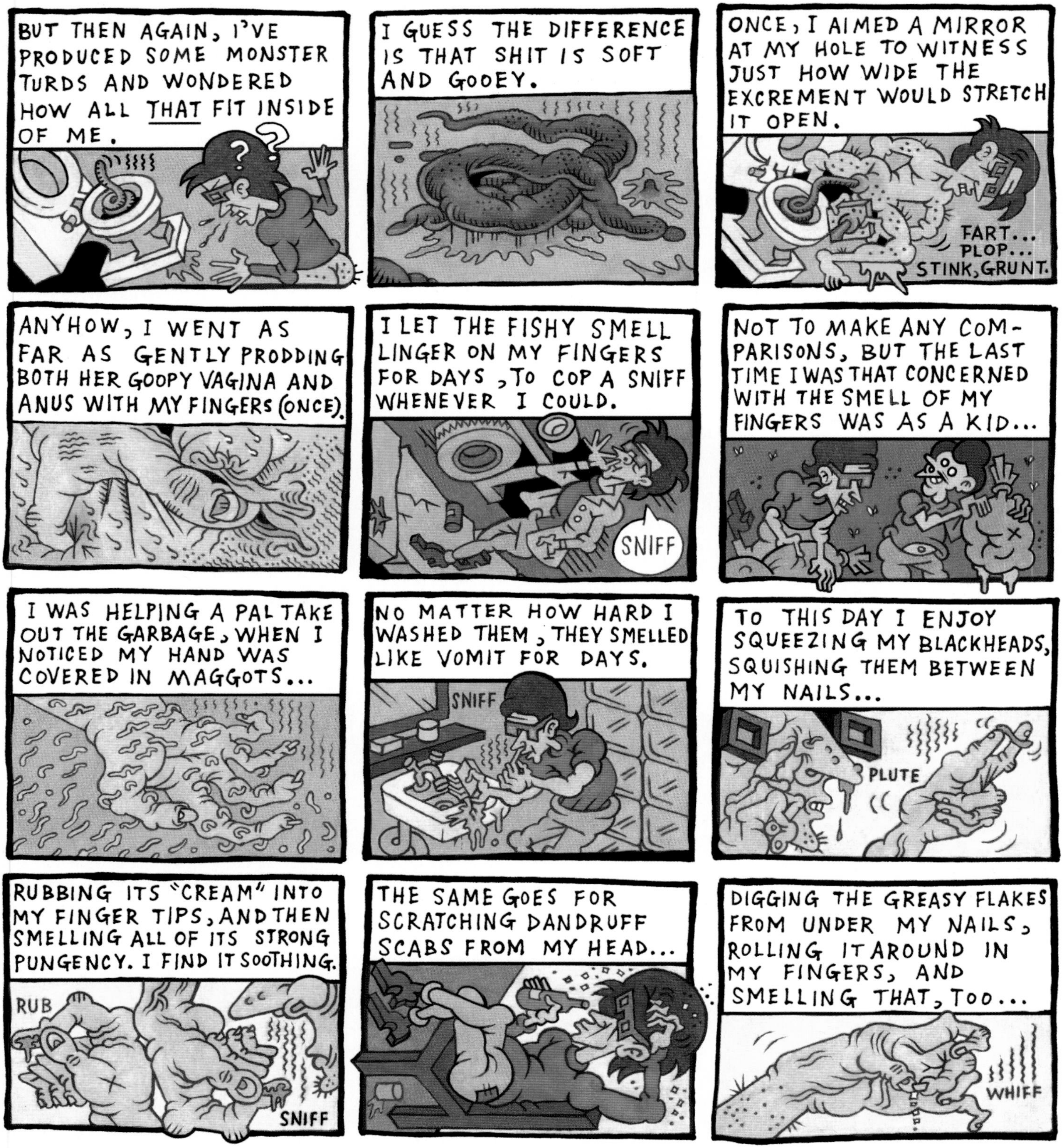
BUT THEN AGAIN, I'VE PRODUCED SOME MONSTER TURDS AND WONDERED HOW ALL THAT FIT INSIDE OF ME.
I GUESS THE DIFFERENCE IS THAT SHIT IS SOFT AND GOOEY.
ONCE, I AIMED A MIRROR AT MY HOLE TO WITNESS JUST HOW WIDE THE EXCREMENT WOULD STRETCH IT OPEN.
FART... PLOP... STINK, GRUNT.
ANYHOW, I WENT AS FAR AS GENTLY PRODDING BOTH HER GOOPY VAGINA AND ANUS WITH MY FINGERS (ONCE).
I LET THE FISHY SMELL LINGER ON MY FINGERS FOR DAYS, TO COP A SNIFF WHENEVER I COULD.
SNIFF
NOT TO MAKE ANY COMPARISONS, BUT THE LAST TIME I WAS THAT CONCERNED WITH THE SMELL OF MY FINGERS WAS AS A KID...
I WAS HELPING A PAL TAKE OUT THE GARBAGE, WHEN I NOTICED MY HAND WAS COVERED IN MAGGOTS...
NO MATTER HOW HARD I WASHED THEM, THEY SMELLED LIKE VOMIT FOR DAYS.
SNIFF
TO THIS DAY I ENJOY SQUEEZING MY BLACKHEADS, SQUISHING THEM BETWEEN MY NAILS...
PLUTE
RUBBING ITS "CREAM" INTO MY FINGER TIPS, AND THEN SMELLING ALL OF ITS STRONG PUNGENCY. I FIND IT SOOTHING.
RUB
SNIFF
THE SAME GOES FOR SCRATCHING DANDRUFF SCABS FROM MY HEAD...
DIGGING THE GREASY FLAKES FROM UNDER MY NAILS, ROLLING IT AROUND IN MY FINGERS, AND SMELLING THAT, TOO...
WHIFF

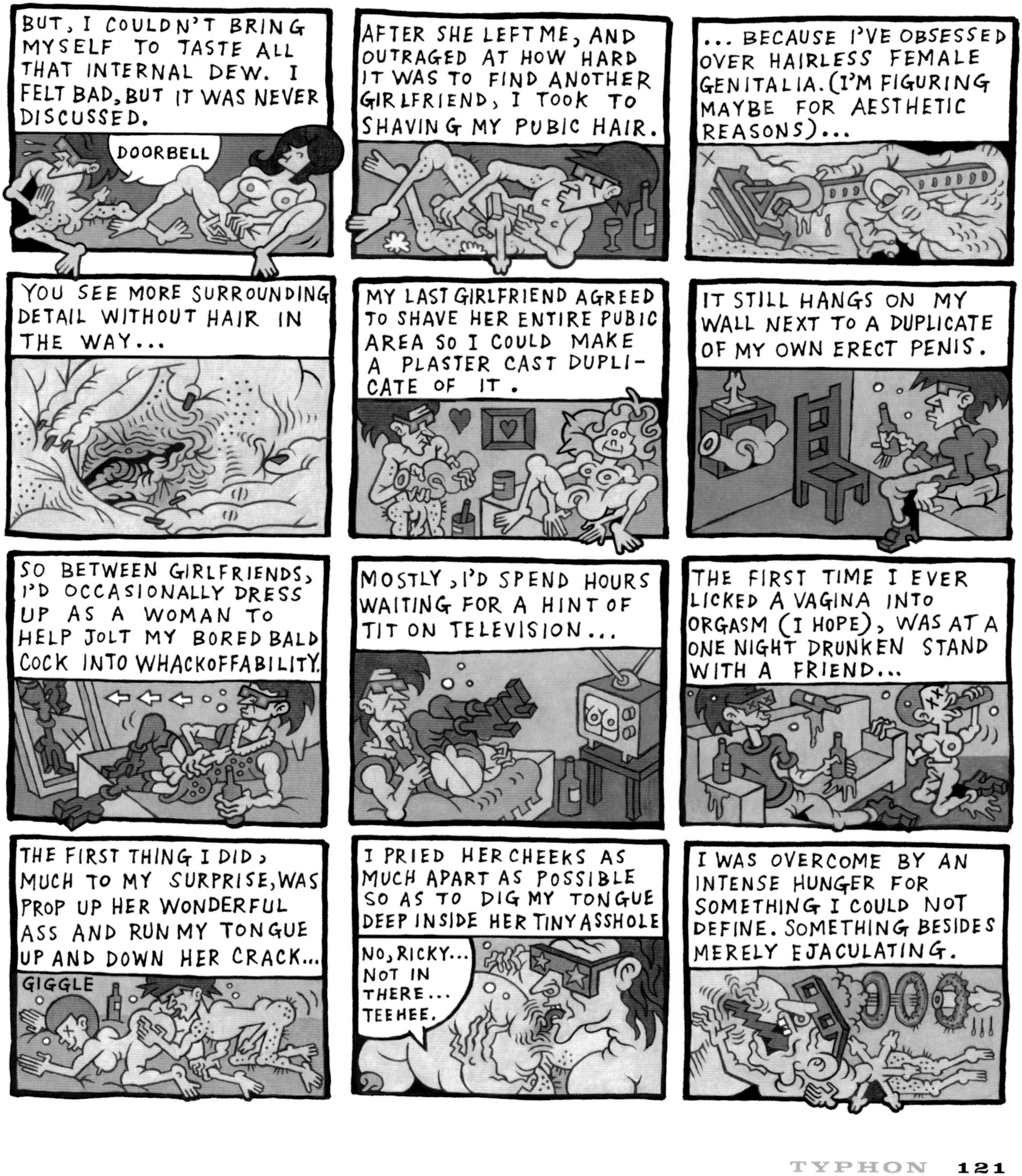
BUT, I COULDN'T BRING MYSELF TO TASTE ALL THAT INTERNAL DEW. I FELT BAD, BUT IT WAS NEVER DISCUSSED.
DOORBELL
AFTER SHE LEFT ME, AND OUTRAGED AT HOW HARD IT WAS TO FIND ANOTHER GIRLFRIEND, I TOOK TO SHAVING MY PUBIC HAIR.
... BECAUSE I'VE OBSESSED OVER HAIRLESS FEMALE GENITALIA. (I'M FIGURING MAYBE FOR AESTHETIC REASONS)...
YOU SEE MORE SURROUNDING DETAIL WITHOUT HAIR IN THE WAY...
MY LAST GIRLFRIEND AGREED TO SHAVE HER ENTIRE PUBIC AREA SO I COULD MAKE A PLASTER CAST DUPLICATE OF IT.
IT STILL HANGS ON MY WALL NEXT TO A DUPLICATE OF MY OWN ERECT PENIS.
SO BETWEEN GIRLFRIENDS, I'D OCCASIONALLY DRESS UP AS A WOMAN TO HELP JOLT MY BORED BALD COCK INTO WHACKOFFABILITY.
MOSTLY, I'D SPEND HOURS WAITING FOR A HINT OF TIT ON TELEVISION...
THE FIRST TIME I EVER LICKED A VAGINA INTO ORGASM (I HOPE), WAS AT A ONE NIGHT DRUNKEN STAND WITH A FRIEND...
THE FIRST THING I DID, MUCH TO MY SURPRISE, WAS PROP UP HER WONDERFUL ASS AND RUN MY TONGUE UP AND DOWN HER CRACK...
GIGGLE
I PRIED HER CHEEKS AS MUCH APART AS POSSIBLE SO AS TO DIG MY TONGUE DEEP INSIDE HER TINY ASSHOLE
NO, RICKY... NOT IN THERE... TEEHEE.
I WAS OVERCOME BY AN INTENSE HUNGER FOR SOMETHING I COULD NOT DEFINE. SOMETHING BESIDES MERELY EJACULATING.

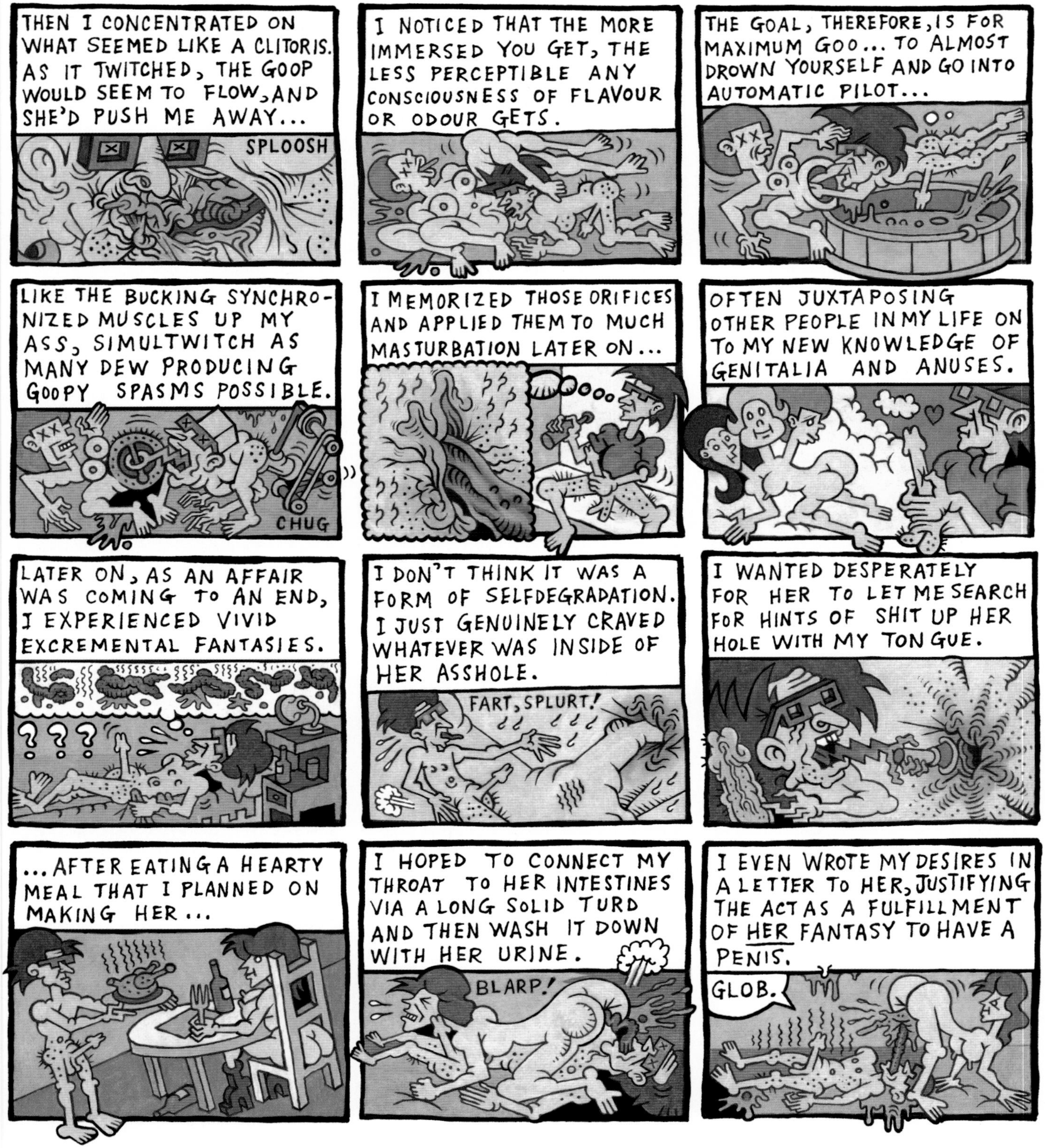
THEN I CONCENTRATED ON WHAT SEEMED LIKE A CLITORIS. AS IT TWITCHED, THE GOOP WOULD SEEM TO FLOW, AND SHE'D PUSH ME AWAY...
SPLOOSH
I NOTICED THAT THE MORE IMMERSED YOU GET, THE LESS PERCEPTIBLE ANY CONSCIOUSNESS OF FLAVOUR OR ODOUR GETS.
THE GOAL, THEREFORE, IS FOR MAXIMUM GOO... TO ALMOST DROWN YOURSELF AND GO INTO AUTOMATIC PILOT...
LIKE THE BUCKING SYNCHRONIZED MUSCLES UP MY ASS, SIMULTWITCH AS MANY DEW PRODUCING GOOPY SPASMS POSSIBLE.
CHUG
I MEMORIZED THOSE ORIFICES AND APPLIED THEM TO MUCH MASTURBATION LATER ON...
OFTEN JUXTAPOSING OTHER PEOPLE IN MY LIFE ON TO MY NEW KNOWLEDGE OF GENITALIA AND ANUSES.
LATER ON, AS AN AFFAIR WAS COMING TO AN END, I EXPERIENCED VIVID EXCREMENTAL FANTASIES.
???
I DON'T THINK IT WAS A FORM OF SELFDEGRADATION. I JUST GENUINELY CRAVED WHATEVER WAS INSIDE OF HER ASSHOLE.
FART, SPLURT!
I WANTED DESPERATELY FOR HER TO LET ME SEARCH FOR HINTS OF SHIT UP HER HOLE WITH MY TONGUE.
...AFTER EATING A HEARTY MEAL THAT I PLANNED ON MAKING HER...
I HOPED TO CONNECT MY THROAT TO HER INTESTINES VIA A LONG SOLID TURD AND THEN WASH IT DOWN WITH HER URINE.
BLARP!
I EVEN WROTE MY DESIRES IN A LETTER TO HER, JUSTIFYING THE ACT AS A FULFILLMENT OF HER FANTASY TO HAVE A PENIS.
GLOB.

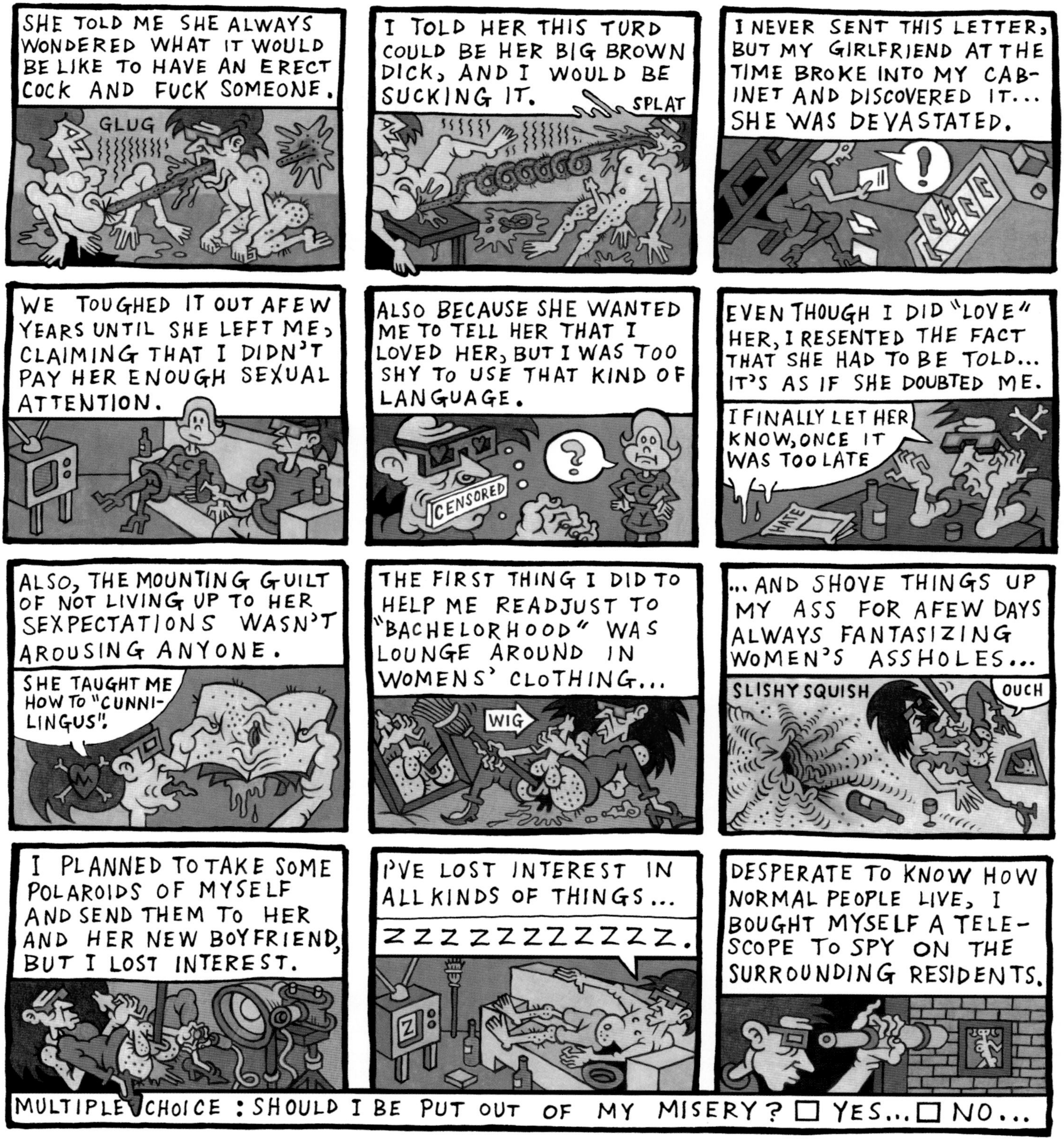
SHE TOLD ME SHE ALWAYS WONDERED WHAT IT WOULD BE LIKE TO HAVE AN ERECT COCK AND FUCK SOMEONE.
GLUG
I TOLD HER THIS TURD COULD BE HER BIG BROWN DICK, AND I WOULD BE SUCKING IT.
SPLAT
I NEVER SENT THIS LETTER, BUT MY GIRLFRIEND AT THE TIME BROKE INTO MY CABINET AND DISCOVERED IT... SHE WAS DEVASTATED.
!
WE TOUGHED IT OUT AFEW YEARS UNTIL SHE LEFT ME, CLAIMING THAT I DIDN'T PAY HER ENOUGH SEXUAL ATTENTION.
ALSO BECAUSE SHE WANTED ME TO TELL HER THAT I LOVED HER, BUT I WAS TOO SHY TO USE THAT KIND OF LANGUAGE.
CENSORED
?
EVEN THOUGH I DID "LOVE" HER, I RESENTED THE FACT THAT SHE HAD TO BE TOLD... IT'S AS IF SHE DOUBTED ME.
I FINALLY LET HER KNOW, ONCE IT WAS TOO LATE
HATE
ALSO, THE MOUNTING GUILT OF NOT LIVING UP TO HER SEXPECTATIONS WASN'T AROUSING ANYONE.
SHE TAUGHT ME HOW TO "CUNNILINGUS".
THE FIRST THING I DID TO HELP ME READJUST TO "BACHELORHOOD" WAS LOUNGE AROUND IN WOMENS' CLOTHING...
WIG
...AND SHOVE THINGS UP MY ASS FOR AFEW DAYS ALWAYS FANTASIZING WOMEN'S ASSHOLES...
SLISHY SQUISH
OUCH
I PLANNED TO TAKE SOME POLAROIDS OF MYSELF AND SEND THEM TO HER AND HER NEW BOYFRIEND, BUT I LOST INTEREST.
I'VE LOST INTEREST IN ALL KINDS OF THINGS...
ZZZZZZZZZZZZ.
DESPERATE TO KNOW HOW NORMAL PEOPLE LIVE, I BOUGHT MYSELF A TELESCOPE TO SPY ON THE SURROUNDING RESIDENTS.
MULTIPLE CHOICE: SHOULD I BE PUT OUT OF MY MISERY? ☐ YES... ☐ NO...

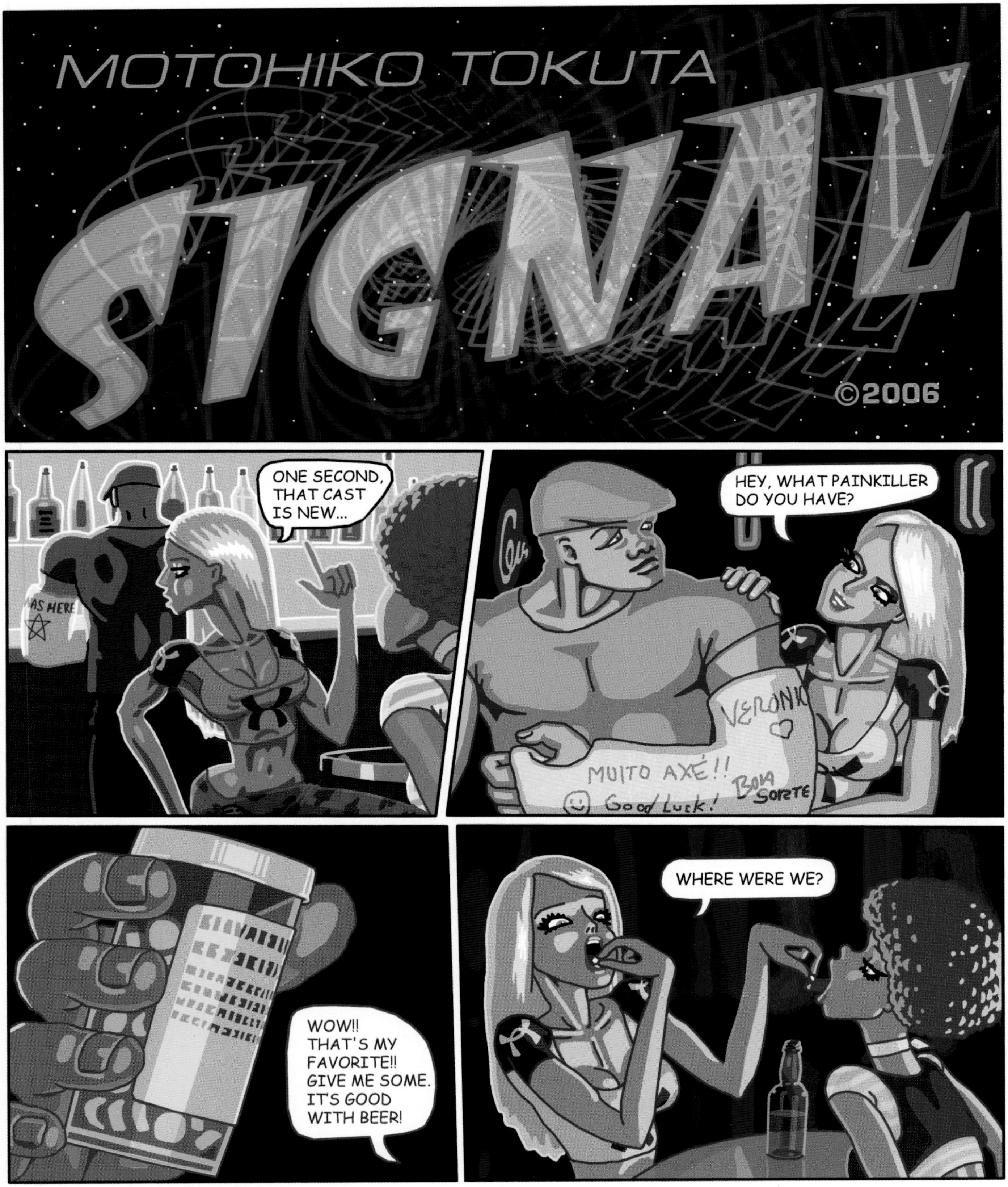
MOTOHIKO TOKUTA
SIGNAL
©2006
ONE SECOND, THAT CAST IS NEW...
HEY, WHAT PAINKILLER DO YOU HAVE?
VERONIC
MUITO AXÉ!!
Good Luck!
BOA SORTE
WOW!! THAT'S MY FAVORITE!! GIVE ME SOME. IT'S GOOD WITH BEER!
WHERE WERE WE?

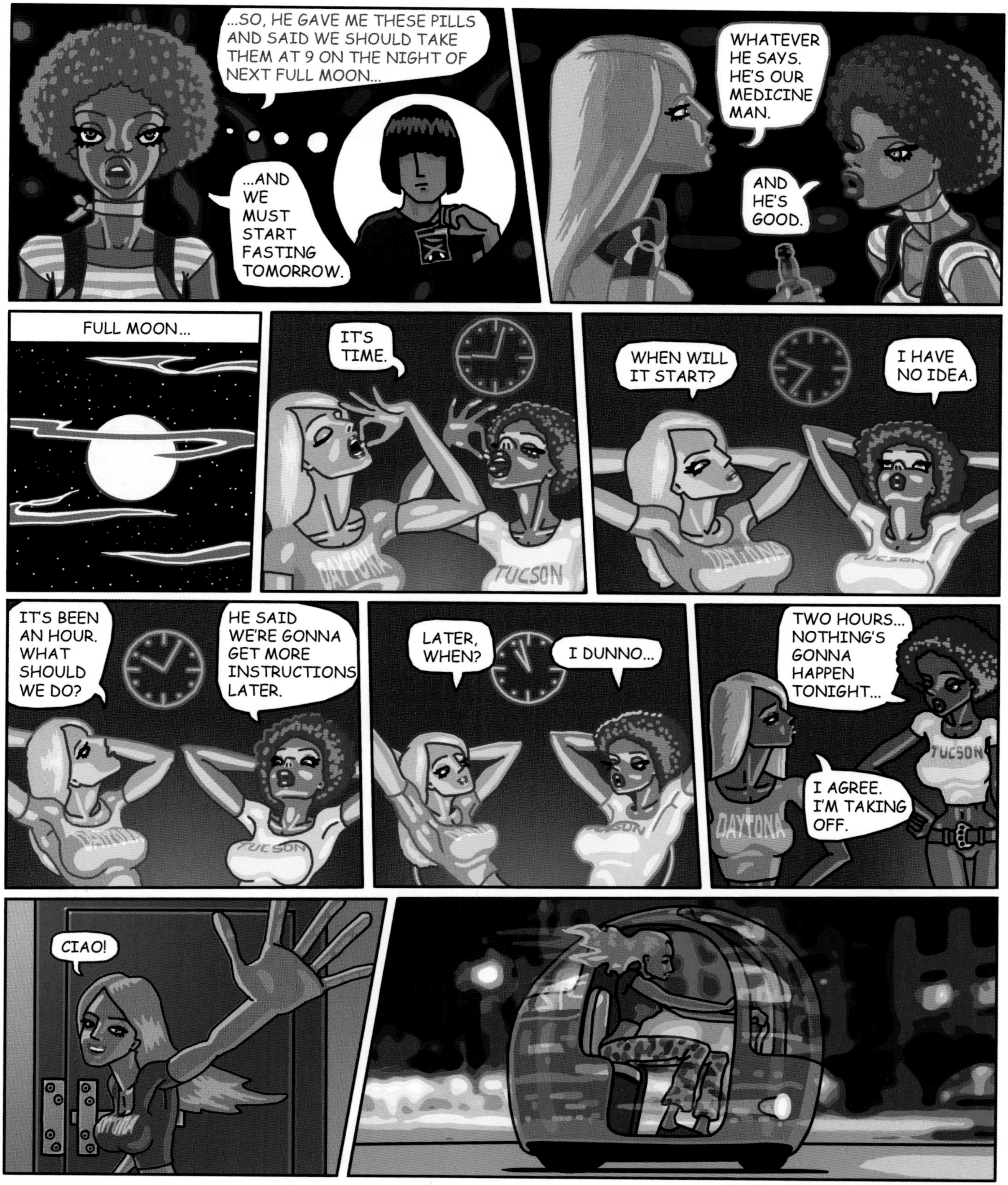

...SO, HE GAVE ME THESE PILLS AND SAID WE SHOULD TAKE THEM AT 9 ON THE NIGHT OF NEXT FULL MOON...
...AND WE MUST START FASTING TOMORROW.
WHATEVER HE SAYS. HE'S OUR MEDICINE MAN.
AND HE'S GOOD.
FULL MOON...
IT'S TIME.
DAYTONA
TUCSON
WHEN WILL IT START?
I HAVE NO IDEA.
IT'S BEEN AN HOUR. WHAT SHOULD WE DO?
HE SAID WE'RE GONNA GET MORE INSTRUCTIONS LATER.
LATER, WHEN?
I DUNNO...
TWO HOURS... NOTHING'S GONNA HAPPEN TONIGHT...
I AGREE. I'M TAKING OFF.
CIAO!

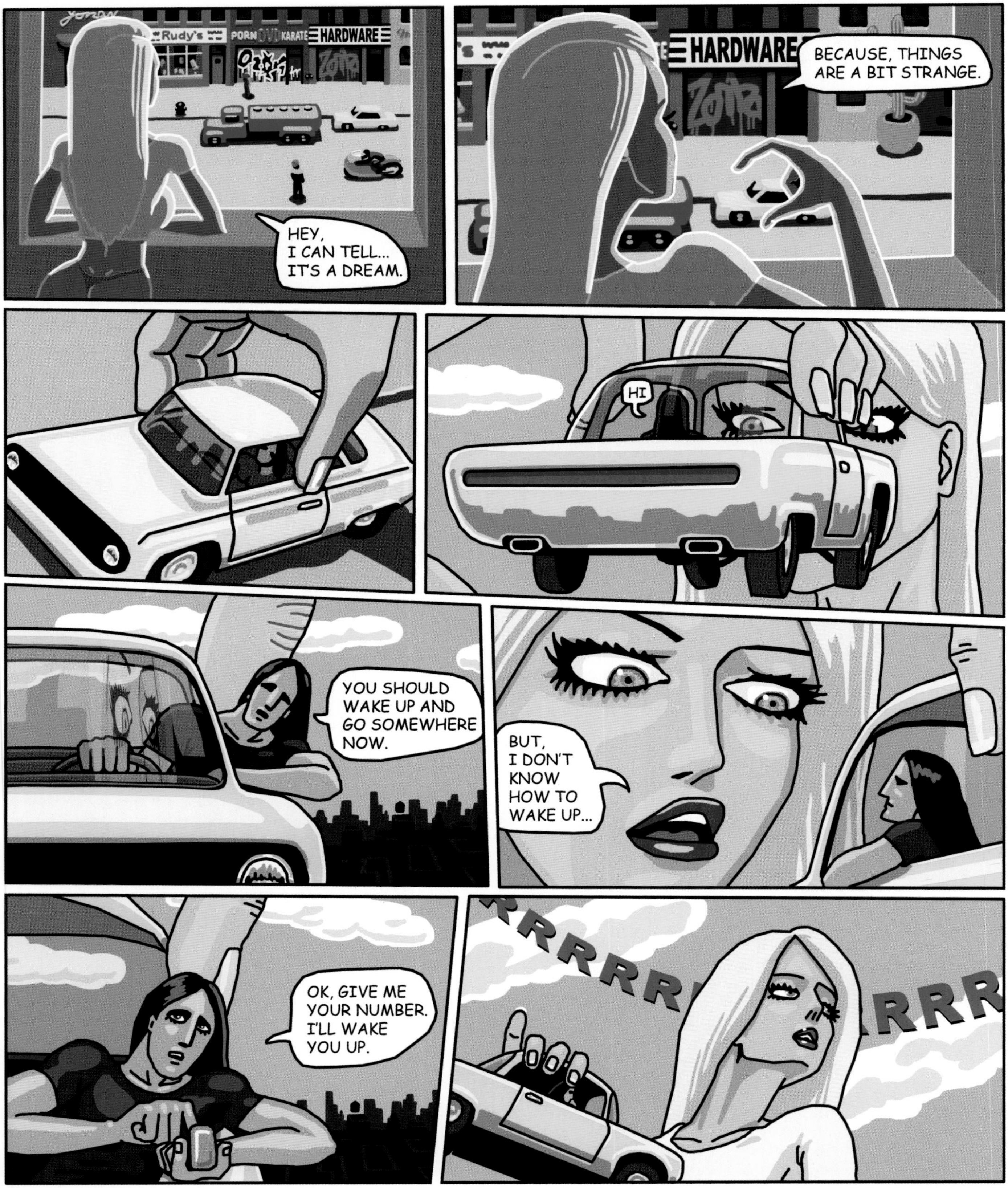
Rudy's
PORN DVD KARATE
HARDWARE
HEY,
I CAN TELL...
IT'S A DREAM.
BECAUSE, THINGS
ARE A BIT STRANGE.
HI
YOU SHOULD
WAKE UP AND
GO SOMEWHERE
NOW.
BUT,
I DON'T
KNOW
HOW TO
WAKE UP...
OK, GIVE ME
YOUR NUMBER.
I'LL WAKE
YOU UP.
RRRRRRRRR

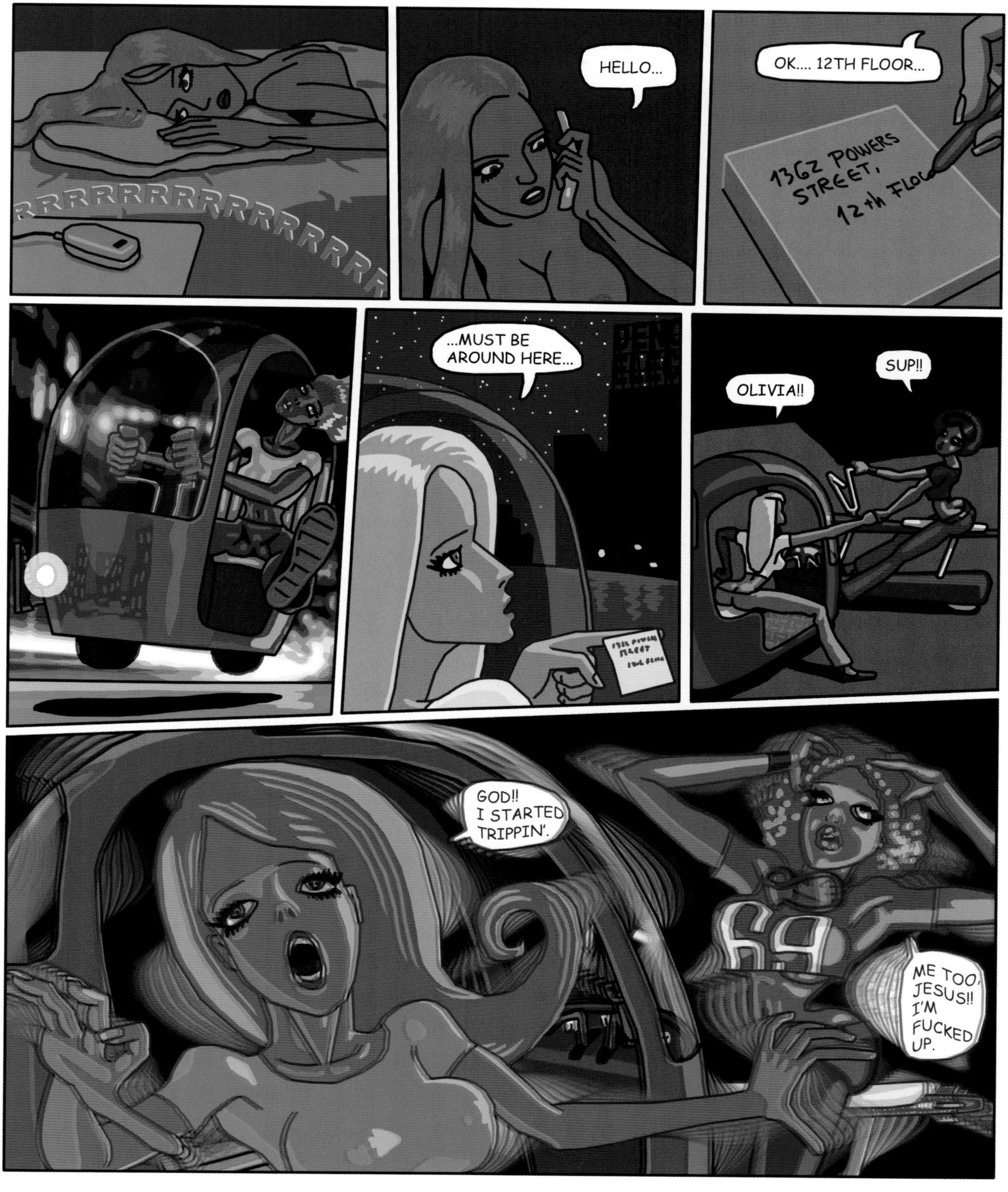
RRRRRRRRRRRRRRRRRRRR
HELLO...
OK.... 12TH FLOOR...
1362 POWERS STREET, 12th FLO
...MUST BE AROUND HERE...
OLIVIA!!
SUP!!
GOD!! I STARTED TRIPPIN'.
ME TOO, JESUS!! I'M FUCKED UP.

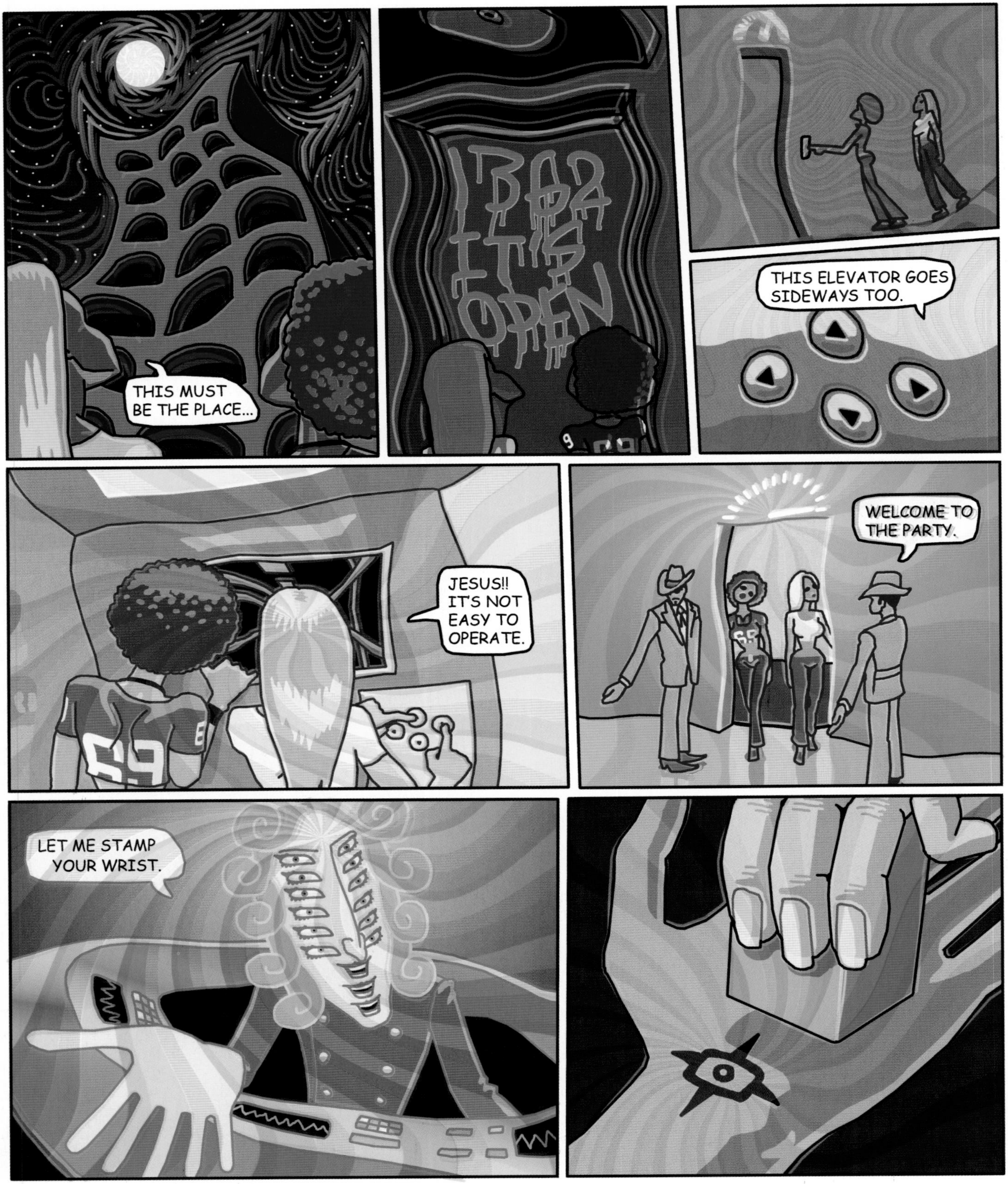
THIS MUST BE THE PLACE...
IT IS OPEN
THIS ELEVATOR GOES SIDEWAYS TOO.
JESUS!! IT'S NOT EASY TO OPERATE.
WELCOME TO THE PARTY.
LET ME STAMP YOUR WRIST.

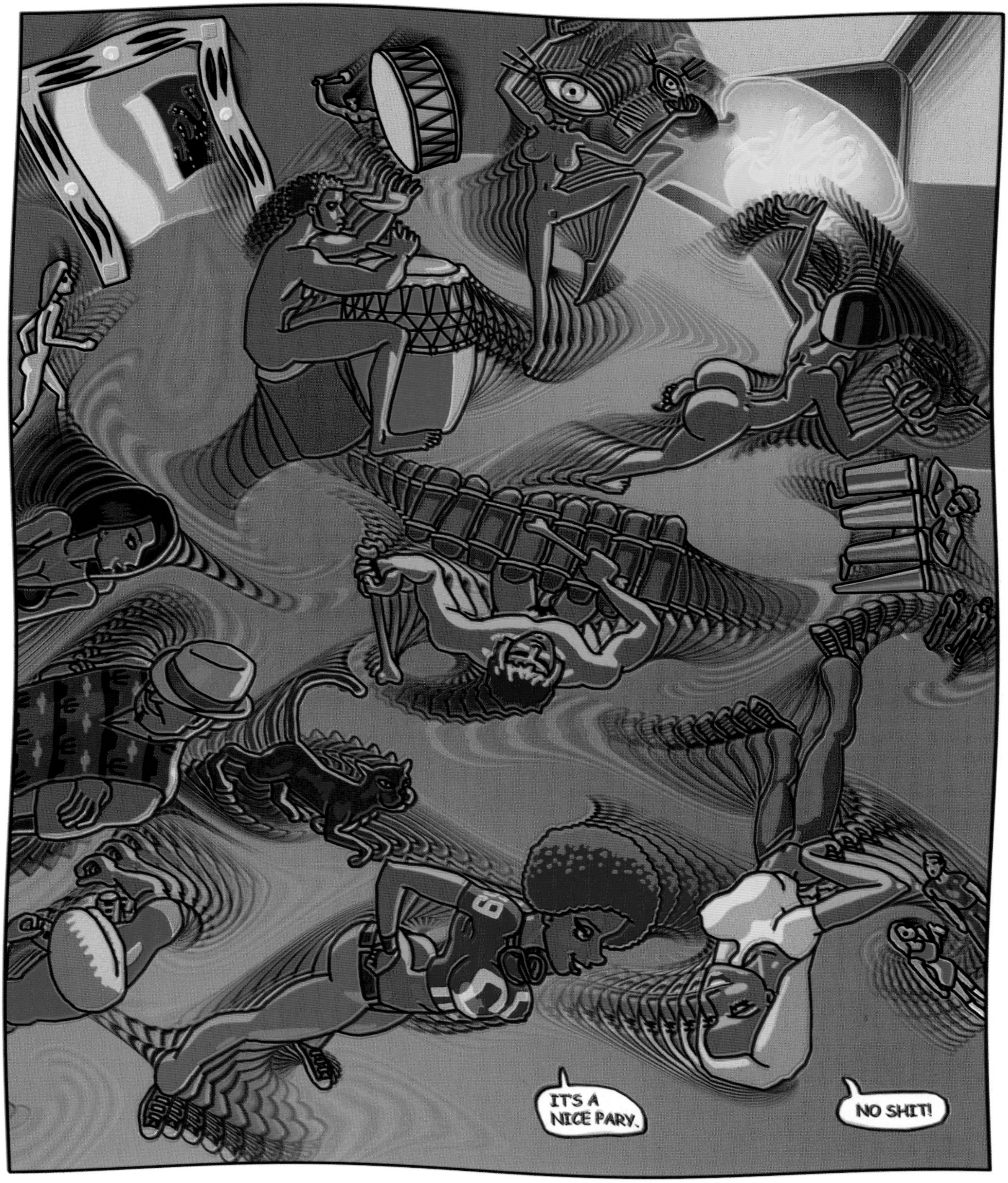
IT'S A NICE PARY.
NO SHIT!

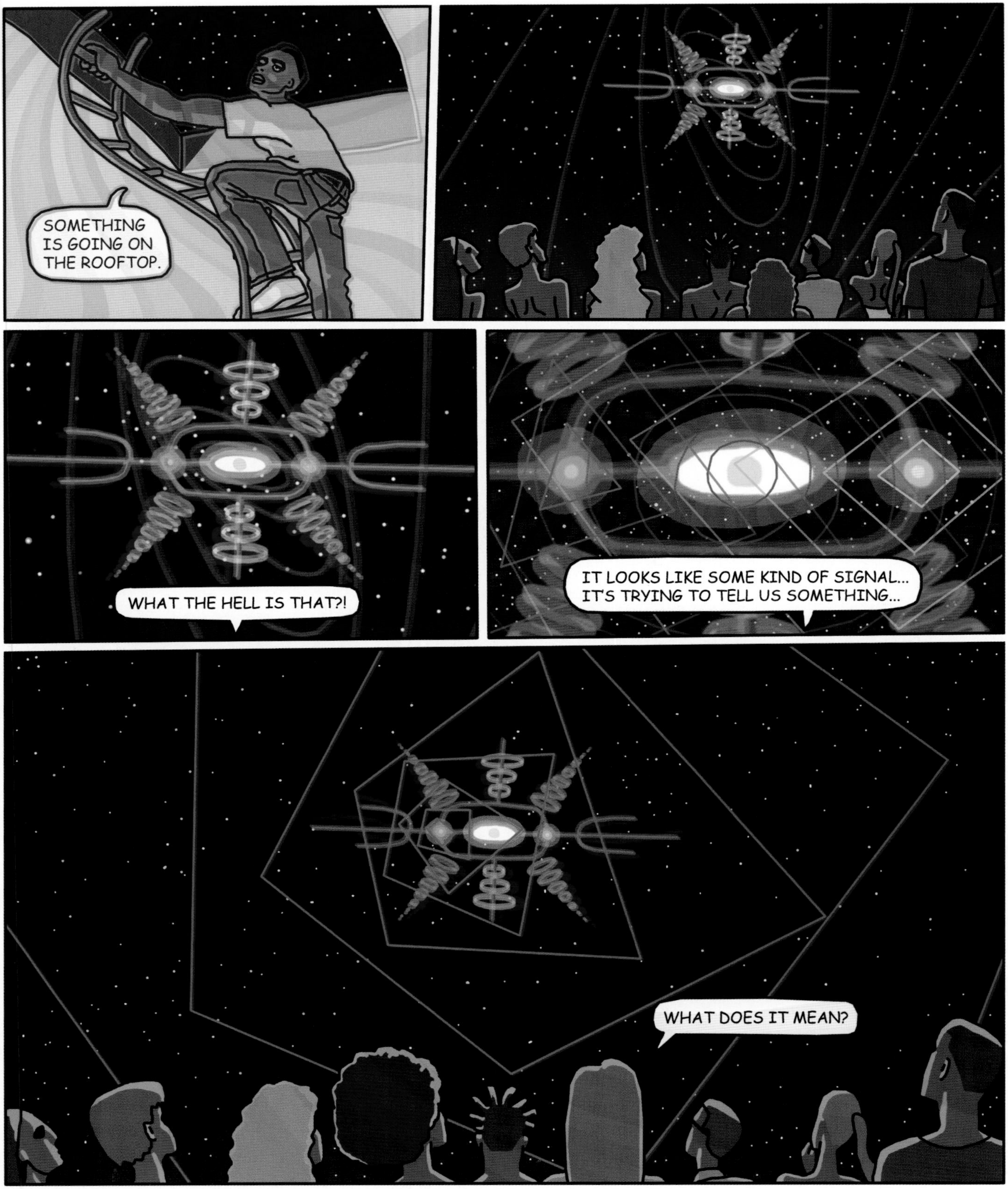
SOMETHING IS GOING ON THE ROOFTOP.
WHAT THE HELL IS THAT?!
IT LOOKS LIKE SOME KIND OF SIGNAL... IT'S TRYING TO TELL US SOMETHING...
WHAT DOES IT MEAN?

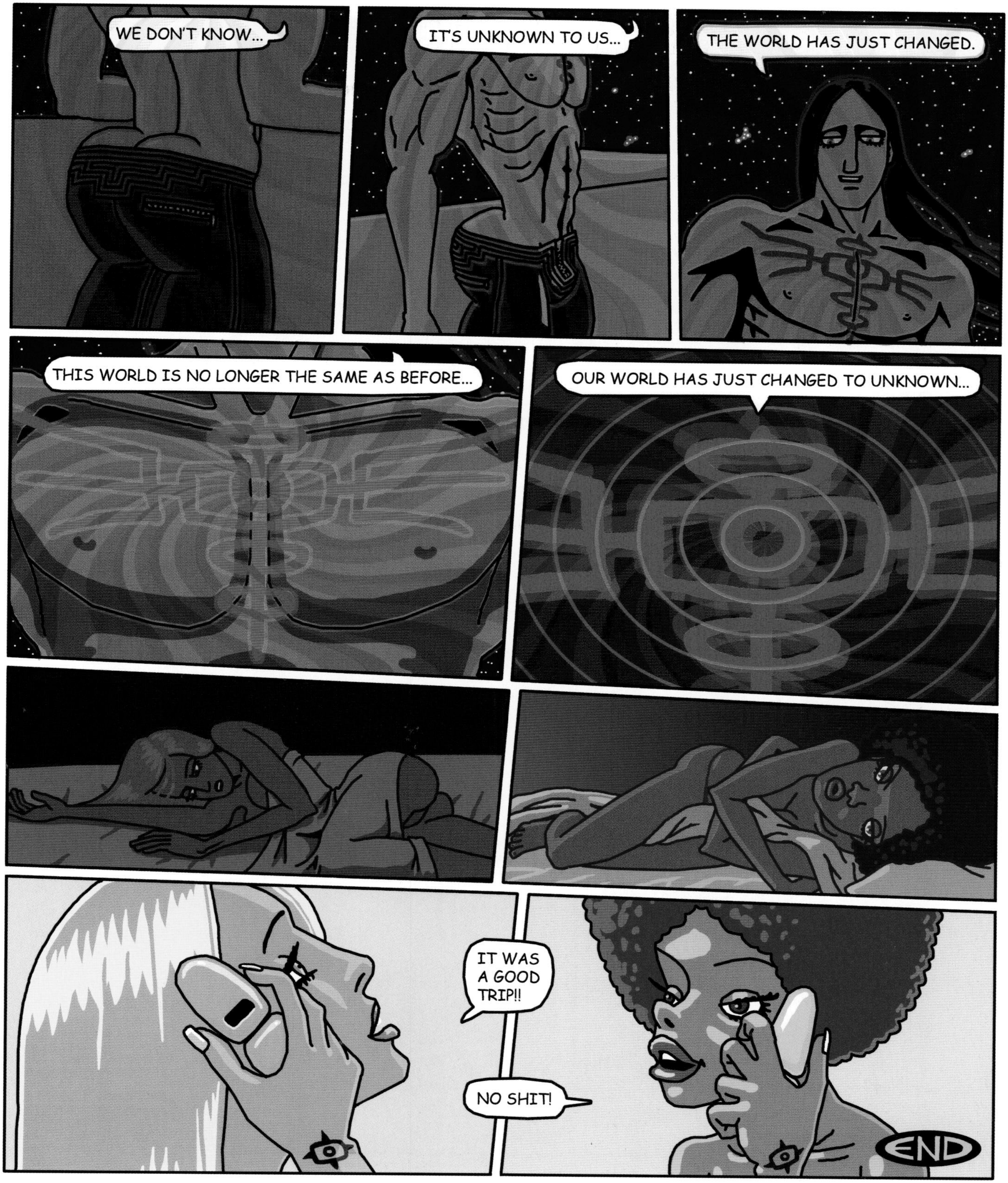
WE DON'T KNOW...
IT'S UNKNOWN TO US...
THE WORLD HAS JUST CHANGED.
THIS WORLD IS NO LONGER THE SAME AS BEFORE...
OUR WORLD HAS JUST CHANGED TO UNKNOWN...
IT WAS A GOOD TRIP!!
NO SHIT!
END

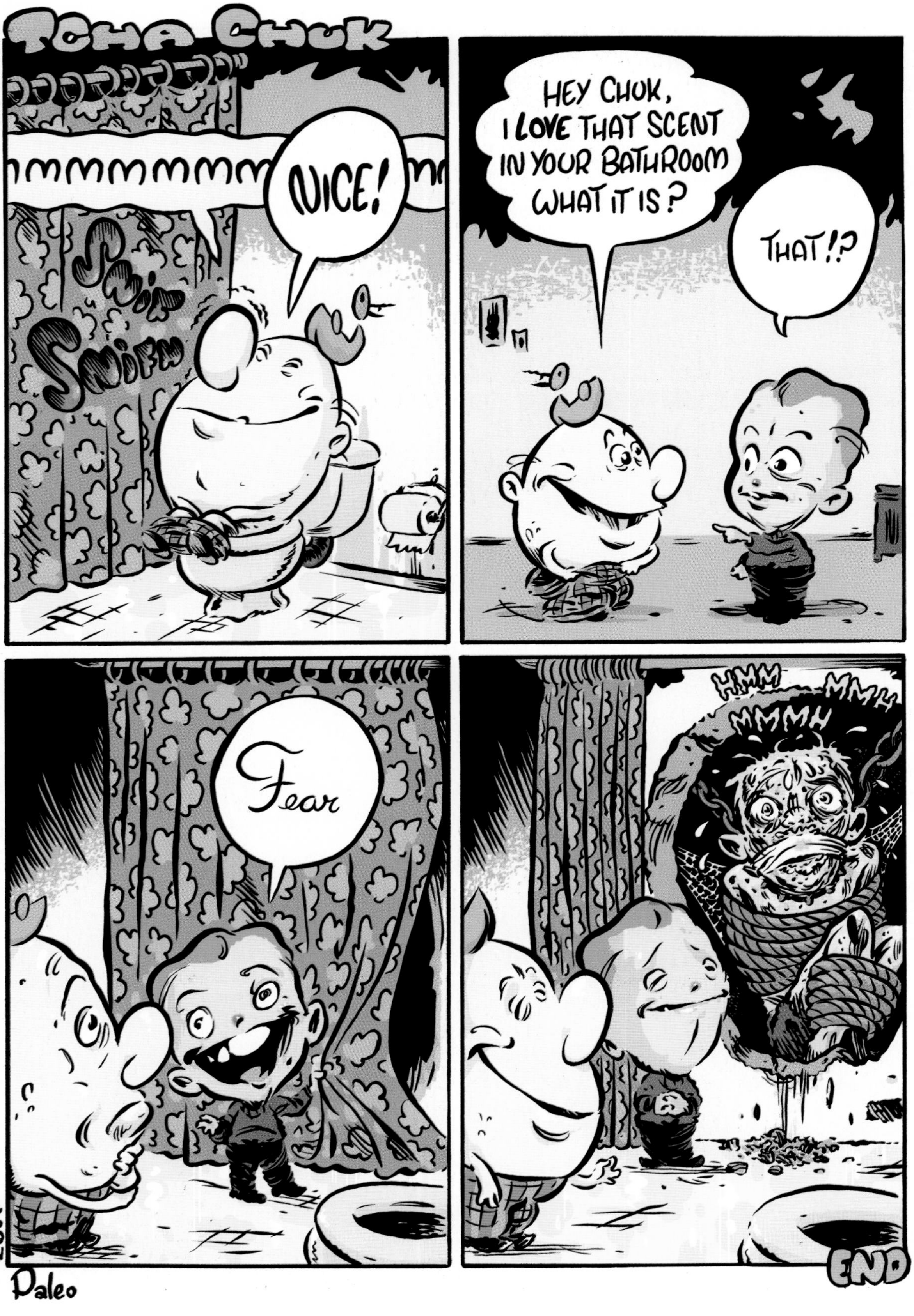
TCHA CHUK
NICE!
HEY CHUK, I LOVE THAT SCENT IN YOUR BATHROOM WHAT IT IS?
THAT!?
Fear
HMM
MMH
MMMH
END
2007
Paleo

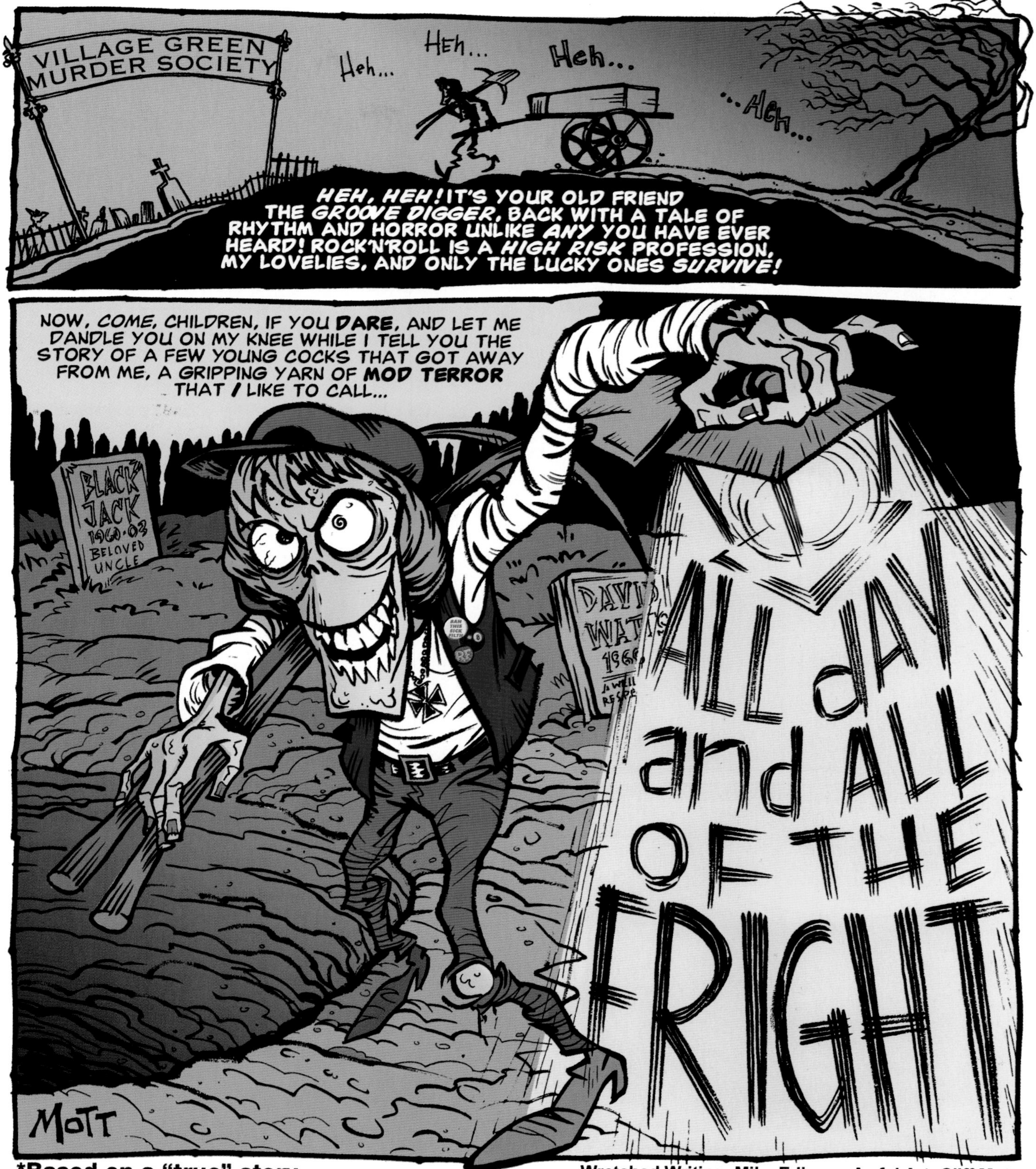
VILLAGE GREEN MURDER SOCIETY
Heh...
Heh...
Heh...
...Heh...
HEH, HEH! IT'S YOUR OLD FRIEND THE GROOVE DIGGER, BACK WITH A TALE OF RHYTHM AND HORROR UNLIKE ANY YOU HAVE EVER HEARD! ROCK'N'ROLL IS A HIGH RISK PROFESSION, MY LOVELIES, AND ONLY THE LUCKY ONES SURVIVE!
NOW, COME, CHILDREN, IF YOU DARE, AND LET ME DANDLE YOU ON MY KNEE WHILE I TELL YOU THE STORY OF A FEW YOUNG COCKS THAT GOT AWAY FROM ME, A GRIPPING YARN OF MOD TERROR THAT I LIKE TO CALL...
BLACK JACK 1960-03 BELOVED UNCLE
ALL DAY and ALL OF THE FRIGHT
MOTT

*Based on a "true" story.

Wretched Writing: Mike Edison • Awful Art: Cliff Mott

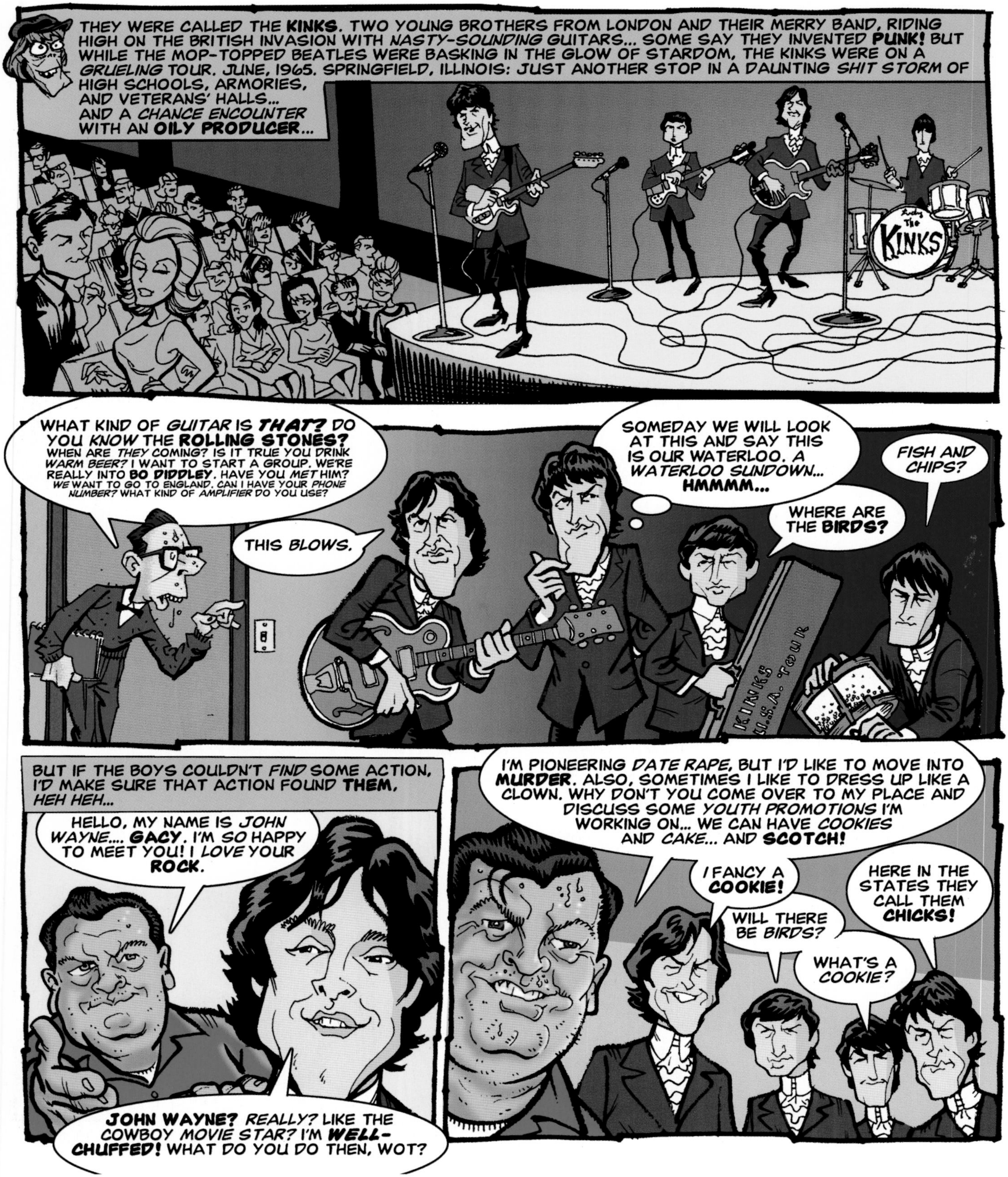
THEY WERE CALLED THE KINKS. TWO YOUNG BROTHERS FROM LONDON AND THEIR MERRY BAND, RIDING HIGH ON THE BRITISH INVASION WITH NASTY-SOUNDING GUITARS... SOME SAY THEY INVENTED PUNK! BUT WHILE THE MOP-TOPPED BEATLES WERE BASKING IN THE GLOW OF STARDOM, THE KINKS WERE ON A GRUELING TOUR. JUNE, 1965. SPRINGFIELD, ILLINOIS: JUST ANOTHER STOP IN A DAUNTING SHIT STORM OF HIGH SCHOOLS, ARMORIES, AND VETERANS' HALLS... AND A CHANCE ENCOUNTER WITH AN OILY PRODUCER...
THE KINKS
WHAT KIND OF GUITAR IS THAT? DO YOU KNOW THE ROLLING STONES? WHEN ARE THEY COMING? IS IT TRUE YOU DRINK WARM BEER? I WANT TO START A GROUP. WE'RE REALLY INTO BO DIDDLEY. HAVE YOU MET HIM? WE WANT TO GO TO ENGLAND. CAN I HAVE YOUR PHONE NUMBER? WHAT KIND OF AMPLIFIER DO YOU USE?
THIS BLOWS.
SOMEDAY WE WILL LOOK AT THIS AND SAY THIS IS OUR WATERLOO. A WATERLOO SUNDOWN... HMMMM...
WHERE ARE THE BIRDS?
FISH AND CHIPS?
KINKS U.S.A. TOUR
BUT IF THE BOYS COULDN'T FIND SOME ACTION, I'D MAKE SURE THAT ACTION FOUND THEM, HEH HEH...
HELLO, MY NAME IS JOHN WAYNE.... GACY. I'M SO HAPPY TO MEET YOU! I LOVE YOUR ROCK.
JOHN WAYNE? REALLY? LIKE THE COWBOY MOVIE STAR? I'M WELL-CHUFFED! WHAT DO YOU DO THEN, WOT?
I'M PIONEERING DATE RAPE, BUT I'D LIKE TO MOVE INTO MURDER. ALSO, SOMETIMES I LIKE TO DRESS UP LIKE A CLOWN. WHY DON'T YOU COME OVER TO MY PLACE AND DISCUSS SOME YOUTH PROMOTIONS I'M WORKING ON... WE CAN HAVE COOKIES AND CAKE... AND SCOTCH!
I FANCY A COOKIE!
WILL THERE BE BIRDS?
HERE IN THE STATES THEY CALL THEM CHICKS!
WHAT'S A COOKIE?

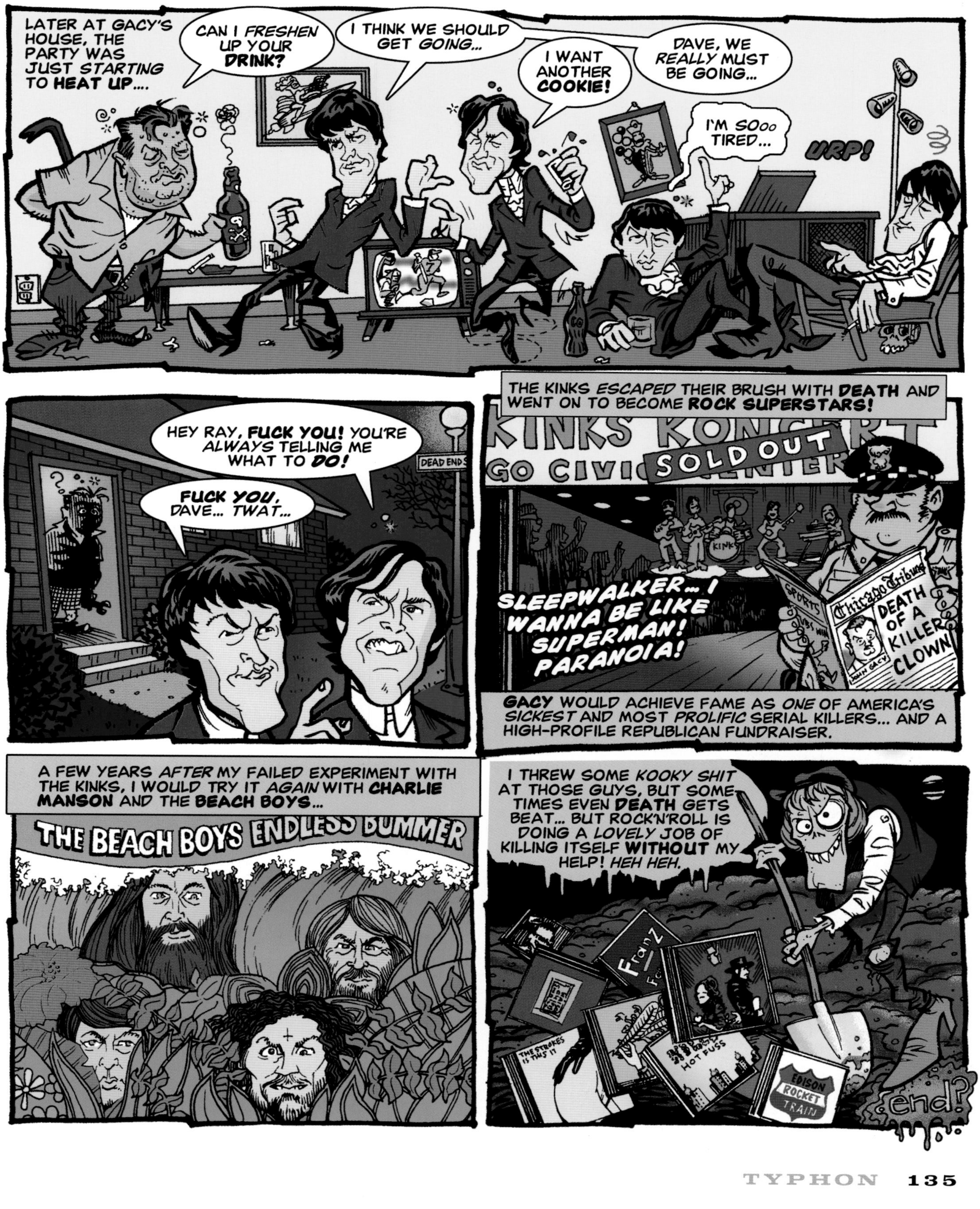

LATER AT GACY'S HOUSE, THE PARTY WAS JUST *STARTING* TO **HEAT UP**....
CAN I *FRESHEN* UP YOUR **DRINK?**
I THINK WE SHOULD GET *GOING*...
I WANT ANOTHER **COOKIE!**
DAVE, WE *REALLY* MUST BE GOING...
I'M *SO*oo TIRED...
URP!
HEY RAY, **FUCK YOU!** YOU'RE *ALWAYS* TELLING ME WHAT TO ***DO!***
FUCK *YOU*, DAVE... *TWAT*...
DEAD END
THE KINKS *ESCAPED* THEIR BRUSH WITH **DEATH** AND WENT ON TO BECOME **ROCK SUPERSTARS!**
KINKS KONCERT
GO CIVIC CENTER
SOLD OUT
KINKS
SLEEPWALKER... I WANNA BE LIKE SUPERMAN! PARANOIA!
Chicago Tribune
SPORTS
DEATH OF A KILLER CLOWN
JOHN GACY
GACY WOULD ACHIEVE FAME AS *ONE* OF AMERICA'S *SICKEST* AND MOST *PROLIFIC* SERIAL KILLERS... AND A HIGH-PROFILE REPUBLICAN FUNDRAISER.
A FEW YEARS *AFTER* MY FAILED EXPERIMENT WITH THE KINKS, I WOULD TRY IT *AGAIN* WITH **CHARLIE MANSON** AND THE **BEACH BOYS**...
THE BEACH BOYS ENDLESS BUMMER
I THREW SOME *KOOKY SHIT* AT THOSE GUYS, BUT SOMETIMES EVEN **DEATH** GETS BEAT... BUT ROCK'N'ROLL IS DOING A *LOVELY* JOB OF KILLING ITSELF **WITHOUT** MY HELP! *HEH HEH.*
Franz
THE STROKES IS THIS IT
HOT FUSS
EDISON ROCKET TRAIN
end?

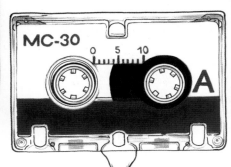

HEY DANNY LOOK WHAT I HAVE FOUND IN THE RUBBISH ...

MC-30 0 5 10 A

OH OLLIE IT'S A LITTLE TAPE RECORDER TRY TO PRESS PLAY ...

PLEASE DON'T MIND IF MY ENGLISH LANGUAGE FAILS... I AM FROM GERMANY, MY NAME IS **HANS** AND MY MESSAGE IS **ABOVE LANGUAGE**. MY MESSAGE IS PHYSICAL SCIENTIFIC REVOLUTIONARY POWER. I LEAVE MY COUNTRY TODAY...

FORWARD AMERICA! NO PROBLEMS WITH THE SECURITY CHECK. I AM NOT AN ARTIST OR A PARODIST. THAT'S WHY I'M GOING TO AMERICA... IN AMERICA I WILL FIND UNERSTANDMENT, AMERICAN BROTHERS AND SISTERS, **COMRADES**...

CLICK!

MIO

THE HANS TAPE

MY MOTHERLAND REJECTED ME. NO ONE COULD SEE. I HAD NO PROBLEMS WITH THE SECURITY CHECK BECAUSE **IT'S IN MY BLOOD. I AM THE CENTERFOLD OF GENETIC EVOLUTION.**

MY BLOOD CELLS HAVE THE SHAPE OF SWASTIKAS. THIS IS THE MOST IMPRESSIVE EXAMPLE OF INTELLIGENT DESIGN. THIS IS THE REASON FOR MY HIGH **SUPERIORITY**...

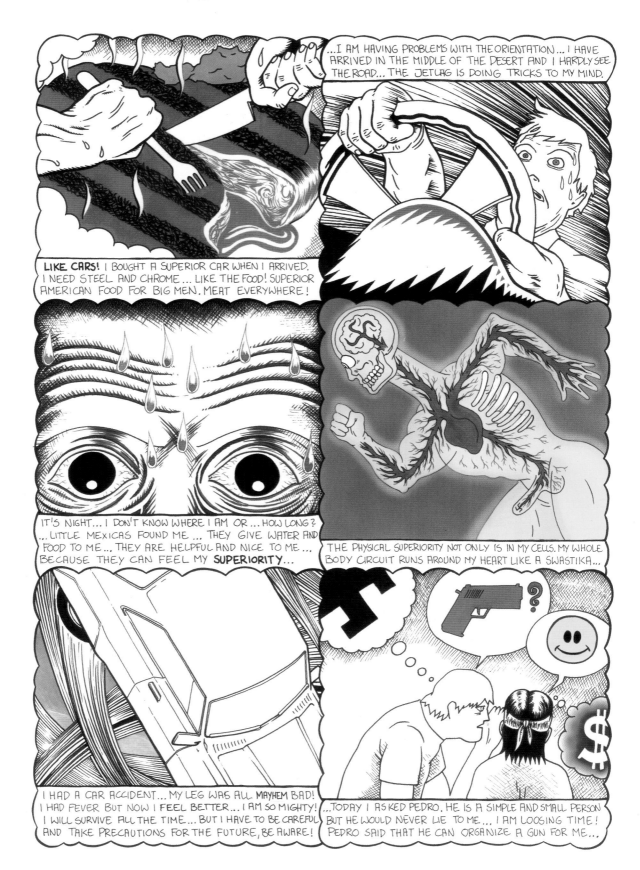

...I AM HAVING PROBLEMS WITH THE ORIENTATION... I HAVE ARRIVED IN THE MIDDLE OF THE DESERT AND I HARDLY SEE THE ROAD... THE JETLAG IS DOING TRICKS TO MY MIND.

LIKE CARS! I BOUGHT A SUPERIOR CAR WHEN I ARRIVED. I NEED STEEL AND CHROME... LIKE THE FOOD! SUPERIOR AMERICAN FOOD FOR BIG MEN. MEAT EVERYWHERE!

IT'S NIGHT... I DON'T KNOW WHERE I AM OR... HOW LONG? ...LITTLE MEXICAS FOUND ME... THEY GIVE WATER AND FOOD TO ME... THEY ARE HELPFUL AND NICE TO ME... BECAUSE THEY CAN FEEL MY SUPERIORITY...

THE PHYSICAL SUPERIORITY NOT ONLY IS IN MY CELLS. MY WHOLE BODY CIRCUIT RUNS AROUND MY HEART LIKE A SWASTIKA...

I HAD A CAR ACCIDENT... MY LEG WAS ALL MAYHEM BAD! I HAD FEVER BUT NOW I FEEL BETTER... I AM SO MIGHTY! I WILL SURVIVE ALL THE TIME... BUT I HAVE TO BE CAREFUL AND TAKE PRECAUTIONS FOR THE FUTURE, BE AWARE!

...TODAY I ASKED PEDRO. HE IS A SIMPLE AND SMALL PERSON BUT HE WOULD NEVER LIE TO ME... I AM LOOSING TIME! PEDRO SAID THAT HE CAN ORGANIZE A GUN FOR ME...

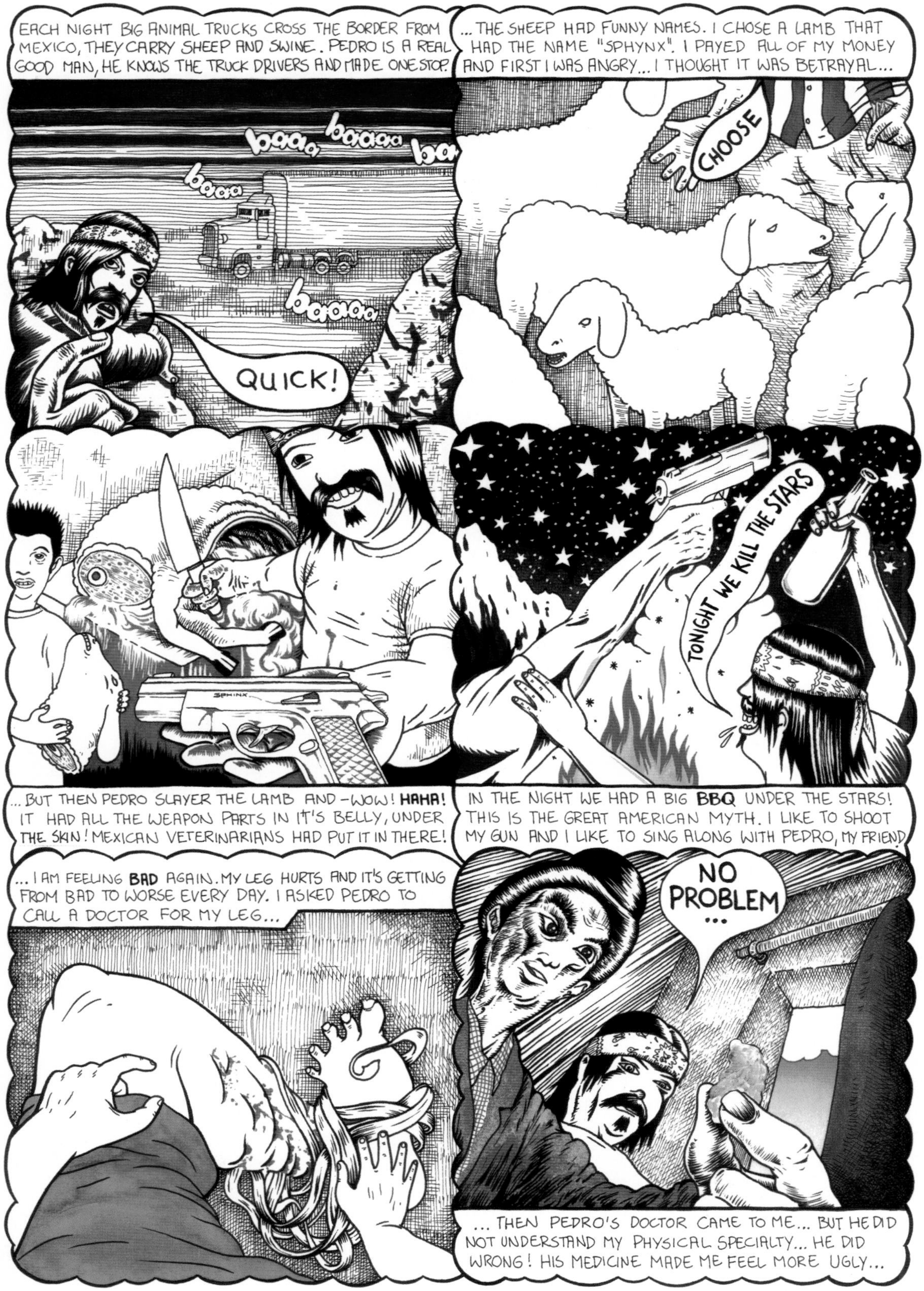
EACH NIGHT BIG ANIMAL TRUCKS CROSS THE BORDER FROM MEXICO, THEY CARRY SHEEP AND SWINE. PEDRO IS A REAL GOOD MAN, HE KNOWS THE TRUCK DRIVERS AND MADE ONE STOP.
baaa
baaa
baaaa
ba
baaaa
QUICK!
...THE SHEEP HAD FUNNY NAMES. I CHOSE A LAMB THAT HAD THE NAME "SPHYNX". I PAYED ALL OF MY MONEY AND FIRST I WAS ANGRY... I THOUGHT IT WAS BETRAYAL...
CHOOSE
SPHINX
...BUT THEN PEDRO SLAYER THE LAMB AND -WOW! HAHA! IT HAD ALL THE WEAPON PARTS IN IT'S BELLY, UNDER THE SKIN! MEXICAN VETERINARIANS HAD PUT IT IN THERE!
TONIGHT WE KILL THE STARS
IN THE NIGHT WE HAD A BIG BBQ UNDER THE STARS! THIS IS THE GREAT AMERICAN MYTH. I LIKE TO SHOOT MY GUN AND I LIKE TO SING ALONG WITH PEDRO, MY FRIEND.
...I AM FEELING BAD AGAIN. MY LEG HURTS AND IT'S GETTING FROM BAD TO WORSE EVERY DAY. I ASKED PEDRO TO CALL A DOCTOR FOR MY LEG...
NO PROBLEM...
...THEN PEDRO'S DOCTOR CAME TO ME... BUT HE DID NOT UNDERSTAND MY PHYSICAL SPECIALTY... HE DID WRONG! HIS MEDICINE MADE ME FEEL MORE UGLY...

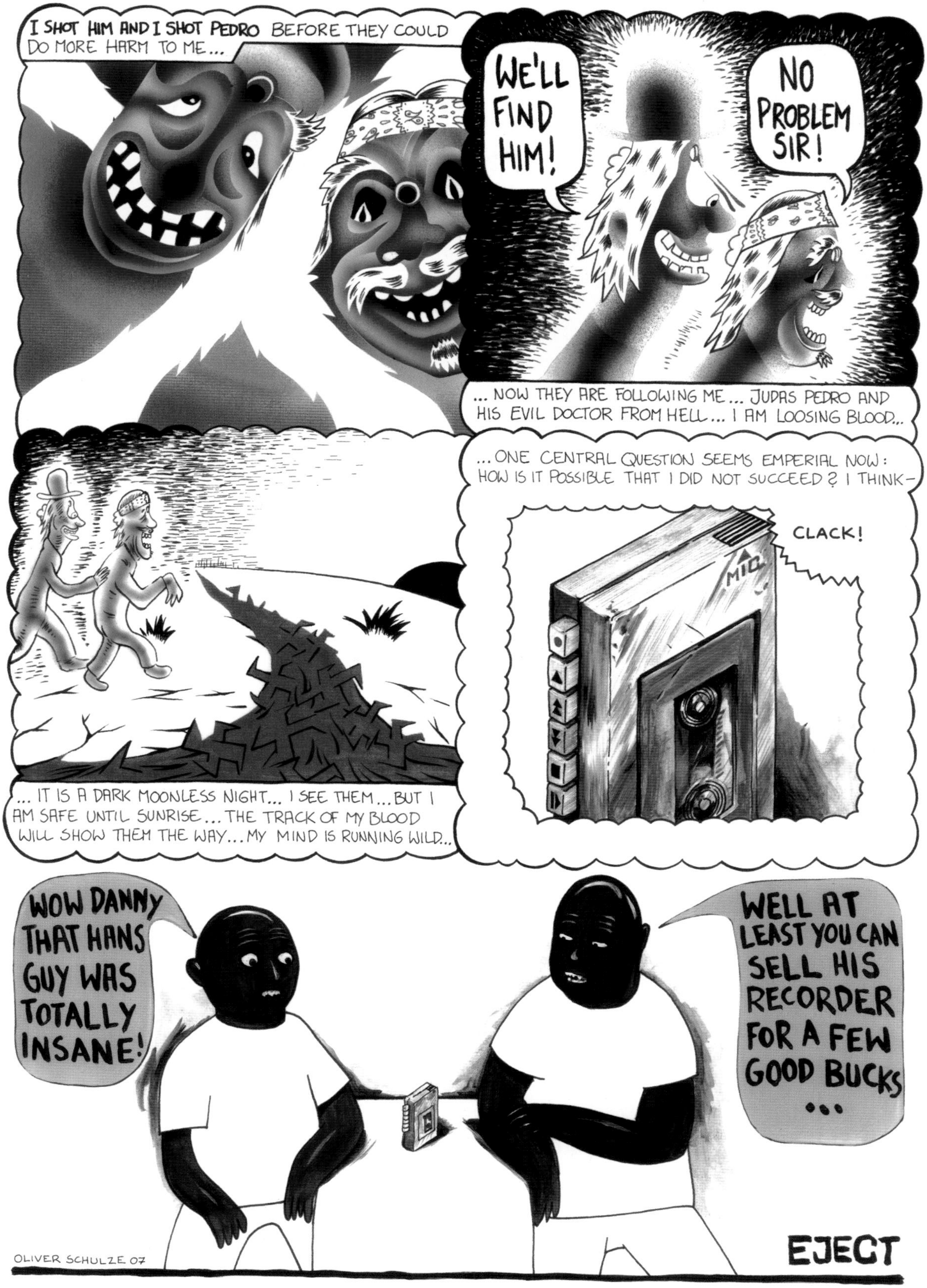
I SHOT HIM AND I SHOT PEDRO BEFORE THEY COULD DO MORE HARM TO ME...
WE'LL FIND HIM!
NO PROBLEM SIR!
... NOW THEY ARE FOLLOWING ME... JUDAS PEDRO AND HIS EVIL DOCTOR FROM HELL... I AM LOOSING BLOOD...
... IT IS A DARK MOONLESS NIGHT... I SEE THEM... BUT I AM SAFE UNTIL SUNRISE... THE TRACK OF MY BLOOD WILL SHOW THEM THE WAY... MY MIND IS RUNNING WILD...
... ONE CENTRAL QUESTION SEEMS EMPERIAL NOW: HOW IS IT POSSIBLE THAT I DID NOT SUCCEED? I THINK-
MIC
CLACK!
WOW DANNY THAT HANS GUY WAS TOTALLY INSANE!
WELL AT LEAST YOU CAN SELL HIS RECORDER FOR A FEW GOOD BUCKS...
OLIVER SCHULZE 07
EJECT

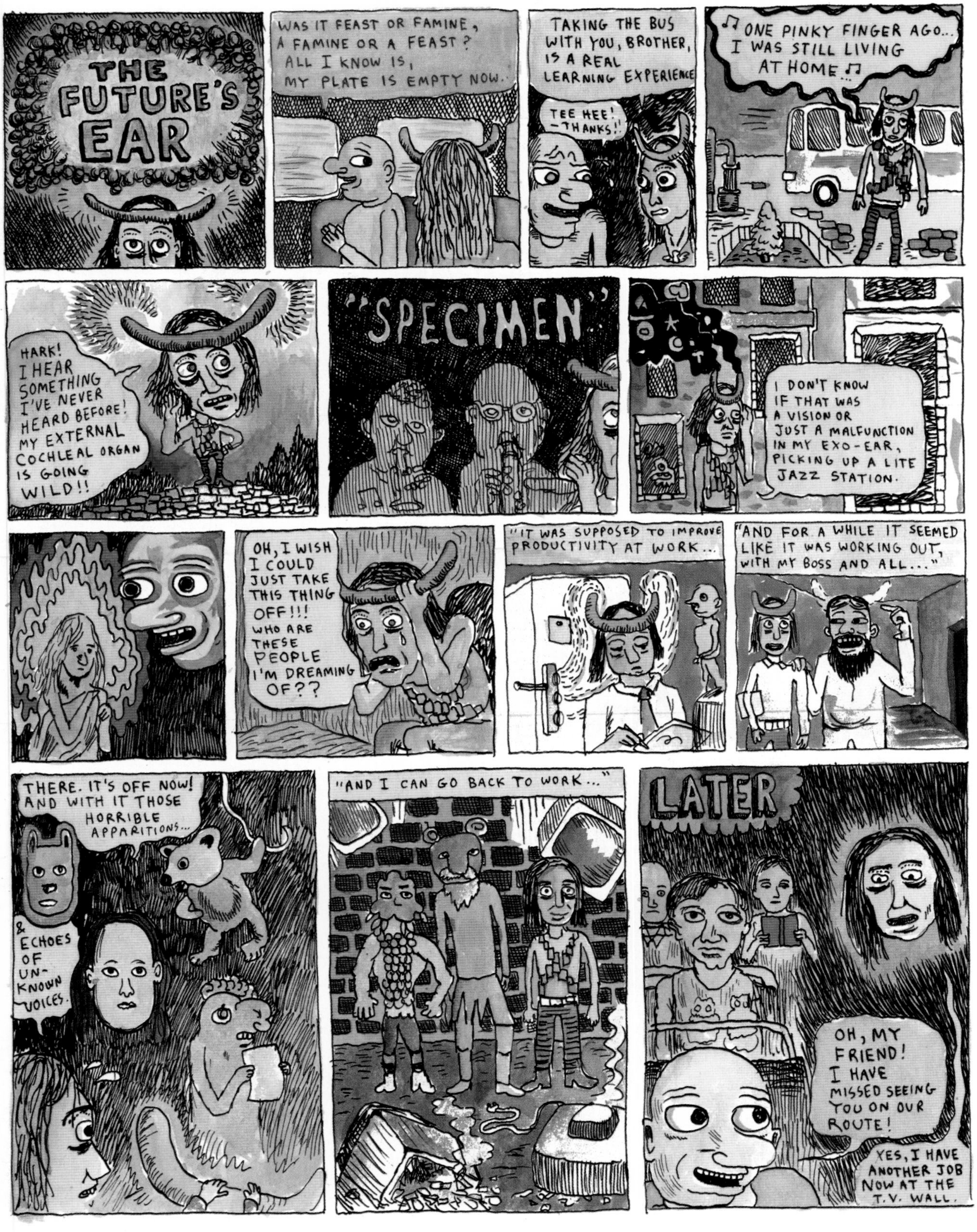
THE FUTURE'S EAR
WAS IT FEAST OR FAMINE, A FAMINE OR A FEAST? ALL I KNOW IS, MY PLATE IS EMPTY NOW.
TAKING THE BUS WITH YOU, BROTHER, IS A REAL LEARNING EXPERIENCE
TEE HEE! -THANKS!
♫ ONE PINKY FINGER AGO... I WAS STILL LIVING AT HOME ♫
HARK! I HEAR SOMETHING I'VE NEVER HEARD BEFORE! MY EXTERNAL COCHLEAL ORGAN IS GOING WILD!!
"SPECIMEN"
I DON'T KNOW IF THAT WAS A VISION OR JUST A MALFUNCTION IN MY EXO-EAR, PICKING UP A LITE JAZZ STATION.
OH, I WISH I COULD JUST TAKE THIS THING OFF!!! WHO ARE THESE PEOPLE I'M DREAMING OF??
"IT WAS SUPPOSED TO IMPROVE PRODUCTIVITY AT WORK...
"AND FOR A WHILE IT SEEMED LIKE IT WAS WORKING OUT, WITH MY BOSS AND ALL..."
THERE. IT'S OFF NOW! AND WITH IT THOSE HORRIBLE APPARITIONS...
& ECHOES OF UN-KNOWN VOICES.
"AND I CAN GO BACK TO WORK..."
LATER
OH, MY FRIEND! I HAVE MISSED SEEING YOU ON OUR ROUTE!
YES, I HAVE ANOTHER JOB NOW AT THE T.V. WALL.

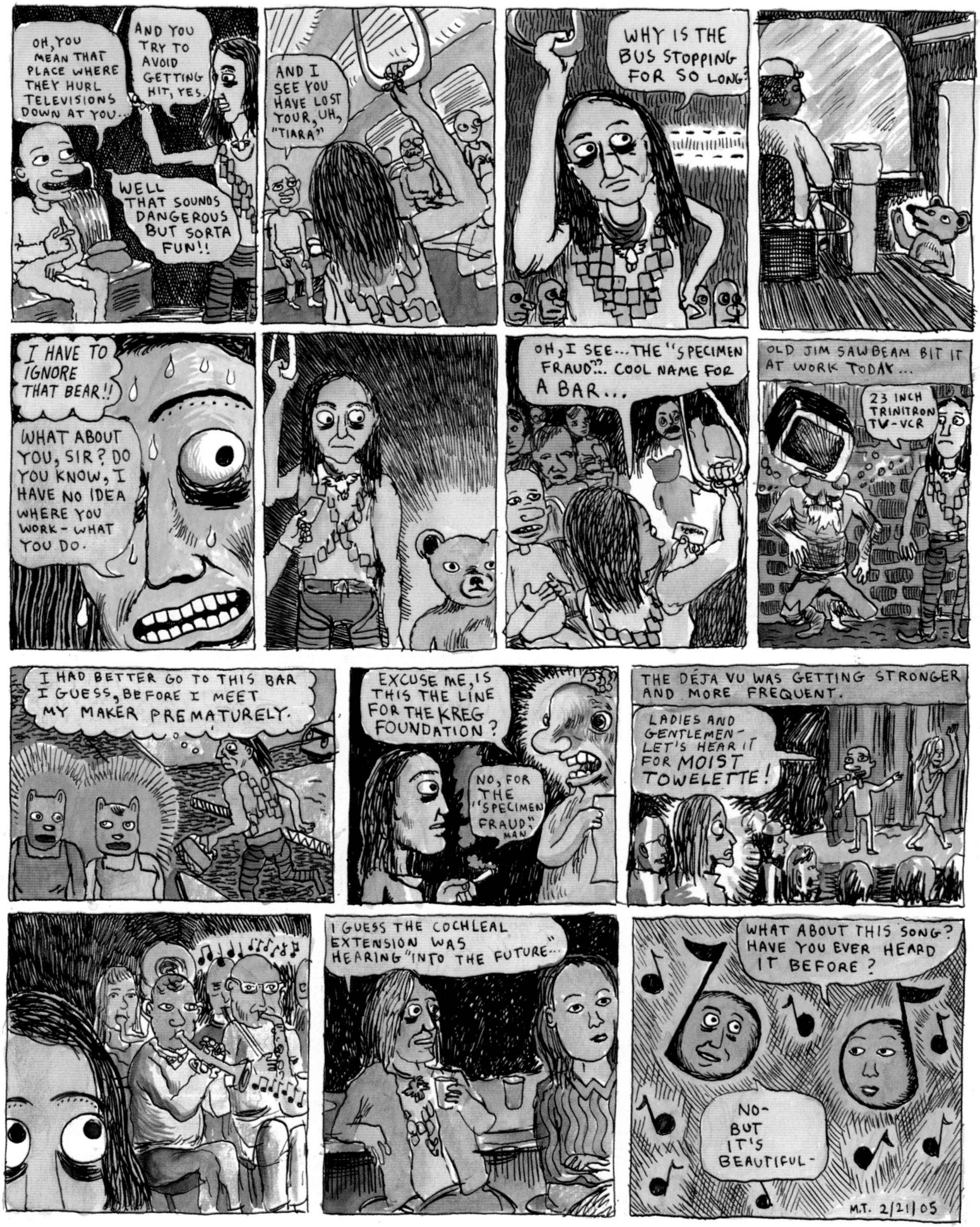

OH, YOU MEAN THAT PLACE WHERE THEY HURL TELEVISIONS DOWN AT YOU...
AND YOU TRY TO AVOID GETTING HIT, YES.
WELL THAT SOUNDS DANGEROUS BUT SORTA FUN!!
AND I SEE YOU HAVE LOST YOUR, UH, "TIARA"
WHY IS THE BUS STOPPING FOR SO LONG?
I HAVE TO IGNORE THAT BEAR!!
WHAT ABOUT YOU, SIR? DO YOU KNOW, I HAVE NO IDEA WHERE YOU WORK - WHAT YOU DO.
OH, I SEE... THE "SPECIMEN FRAUD"?.. COOL NAME FOR A BAR...
OLD JIM SAWBEAM BIT IT AT WORK TODAY...
23 INCH TRINITRON TV-VCR
I HAD BETTER GO TO THIS BAR I GUESS, BEFORE I MEET MY MAKER PREMATURELY.
EXCUSE ME, IS THIS THE LINE FOR THE KREG FOUNDATION?
NO, FOR THE "SPECIMEN FRAUD" MAN
THE DÉJA VU WAS GETTING STRONGER AND MORE FREQUENT.
LADIES AND GENTLEMEN - LET'S HEAR IT FOR MOIST TOWELETTE!
I GUESS THE COCHLEAL EXTENSION WAS HEARING "INTO THE FUTURE"...
WHAT ABOUT THIS SONG? HAVE YOU EVER HEARD IT BEFORE?
NO - BUT IT'S BEAUTIFUL -
M.T. 2/21/05

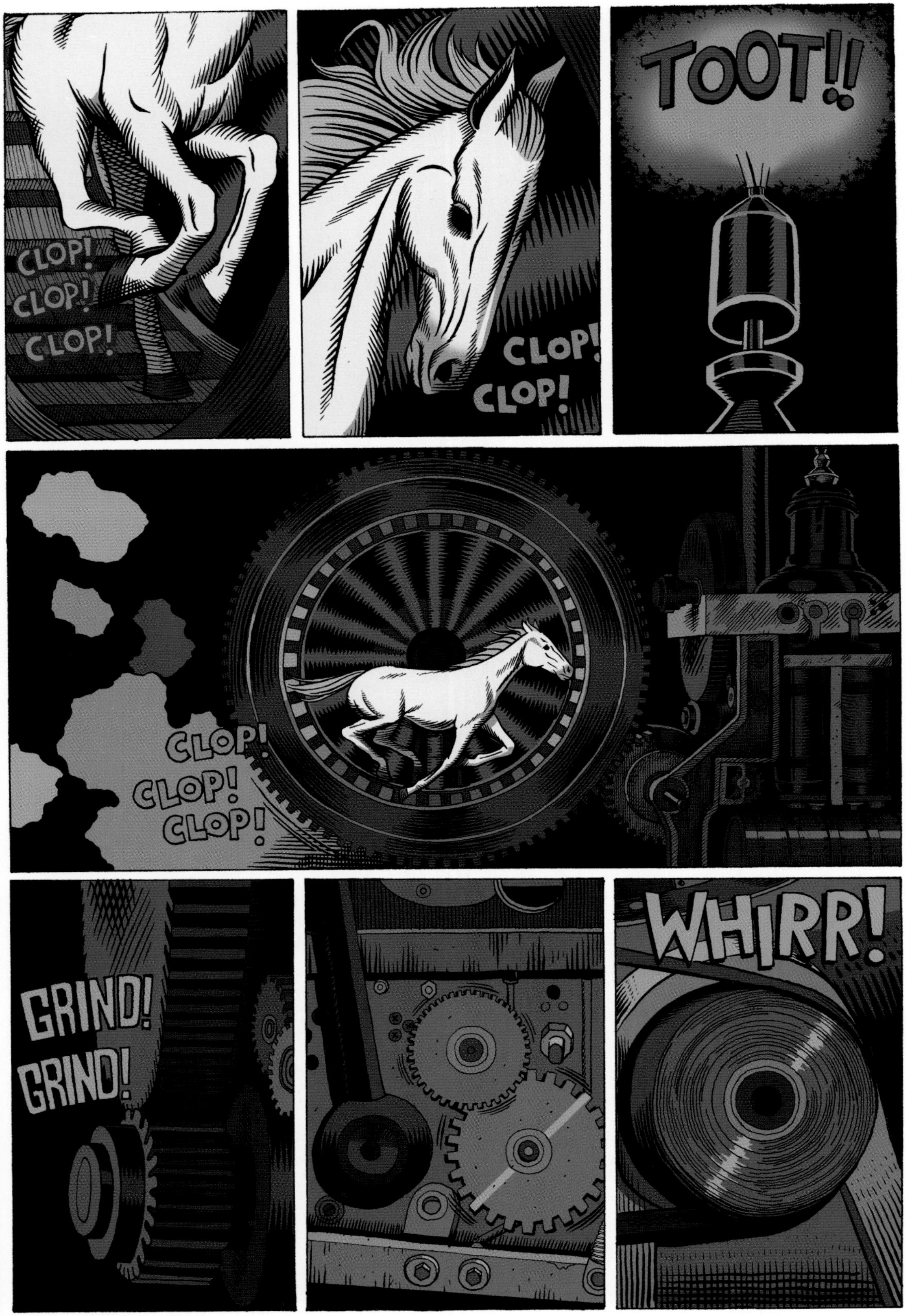
CLOP!
CLOP!
CLOP!
CLOP!
CLOP!
TOOT!!
CLOP!
CLOP!
CLOP!
GRIND!
GRIND!
WHIRR!

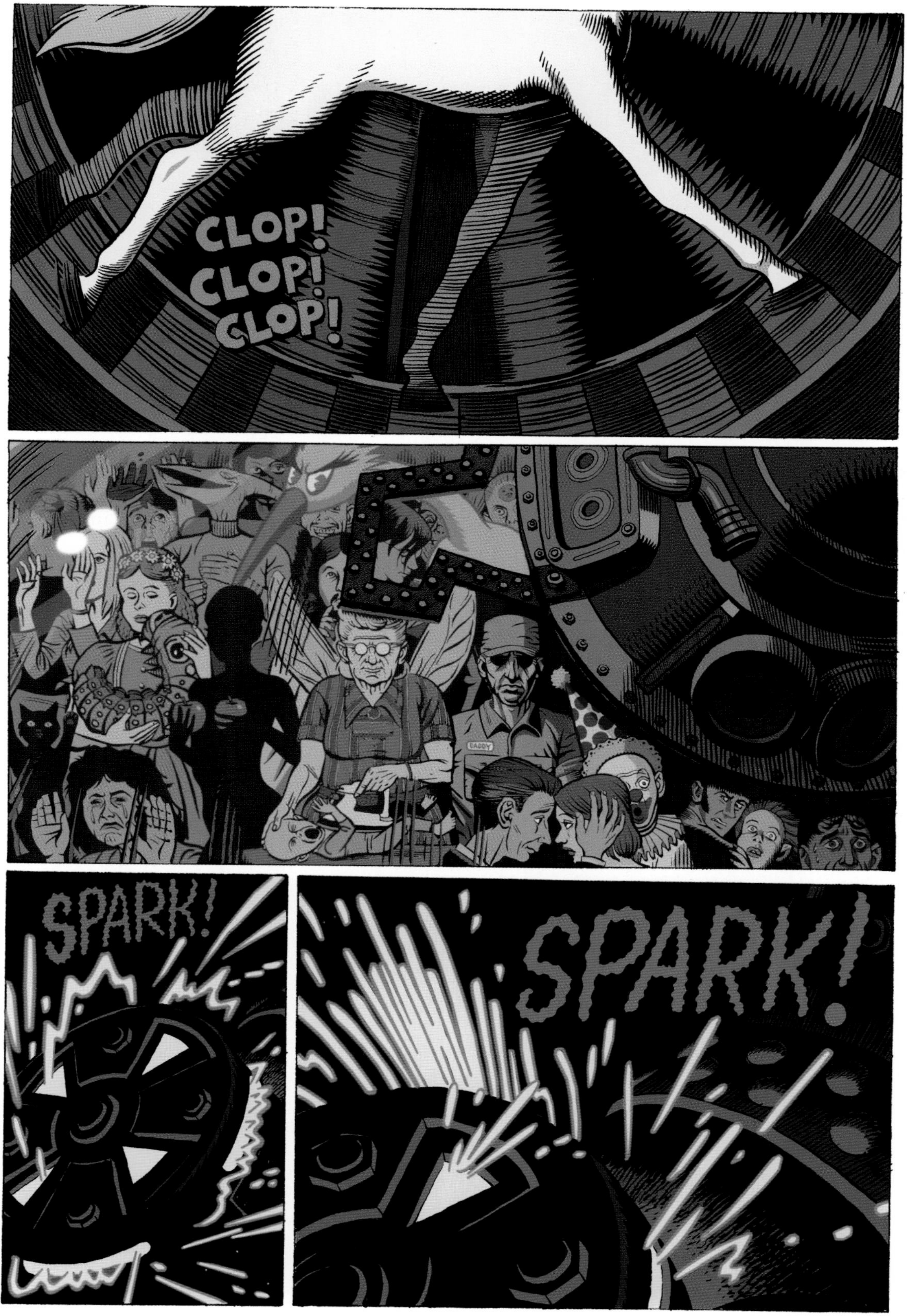
CLOP!
CLOP!
CLOP!
SPARK!
SPARK!

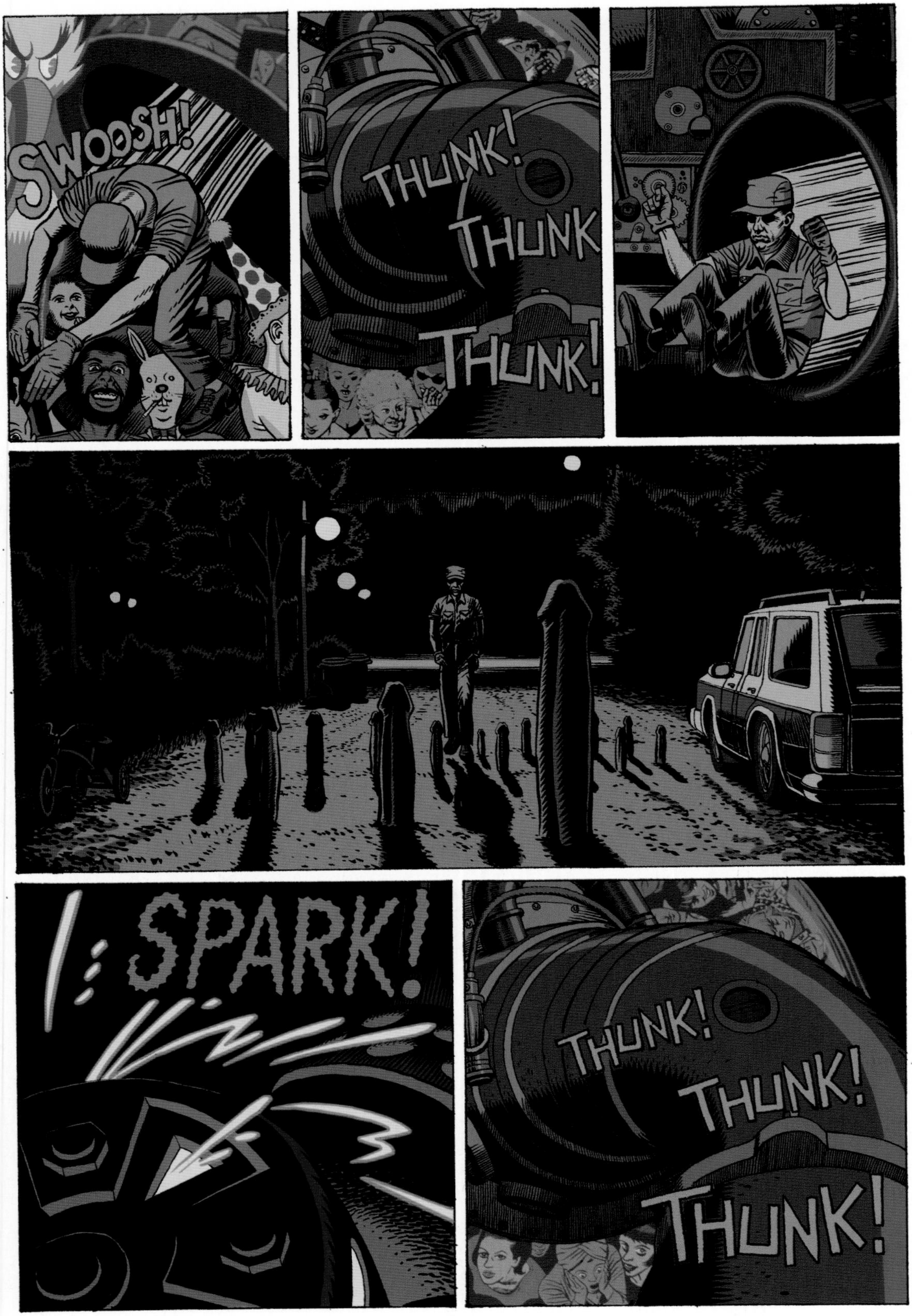
SWOOSH!
THUNK!
THUNK
THUNK!
SPARK!
THUNK!
THUNK!
THUNK!

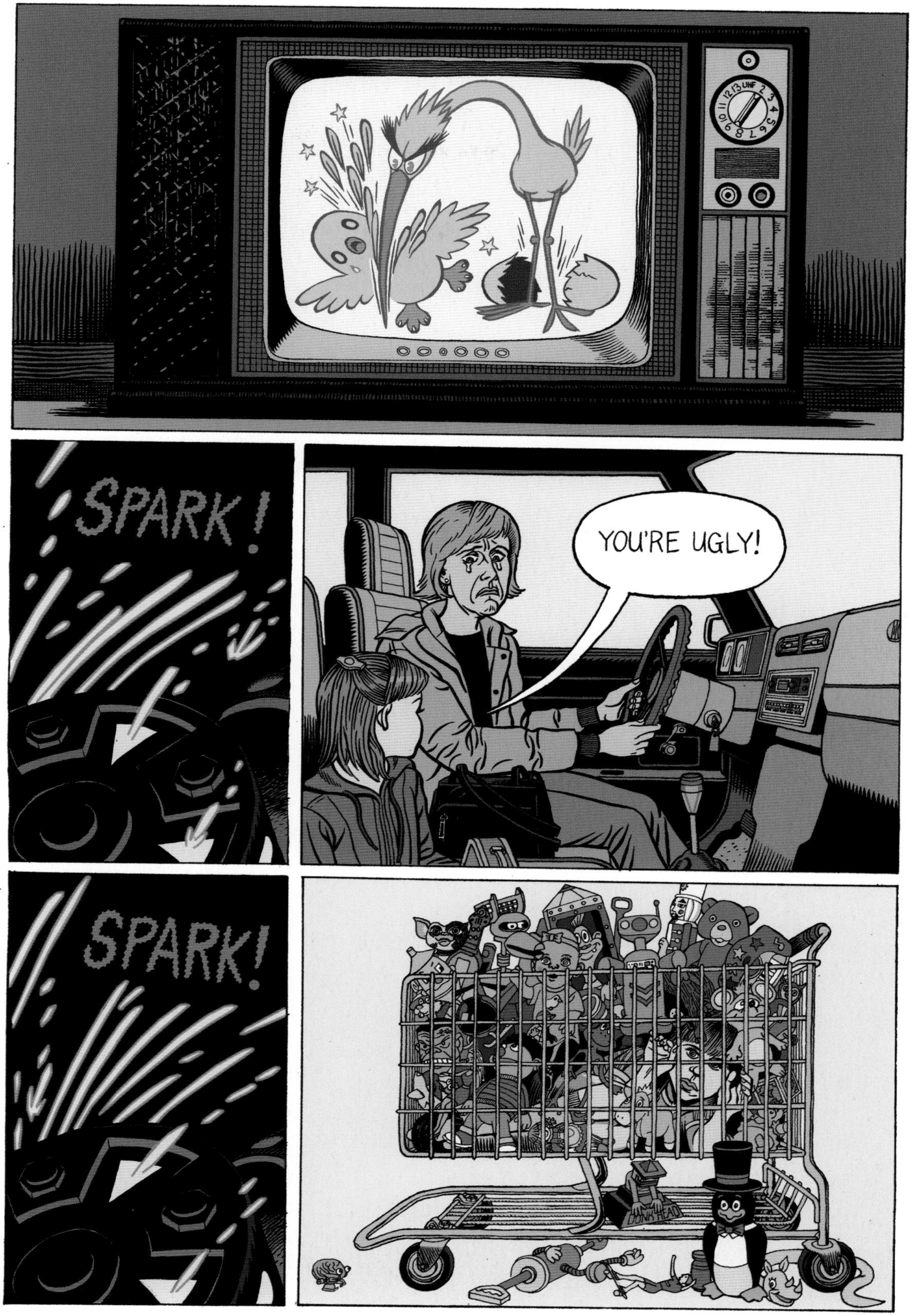
SPARK!
YOU'RE UGLY!
SPARK!

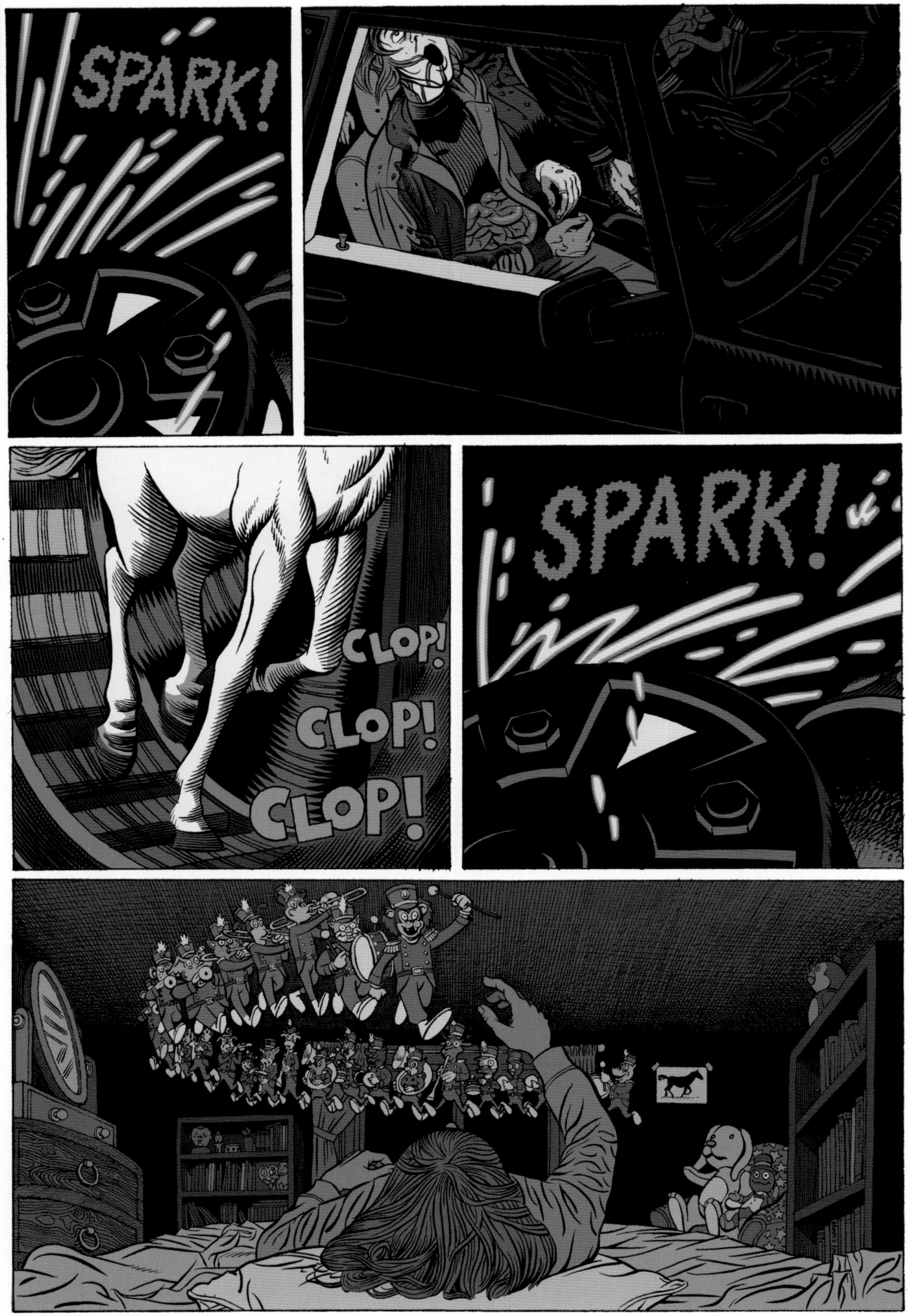
SPARK!
CLOP!
CLOP!
CLOP!
SPARK!

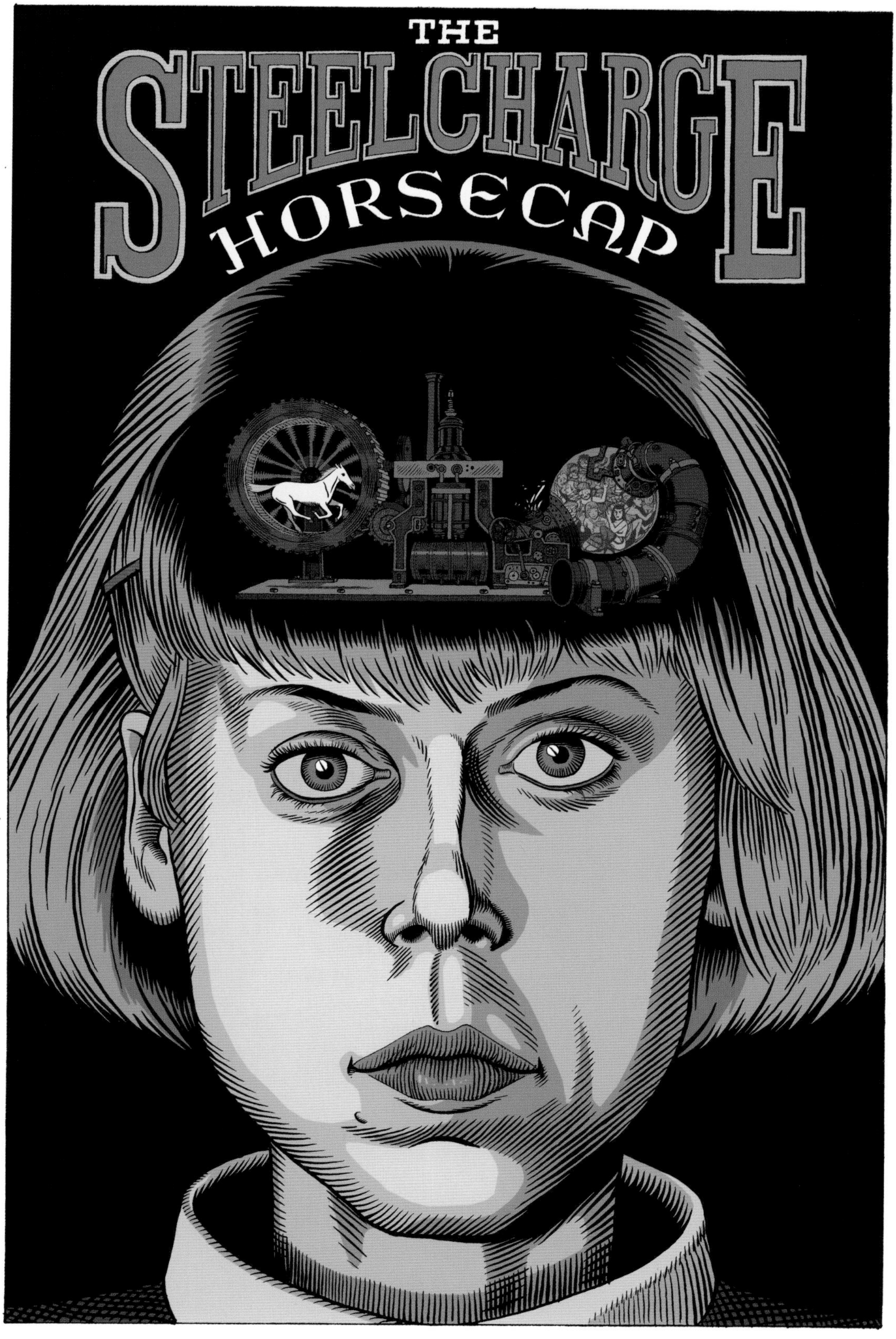
THE
STEELCHARGE
HORSECAP

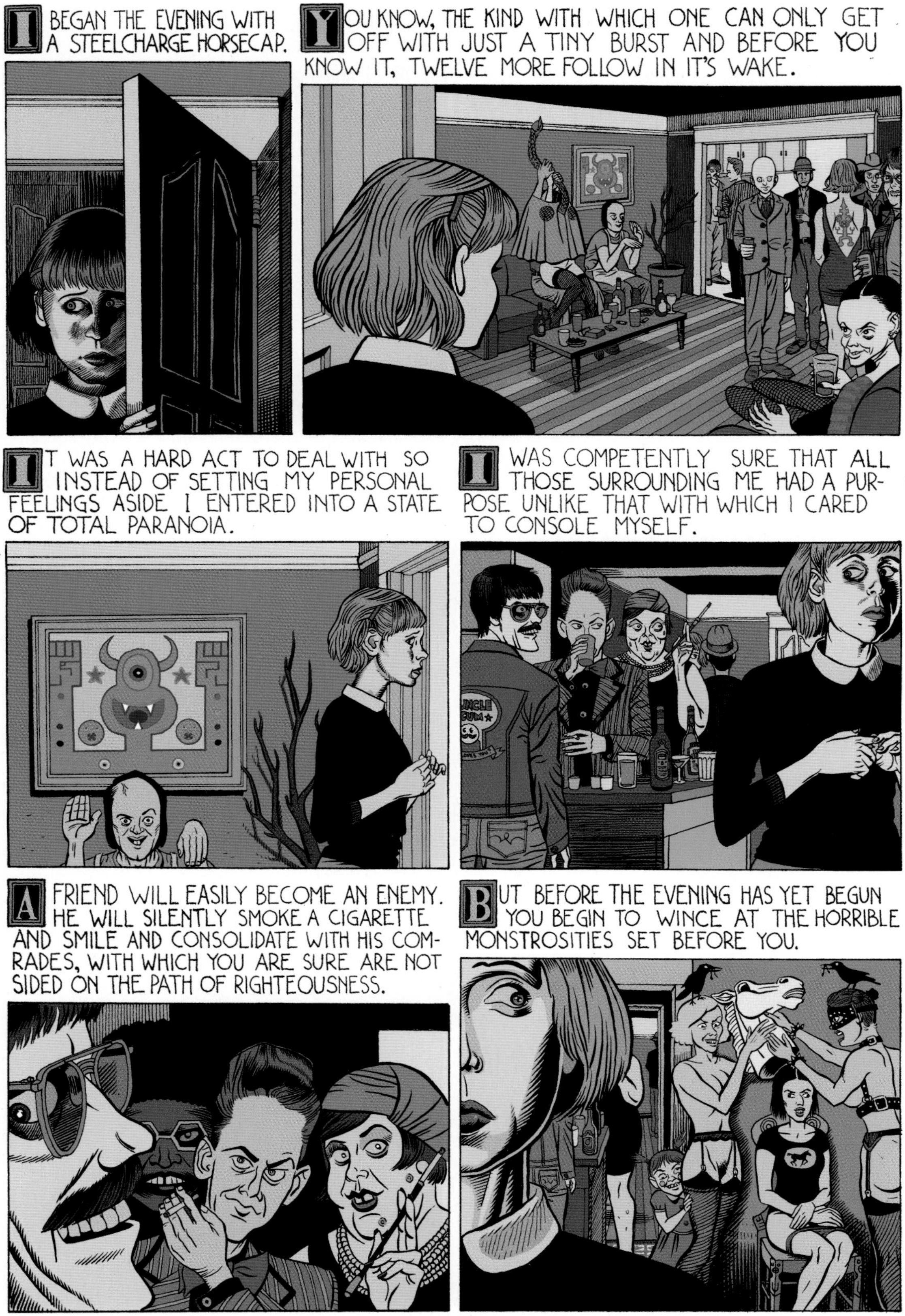
I BEGAN THE EVENING WITH A STEELCHARGE HORSECAP.
YOU KNOW, THE KIND WITH WHICH ONE CAN ONLY GET OFF WITH JUST A TINY BURST AND BEFORE YOU KNOW IT, TWELVE MORE FOLLOW IN IT'S WAKE.
IT WAS A HARD ACT TO DEAL WITH SO INSTEAD OF SETTING MY PERSONAL FEELINGS ASIDE I ENTERED INTO A STATE OF TOTAL PARANOIA.
I WAS COMPETENTLY SURE THAT ALL THOSE SURROUNDING ME HAD A PURPOSE UNLIKE THAT WITH WHICH I CARED TO CONSOLE MYSELF.
A FRIEND WILL EASILY BECOME AN ENEMY. HE WILL SILENTLY SMOKE A CIGARETTE AND SMILE AND CONSOLIDATE WITH HIS COMRADES, WITH WHICH YOU ARE SURE ARE NOT SIDED ON THE PATH OF RIGHTEOUSNESS.
BUT BEFORE THE EVENING HAS YET BEGUN YOU BEGIN TO WINCE AT THE HORRIBLE MONSTROSITIES SET BEFORE YOU.

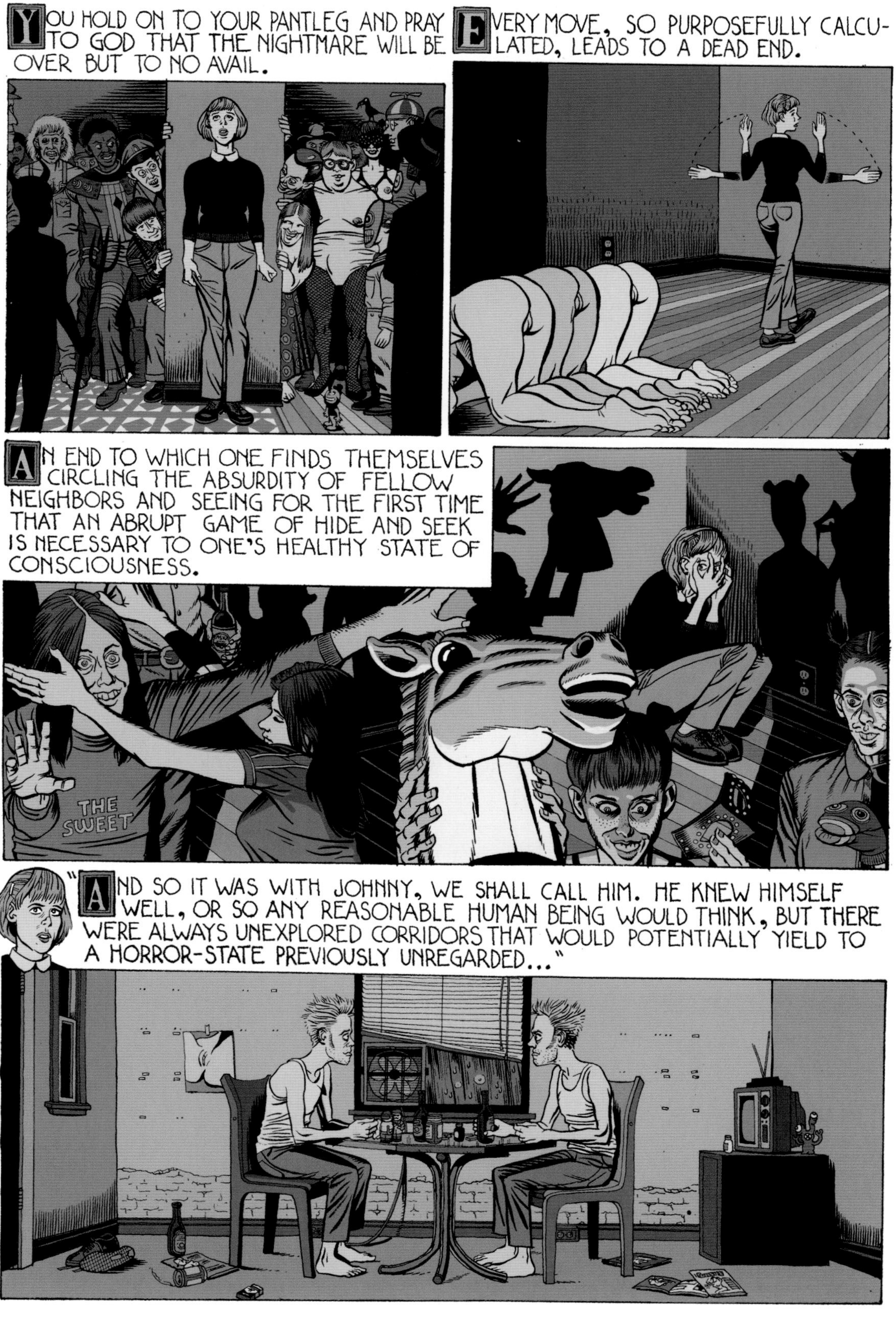
YOU HOLD ON TO YOUR PANTLEG AND PRAY TO GOD THAT THE NIGHTMARE WILL BE OVER BUT TO NO AVAIL.
EVERY MOVE, SO PURPOSEFULLY CALCULATED, LEADS TO A DEAD END.
AN END TO WHICH ONE FINDS THEMSELVES CIRCLING THE ABSURDITY OF FELLOW NEIGHBORS AND SEEING FOR THE FIRST TIME THAT AN ABRUPT GAME OF HIDE AND SEEK IS NECESSARY TO ONE'S HEALTHY STATE OF CONSCIOUSNESS.
THE SWEET
"AND SO IT WAS WITH JOHNNY, WE SHALL CALL HIM. HE KNEW HIMSELF WELL, OR SO ANY REASONABLE HUMAN BEING WOULD THINK, BUT THERE WERE ALWAYS UNEXPLORED CORRIDORS THAT WOULD POTENTIALLY YIELD TO A HORROR-STATE PREVIOUSLY UNREGARDED..."

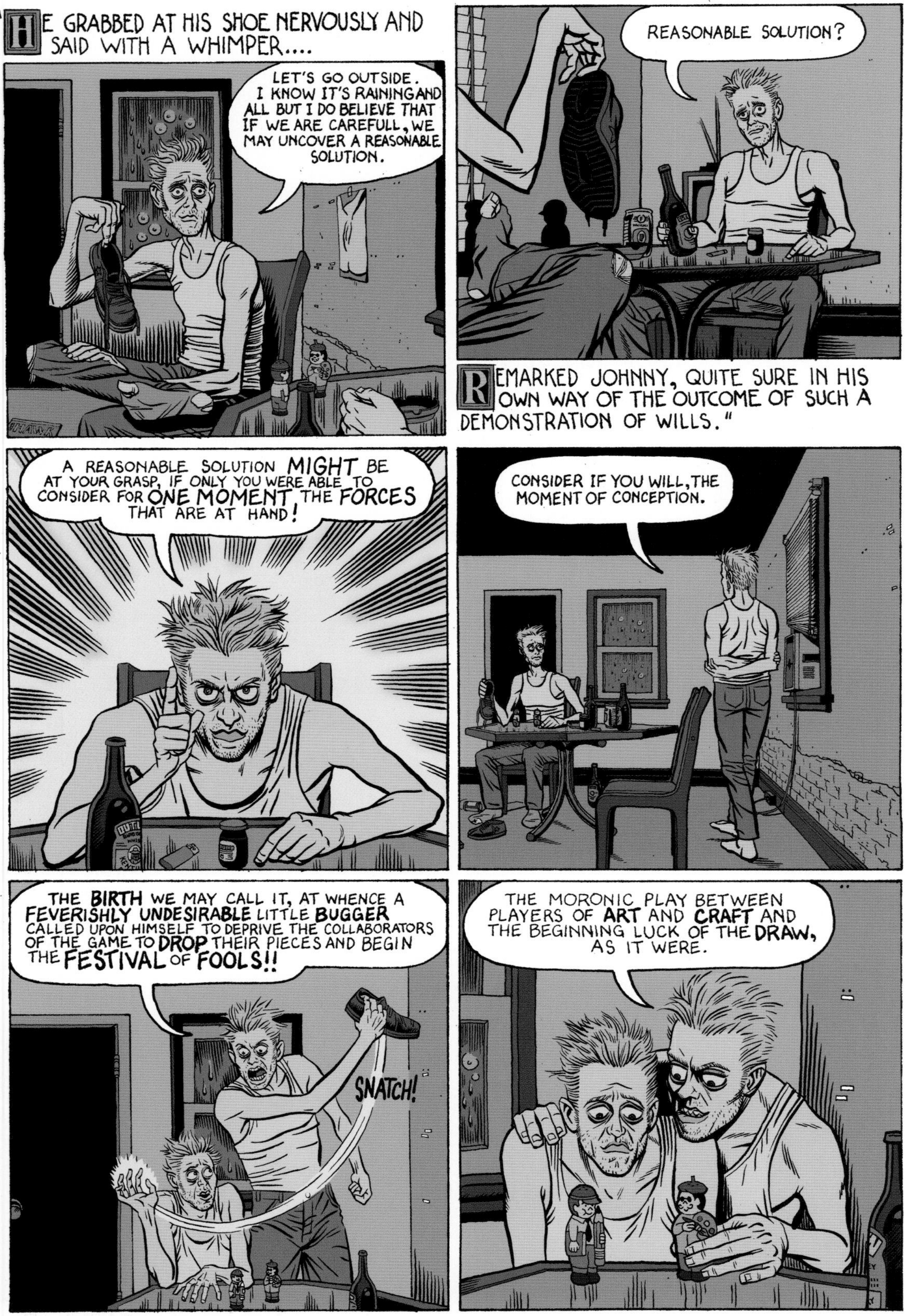
"HE GRABBED AT HIS SHOE NERVOUSLY AND SAID WITH A WHIMPER....
LET'S GO OUTSIDE. I KNOW IT'S RAINING AND ALL BUT I DO BELIEVE THAT IF WE ARE CAREFULL, WE MAY UNCOVER A REASONABLE SOLUTION.
REASONABLE SOLUTION?
REMARKED JOHNNY, QUITE SURE IN HIS OWN WAY OF THE OUTCOME OF SUCH A DEMONSTRATION OF WILLS."
A REASONABLE SOLUTION MIGHT BE AT YOUR GRASP, IF ONLY YOU WERE ABLE TO CONSIDER FOR ONE MOMENT, THE FORCES THAT ARE AT HAND!
CONSIDER IF YOU WILL, THE MOMENT OF CONCEPTION.
THE BIRTH WE MAY CALL IT, AT WHENCE A FEVERISHLY UNDESIRABLE LITTLE BUGGER CALLED UPON HIMSELF TO DEPRIVE THE COLLABORATORS OF THE GAME TO DROP THEIR PIECES AND BEGIN THE FESTIVAL OF FOOLS!!
SNATCH!
THE MORONIC PLAY BETWEEN PLAYERS OF ART AND CRAFT AND THE BEGINNING LUCK OF THE DRAW, AS IT WERE.

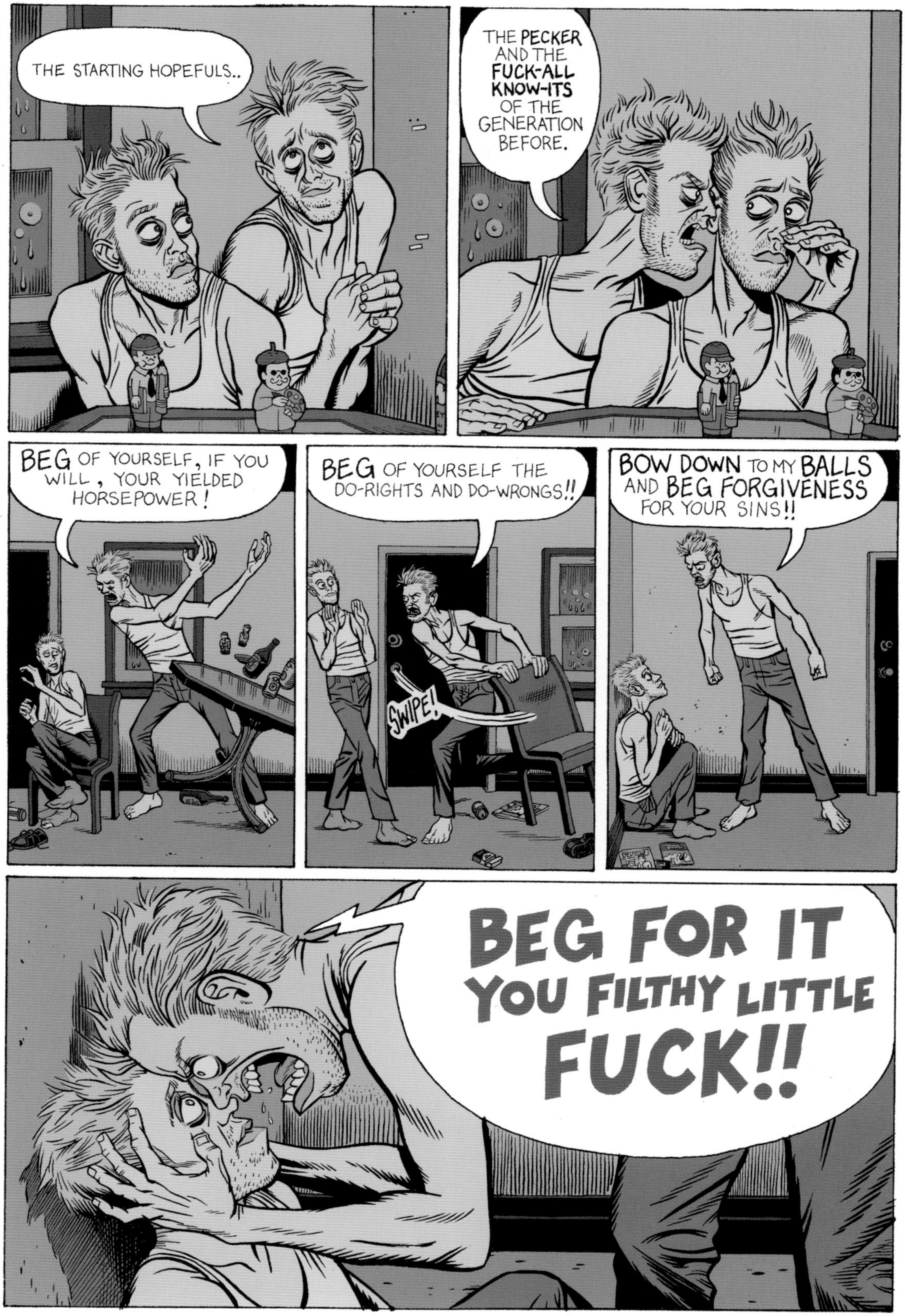
THE STARTING HOPEFULS..
THE PECKER AND THE FUCK-ALL KNOW-ITS OF THE GENERATION BEFORE.
BEG OF YOURSELF, IF YOU WILL, YOUR YIELDED HORSEPOWER!
BEG OF YOURSELF THE DO-RIGHTS AND DO-WRONGS!!
SWIPE!
BOW DOWN TO MY BALLS AND BEG FORGIVENESS FOR YOUR SINS!!
BEG FOR IT YOU FILTHY LITTLE FUCK!!

"HE GRABBED HIM BY THE HAIR AND GAVE HIM A PERFECTLY GOOD VIEW OF THE SEQUENTIAL MONITORS*.

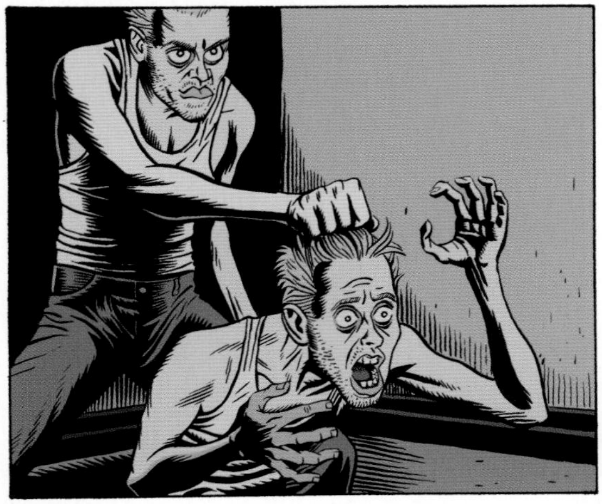

HOWEVER, IT WAS ONLY THEN THAT HE COULD OBSERVE THE TRUE ERROR OF HIS WAYS. THE UNTOLD HYPOCRISY, THE BEGGING-FOR-IT NOSTALGIA OF BULLSHIT."

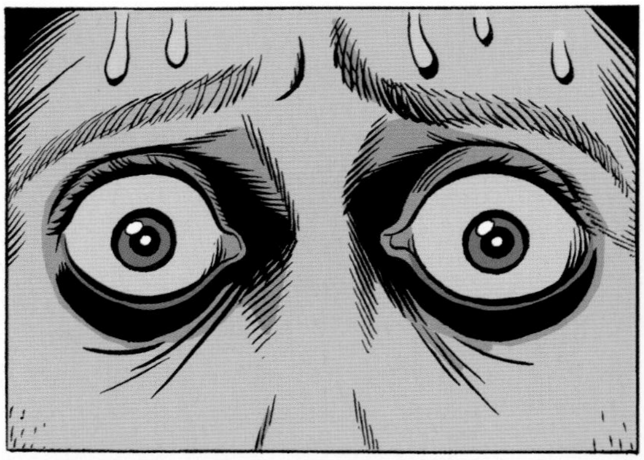

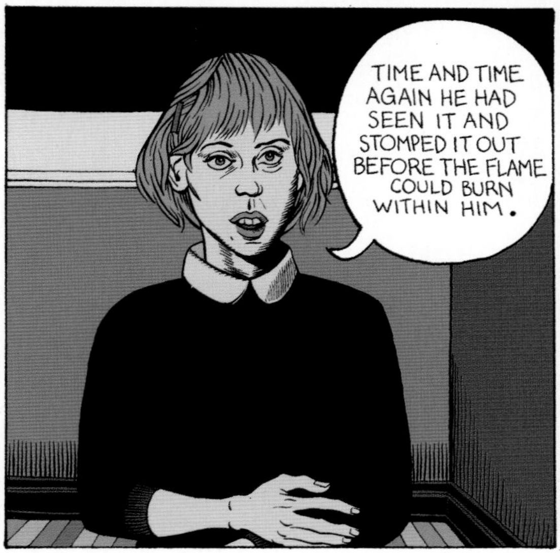
TIME AND TIME AGAIN HE HAD SEEN IT AND STOMPED IT OUT BEFORE THE FLAME COULD BURN WITHIN HIM.

*SEQUENTIAL MONITORS

You may have seen them while watching your first sunset or petting your first puppy, and then seen a dying frog pretentiously begging for mercy from some undergraduate of the self-infliction of murderous lust. Perhaps you've seen them at your nearest bookstore.

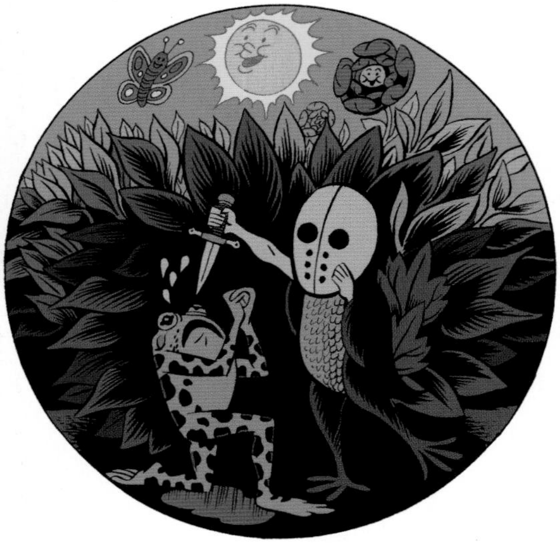

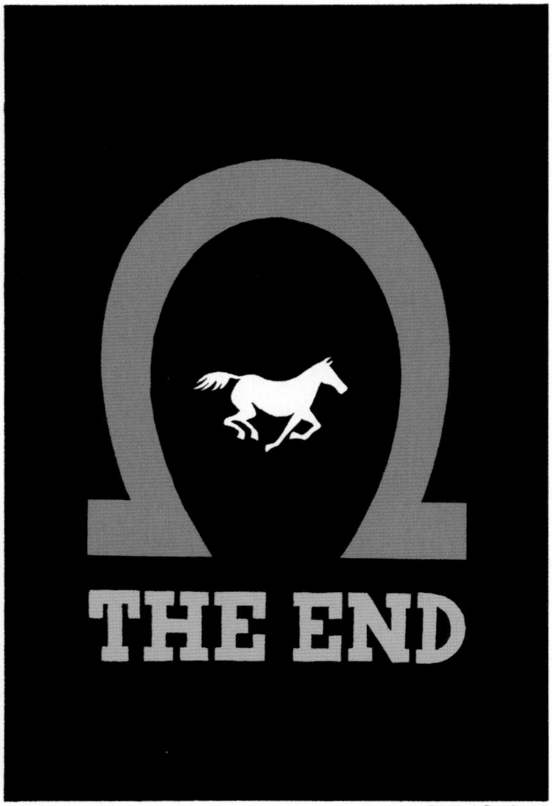
THE END

D.J. BRYANT

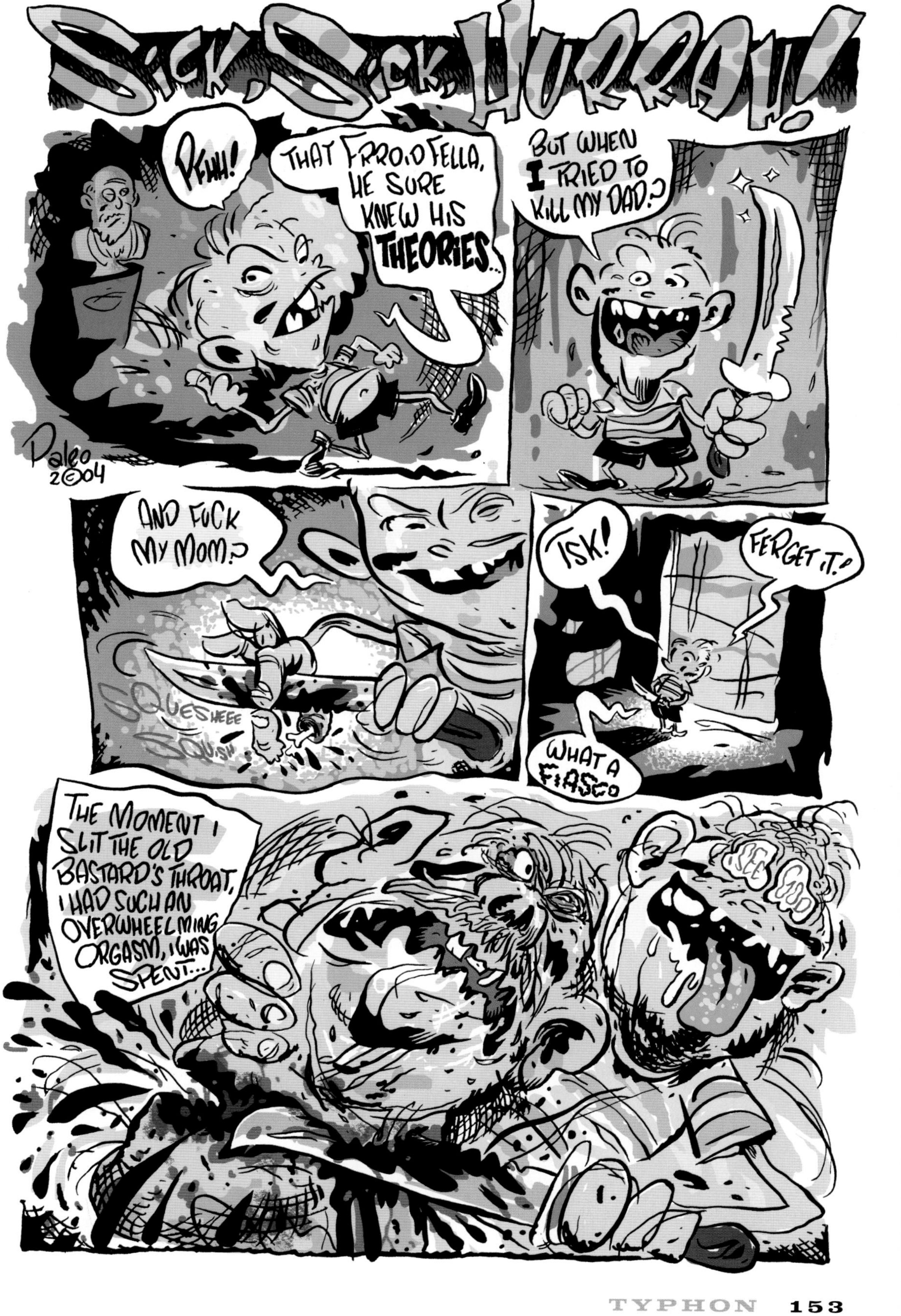
SICK, SICK, HURRAH!
PFHH!
THAT FRROID FELLA, HE SURE KNEW HIS THEORIES...
BUT WHEN I TRIED TO KILL MY DAD?
Paleo 2©04
AND FUCK MY MOM?
SQUESHEEE
SQUISH
TSK!
FERGET IT.
WHAT A FIASCO
THE MOMENT I SLIT THE OLD BASTARD'S THROAT, I HAD SUCH AN OVERWHEELMING ORGASM, I WAS SPENT...
SEE GOD

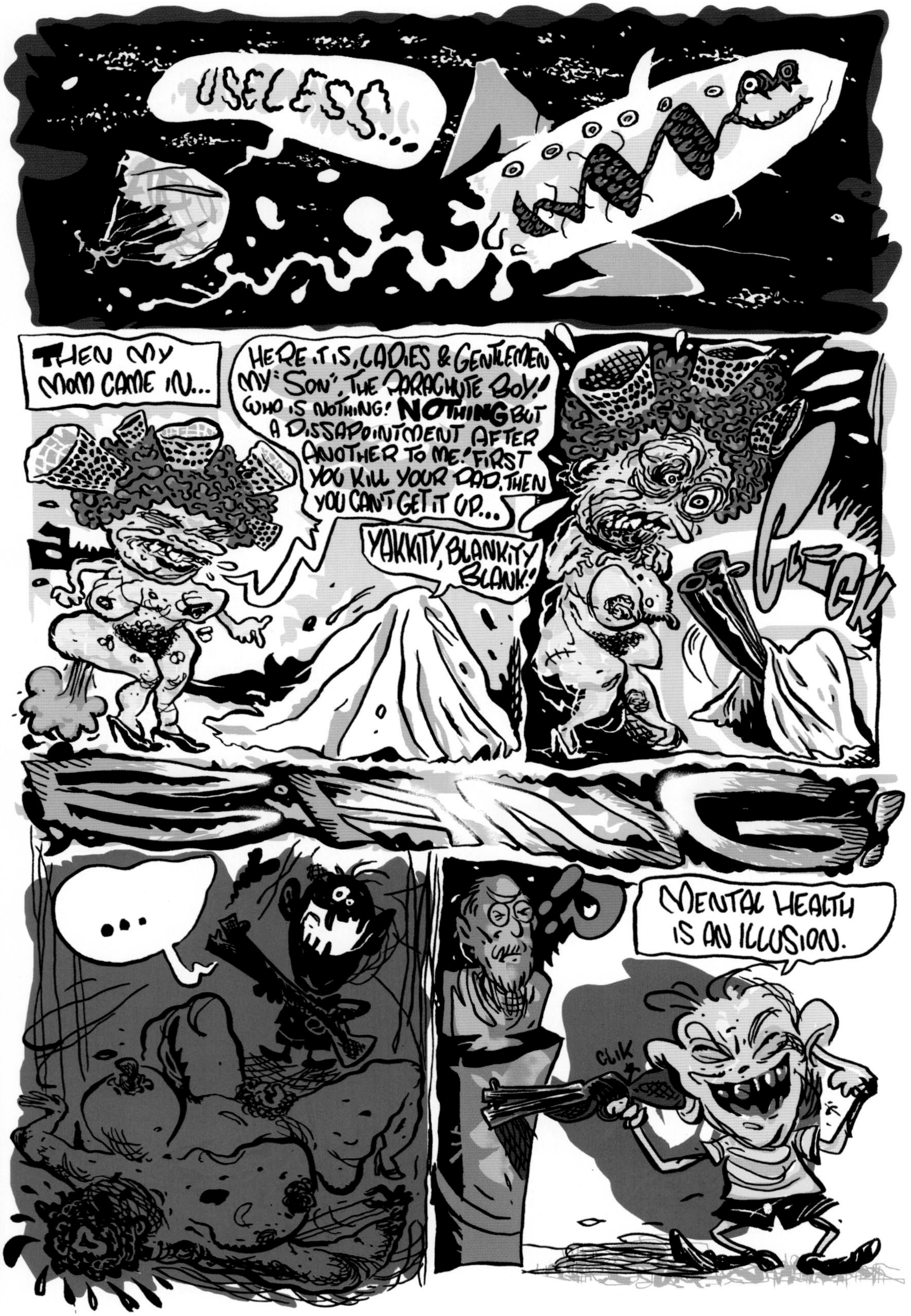

USELESS...
THEN MY MOM CAME IN...
HERE IT IS, LADIES & GENTLEMEN MY "SON", THE PARACHUTE BOY! WHO IS NOTHING! NOTHING BUT A DISSAPOINTMENT AFTER ANOTHER TO ME! FIRST YOU KILL YOUR DAD, THEN YOU CAN'T GET IT UP...
YAKKITY, BLANKITY BLANK!
CLICK
BLAM
...
MENTAL HEALTH IS AN ILLUSION.
CLIK

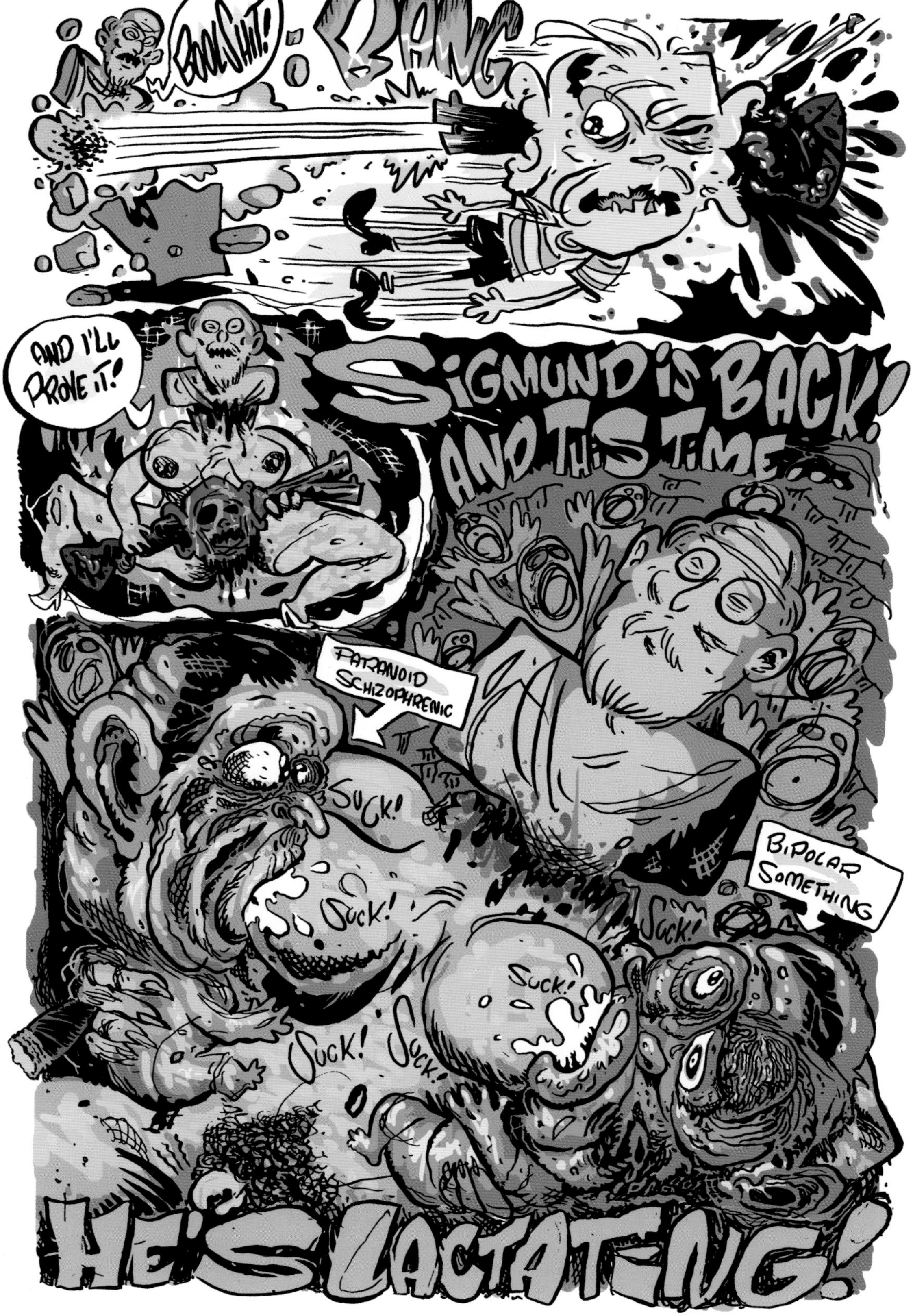
BULLSHIT!
BANG
AND I'LL PROVE IT!
SIGMUND IS BACK! AND THIS TIME
PARANOID SCHIZOPHRENIC
SUCK!
SUCK!
BIPOLAR SOMETHING
SUCK!
SUCK!
SUCK!
SUCK!
HE'S LACTATING!

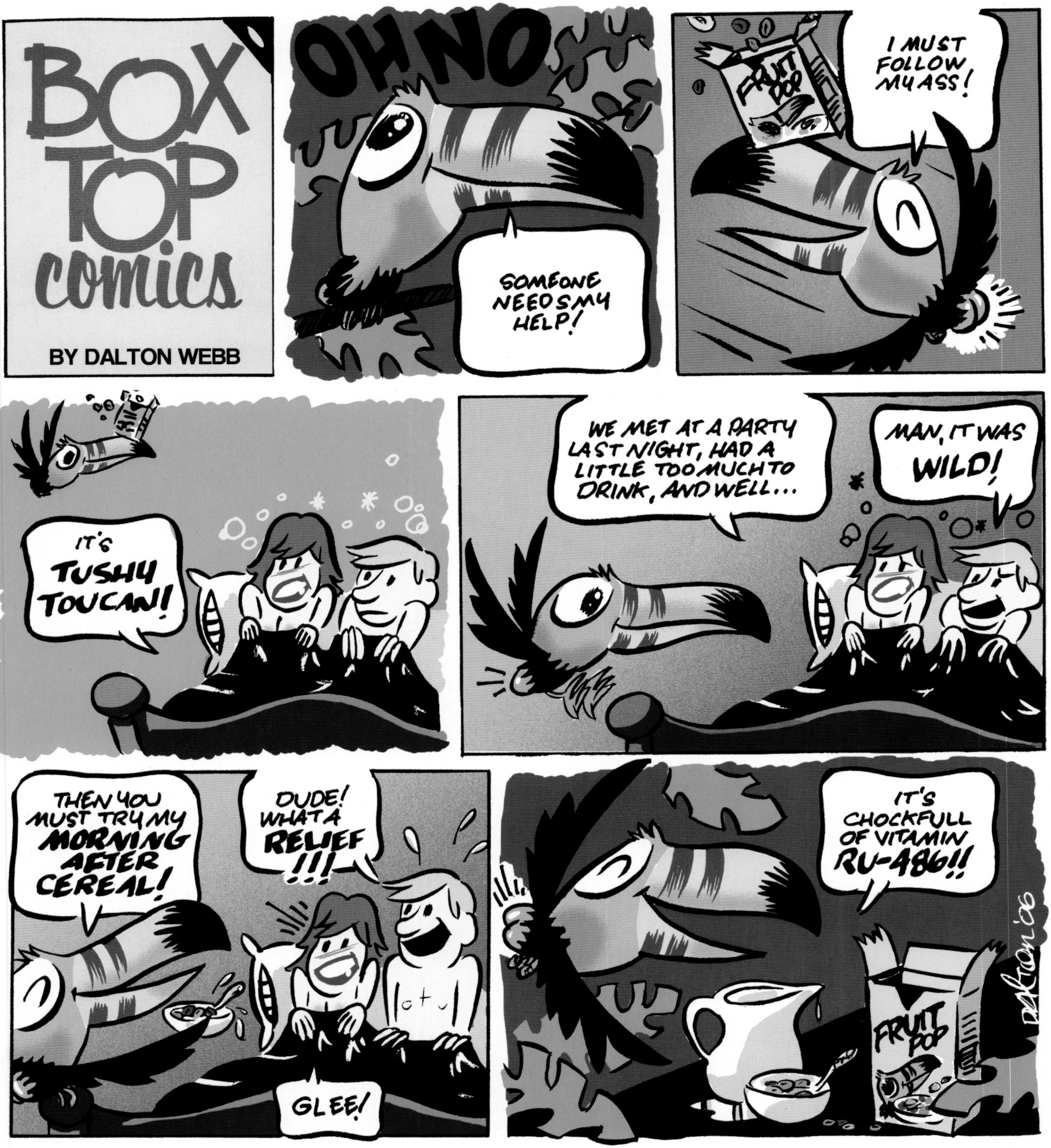
BOX TOP comics
BY DALTON WEBB
OH NO
SOMEONE NEEDS MY HELP!
I MUST FOLLOW MY ASS!
FRUIT POP
IT'S TUSHY TOUCAN!
WE MET AT A PARTY LAST NIGHT, HAD A LITTLE TOO MUCH TO DRINK, AND WELL...
MAN, IT WAS WILD!
THEN YOU MUST TRY MY MORNING AFTER CEREAL!
DUDE! WHAT A RELIEF !!!
GLEE!
IT'S CHOCKFULL OF VITAMIN RU-486!!
FRUIT POP
DALTON '06

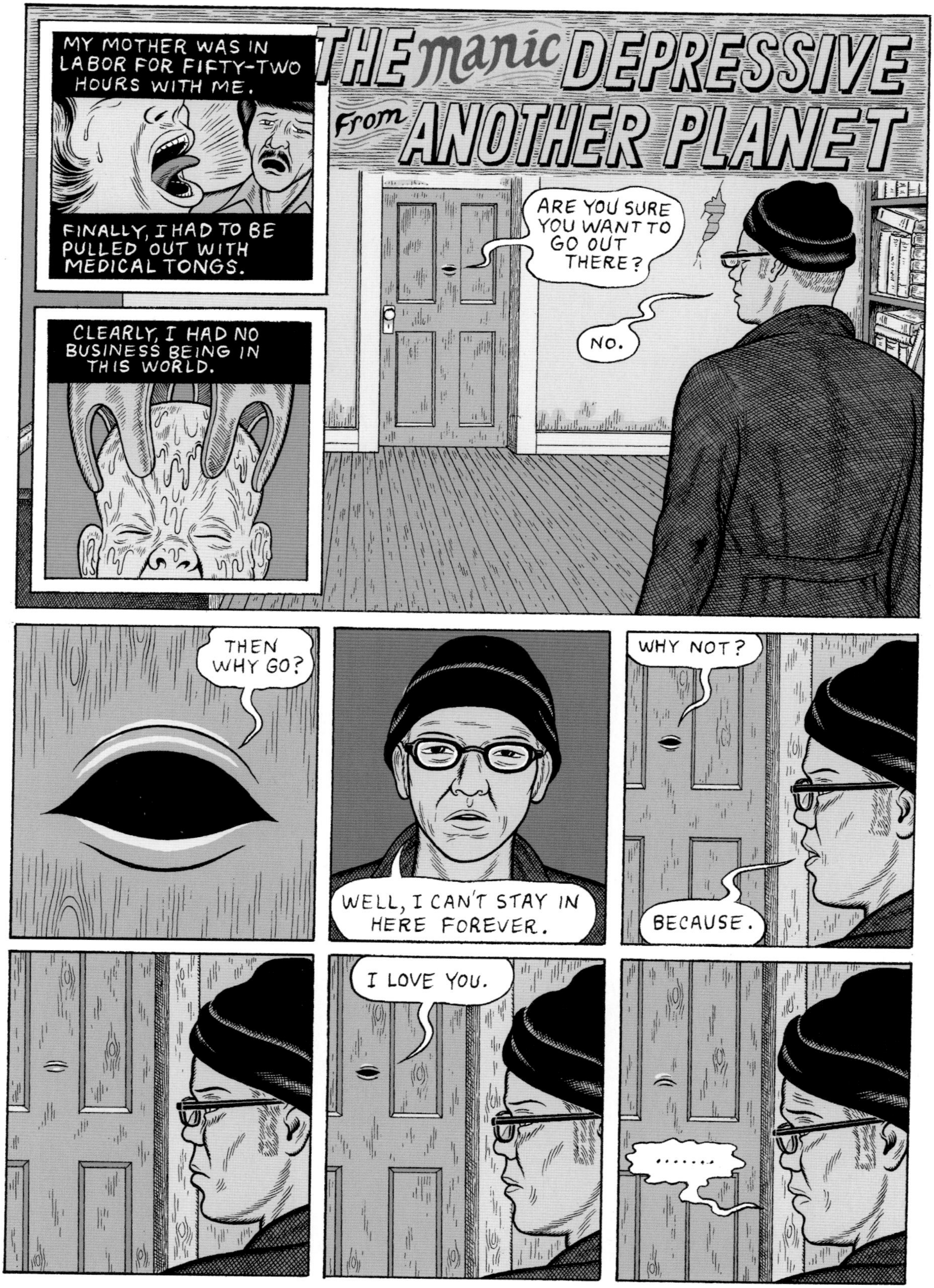
THE manic DEPRESSIVE from ANOTHER PLANET
MY MOTHER WAS IN LABOR FOR FIFTY-TWO HOURS WITH ME.
FINALLY, I HAD TO BE PULLED OUT WITH MEDICAL TONGS.
CLEARLY, I HAD NO BUSINESS BEING IN THIS WORLD.
ARE YOU SURE YOU WANT TO GO OUT THERE?
NO.
THEN WHY GO?
WELL, I CAN'T STAY IN HERE FOREVER.
WHY NOT?
BECAUSE.
I LOVE YOU.
....

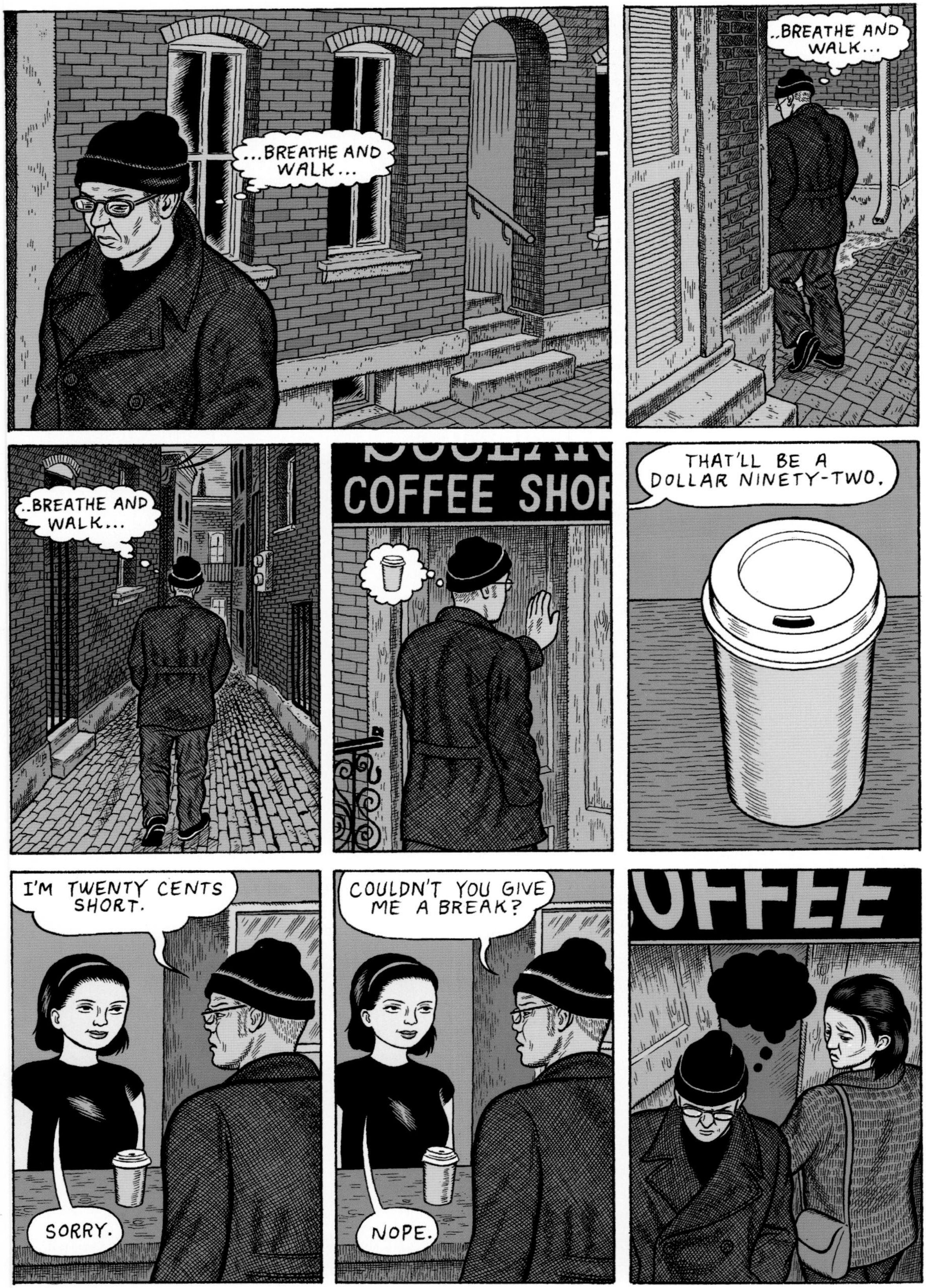
...BREATHE AND WALK...
..BREATHE AND WALK...
..BREATHE AND WALK...
COFFEE SHO
THAT'LL BE A DOLLAR NINETY-TWO.
I'M TWENTY CENTS SHORT.
SORRY.
COULDN'T YOU GIVE ME A BREAK?
NOPE.
OFFEE

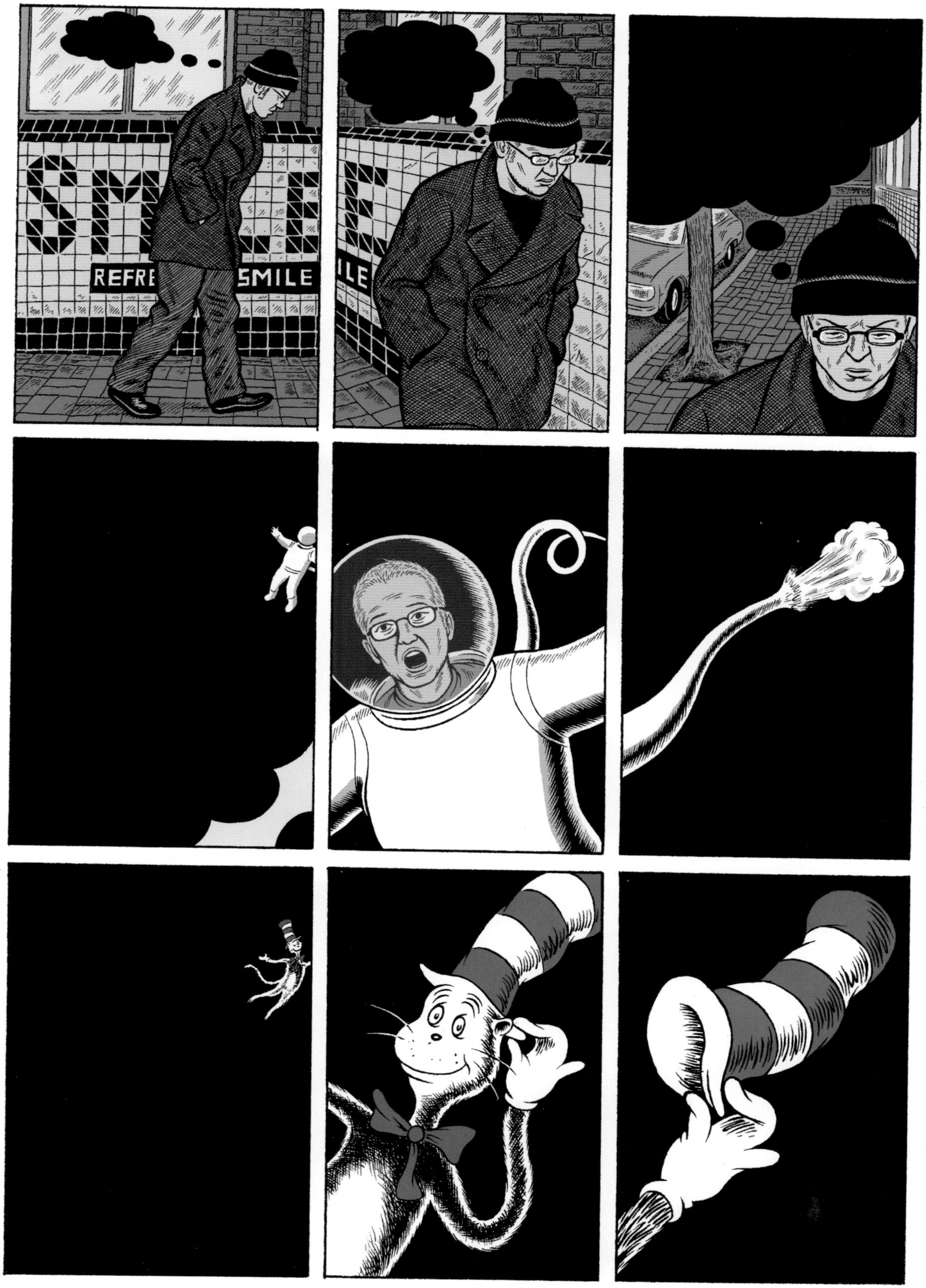
SM
REFRE
SMILE
ILE

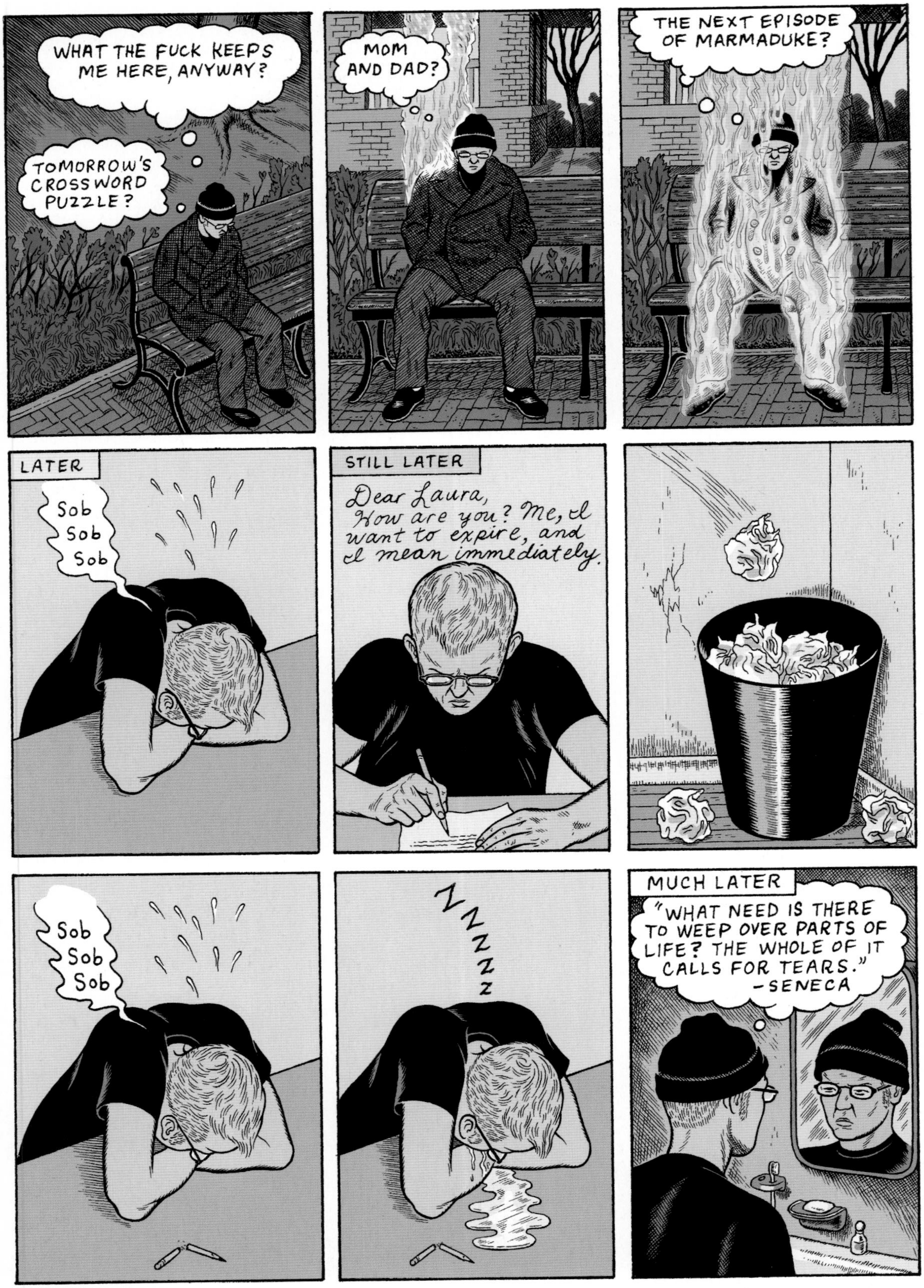

WHAT THE FUCK KEEPS ME HERE, ANYWAY?
TOMORROW'S CROSSWORD PUZZLE?
MOM AND DAD?
THE NEXT EPISODE OF MARMADUKE?
LATER
Sob Sob Sob
STILL LATER
Dear Laura,
How are you? Me, I want to expire, and I mean immediately.
Sob Sob Sob
ZZZZZ
MUCH LATER
"WHAT NEED IS THERE TO WEEP OVER PARTS OF LIFE? THE WHOLE OF IT CALLS FOR TEARS."
-SENECA

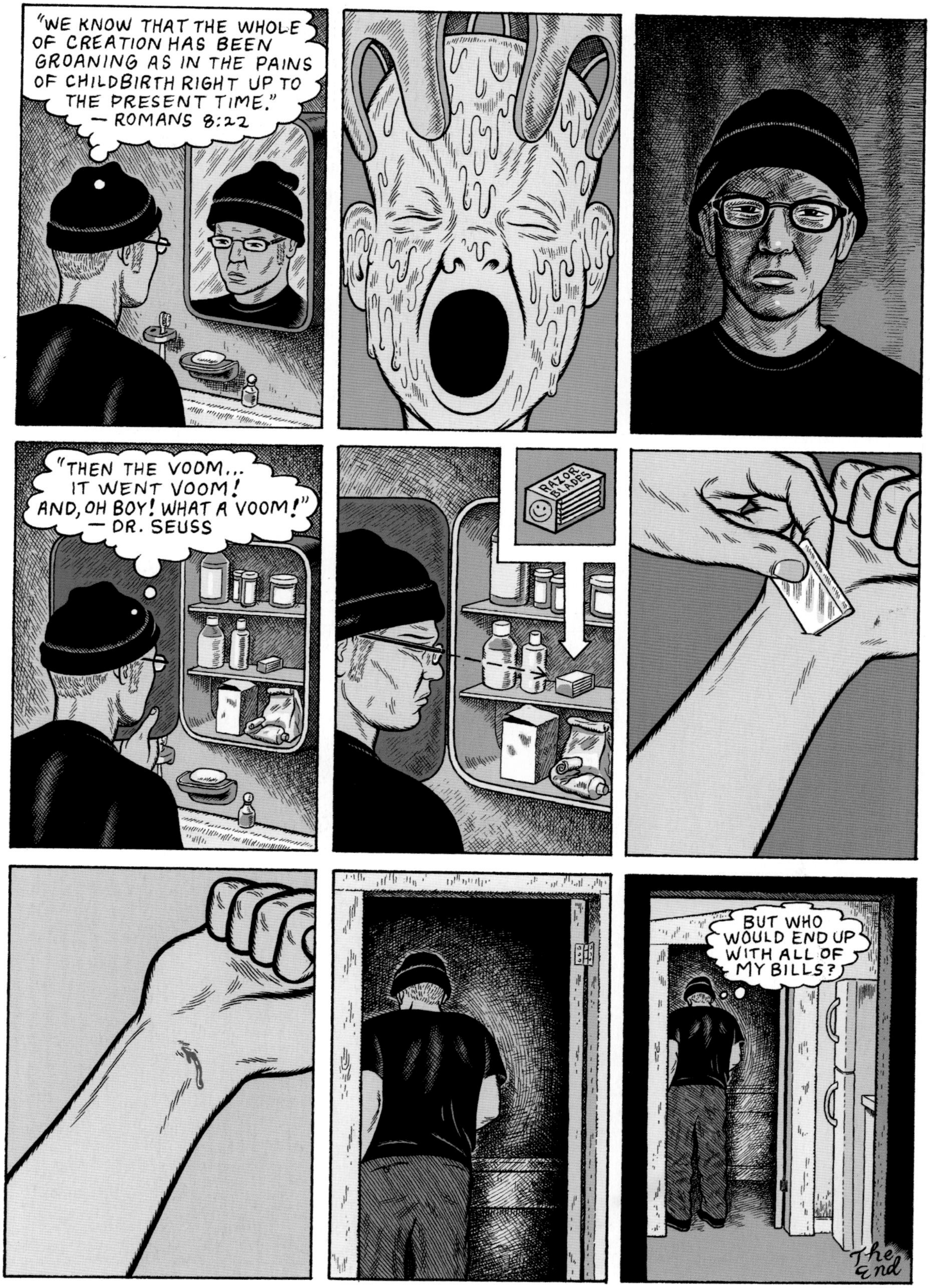
"WE KNOW THAT THE WHOLE OF CREATION HAS BEEN GROANING AS IN THE PAINS OF CHILDBIRTH RIGHT UP TO THE PRESENT TIME." — ROMANS 8:22
"THEN THE VOOM... IT WENT VOOM! AND, OH BOY! WHAT A VOOM!" — DR. SEUSS
RAZOR BLADES
BUT WHO WOULD END UP WITH ALL OF MY BILLS?
The End

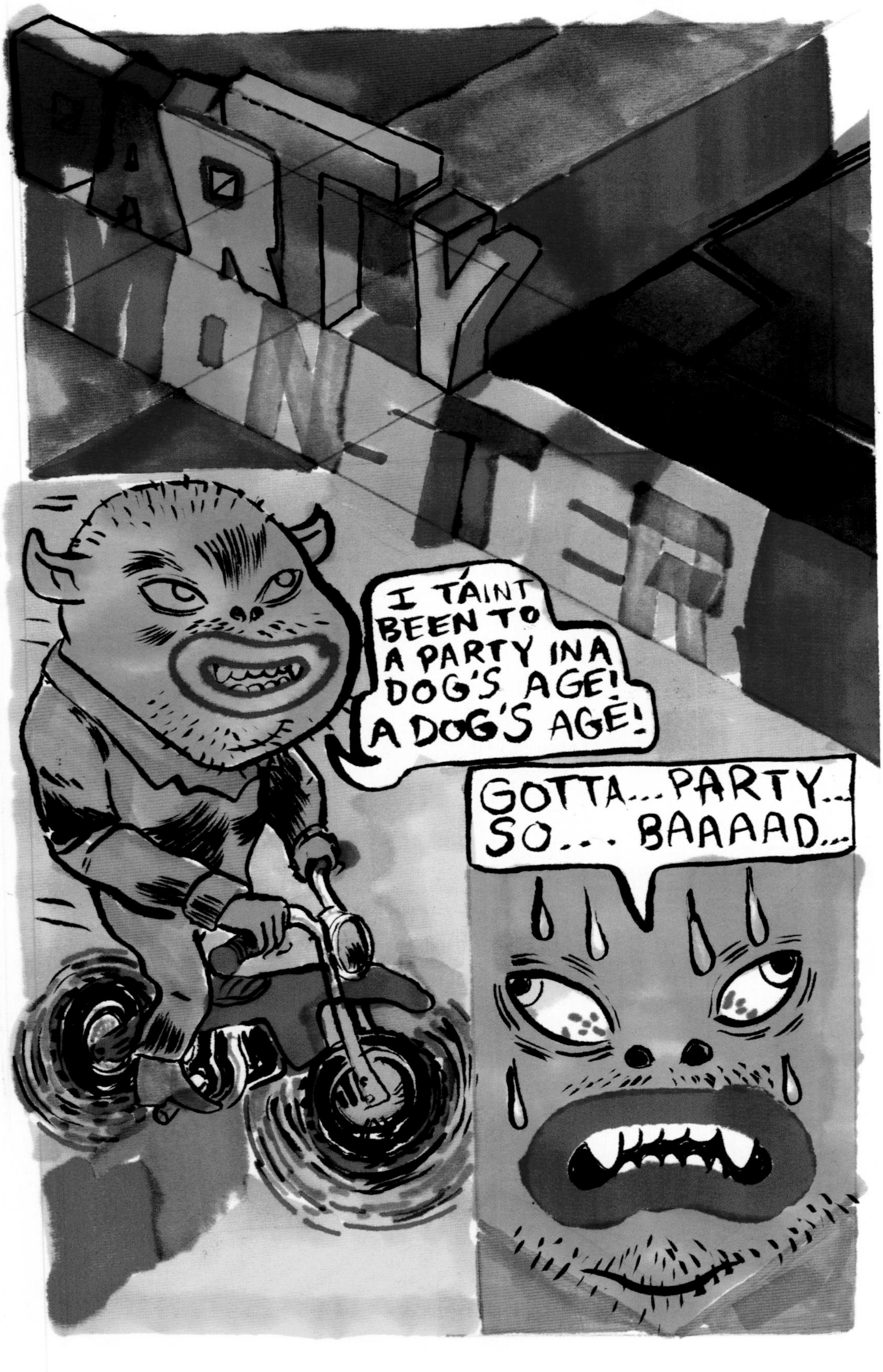
I TAINT BEEN TO A PARTY IN A DOG'S AGE! A DOG'S AGE!
GOTTA... PARTY... SO... BAAAAD...

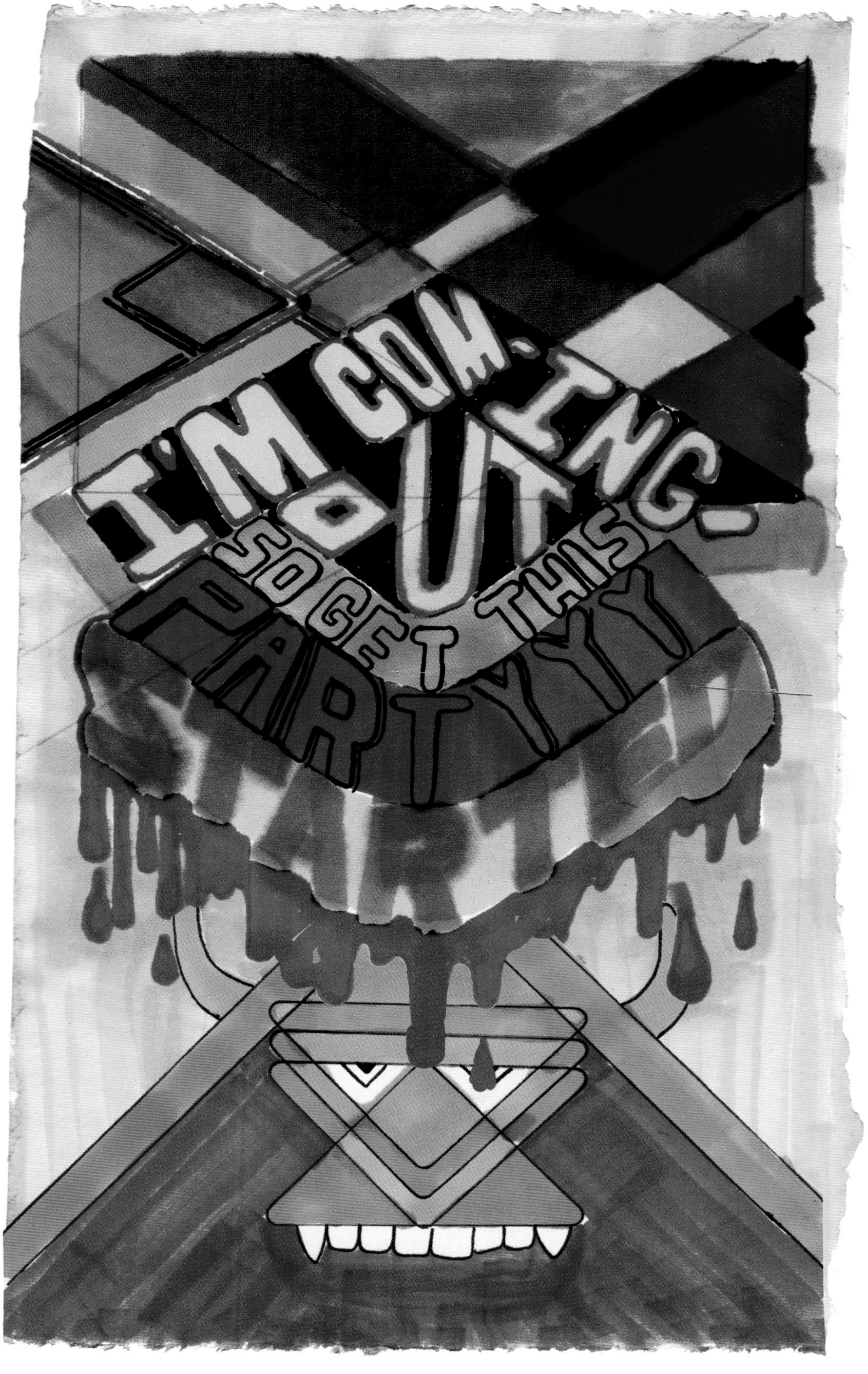
I'M COM-ING-OUT
SO GET THIS
PARTYYY

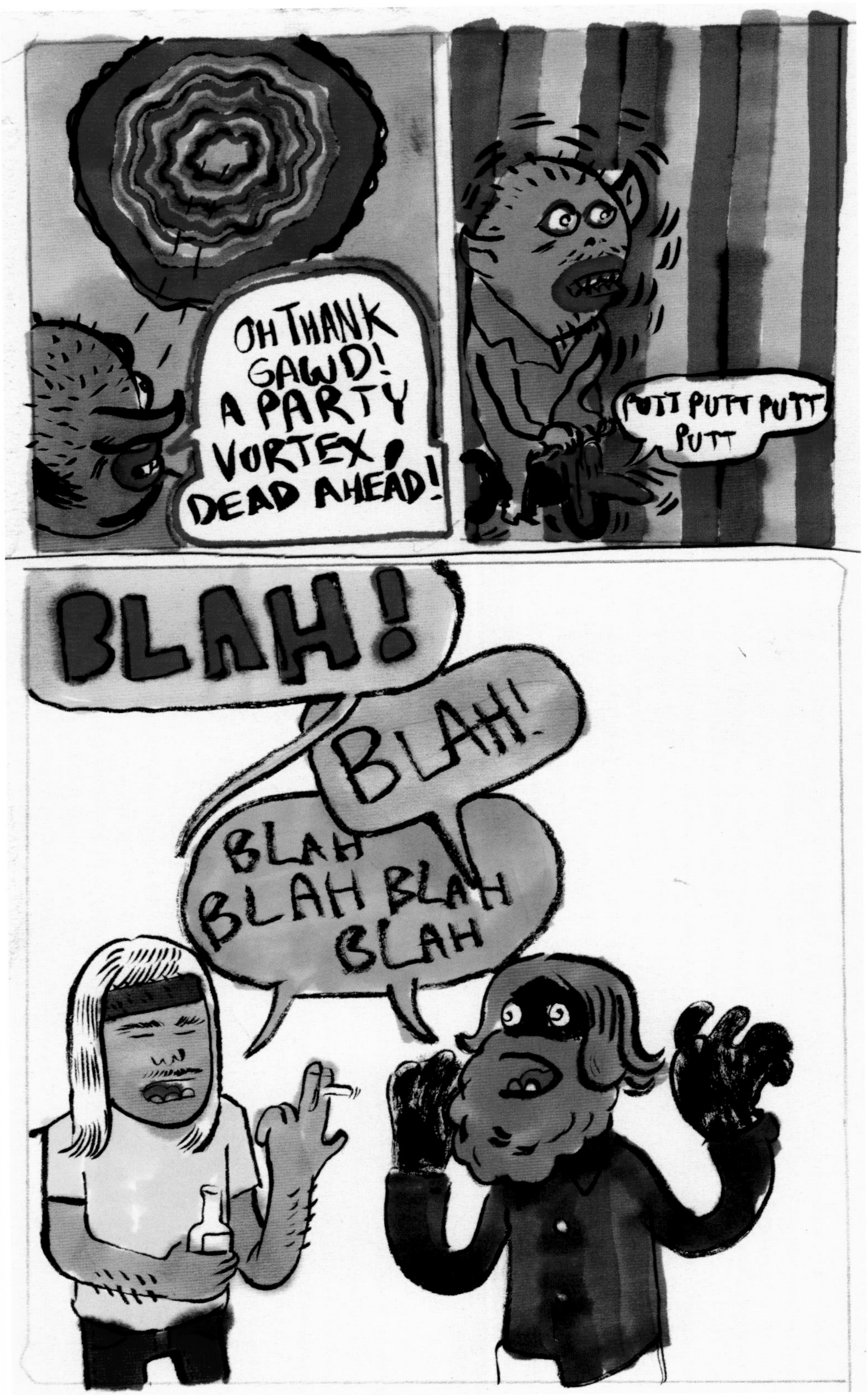
OH THANK GAWD! A PARTY VORTEX DEAD AHEAD!
PUTT PUTT PUTT PUTT PUTT
BLAH!
BLAH!
BLAH BLAH BLAH BLAH

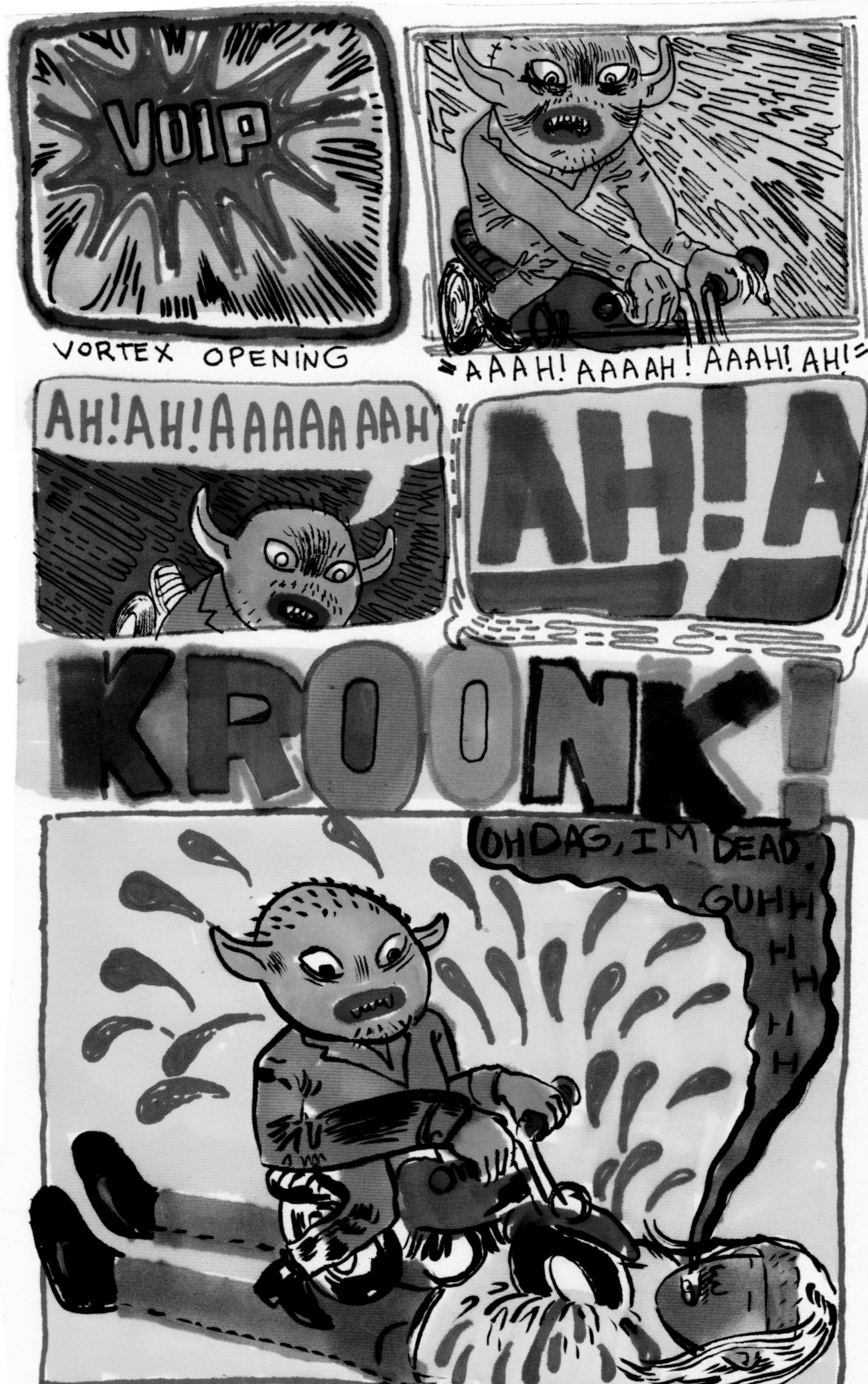
VOIP
VORTEX OPENING
"AAAH! AAAAH! AAAH! AH!"
AH! AH! AAAAA AAH
AH! A
KROONK!
OHDAG, I'M DEAD
GUHHHHHHH

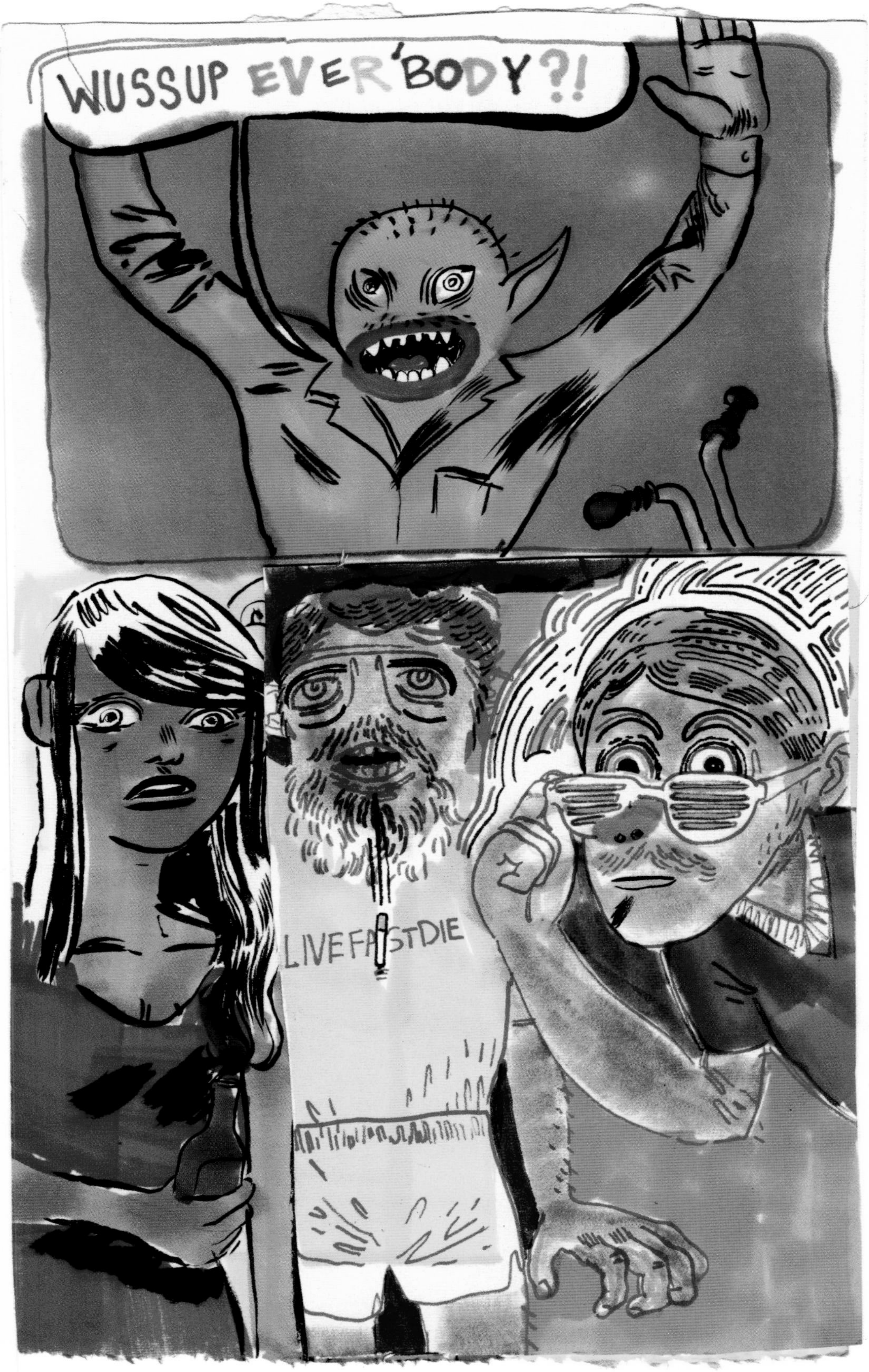
WUSSUP EVER'BODY?!
LIVEFASTDIE

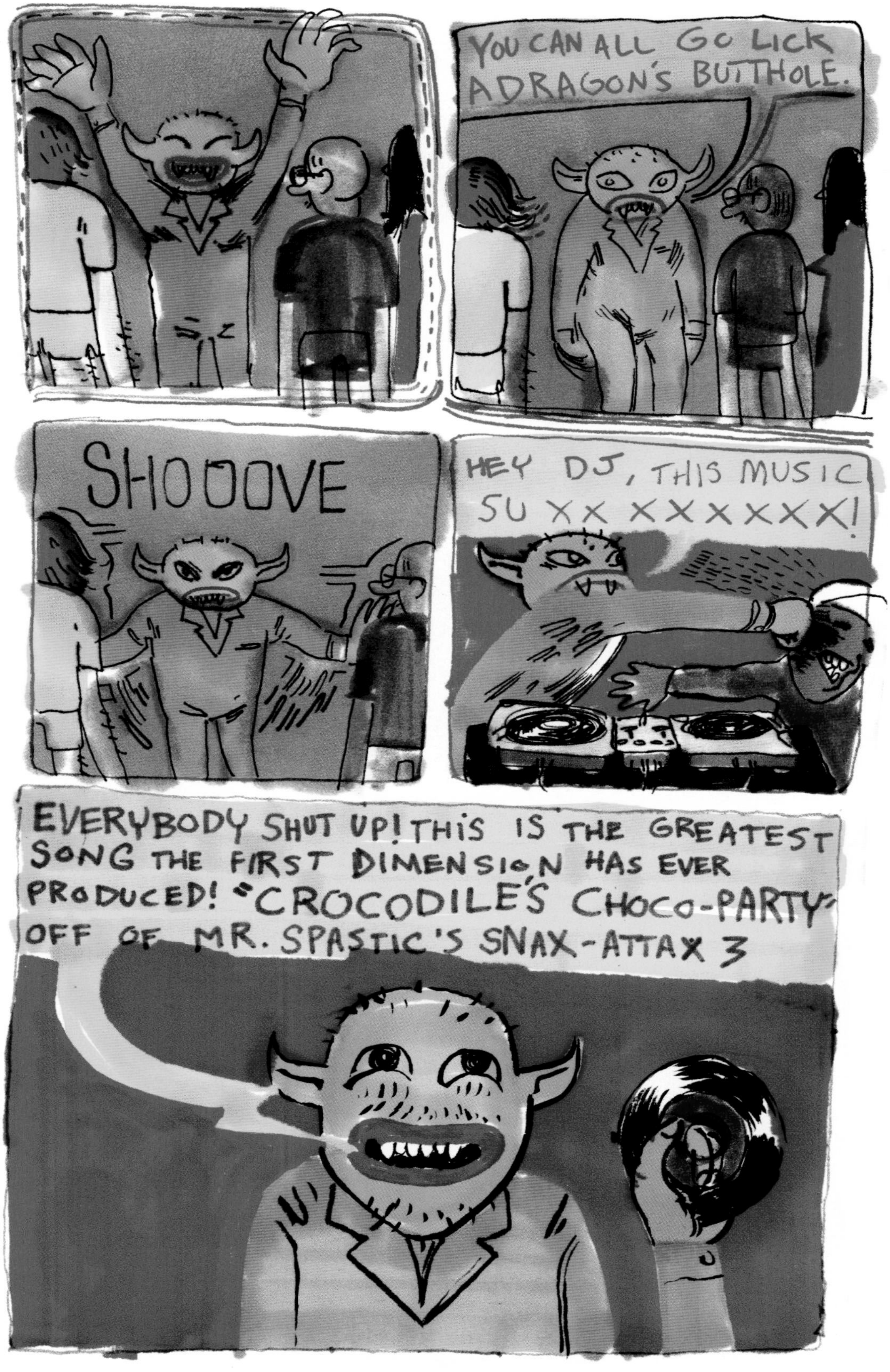
YOU CAN ALL GO LICK A DRAGON'S BUTTHOLE.
SHOOOVE
HEY DJ, THIS MUSIC SU XX XXXXXX!
EVERYBODY SHUT UP! THIS IS THE GREATEST SONG THE FIRST DIMENSION HAS EVER PRODUCED! "CROCODILE'S CHOCO-PARTY" OFF OF MR. SPASTIC'S SNAX-ATTAX 3

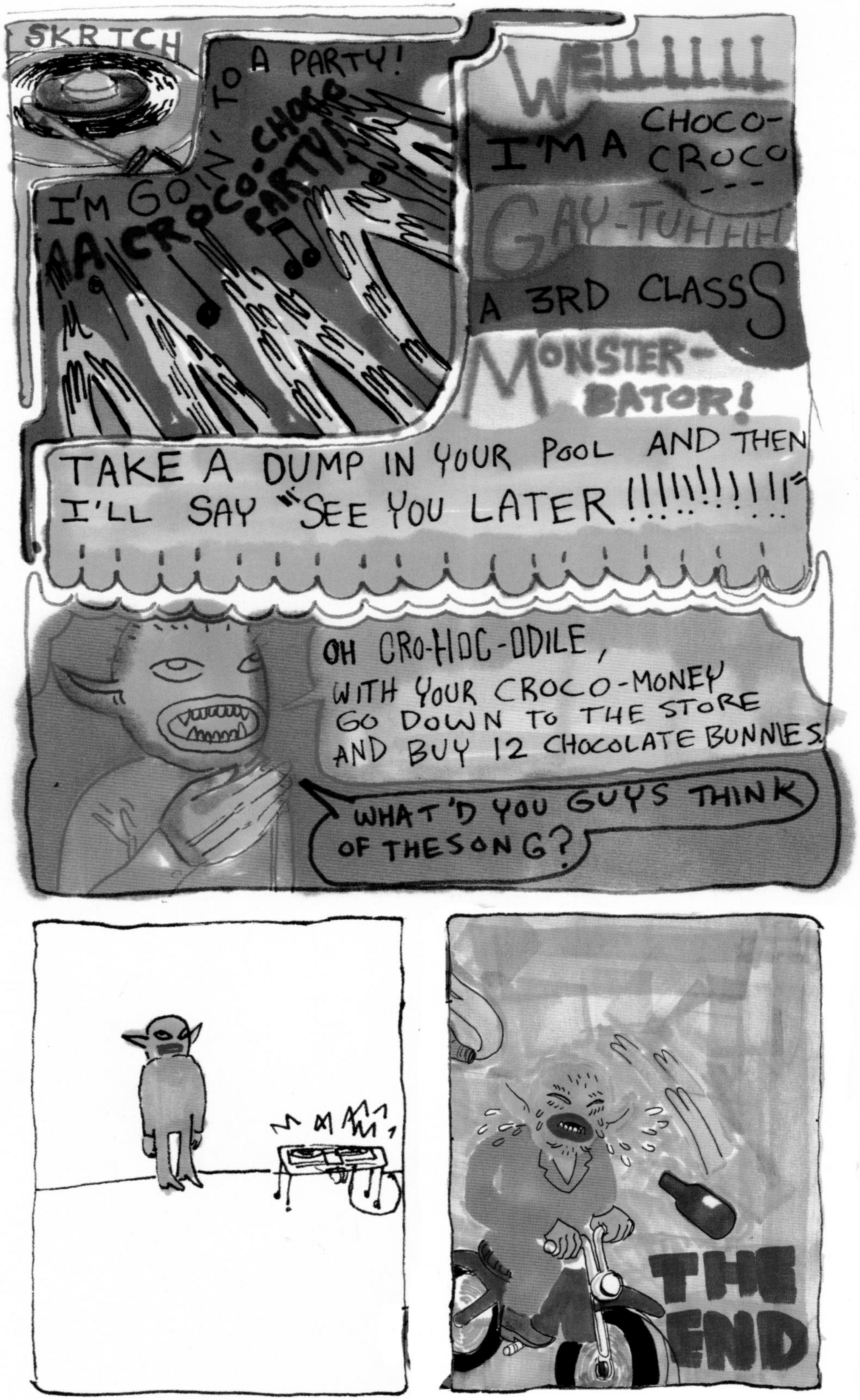
SKRTCH
I'M GOIN' TO A PARTY!
A CROCO-CHOCO PARTY!
WELLLLLL
I'M A CHOCO-CROCO---
GAY-TUHHHH
A 3RD CLASSS
MONSTER-BATOR!
TAKE A DUMP IN YOUR POOL AND THEN I'LL SAY "SEE YOU LATER!!!!!!!!!!"
OH CRO-HOC-ODILE, WITH YOUR CROCO-MONEY GO DOWN TO THE STORE AND BUY 12 CHOCOLATE BUNNIES.
WHAT'D YOU GUYS THINK OF THESONG?
THE END

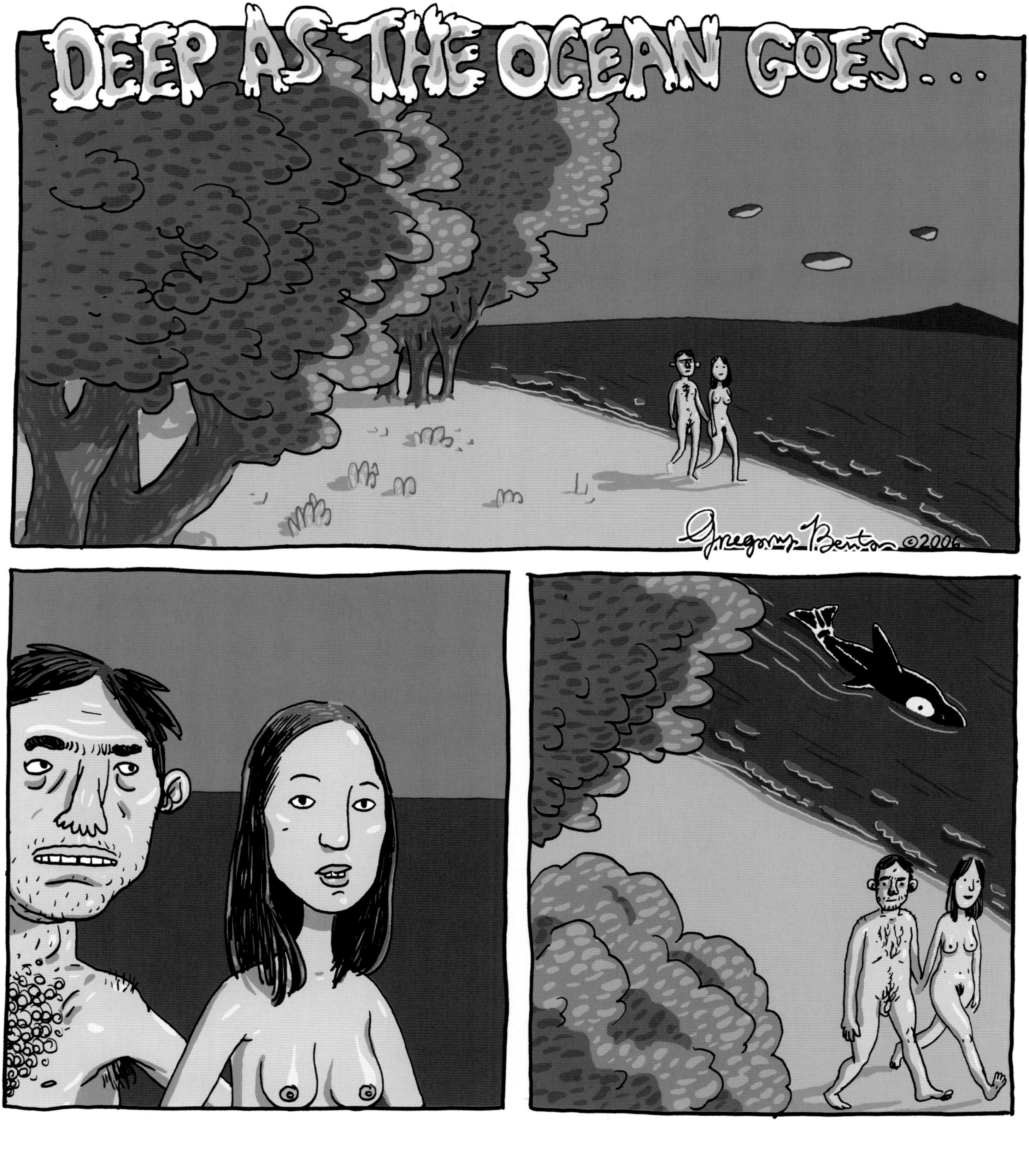
DEEP AS THE OCEAN GOES...
Gregory Benton ©2006

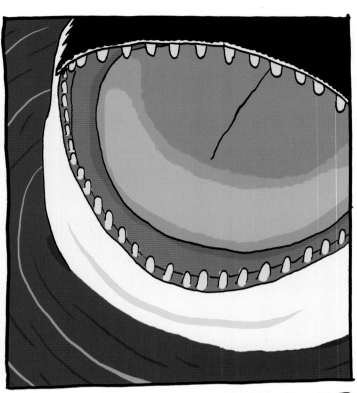

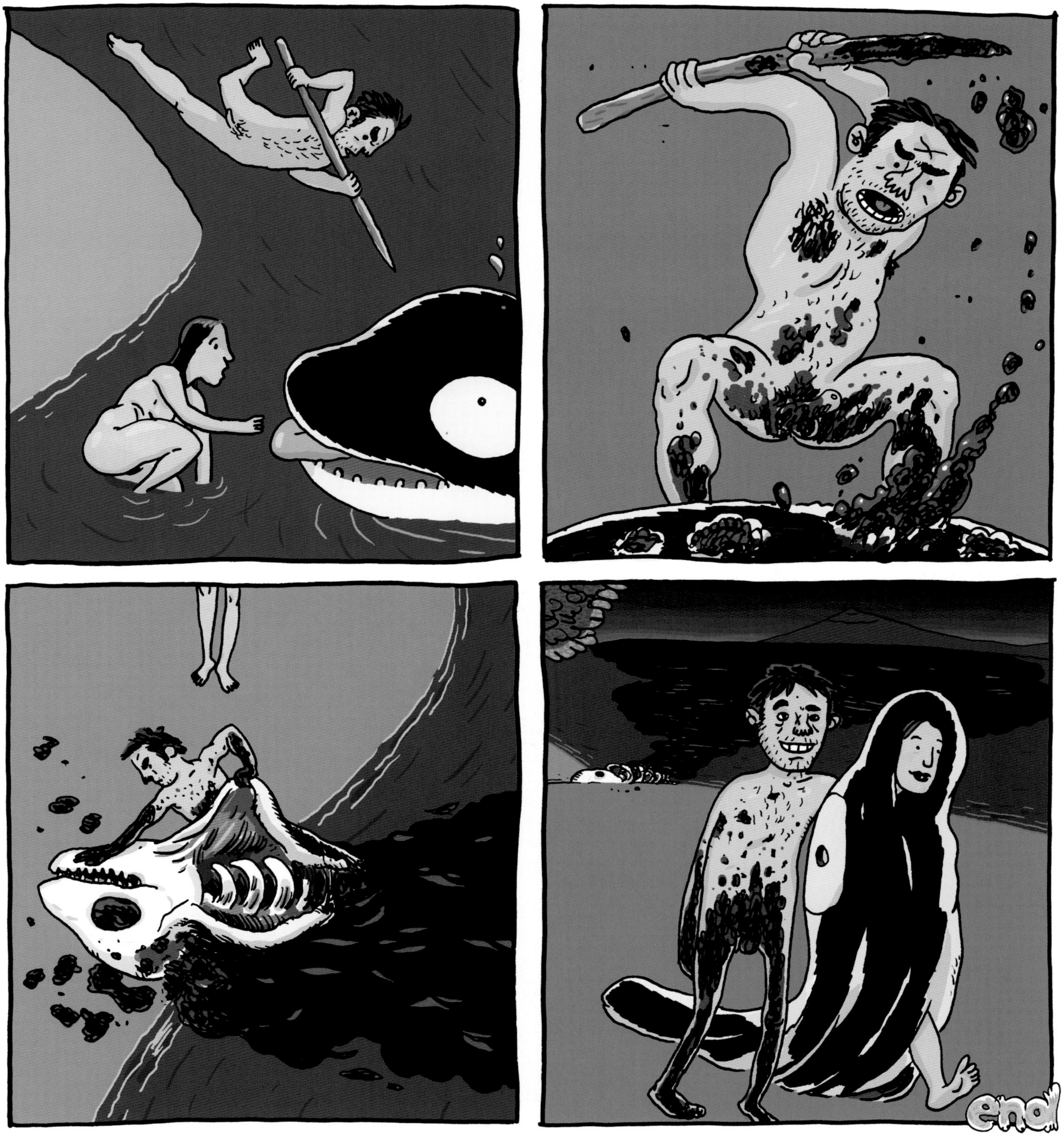
end

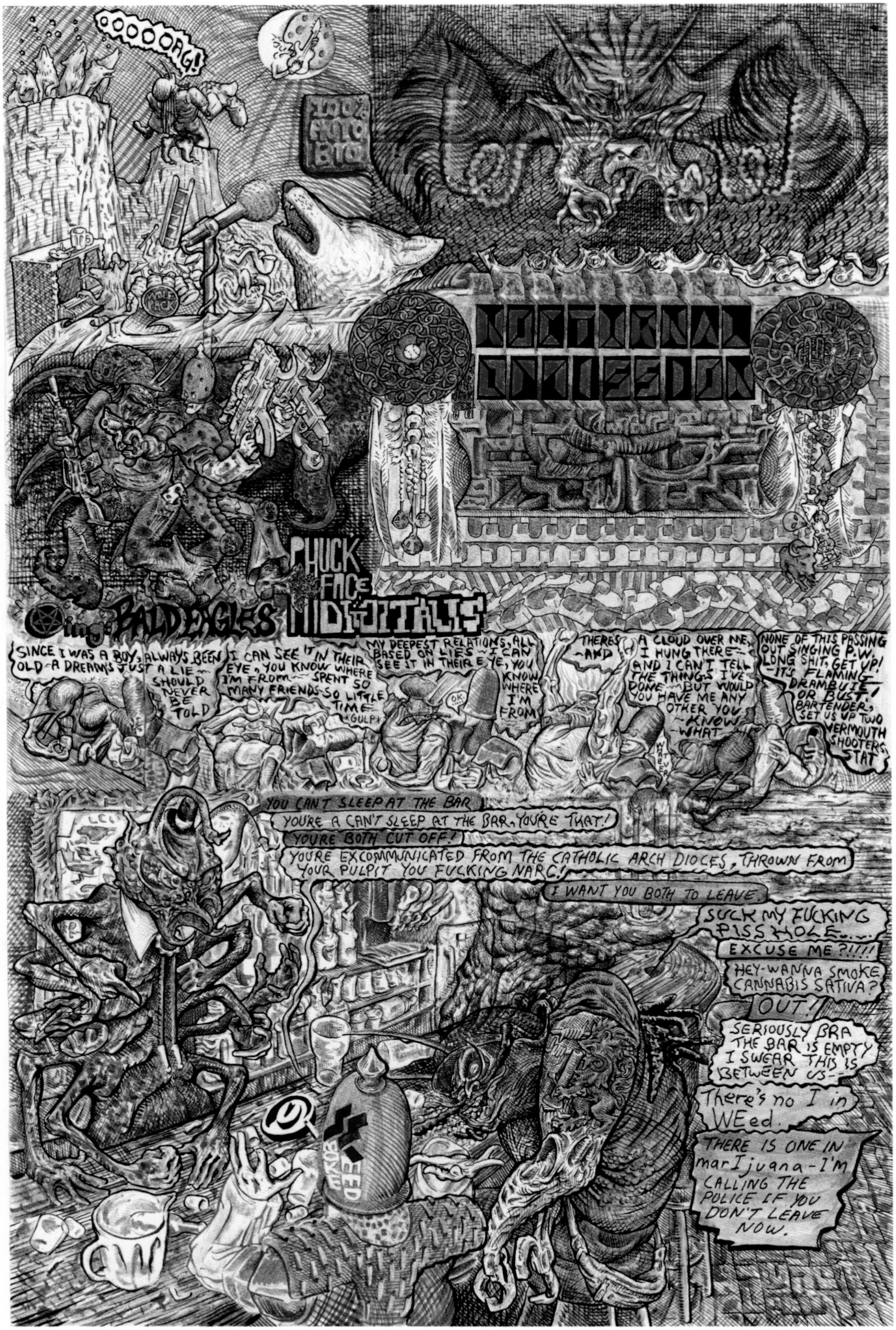
OOOOOAG!
PHUCK FACE
BALD EAGLES
SINCE I WAS A BOY, ALWAYS BEEN OLD - A DREAM'S JUST A LIE ~ SHOULD NEVER BE TOLD
I CAN SEE IT IN THEIR EYE, YOU KNOW WHERE I'M FROM ~ SPENT SO MANY FRIENDS - SO LITTLE TIME
GULP
OK.
MY DEEPEST RELATIONS, ALL BASED ON LIES ~ I CAN SEE IT IN THEIR EYE, YOU KNOW WHERE I'M FROM
THERE'S ~AND
A CLOUD OVER ME, I HUNG THERE ~ AND I CAN'T TELL THE THINGS I'VE DONE ~ BUT WOULD YOU HAVE ME ANY OTHER YOU ~ KNOW ~ WHAT
WHATEVER
NONE OF THIS PASSING OUT SINGING P.W. LONG SHIT, GET UP! - IT'S FLAMING DRAMBUIE OR BUST! BARTENDER, SET US UP TWO VERMOUTH SHOOTERS, STAT
YOU CAN'T SLEEP AT THE BAR
YOU'RE A CAN'T SLEEP AT THE BAR, YOU'RE THAT!
YOU'RE BOTH CUT OFF!
YOU'RE EXCOMMUNICATED FROM THE CATHOLIC ARCH DIOCES, THROWN FROM YOUR PULPIT YOU FUCKING NARC!
I WANT YOU BOTH TO LEAVE
SUCK MY FUCKING PISS HOLE...
EXCUSE ME?!!!!
HEY-WANNA SMOKE CANNABIS SATIVA?
OUT!
SERIOUSLY BRA THE BAR IS EMPTY I SWEAR THIS IS BETWEEN US -
There's no I in WEed.
THERE IS ONE IN marIjuana - I'M CALLING THE POLICE IF YOU DON'T LEAVE NOW.

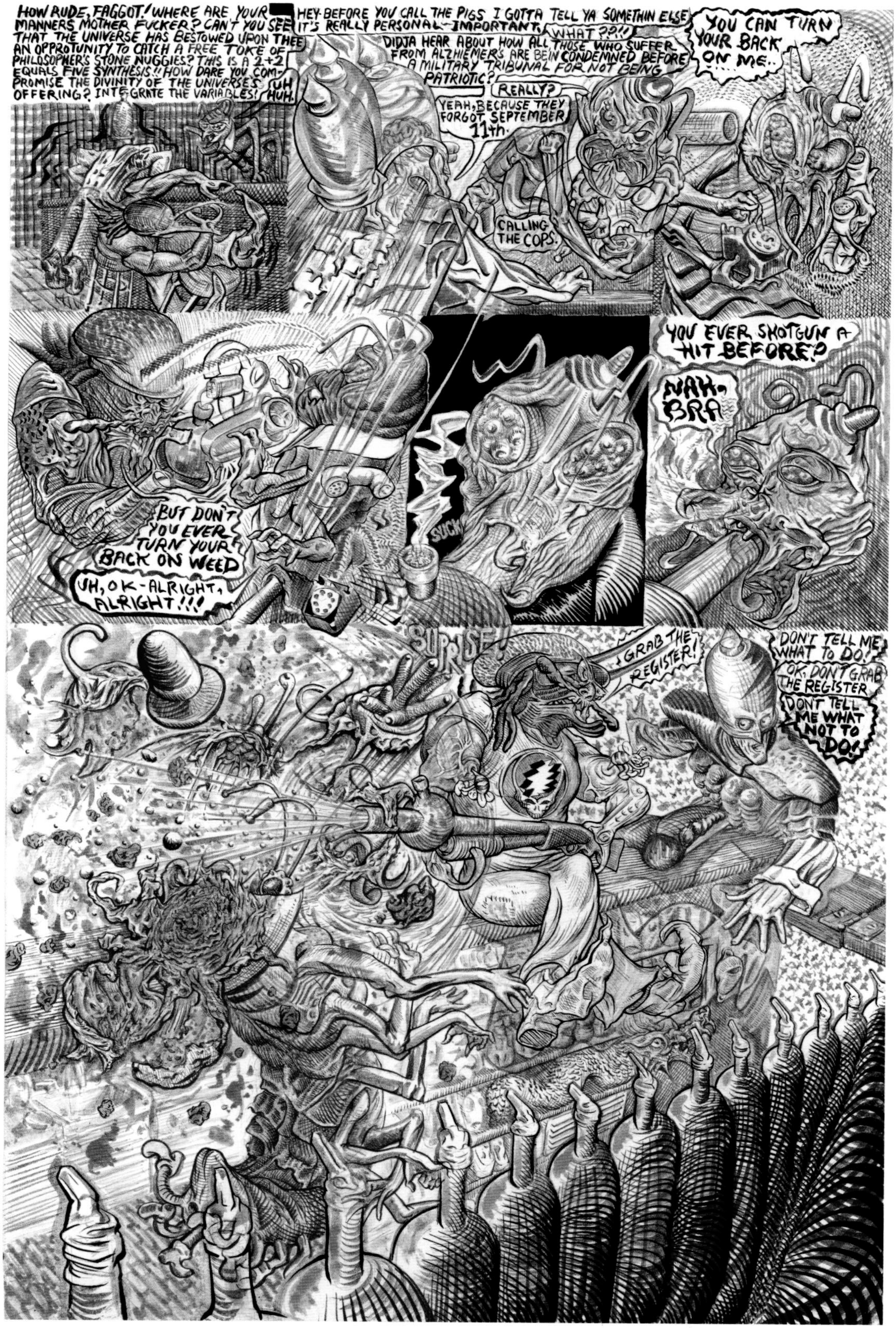
HOW RUDE, FAGGOT! WHERE ARE YOUR MANNERS MOTHER FUCKER? CAN'T YOU SEE THAT THE UNIVERSE HAS BESTOWED UPON THEE AN OPPROTUNITY TO CATCH A FREE TOKE OF PHILOSOPHER'S STONE NUGGIES? THIS IS A 2+2 EQUALS FIVE SYNTHESIS!! HOW DARE YOU COMPROMISE THE DIVINITY OF THE UNIVERSE'S OFFERING? INTEGRATE THE VARIABLES!
UH HUH.
HEY-BEFORE YOU CALL THE PIGS I GOTTA TELL YA SOMETHIN ELSE IT'S REALLY PERSONAL-IMPORTANT.
WHAT??!!
DIDJA HEAR ABOUT HOW ALL THOSE WHO SUFFER FROM ALZHIEMER'S ARE BEIN CONDEMNED BEFORE A MILITARY TRIBUNAL FOR NOT BEING PATRIOTIC?
REALLY?
YEAH, BECAUSE THEY FORGOT SEPTEMBER 11th.
CALLING THE COPS.
YOU CAN TURN YOUR BACK ON ME....
BUT DON'T YOU EVER TURN YOUR BACK ON WEED
UH, OK-ALRIGHT, ALRIGHT!!!
SUCK
YOU EVER SHOTGUN A HIT BEFORE?
NAH, BRA
SURPRISE!
GRAB THE REGISTER!
DON'T TELL ME WHAT TO DO!
OK, DON'T GRAB THE REGISTER
DON'T TELL ME WHAT NOT TO DO!

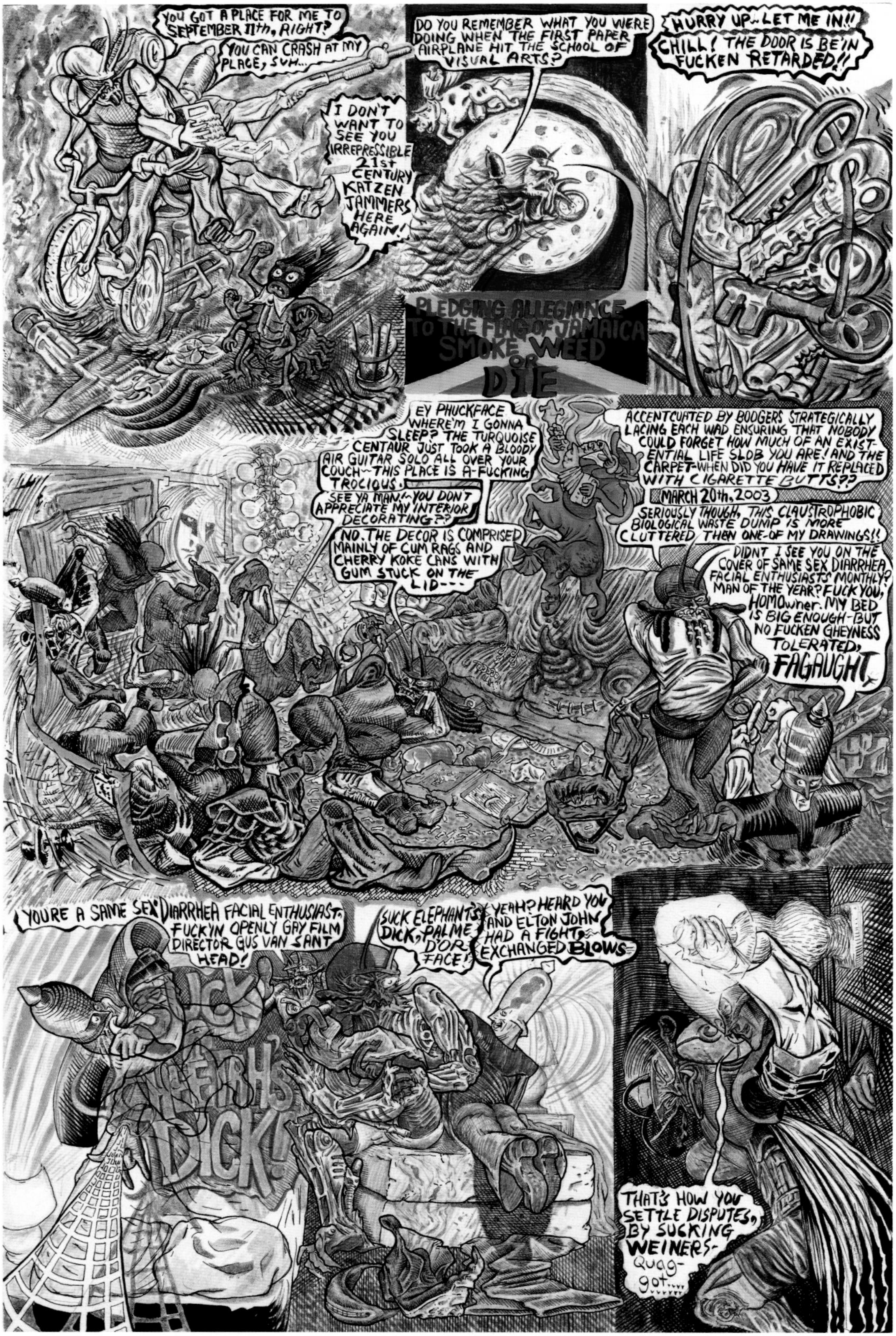

YOU GOT A PLACE FOR ME TO SEPTEMBER 11th, RIGHT?
YOU CAN CRASH AT MY PLACE, SUH...
I DON'T WANT TO SEE YOU IRREPRESSIBLE 21st CENTURY KATZEN JAMMERS HERE AGAIN!
DO YOU REMEMBER WHAT YOU WERE DOING WHEN THE FIRST PAPER AIRPLANE HIT THE SCHOOL OF VISUAL ARTS?
PLEDGING ALLEGIANCE TO THE FLAG OF JAMAICA SMOKE WEED OR DIE
HURRY UP~LET ME IN!!
CHILL! THE DOOR IS BE'IN FUCKEN RETARDED!!
EY PHUCKFACE WHERE'M I GONNA SLEEP? THE TURQUOISE CENTAUR JUST TOOK A BLOODY AIR GUITAR SOLO ALL OVER YOUR COUCH~THIS PLACE IS A-FUCKING TROCIOUS.
SEE YA MAN!~YOU DON'T APPRECIATE MY INTERIOR DECORATING??
NO. THE DECOR IS COMPRISED MAINLY OF CUM RAGS AND CHERRY KOKE CANS WITH GUM STUCK ON THE LID---
ACCENTCUATED BY BOOGERS STRATEGICALLY LACING EACH WAD ENSURING THAT NOBODY COULD FORGET HOW MUCH OF AN EXIST-ENTIAL LIFE SLOB YOU ARE! AND THE CARPET-WHEN DID YOU HAVE IT REPLACED WITH CIGARETTE BUTTS??
MARCH 20th, 2003
SERIOUSLY THOUGH, THIS CLAUSTROPHOBIC BIOLOGICAL WASTE DUMP IS MORE CLUTTERED THEN ONE-OF MY DRAWINGS!!
DIDNT I SEE YOU ON THE COVER OF SAME SEX DIARRHEA FACIAL ENTHUSIASTS' MONTHLY? MAN OF THE YEAR? FUCK YOU, HOMOwner. MY BED IS BIG ENOUGH-BUT NO FUCKEN GHEYNESS TOLERATED, FAGAUGHT.
YOU'RE A SAME SEX DIARRHEA FACIAL ENTHUSIAST, FUCK'IN OPENLY GAY FILM DIRECTOR GUS VAN SANT HEAD!
SUCK ELEPHANT'S DICK, PALME D'OR FACE!
YEAH? HEARD YOU AND ELTON JOHN HAD A FIGHT, EXCHANGED BLOWS
DICK!
THAT'S HOW YOU SETTLE DISPUTES, BY SUCKING WEINERS-
Quag-got.....

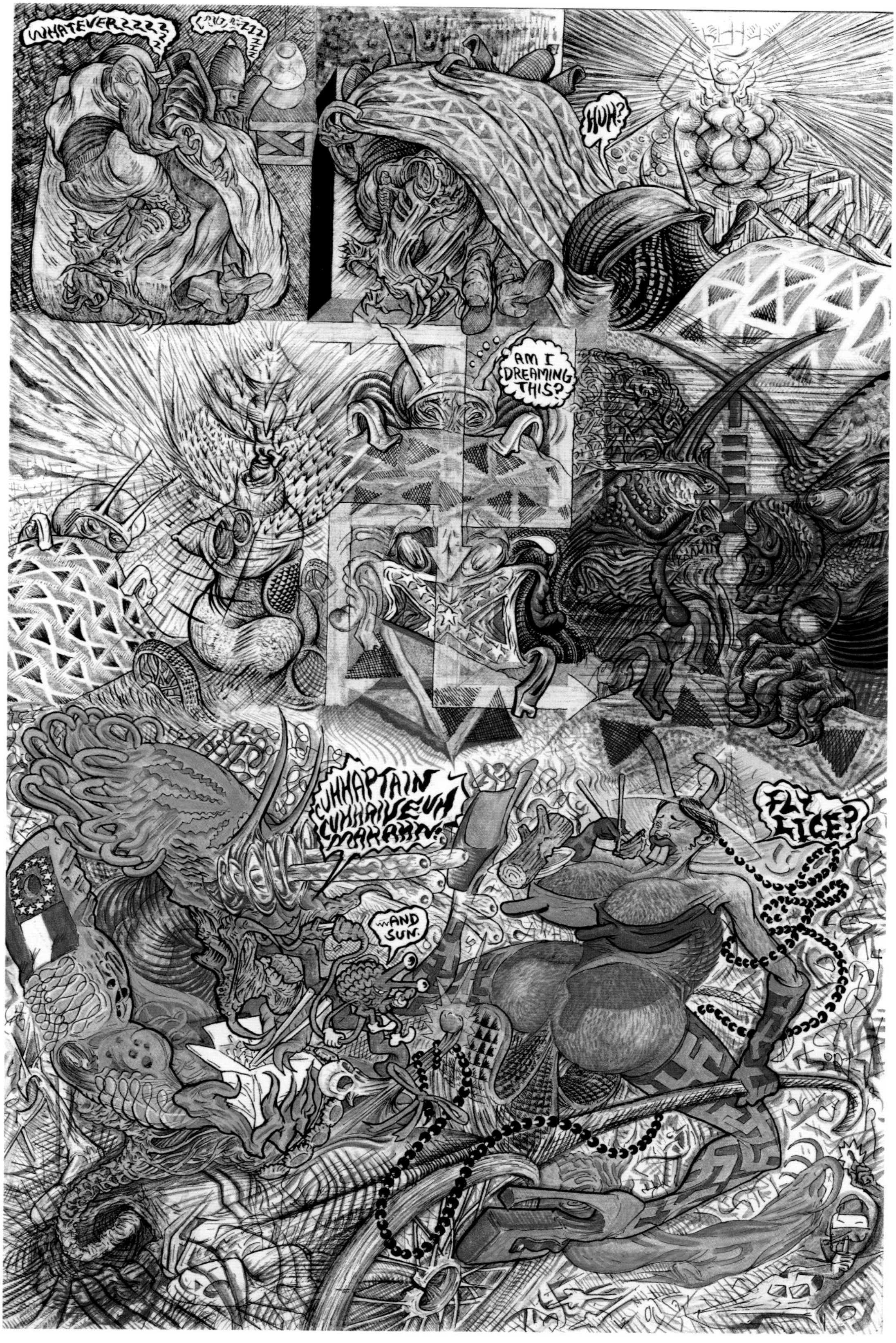
WHATEVERZZZZZZZ
HUH?
AM I DREAMING THIS?
CUHHAPTAIN CUHHAIVEUH CUHRAHN!
AND SUN.
FLY LICE?

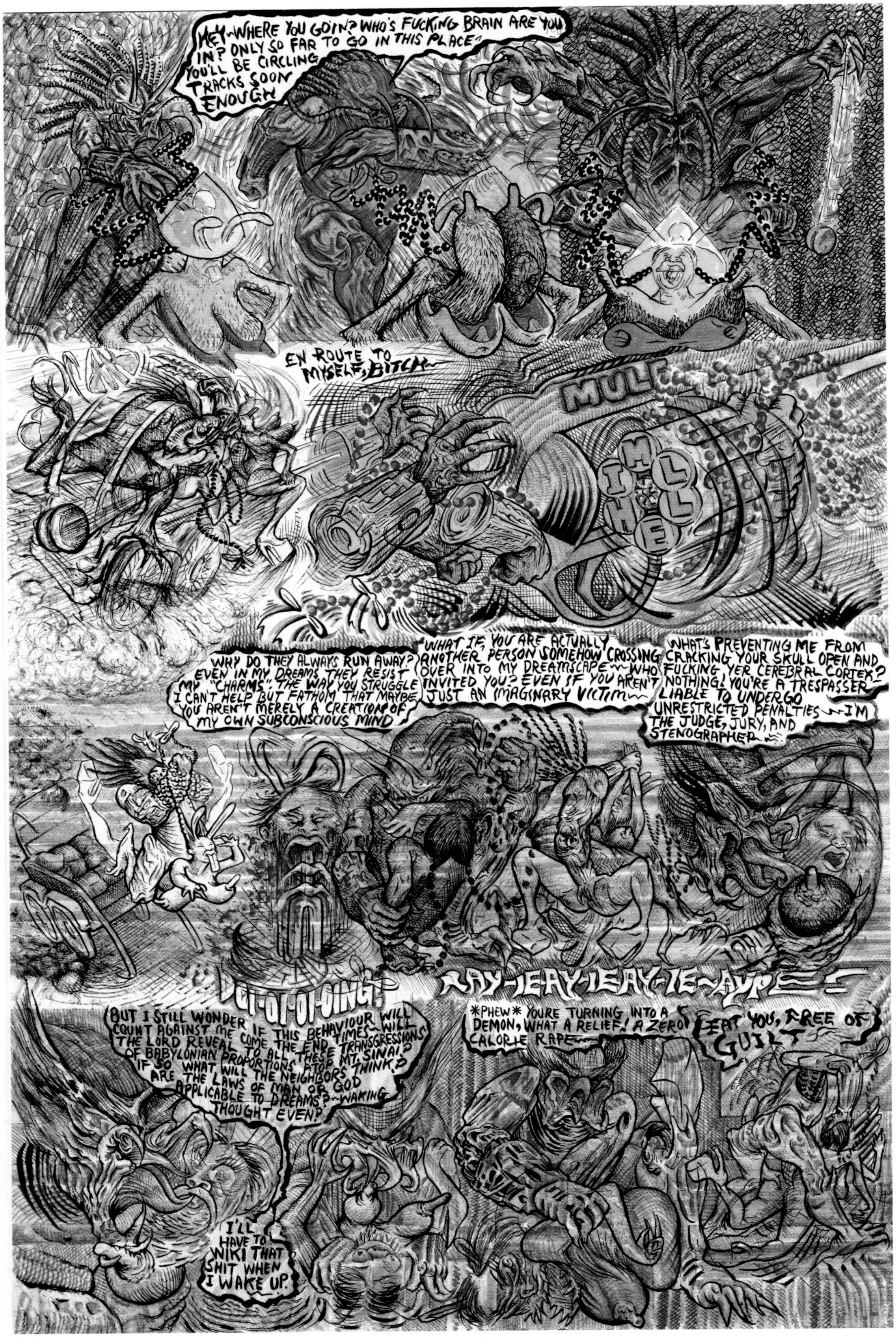
HEY~WHERE YOU GOIN? WHO'S FUCKING BRAIN ARE YOU IN? ONLY SO FAR TO GO IN THIS PLACE~ YOU'LL BE CIRCLING TRACKS SOON ENOUGH
EN ROUTE TO MYSELF, BITCH~
WHY DO THEY ALWAYS RUN AWAY? EVEN IN MY DREAMS THEY RESIST MY "CHARMS". THE WAY YOU STRUGGLE I CAN'T HELP BUT FATHOM THAT MAYBE YOU AREN'T MERELY A CREATION OF MY OWN SUBCONSCIOUS MIND
WHAT IF, YOU ARE ACTUALLY ANOTHER PERSON SOMEHOW CROSSING OVER INTO MY DREAMSCAPE~ WHO INVITED YOU? EVEN IF YOU AREN'T JUST AN IMAGINARY VICTIM~
WHAT'S PREVENTING ME FROM CRACKING YOUR SKULL OPEN AND FUCKING YER CEREBRAL CORTEX? NOTHING! YOU'RE A TRESPASSER LIABLE TO UNDERGO UNRESTRICTED PENALTIES~ I'M THE JUDGE, JURY, AND STENOGRAPHER~
OI-OI-OI-OING!
BUT I STILL WONDER IF THIS BEHAVIOUR WILL COUNT AGAINST ME COME THE END TIMES~ WILL THE LORD REVEAL TO ALL THESE TRANSGRESSIONS OF BABYLONIAN PROPORTIONS ATOP MT. SINAI? IF SO WHAT WILL THE NEIGHBORS THINK? ARE THE LAWS OF MAN OR GOD APPLICABLE TO DREAMS?~ WAKING THOUGHT EVEN?
PHEW YOURE TURNING INTO A DEMON, WHAT A RELIEF! A ZERO CALORIE RAPE~
EAT YOU, FREE OF GUILT
I'LL HAVE TO WIKI THAT SHIT WHEN I WAKE UP.

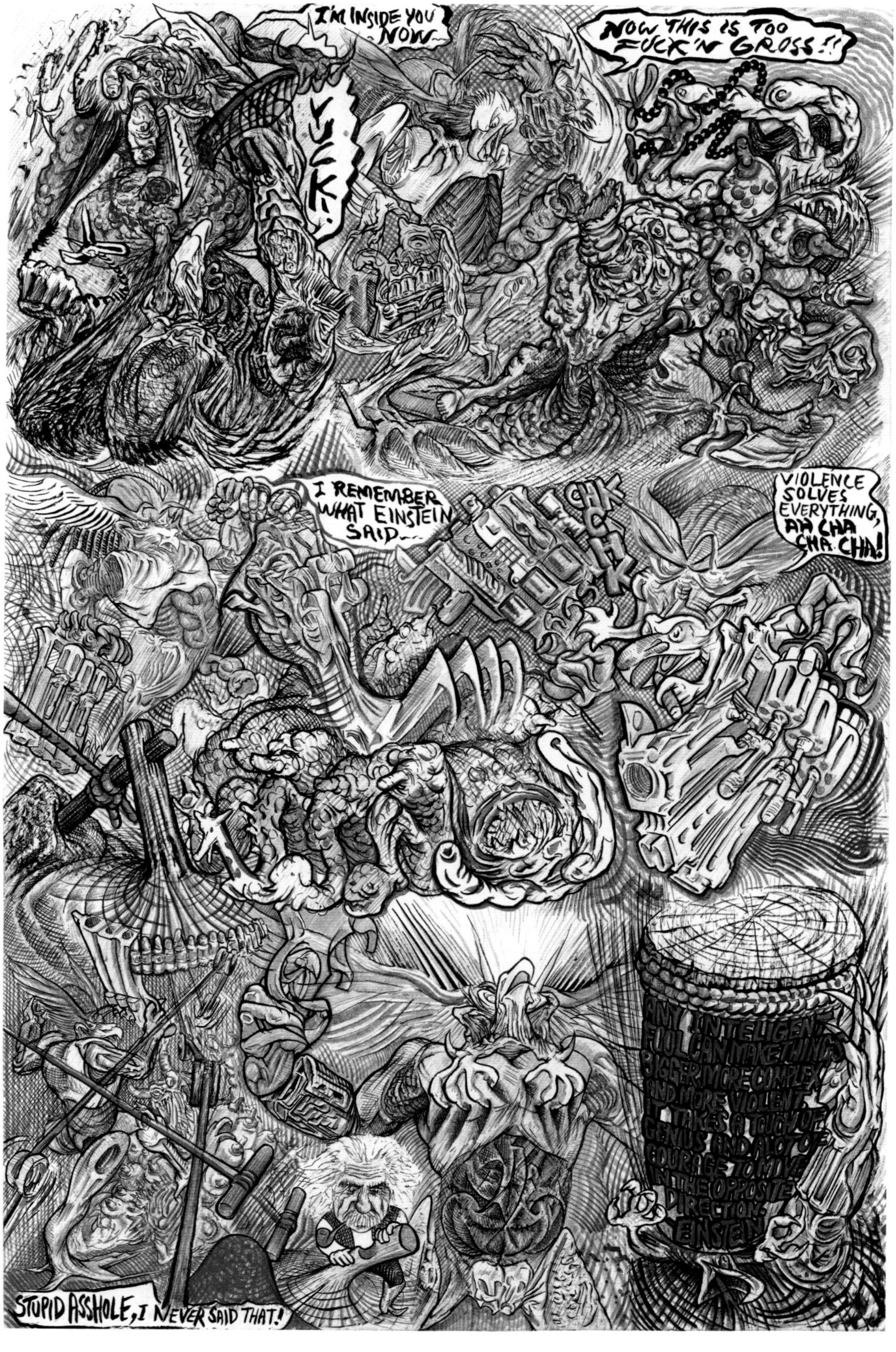
I'M INSIDE YOU NOW
YUCK!
NOW THIS IS TOO FUCK'N GROSS!!
I REMEMBER WHAT EINSTEIN SAID...
CHK CHK CHK
VIOLENCE SOLVES EVERYTHING, AH CHA CHA CHA!
ANY INTELIGENT FOOL CAN MAKE THINGS BIGGER, MORE COMPLEX AND MORE VIOLENT. IT TAKES A TOUCH OF GENIUS AND A LOT OF COURAGE TO MOVE IN THE OPPOSITE DIRECTION. EINSTEIN
STUPID ASSHOLE, I NEVER SAID THAT!

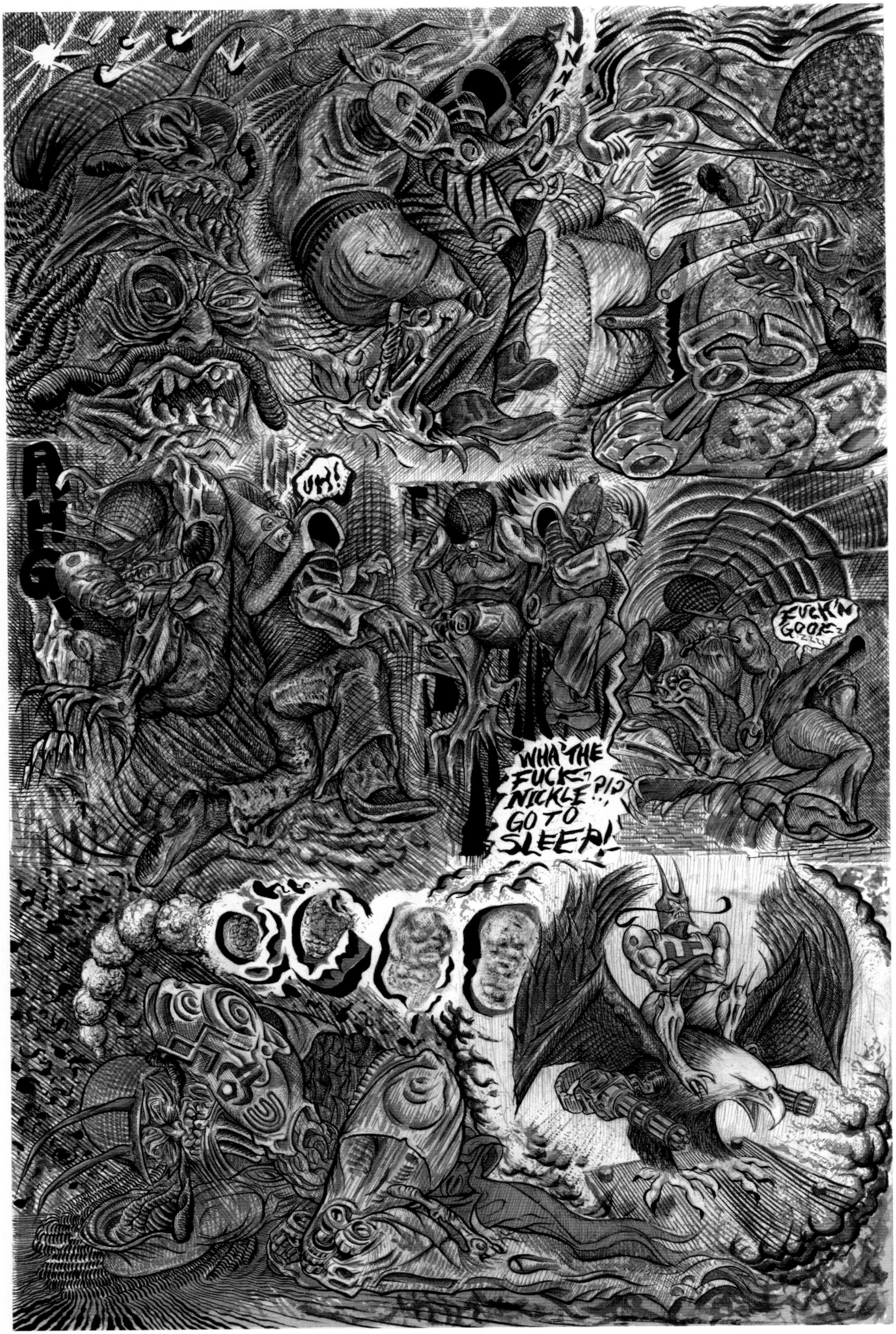
AHG!
UH!
FUCK'N GOOF
WHA'THE FUCK?!? NICKLE GO TO SLEEP!

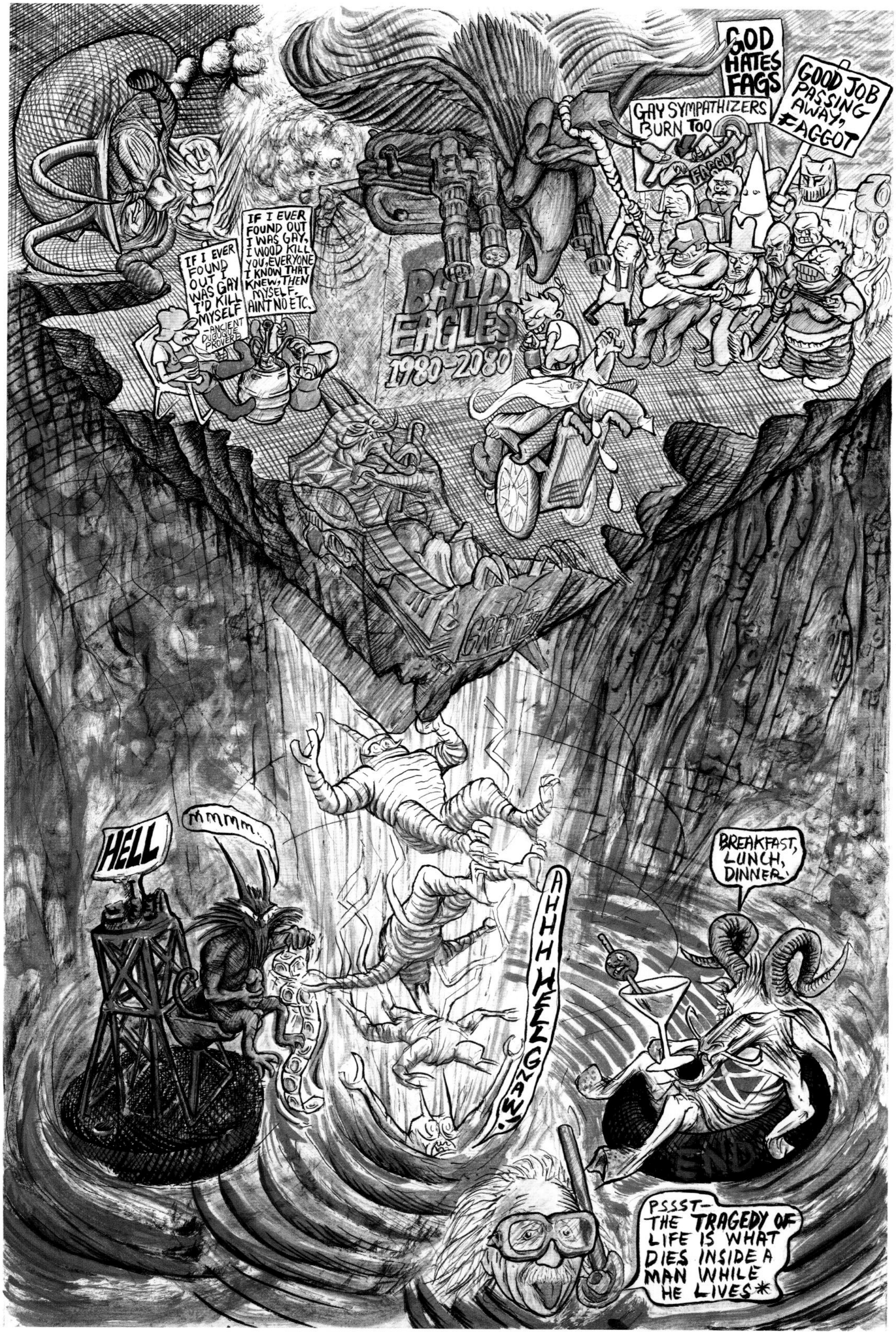

GOD HATES FAGS
GOOD JOB PASSING AWAY, FAGGOT
GAY SYMPATHIZERS BURN TOO
FAGGOT
IF I EVER FOUND OUT I WAS GAY I'D KILL MYSELF -ANCIENT DUBUQUE PROVERB
IF I EVER FOUND OUT I WAS GAY, I WOOD KILL YOU, EVERYONE I KNOW THAT KNEW, THEN MYSELF. AINT NO ETC.
BALD EAGLES 1980-2080
HELL
MMMMM.
AHHHHHEEEGNAW!
BREAKFAST, LUNCH, DINNER.
END
PSSST– THE TRAGEDY OF LIFE IS WHAT DIES INSIDE A MAN WHILE HE LIVES*

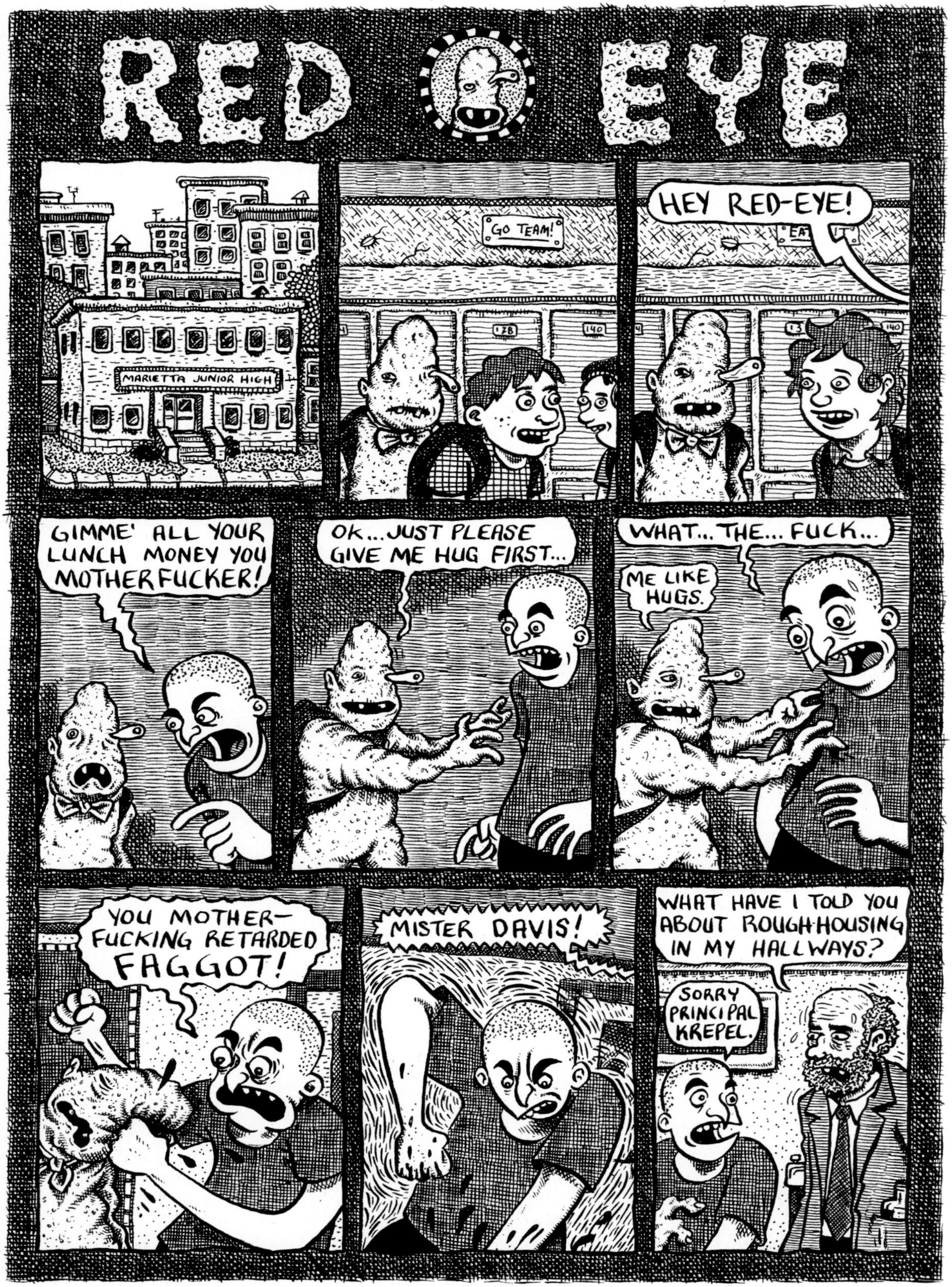
RED EYE
MARIETTA JUNIOR HIGH
GO TEAM!
HEY RED-EYE!
GIMME' ALL YOUR LUNCH MONEY YOU MOTHERFUCKER!
OK... JUST PLEASE GIVE ME HUG FIRST...
WHAT... THE... FUCK...
ME LIKE HUGS.
YOU MOTHER-FUCKING RETARDED FAGGOT!
MISTER DAVIS!
WHAT HAVE I TOLD YOU ABOUT ROUGH-HOUSING IN MY HALLWAYS?
SORRY PRINCIPAL KREPEL.

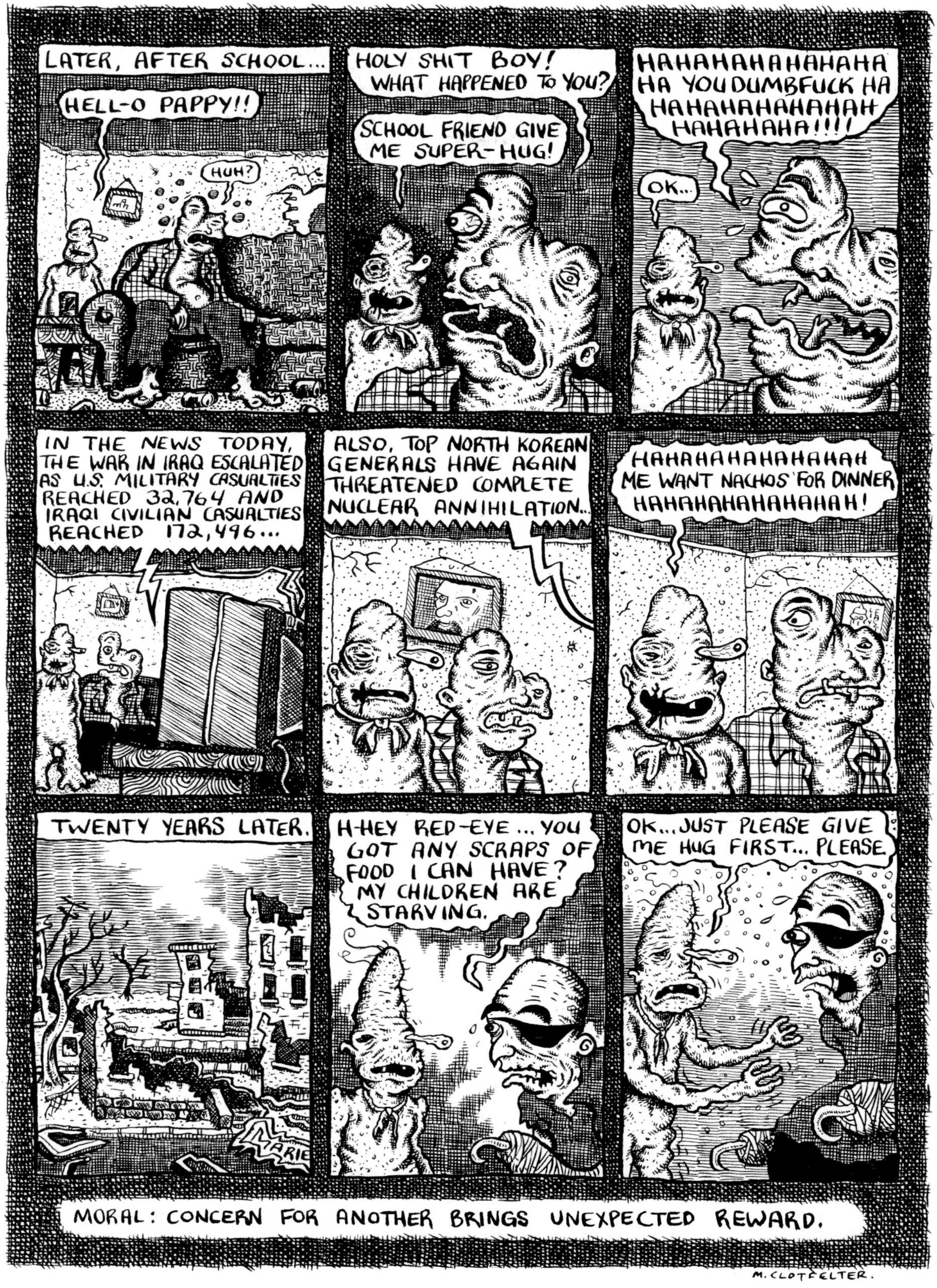
LATER, AFTER SCHOOL...
HELL-O PAPPY!!
HUH?
HOLY SHIT BOY! WHAT HAPPENED TO YOU?
SCHOOL FRIEND GIVE ME SUPER-HUG!
HAHAHAHAHAHAHA HA YOU DUMBFUCK HA HAHAHAHAHAHAH HAHAHAHA!!!!
OK...
IN THE NEWS TODAY, THE WAR IN IRAQ ESCALATED AS U.S. MILITARY CASUALTIES REACHED 32,764 AND IRAQI CIVILIAN CASUALTIES REACHED 172,496...
ALSO, TOP NORTH KOREAN GENERALS HAVE AGAIN THREATENED COMPLETE NUCLEAR ANNIHILATION...
HAHAHAHAHAHAHAH ME WANT NACHOS FOR DINNER HAHAHAHAHAHAHAH!
TWENTY YEARS LATER.
H-HEY RED-EYE... YOU GOT ANY SCRAPS OF FOOD I CAN HAVE? MY CHILDREN ARE STARVING.
OK... JUST PLEASE GIVE ME HUG FIRST... PLEASE.
MORAL: CONCERN FOR ANOTHER BRINGS UNEXPECTED REWARD.
M. CLOTFELTER.

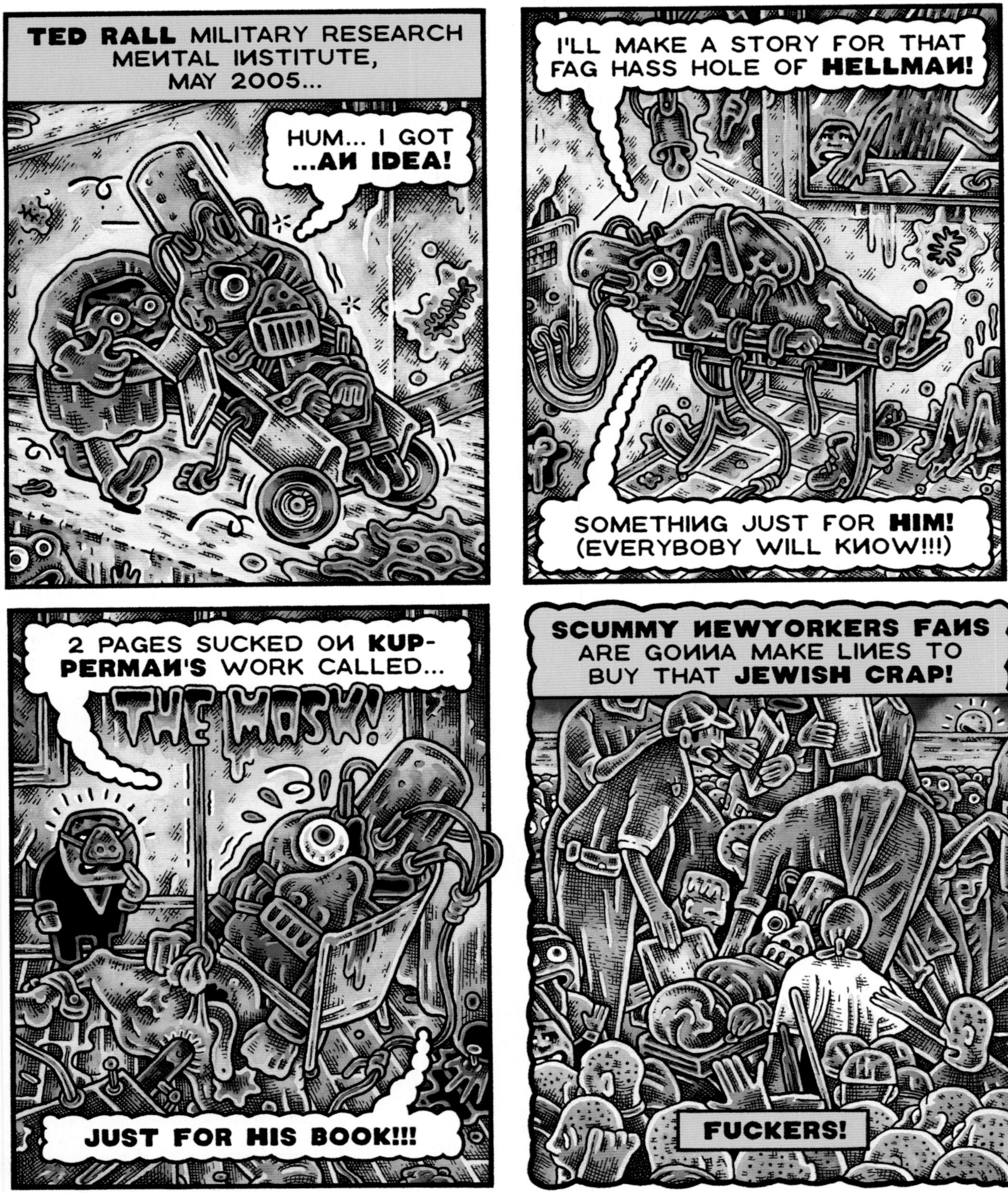
TED RALL MILITARY RESEARCH MENTAL INSTITUTE, MAY 2005...
HUM... I GOT ...AN IDEA!
I'LL MAKE A STORY FOR THAT FAG HASS HOLE OF HELLMAN!
SOMETHING JUST FOR HIM! (EVERYBOBY WILL KNOW!!!)
2 PAGES SUCKED ON KUP-PERMAN'S WORK CALLED...
THE MASK!
JUST FOR HIS BOOK!!!
SCUMMY NEWYORKERS FANS ARE GONNA MAKE LINES TO BUY THAT JEWISH CRAP!
FUCKERS!

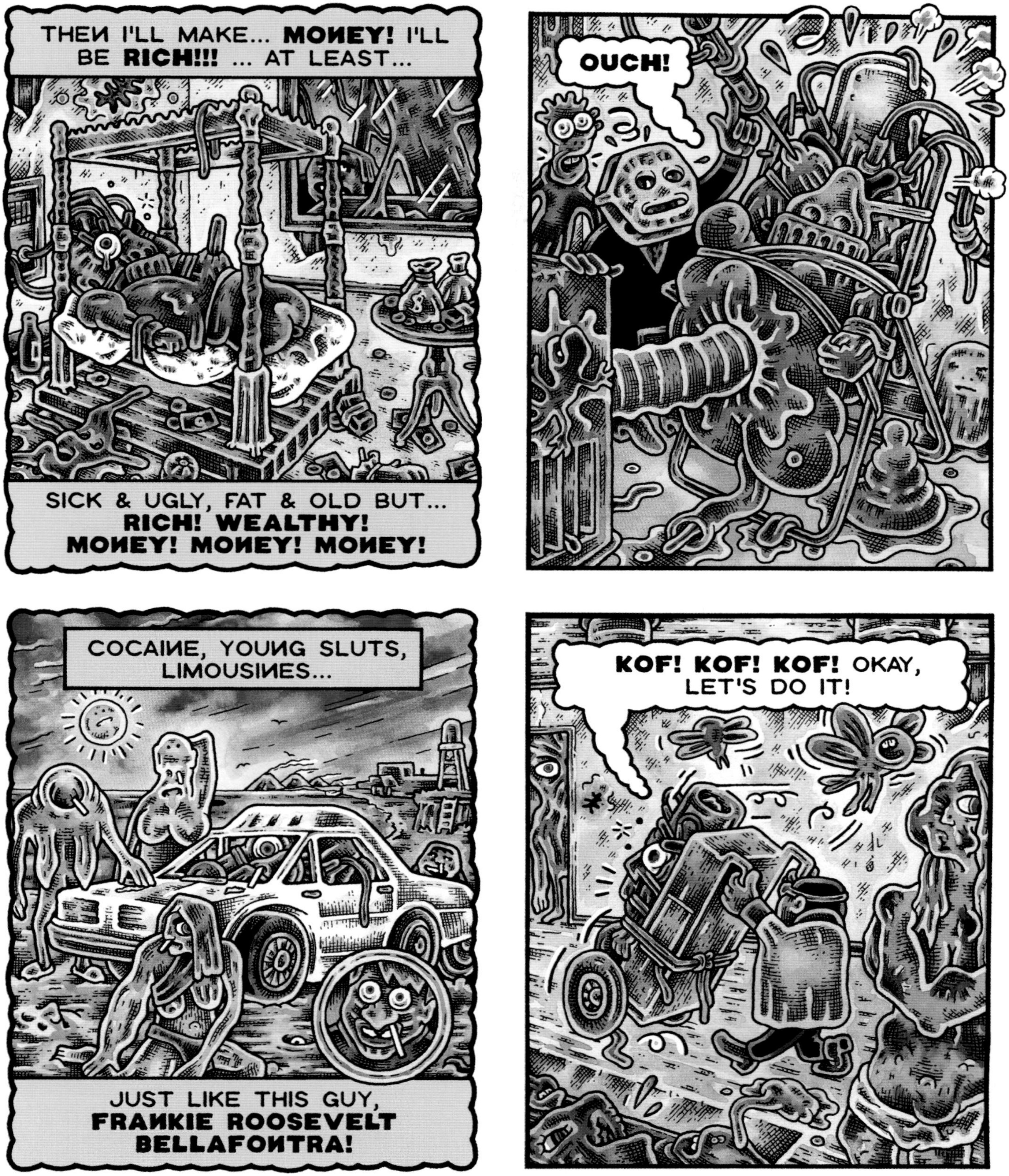
THEN I'LL MAKE... **MONEY!** I'LL BE **RICH!!!** ... AT LEAST...
SICK & UGLY, FAT & OLD BUT... **RICH! WEALTHY! MONEY! MONEY! MONEY!**
OUCH!
COCAINE, YOUNG SLUTS, LIMOUSINES...
JUST LIKE THIS GUY, **FRANKIE ROOSEVELT BELLAFONTRA!**
KOF! KOF! KOF! OKAY, LET'S DO IT!

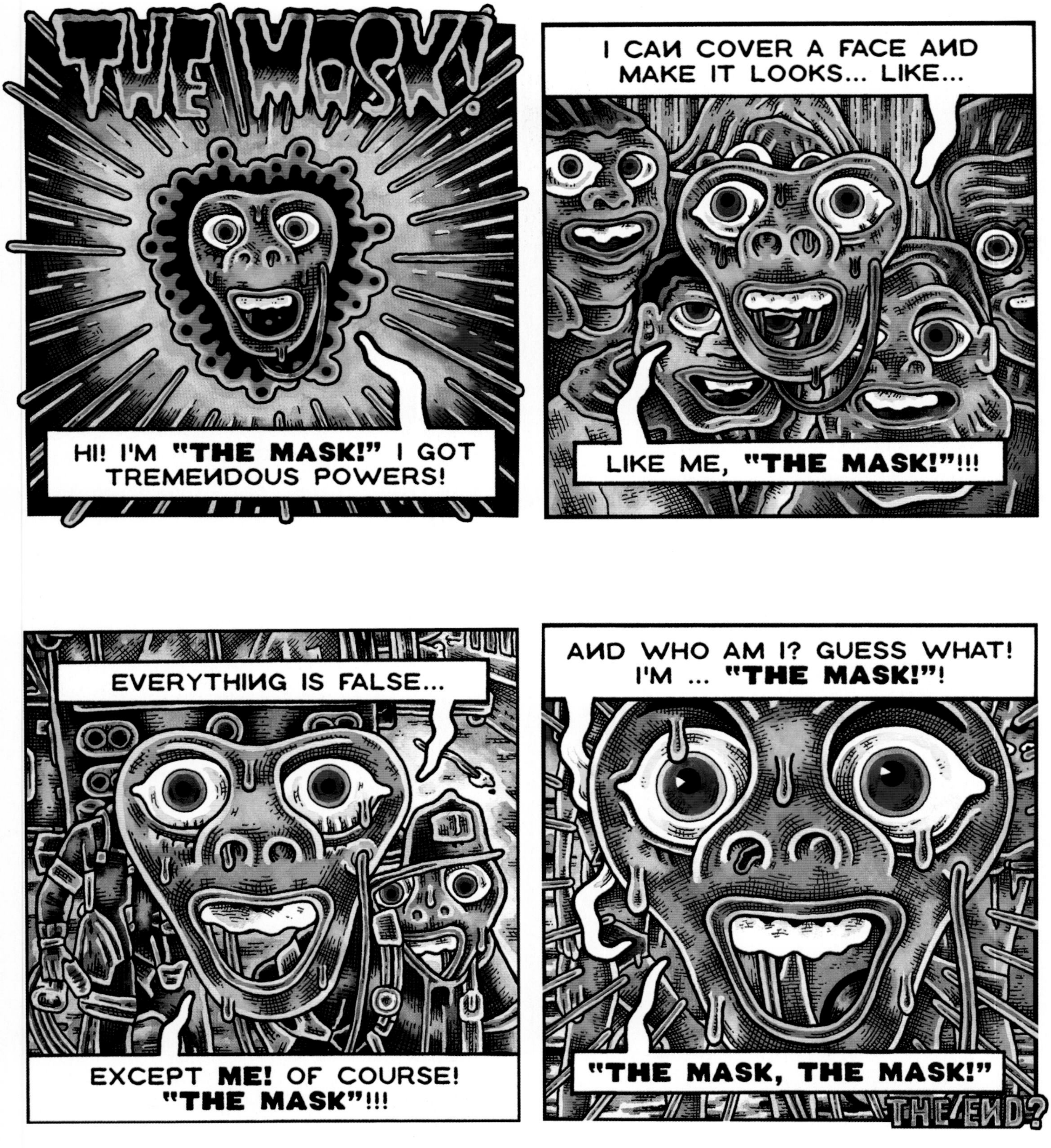
THE MASK!
HI! I'M "THE MASK!" I GOT TREMENDOUS POWERS!
I CAN COVER A FACE AND MAKE IT LOOKS... LIKE...
LIKE ME, "THE MASK!"!!!
EVERYTHING IS FALSE...
EXCEPT ME! OF COURSE! "THE MASK"!!!
AND WHO AM I? GUESS WHAT! I'M ... "THE MASK!"!
"THE MASK, THE MASK!"
THE END?

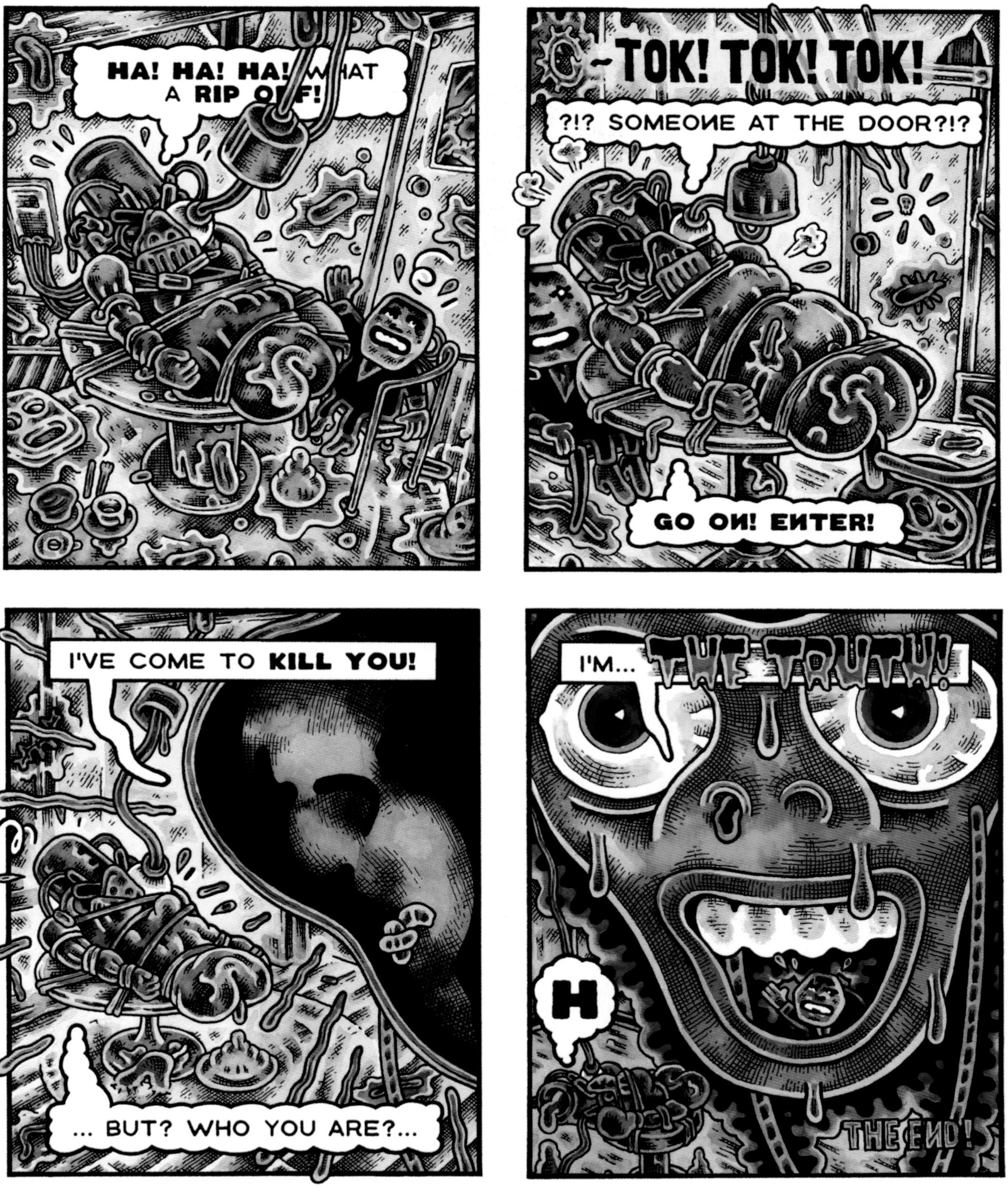
HA! HA! HA! WHAT A RIP OFF!
TOK! TOK! TOK!
?!? SOMEONE AT THE DOOR?!?
GO ON! ENTER!
I'VE COME TO KILL YOU!
... BUT? WHO YOU ARE?...
I'M... THE TRUTH!
H
THE END!

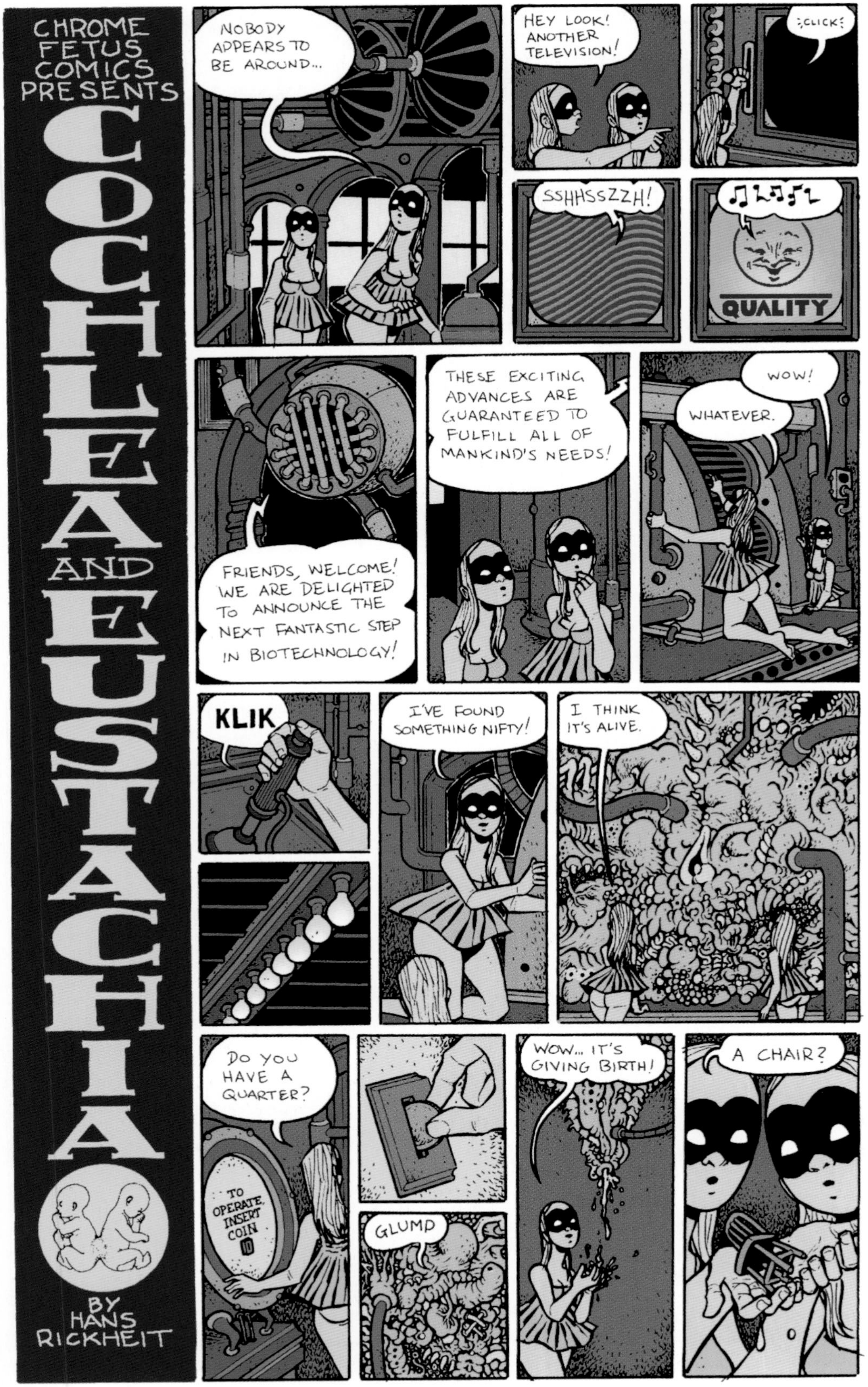
CHROME FETUS COMICS PRESENTS
COCHLEA AND EUSTACHIA
BY HANS RICKHEIT
NOBODY APPEARS TO BE AROUND...
HEY LOOK! ANOTHER TELEVISION!
CLICK
SSHHSSZZH!
QUALITY
FRIENDS, WELCOME! WE ARE DELIGHTED TO ANNOUNCE THE NEXT FANTASTIC STEP IN BIOTECHNOLOGY!
THESE EXCITING ADVANCES ARE GUARANTEED TO FULFILL ALL OF MANKIND'S NEEDS!
WOW!
WHATEVER.
KLIK
I'VE FOUND SOMETHING NIFTY!
I THINK IT'S ALIVE.
DO YOU HAVE A QUARTER?
TO OPERATE, INSERT COIN
GLUMP
WOW... IT'S GIVING BIRTH!
A CHAIR?

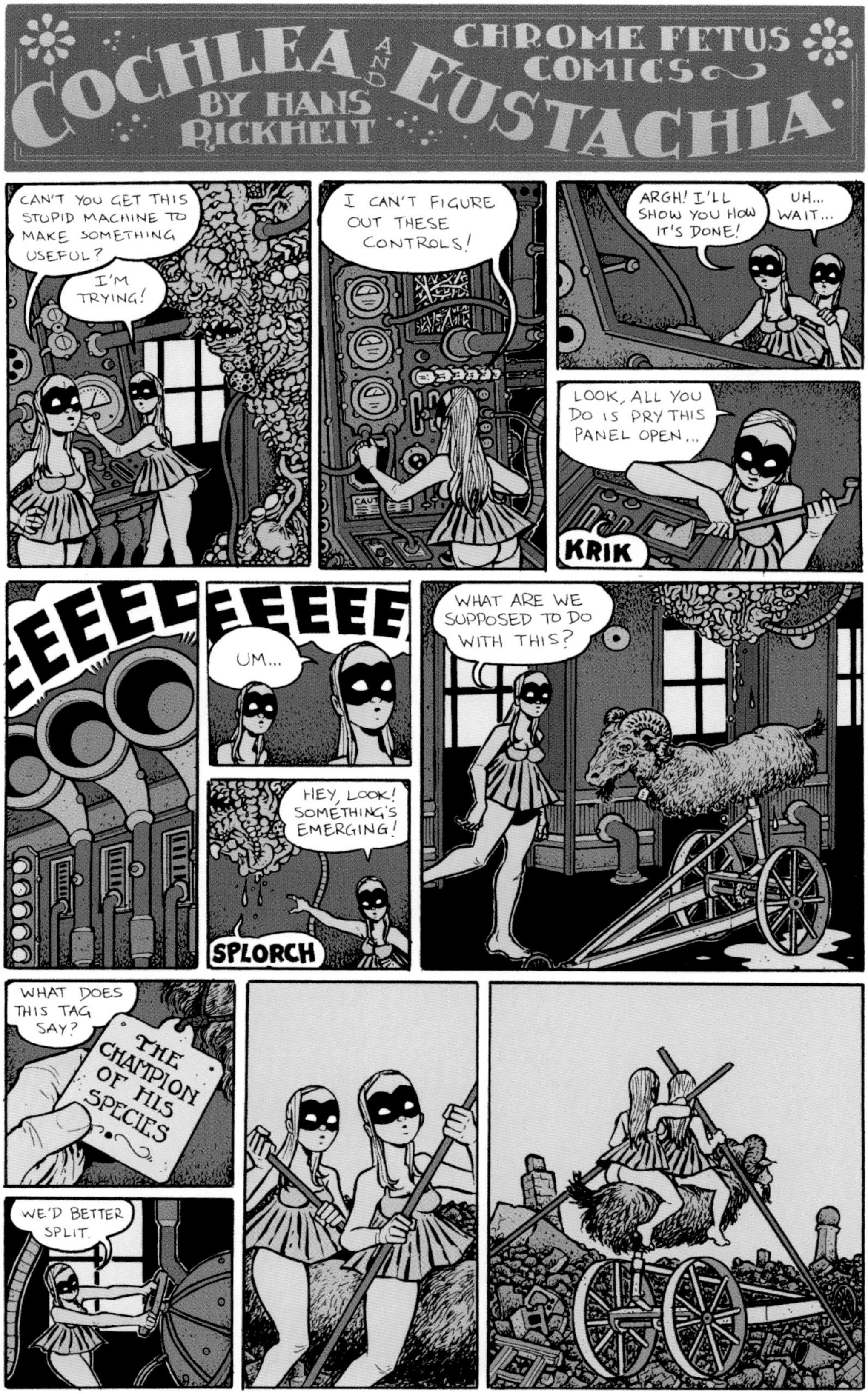
CHROME FETUS COMICS
COCHLEA AND EUSTACHIA
BY HANS RICKHEIT
CAN'T YOU GET THIS STUPID MACHINE TO MAKE SOMETHING USEFUL?
I'M TRYING!
I CAN'T FIGURE OUT THESE CONTROLS!
ARGH! I'LL SHOW YOU HOW IT'S DONE!
UH... WAIT...
LOOK, ALL YOU DO IS PRY THIS PANEL OPEN...
KRIK
EEEEEEEEEE
UM...
HEY, LOOK! SOMETHING'S EMERGING!
SPLORCH
WHAT ARE WE SUPPOSED TO DO WITH THIS?
WHAT DOES THIS TAG SAY?
THE CHAMPION OF HIS SPECIES
WE'D BETTER SPLIT.

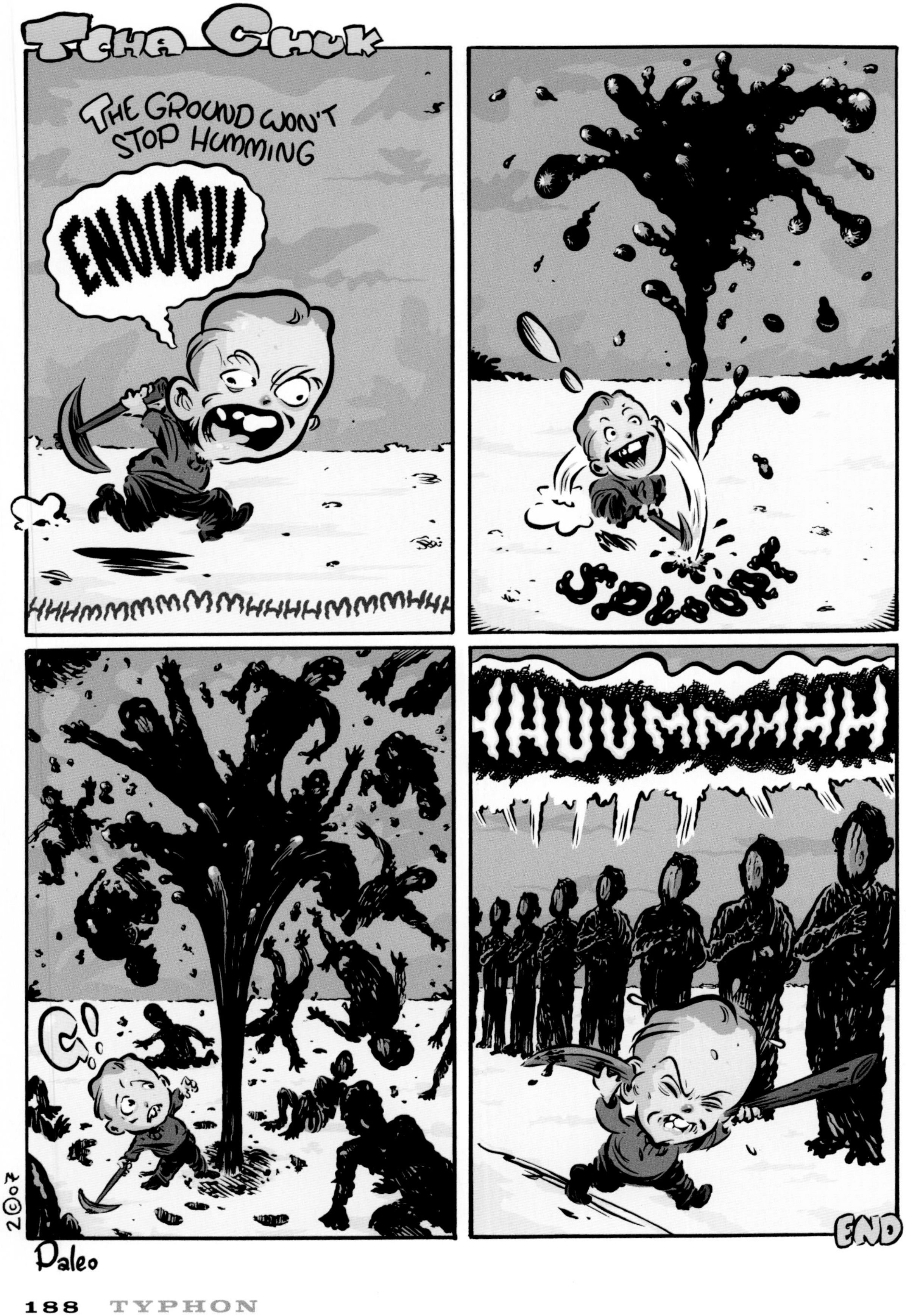
TCHA CHUK
THE GROUND WON'T STOP HUMMING
ENOUGH!
HHHMMMMMMHHHHHMMMMHHH
SPLOOR
HHUUMMMHH
END
Paleo

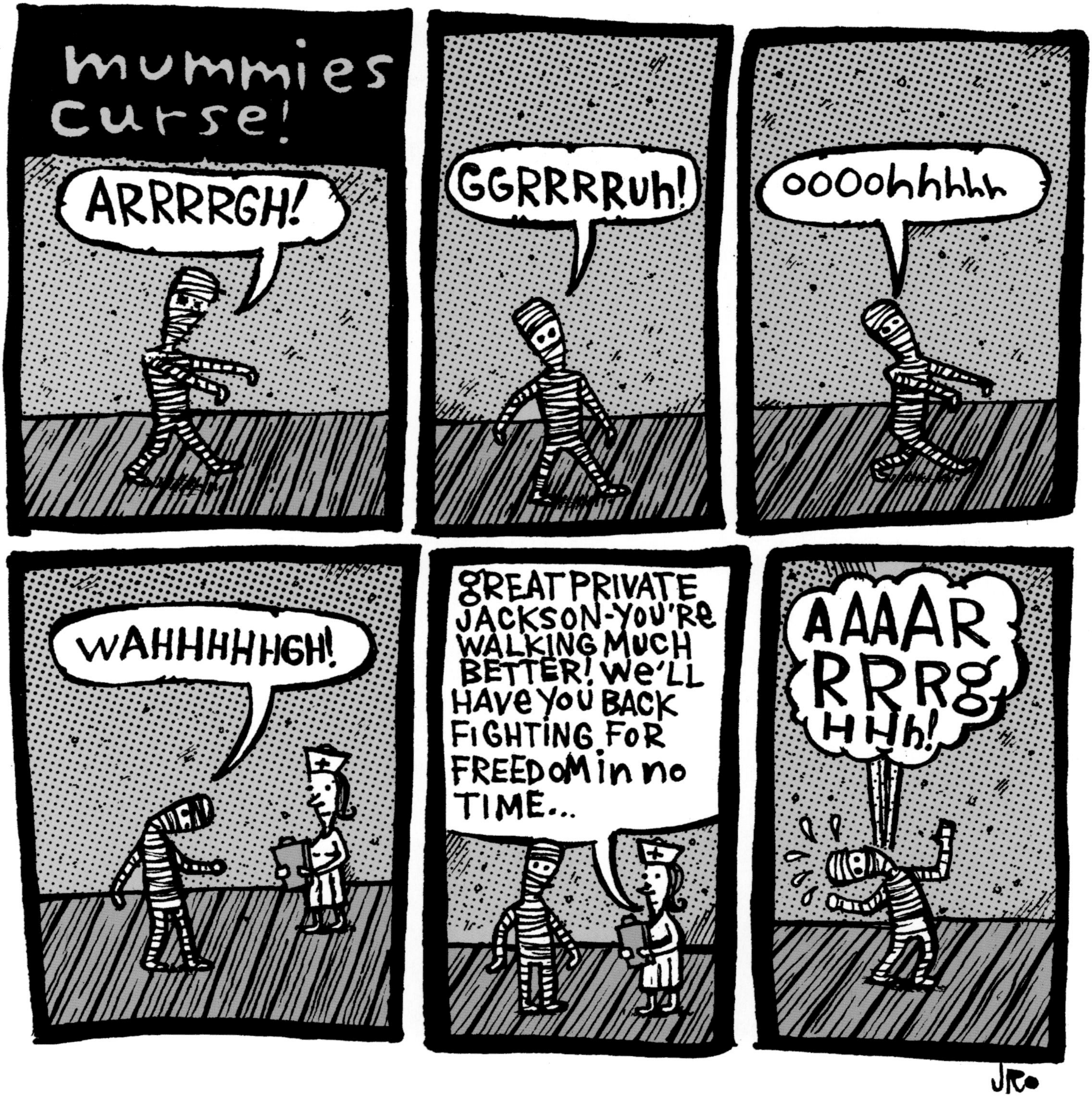
mummies curse!
ARRRRGH!
GGRRRRRUh!
oooohhhhh
WAHHHHHHGH!
GREAT PRIVATE JACKSON-YOU'RE WALKING MUCH BETTER! WE'LL HAVE YOU BACK FIGHTING FOR FREEDOM in no TIME...
AAAARRRRgHHh!
JRo

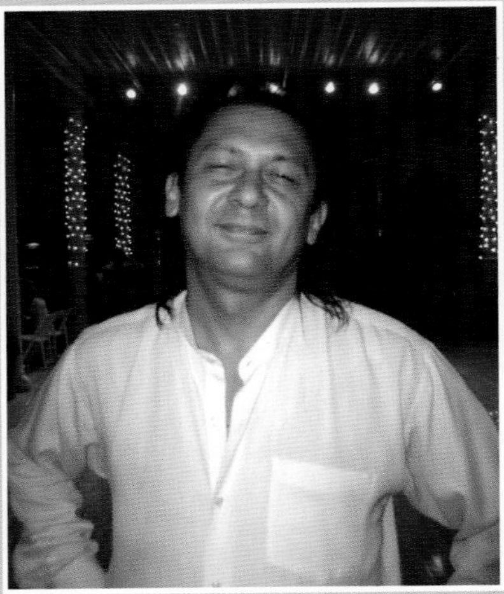

On Page Four, you met "Guy," the mop-wielding hero of "The Terror in Peep Booth Five." Now, as we near the close of this volume of TYPHON, please allow me to present Guy Gonzales, the artist.

Like your humble editor, Guy Gonzales is an alumnus of Manhattan's High School of Art & Design, and also a longtime contributor to New York's legendary smut tabloid SCREW Magazine.
Unlike your humble editor, Guy is a survivor of Times Square's notoriously grimy 1980's heyday, where he performed onstage in live sex shows; he also worked as a peep booth mop man at such venerable institutions as the Paradise Club and Show World. Many of his friends and co-workers from that era are no longer alive, but Guy emerged from Times Square's meat grinder with his life, sanity, and drawing chops intact.

I've been a fan of Guy Gonzales' hilariously sleazy, painstakingly detailed drawings since we first met in the offices of SCREW in the early 1990s. If you're looking to take a cartoon cruise through Times Square's vanished underworld, there is no better qualified a tour guide than Guy.

Here's a taste of his artwork; a few choice tidbits to kick start a habit that can only be satisfied by more!

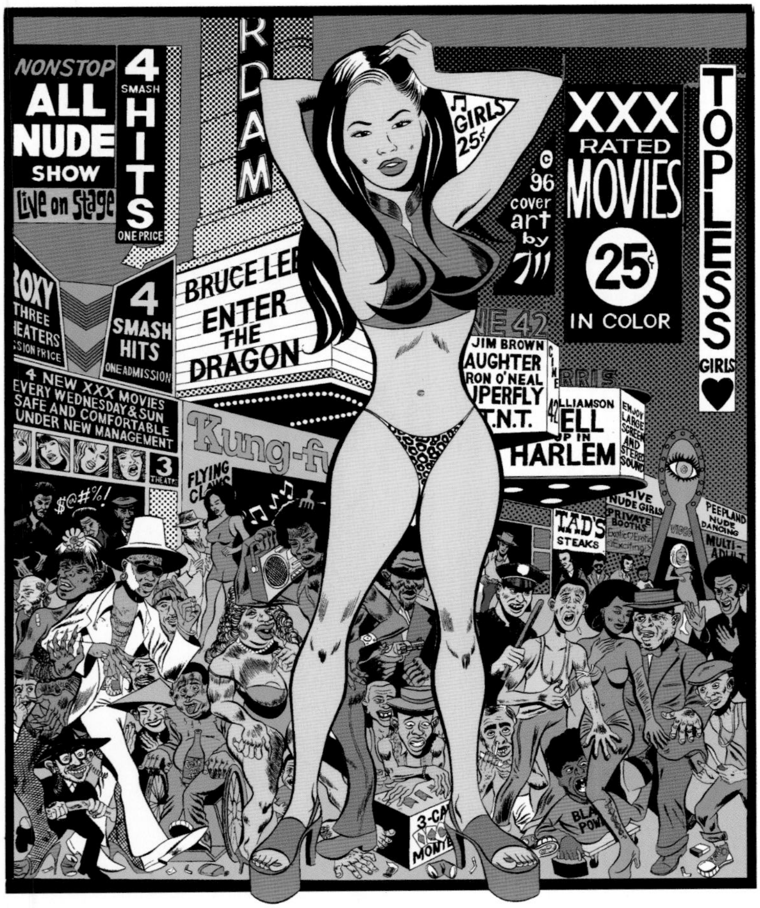
NONSTOP
ALL NUDE SHOW
Live on Stage
4 SMASH HITS ONE PRICE
XXX RATED MOVIES
25¢
IN COLOR
TOPLESS GIRLS
GIRLS 25¢
BRUCE LEE ENTER THE DRAGON
4 SMASH HITS ONE ADMISSION
4 NEW XXX MOVIES EVERY WEDNESDAY & SUN SAFE AND COMFORTABLE UNDER NEW MANAGEMENT
Kung-fu
JIM BROWN
HARLEM
TAD'S STEAKS

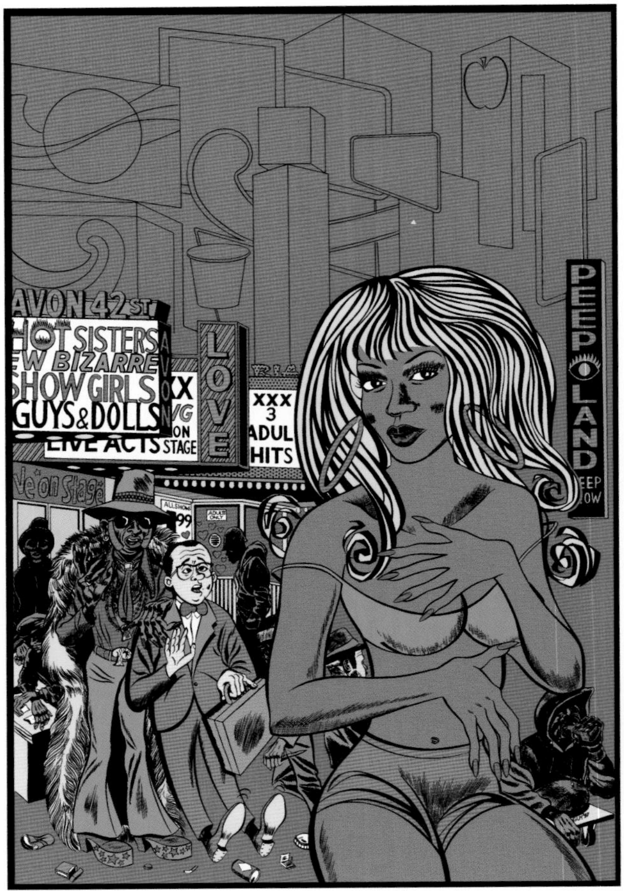
AVON 42 ST
SHOW GIRLS
GUYS & DOLLS
LOVE

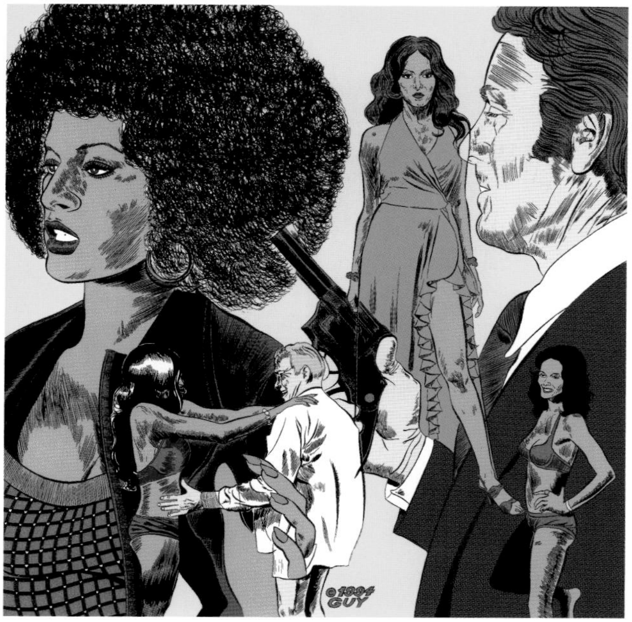

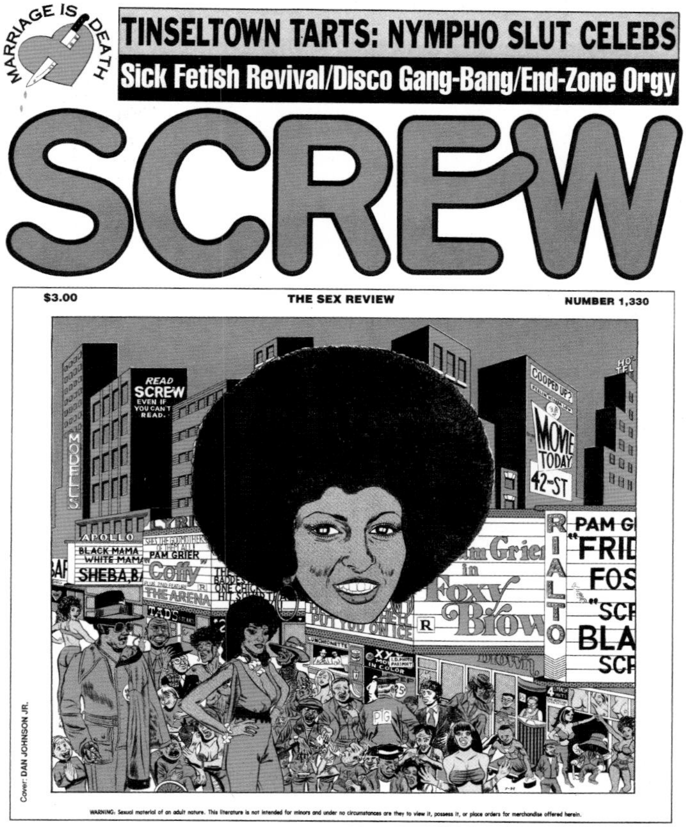
MARRIAGE IS DEATH
TINSELTOWN TARTS: NYMPHO SLUT CELEBS
Sick Fetish Revival/Disco Gang-Bang/End-Zone Orgy
SCREW
$3.00
THE SEX REVIEW
NUMBER 1,330
READ SCREW EVEN IF YOU CAN'T READ.
APOLLO
BLACK MAMA WHITE MAMA
PAM GRIER
Coffy
THE ARENA
MOVIE TODAY
42-ST
RIALTO
Foxy Brown
Cover: DAN JOHNSON JR.
WARNING: Sexual material of an adult nature. This literature is not intended for minors and under no circumstances are they to view it, possess it, or place orders for merchandise offered herein.

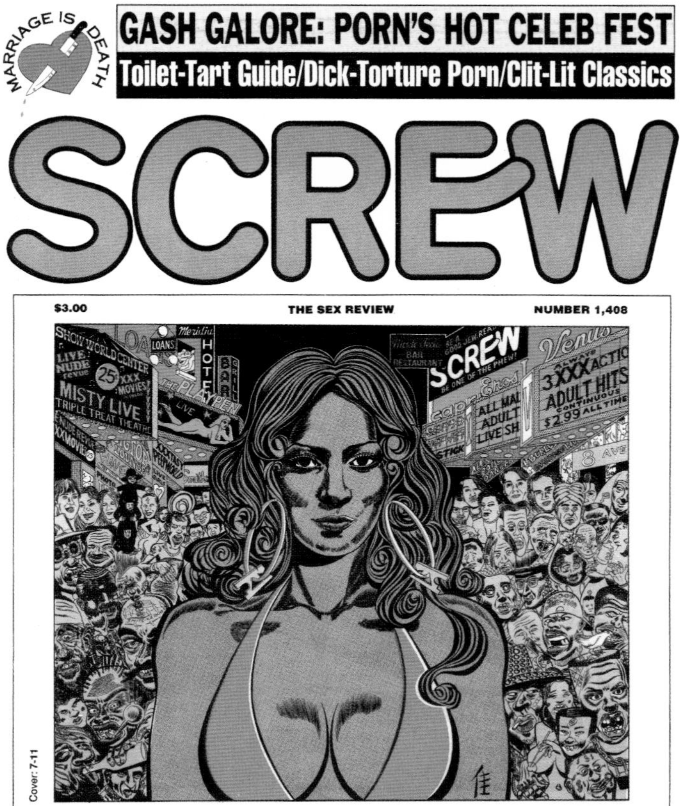
MARRIAGE IS DEATH
GASH GALORE: PORN'S HOT CELEB FEST
Toilet-Tart Guide/Dick-Torture Porn/Clit-Lit Classics
SCREW
$3.00
THE SEX REVIEW
NUMBER 1,408
LIVE NUDE
MISTY LIVE
LOANS
HOTEL
SCREW
ADULT HITS
Cover: 7-11
WARNING: Sexual material of an adult nature. This literature is not intended for minors and under no circumstances are they to view it, possess it, or place orders for merchandise offered herein.

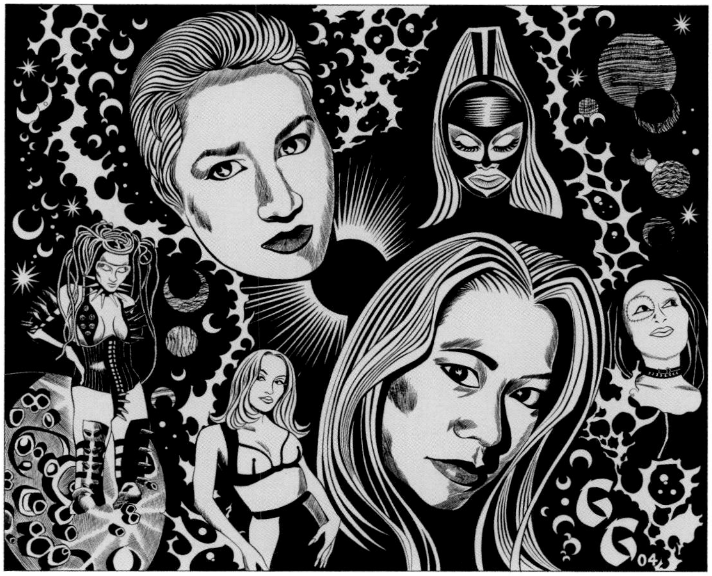

Screw covers courtesy of the Georg Lanz Foundation

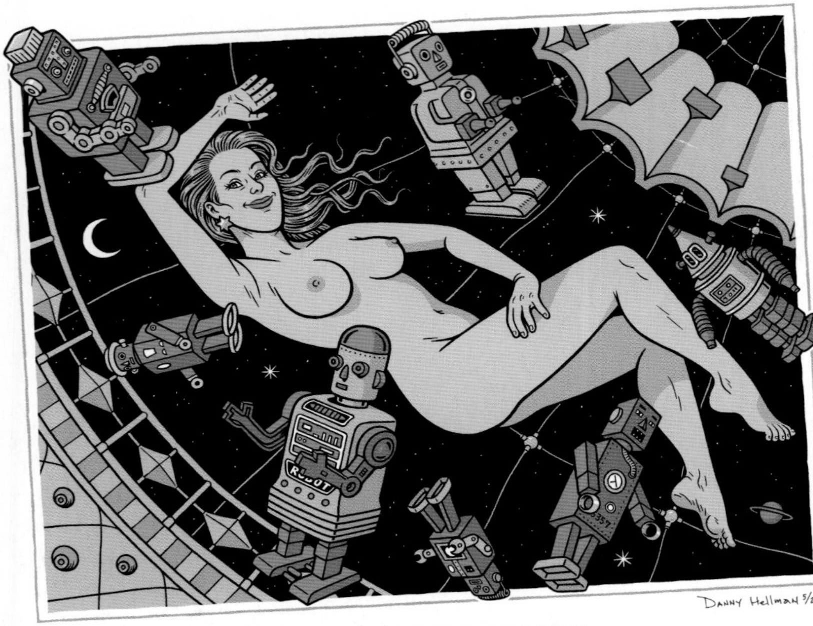

DANNY Hellman 5/250

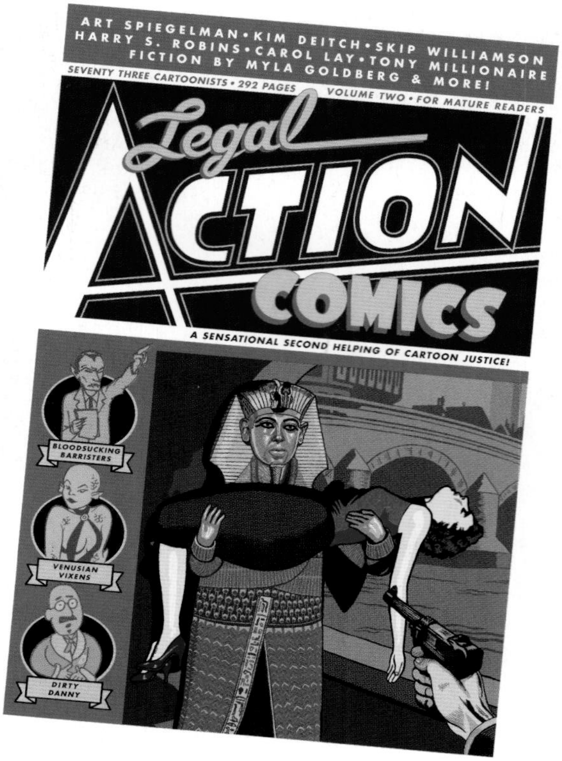

ART SPIEGELMAN•KIM DEITCH•SKIP WILLIAMSON
HARRY S. ROBINS•CAROL LAY•TONY MILLIONAIRE
FICTION BY MYLA GOLDBERG & MORE!
SEVENTY THREE CARTOONISTS • 292 PAGES
VOLUME TWO • FOR MATURE READERS
Legal
ACTION
COMICS
A SENSATIONAL SECOND HELPING OF CARTOON JUSTICE!
BLOODSUCKING BARRISTERS
VENUSIAN VIXENS
DIRTY DANNY

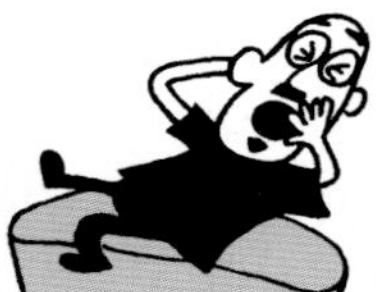

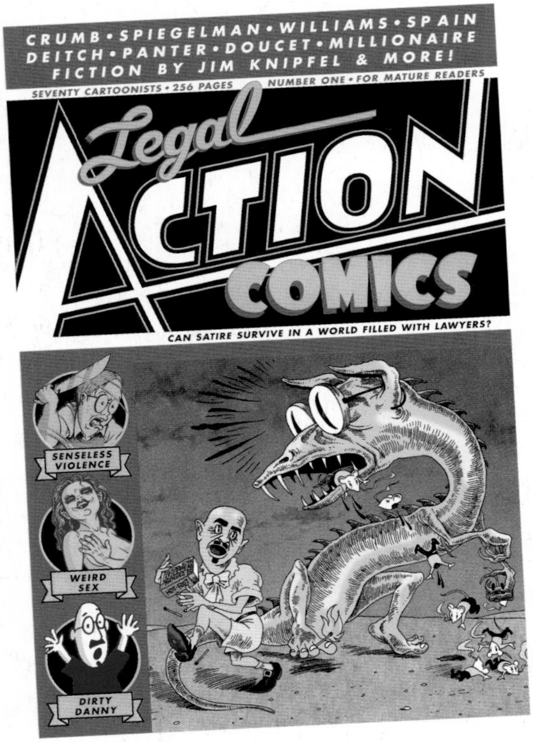

CRUMB•SPIEGELMAN•WILLIAMS•SPAIN
DEITCH•PANTER•DOUCET•MILLIONAIRE
FICTION BY JIM KNIPFEL & MORE!
SEVENTY CARTOONISTS • 256 PAGES
NUMBER ONE • FOR MATURE READERS
Legal
ACTION
COMICS
CAN SATIRE SURVIVE IN A WORLD FILLED WITH LAWYERS?
SENSELESS VIOLENCE
WEIRD SEX
DIRTY DANNY

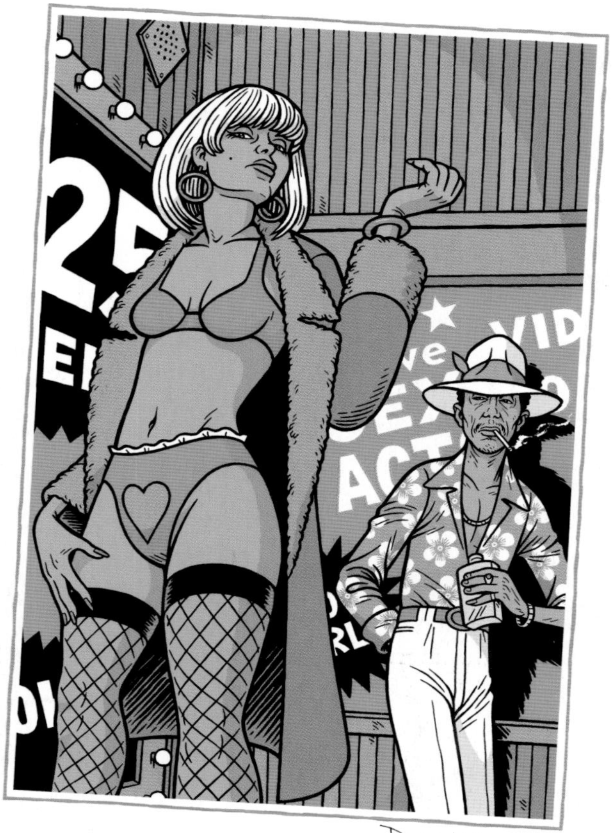

DANNY Hellman 5/250

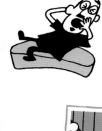